SLOW TRAVEL

The Cotswolds

Local, characterful guides to Britain's special places

Including Stratford-upon-Avon, Oxford & Bath

Caroline Mil

T0034924

EDITION 3

Bradt Guides Ltd, UK
The Globe Pequot Press Inc, USA

Third edition published March 2024
First published 2011
Bradt Guides Ltd
31a High Street, Chesham, Buckinghamshire, HP5 1BW, England
www.bradtguides.com
Print edition published in the USA by The Globe Pequot Press Inc,
PO Box 480, Guilford, Connecticut 06437-0480

Text copyright © 2024 Bradt Guides Ltd
Maps copyright © 2024 Bradt Guides Ltd; includes map data © OpenStreetMap contributors
Photographs copyright © 2024 Individual photographers (see below)
Project Manager: Emma Gibbs
Cover research: Pepi Bluck, Perfect Picture

The author and publisher have made every effort to ensure the accuracy of the information
in this book at the time of going to press. However, they cannot accept any responsibility
for any loss, injury or inconvenience resulting from the use of information contained in this
guide. All rights reserved. No part of this publication may be reproduced, stored in a retrieval
system, or transmitted in any form or by any means, electronic, mechanical, photocopying,
recording or otherwise without the prior consent of the publisher.

ISBN: 9781804691717

British Library Cataloguing in Publication Data
A catalogue record for this book is available from the British Library

Photographs
© individual photographers and organisations credited beside images & also from picture
libraries and organisations credited as follows: Alamy.com (A); AWLimages.com (AWL);
Dreamstime.com (D); Shutterstock.com (S); Society of Antiquaries of London, Kelmscott
Manor (SAL); Superstock.com (SS)
Front cover Lower Slaughter, Gloucestershire (Luigi Vaccarella/4Corners Images)
Back cover Chipping Campden (Dave Knibbs/S)
Title page Dry-stone wall in Gloucestershire (nagelestock.com/A)

Maps David McCutcheon FBCart.S. FRGS

Typeset by Ian Spick, Bradt Guides
Production managed by Zenith Media printed in the UK
Digital conversion by www.dataworks.co.in

Paper used for this product comes from sustainably managed forests, recycled and controlled
sources.

AUTHOR

Caroline Mills is a country girl. While she loves to visit the towns and cities of the world, she likes nothing better than to return to the farm where she lives with her husband and three children, on the edge of the Cotswolds. Having moved no more than five miles from where she grew up – also in the Cotswolds – she has been able to call the region home for more than 50 years. With a

keen desire to see the area maintain its identity, keeping old traditions alive, and with a passionate love of the countryside in which she lives, Caroline is well placed to paint a very personal picture of this special place. It is this vast in-depth knowledge of the region that led her to write *Slow Travel The Cotswolds* for Bradt.

AUTHOR'S STORY

Forgive me for being frivolously biased, but I have decided that I live in the most beautiful part of the UK! I knew it all along really, but initially researching, then updating this book has cemented my thoughts and now I want to shout it out loud.

The Cotswolds might not be as dramatic as the Scottish glens, as rugged as the North York Moors or even as picturesque as the Lake District on certain days. But what it does have is a comforting feeling that everything is right with the world, if only for a brief moment in time.

When Bradt asked if I would like to write a book on the Cotswolds more than a decade ago, I jumped at the chance to explore the area some more. And then my blood ran cold. Another book on the Cotswolds – how do I make it different? How often can I write about honey-coloured stone, and which villages do I include when so many of them look appealing? Am I the right person to write about the area when, I'm ashamed to say, I often take where I live for granted as I go about my day-to-day life?

An aspect I love about preparing a new edition is finding out new things, be that new to everyone or simply new to me – a newly opened visitor attraction or an undiscovered village, or garden, or a pub that was down on its luck and brought back from the brink. Unexpected finds, a jigsaw piece of history, another passionate person to talk to. I love research and I hope this freshness comes through with this third edition.

I realise that it will take more than my lifetime to really discover the Cotswolds. I've made more than a start, but I'd like to stand and stare (page 9) for longer.

ACKNOWLEDGEMENTS

This book would not be what it is without the input of those living and working in the Cotswolds who generously gave up their time to talk – thank you. On a professional level, my thanks to the ever-patient Anna Moores, Emma Gibbs and all the team at Bradt, and to David McCutcheon for the creation of the maps and Ian Spick for making the copy look fantastic. And on a personal level, to my wonderful husband and to my children who sometimes barely see Mummy for several weeks as she goes about her work, but have nonetheless learnt patience, where the vacuum cleaner is kept and how to cook a roast dinner. *Slow Travel The Cotswolds* is dedicated to the farmers of the Cotswolds who have, for generations, cared for and been the guardians of this unique landscape, and to my parents, who introduced me to this wonderful area while I was a babe in arms. Thank you.

FEEDBACK REQUEST

At Bradt Guides we're aware that guidebooks start to go out of date on the day they're published – and that you, our readers, are out there in the field doing research of your own. You'll find out before us when a fine new family-run hotel opens or a favourite restaurant changes hands and goes downhill. So why not tell us about your experiences? Contact us on ✆ 01753 893444 or ✉ info@bradtguides.com. We will forward emails to the author who may post updates on the Bradt website at ⟡ bradtguides.com/updates. Alternatively, you can add a review of the book to Amazon, or share your adventures with us on social: ⓕ, ✖, ⧉ BradtGuides; ✖, ⧉ CarolineMills99.

CONTENTS

SUGGESTED PLACES TO BASE YOURSELF

These bases make ideal starting points for exploring localities the Slow way.

N

0
0
5 miles
10kms

CHIPPING CAMPDEN page 93
The starting point – and finish – of the Cotswold Way.

WINCHCOMBE page 182
Winchcombe is a must for those taking to the footpaths.

PAINSWICK page 305
In close proximity to nature reserves of international importance.

CHIPPING NORTON page 132
Perfect for exploring the eastern fringes of the Cotswolds.

CHAPTER 1
page 27

CHAPTER 2
page 80

CHAPTER 3
page 118

CHAPTER 4
page 154

CHAPTER 5
page 204

WORCESTER

Worcestershire

Warwickshire

Stratford-upon-Avon

BANBURY

Evesham

Broadway

Chipping Campden

Moreton-in-Marsh

Chipping Norton

Chalbury

Winchcombe

Stow-on-the-Wold

Burford

CHELTENHAM

Northleach

Oxfordshire

Gloucestershire

GLOUCESTER

Avon

Stour

Severn

Evenlode

Windrush

Cherwell

M40

M42

A422

A46

A44

A429

A429

A361

A44

A40

A436

A40

A417

M5

M5

M50

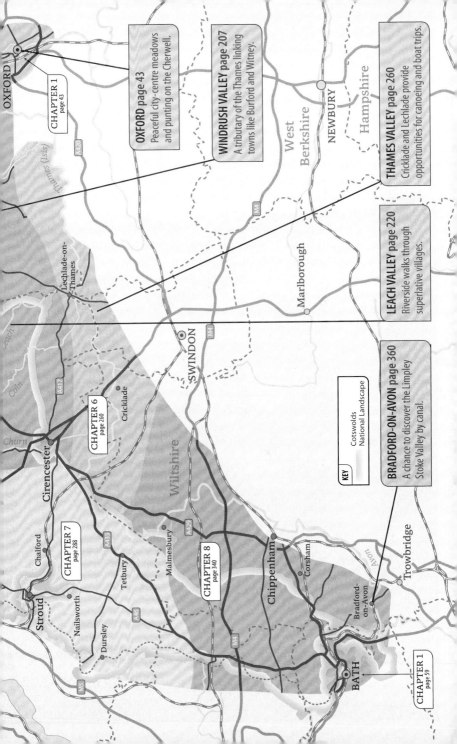

OXFORD

CHAPTER 1
page 43

OXFORD page 43
Peaceful city-centre meadows and punting on the Cherwell.

WINDRUSH VALLEY page 207
A tributary of the Thames linking towns like Burford and Witney.

THAMES VALLEY page 260
Cricklade and Lechlade provide opportunities for canoeing and boat trips.

LEACH VALLEY page 220
Riverside walks through superlative villages.

BRADFORD-ON-AVON page 360
A chance to discover the Limpley Stoke Valley by canal.

NEWBURY

West Berkshire

Hampshire

Thames (Isis)

Lechlade-on-Thames

Coln

Leach

MARLBOROUGH

SWINDON

Churn

CHAPTER 6
page 260

Cricklade

Cirencester

Wiltshire

KEY
Cotswolds
National Landscape

CHAPTER 7
page 288

Chalford

Stroud

Nailsworth

Dursley

Tetbury

Malmesbury

CHAPTER 8
page 340

Chippenham

Corsham

Avon

Bradford-on-Avon

Trowbridge

BATH

CHAPTER 1
page 59

GOING SLOW IN

THE COTSWOLDS

What is this life if, full of care,
We have no time to stand and stare.
No time to stand beneath the boughs
And stare as long as sheep or cows.
W H Davies, *Leisure*

There are two reasons to begin this guide with a few lines from William Henry Davies, other than it being an effective piece of poetry. First, W H Davies was a one-time traveller of sorts (more vagrant than tourist) and he was a resident of the Cotswolds. Admittedly, he wrote the poem *Leisure* in 1911, long before he settled in the Cotswolds but, nevertheless, he chose to spend the last years of his life in the area. Secondly, in a few short lines, the poem sums up what going slow in the Cotswolds is all about.

In parts of the Cotswolds it is indeed impossible to do anything but go slow – narrow and contorted lanes wind their way up steep hillsides, and many villages seem decades away from the modern world. That's not to say that the Cotswolds is backward-looking, but if, as I was one Sunday evening, you happen to be gently rocking in a chair beside the embers of a log fire in one of the Cotswolds' charismatic village pubs, that pressing business meeting arranged for the following morning suddenly seems slightly less important.

The rounded landscape of the Cotswolds feels cosy, snuggly and warm, even in the depths of winter. There's little that's raw, jagged or sharp about the landscape and the sense of harmony between people and the land feels comfortingly organic. With 86% of the Cotswolds being farmland, the relationship between the two is where the story of the region begins.

◄ Naunton church peeks out among the rolling hills (page 171).

THE SLOW MINDSET

Hilary Bradt, Founder, Bradt Guides

> We shall not cease from exploration
> And the end of all our exploring
> Will be to arrive where we started
> And know the place for the first time.
>
> T S Eliot, 'Little Gidding', *Four Quartets*

This series evolved, slowly, from a Bradt editorial meeting when we started to explore ideas for guides to our favourite part of the world – Great Britain. We wanted to get away from the usual 'top sights' formula and encourage our authors to bring out the nuances and local differences that make up a sense of place – such things as food, building styles, nature, geology, or local people and what makes them tick. Our aim was to create a series that celebrates the present, focusing on sustainable tourism, rather than taking a nostalgic wallow in the past.

So without our realising it at the time, we had defined 'Slow Travel', or at least our concept of it. For the beauty of the Slow movement is that there is no fixed definition; we adapt the philosophy to fit our individual needs and aspirations. Thus Carl Honoré, author of *In Praise of Slow*, writes: 'The Slow Movement is a cultural revolution against the notion that faster is always better. It's not about doing everything at a snail's pace, it's about seeking to do everything at the right speed. Savouring the hours and minutes rather than just counting them. Doing everything as well as possible, instead of as fast as possible. It's about quality over quantity in everything from work to food to parenting.' And travel.

So take time to explore. Don't rush it, get to know an area – and the people who live there – and you'll be as delighted as the authors by what you find.

You can't avoid noticing geology wherever you go. The distinctive local limestone makes the Cotswolds what they are today, both in the natural rock formations that remain and in the buildings in towns and villages. The colour of the stone varies from creamy white to a deep golden brown but its composition remains the same. Formed in the Jurassic age – 140 to 210 million years ago – when the area was awash with sea creatures, layers of sedimentary rock known as oolite were laid down. This oolitic limestone is so called because the small round particles, or ooids, look like fish eggs. Some eons later man came along and started digging up this stone for houses, animal shelters and walls to enclose livestock.

The Cotswolds stretch from Bath in the southwest towards Stratford-upon-Avon in the northeast and covers six historic counties: Somerset, Wiltshire, Gloucestershire, Worcestershire, Oxfordshire and Warwickshire. To some extent the Cotswolds divide into two. The western side is dominated by a striking line of hills that rise to 1,080ft above sea level, running from Bath to a point east of Evesham. This escarpment overlooks the Severn Valley, the Forest of Dean and the Welsh hills beyond. Yet the escarpment, while it may look like one long ridge from a distance, is actually made up of many lumps and bumps between both wet and dry valleys that weave through the landscape. Its character is very different from the eastern side, a plateau where the land levels out to a gentler scene with rolling hills, river valleys and agricultural plains. These are interspersed with a spattering of towns and villages that evolved with purpose – as the meeting points for the farmers and merchants who also made their mark on the landscape. For while the Cotswolds are predominantly a rural idyll now, they were by no means an industrial backwater. The quality of the stone architecture of the towns and villages that give the landscape such appeal is a potent reminder of the area's once thriving and prosperous industries.

Evidence of prehistoric man crops up here and there with Neolithic burial chambers, found mainly on the western escarpment. The Bronze Age and Iron Age residents built hillforts, many of which can still be seen clearly. When the Romans arrived, they too made their mark on the Cotswolds, in the form of villas such as Chedworth. One particularly prominent legacy of their presence is the Fosse Way, a road that runs the length of the Cotswolds from Bath through Cirencester to Moreton-in-Marsh and beyond to the Lincolnshire Wolds.

One of the most plausible explanations for the Cotswolds name is that 'wolds' means 'open hillsides' and 'cotes' denotes 'sheep enclosures'. Hence the 'Cotswolds' (or 'hills covered in sheep') became renowned for these woolly beasts and later the wool itself. The Cotswolds' finest hour came in the late Middle Ages when the sheep – and their prized wool – had made a name for themselves internationally. Merchants came from all over Europe to trade, 'wool towns' sprang up across the region and the wealth was pumped into magnificent houses, market halls and churches.

The woollen cloth industry began to boom during the 17th and 18th centuries, particularly along the river valleys where mills sprang up. But it was not to last; competition from large-scale mechanised mills in Yorkshire and then cheap imports thwarted the industry and the area gave way to a wave of artists and craftsmen and women as the Arts and Crafts Movement began, most notably William Morris, who made the Cotswolds his home and an inspiration for his work, together with numerous other associates, including several of the Pre-Raphaelite Brotherhood.

While many of the sheep have gone from the hillsides, agriculture still plays a lively part in the local economy, as does quarrying for the sought-after stone that has made the landscape in more senses than one.

However, I can't deny that since the first edition of *Slow Travel The Cotswolds* was published in 2011, the pace of change within the region has escalated exponentially. Even without looking through rose-tinted glasses, disheartening development is changing the character of the Cotswolds, particularly in the north and east of the region, with multiple once-unassuming little farmsteads replaced by giant, eclipsing 'country' piles, often as immaculate second homes, with manicured landscape-sized lawns and pretentious entrance gates.

Besides that, it has been reassuring to meet individuals and small communities that suppress that pace and offer a gentler vision. One of those new-to-me places I refer to in my author's story on page 13, which I discovered while researching this edition, is Nomad Letterpress. This tiny printing and publishing house resides in a tumbledown property in Whittington (page 197), east of Cheltenham. Tall overgrowth hides it from the world but inside a small community creates exquisite works of art; printed books using 'old-fashioned' third-dimension methods with letterpress machines. Well-thumbed wooden filing cabinets of archaic age showcase shiny metal characters. The procedure takes time. The creative vibe and the passion for slow is overwhelming.

Among a hotchpotch of papers pinned to a door, one, revealing itself behind another, caught my eye on a recent visit to the printworks. It was a quote written by eminent New York typographer, letterpress printer and filmmaker, Lowell Bodger. It read, 'When everyone and everything else is speeding up, it might be one's responsibility to move even more slowly than before. If the only possible change of speed is to slow down, so the only available change of direction is backward.' I think it sums up where we are – and, perhaps, where we need to go – in the Cotswolds succinctly.

Visitors can (re)awaken their senses by sampling the sights, sounds and smells of the area, immersing themselves in the landscape, tasting its fruits and encountering an altogether more organic experience – and a slower pace of life. The Cotswolds has a character like no other.

A NATIONAL LANDSCAPE OF OUTSTANDING NATURAL BEAUTY

Much of the Cotswolds is designated as a National Landscape (formerly known as an Area of Outstanding Natural Beauty), a status close to that of a National Park; indeed the Cotswolds Conservation Board is promoting the case for it to become a national park. Covering 787 square miles, it is the largest of all the National Landscapes in England and Wales. National Landscapes are designed to 'conserve and enhance the natural beauty of their landscapes while also taking account of agriculture, forestry, rural industries and the economic and social needs of local communities'. This sits very well with the ethos behind slow tourism.

The region has strikingly special attributes and the Cotswolds Conservation Board, which manages it, has identified numerous landscape types and elements that are keynotes to the Cotswolds. These include more than 4,000 miles of dry-stone walls (longer than the Great Wall of China), ancient woodland, unimproved grassland, vernacular stone buildings, archaeological sites, settlement patterns and historic parkland.

The National Landscape has more than 400 Cotswold Voluntary Wardens who, in connection with the Cotswold Way Association, carry out conservation work and lead guided walks. Each warden cares for a particular area and has special knowledge of his or her patch. The Cotswolds Conservation Board website (⌀ cotswolds-nl. org.uk) is a good starting point for finding out about activities such as guided walks (led by the voluntary wardens) and themed events. Volunteers are also involved in work-party projects such as dry-stone walling (page 14), hedging and tree planting, providing the perfect way in which to become involved with an aspect of the Cotswolds landscape. National Landscape events are listed on the Board's website and in the free *Cotswold Lion* magazine (available to download from ⌀ cotswolds-nl.org.uk/about-us/cotswold-lion-magazine).

DRY AS A STONE – COTSWOLD WALLS

One of the most important and integral features of the Cotswolds are the miles of aesthetically pleasing dry-stone walls that break up the landscape, whether with lichens and mosses subtly weathering the stone into its famous mottled colours, cascaded with vibrant aubrietia in a cottage garden, or extending into the horizon enclosing a great estate, capped with coping stones.

Wychwood Forest Trust (page 252) runs one-day dry-stone walling courses near Witney in the Oxfordshire Cotswolds. These courses are open to anyone. They make a memorable way to be outdoors, at one with your surroundings, as well as giving something back to the area. The walls that are built during the courses are 'proper' dry-stone walls that will be around for centuries

not a makeshift partition ready to be pulled down again at the end of the weekend.

I went along to a course run by the Trust at Singe Wood (one of its nature reserves), and learnt much about this iconic Cotswold feature.

Our tutor was Toby Smith, the Trust's Countryside and Reserves Manager and instructor of rural skills. He demonstrated the different kinds of stones used – walling stone is different from building stone – and how they differ according to the area of the Cotswolds from which they're quarried. My trio of companions on the course and I learnt how some perish over time once the frost and heat travel into the sedimentary layers, delaminating the stone, when to mix old stone with new and when it's time to start

Leaving the car behind really helps you get to grips with some parts of the Cotswolds. Besides, there is no other feeling like it than to climb one of the Cotswold hills under some seasonal sunshine, peek your head over the summit and find the rest of the world laid out before you. To wander the full 102 miles of the Cotswold Way, designated as a National Trail and waymarked with acorn motifs, in one hit requires some preparation – and in truth, you miss out on so much more that the Cotswolds have to offer. So the Cotswolds Conservation Board has come up with a series of **Cotswold Way circular walks** of varying lengths that take up some of the very best sections of the Cotswold Way combined with other public footpaths and bridleways. You can download maps for the circular walks from their website along with short walks to explore the National Landscape using wheelchairs, mobility scooters or pushchairs. Also on its website is information about national **cycle routes** and paths that run through the area, and bridleways (which can also be used by cyclists). **Horseriding** is extremely popular in the Cotswolds, with riding schools dotted across the area, many of them offering treks through the again with fresh stone. We found out about the different qualities of the stone– what to listen for when you tap one and how long it takes to weather.

'An experienced waller,' said Toby, 'will think one step ahead all the time to conserve energy and get to the end result quicker.' That was what he wanted us to do as we went about sorting the stone, getting an eye for the right-sized piece, and making sure that it had a good long 'tail' to tie the two sides of the wall together like a jigsaw puzzle, before chipping with a scutch hammer, which we were taught to use, and shaping, then laying the stone down and filling the middle with 'hearting' – the smaller rubble that helps to hold the wall together.

Tools down, I looked along the length of the wall that we had completed. The aesthetic beauty lay in its rhythm – the layers and the irregular pattern of the stone. I'd spent a day beside woodland with the scent of crushed ground ivy and inky gloss of ripening blackberries, a gentle breeze that had quashed any notion of the physical hard work, and the therapeutic, tap tap, of the walling hammer striking stone echoing across the neighbouring meadows. I left with the knowledge that the wall will still be there long after I've gone.

For information on dry-stone walling courses, and other rural-skills workshops, visit ⊘ wychwoodforesttrust.co.uk. The proceeds of all the courses go to support the work of the Wychwood Forest Trust.

countryside. Some 44 miles of the long-distance Sabrina Way riding route are through the Cotswolds, while the Claude Duval Bridle Route, named after a notorious highwayman, is in the east of the region and covers 50 miles through north Oxfordshire and Gloucestershire.

A TASTE OF THE COTSWOLDS

There was a time when British food was considered lacklustre and dull, a poor relation to the gourmet cuisine of continental neighbours. Not so in the Cotswolds, whose farming traditions go back centuries. Pubs, restaurants and cafés are plentiful in the Cotswolds with many using the wealth of produce from the doorstep and, while there are still bland menus out there, I'd say that there are more places to eat with excellent food than there are with indifferent menus.

Perhaps that's unsurprising given the enormous choice of local, seasonal and organic food that is produced in the Cotswolds – and which you can also get your hands on at a plentiful supply of farmers'

THE COTSWOLD LION

Few breeds of animal can claim to have helped shape the economic history of England and create an entire landscape based upon their fame, but the Cotswold sheep is one of them. Descended from the flocks that grazed the Cotswold hills in Roman times, it was originally a rugged animal whose characteristics evolved over time. To my mind, the Romans' greatest legacy to the area is their introduction of this breed.

Its wool was already recognised as important and of good quality by the Romans and became known as the Golden fleece because it generated so much wealth. It was exported during Saxon times but had its heyday in the Middle Ages, when the sheep became known as the Cotswold lion. The sheep grew large, their coats heavy and thick owing to the herb- and grass-rich limestone pastures on which they grazed; they were big, strong and hardy. This gave the Cotswold lion a second golden age in the 19th century when, rather than wool, rams were in huge demand. They were exported all over the world for breeding to generate the tasty meat for which the sheep had now become renowned. But as Victorian-sized families disappeared, the need for large meat joints declined.

Today, numbers are increasing again. With a renewed emphasis on low-impact farming, the Cotswold lion's traditional qualities are the focus of attention. The breed has evolved further, so it is much larger than its 15th-century forebears and creates outstandingly flavoursome meat as well as special-quality long fleece.

I spoke to Steve Higgins, sheep farmer and judge of the Cotswold sheep breed at Moreton Show (page 151). I asked him what a judge is looking for to find a champion Cotswold lion at agricultural shows.

markets, organic farm shops or, indeed, by visiting the place where the food and drink is produced. Visit **Winstones Cotswolds Ice Cream** (page 330) and you'll probably see some of the cows sitting outside the ice-cream parlour enjoying the same view of Stroud as you are; head to **Cotswold Lavender** (page 108) during the summer and you can sample lavender shortbread while overlooking the purple hues; or take a tour at **Cotswolds Distillery** (page 144) and see how its gin is made.

If you like fresh milk, you can purchase milk that pours from a tap at **Gorsehill Abbey Farm** at Willersey (page 103) or rare-breed meat from Conygree Farm, based on the National Trust's **Sherborne Estate** (page 209), whose cattle are kept to help maintain the look of the Cotswolds. If it's **Cotswold lamb** that you wish to taste, make sure that you check it is the meat of the actual Cotswold sheep rare breed and not simply meat from sheep grazed *in* the Cotswolds.

'First, the fleece is naturally very important,' Steve explained. 'The crimp or curl should be uniform and the staple [the natural clusters of wool] should be long and wide when parted. The lustre of the fleece must be good; there should be a yellow tinge to the root.'

Steve continued, 'The sheep should have a good, wide head with a white and black nose. The "top knot", the distinguishing feature of the Cotswold sheep, should be left on rather than sheared for judging. There is usually a compromise, balancing the shape and size of the sheep alongside the quality of the wool. It's got to be big – the Cotswold is one of the biggest breeds in Britain. Otherwise, it comes down to "I like the look of that one!"'

It is the male sheep that grows the longest wool and the first shear is always the best wool. Because the sheep were kept especially for their wool, the animals were that much older. Therefore the meat was actually mutton, which is why they became renowned for their flavour. However, today Cotswold sheep are kept more for their meat than their wool (although there is a demand for it, to use in crafts, insulation and mattresses). The Cotswold sheep is bigger boned so it creates a large joint. There is more fat and more marbling than modern breeds and this gives the meat its flavour; it is a very traditional joint of meat.

According to the Cotswold Sheep Society (cotswoldsheepsociety.co.uk), which has around a hundred members, there are approximately 2,000 breeding ewes. That still makes the Cotswold sheep a rare breed, but numbers are increasing as demand for the delicious meat develops. As for the character of the breed, 'They are very docile and easy to handle,' said Steve. 'They are the sheep with manners.'

CHEESE & ALE

It might not be obvious at first glance but the Cotswolds has built quite a reputation for both cheese and ale with numerous artisan cheesemakers and craft breweries established over the last ten years. The desire to create quality products with low food miles is evident – many of the cheese dairies are on-farm, using milk from the farmer's own dairy herd.

Put all the **cheeses** produced in the Cotswolds together and you won't just have a platter, but an entire chiller cabinet! All the producers are passionate about cheese and cheesemaking, like **King Stone Dairy** at Chedworth, creating the deliciously gooey Rollright, washed-rind Evenlode and the buttery Moreton, a Cotswold take on an Alpine cheese; or **Simon Weaver** producing a Cotswold Brie at Cotswold Organic Dairy in the Slaughters (page 171) and **Cerney Cheese**,

DAVIDMARTYN/D

NICK TURNER/COTSWOLDS.COM

FARMSHOP

CAROLINE MILLS

MARIE LOUISE FRENCH

creating a notable goat's cheese, Cerney Ash. Without thinking too hard, I've counted ten cheesemakers.

Of course, cheese washes down very well with an **ale** and the Cotswolds is filled with breweries. Only recently I decided to carry out a taste test and picked up five beers from five different breweries – all within a ten-mile radius around the north Cotswolds. Some, like **Hook Norton Brewery** (page 128) and **Donnington Ales** (page 165), both possible to visit, have been around for over a century and have countrywide reputations. Others, like **Chadlington** and the **North Cotswold Brewery** at Stretton-on-Fosse, are microbreweries, established far more recently. Hawkstone, the one-time **Cotswold Brewing Company**, created one of the UK's first lagers in 2005. It was delicious then, and has more recently been noticed and taken up by Jeremy Clarkson, sending the renamed Bourton-on-the-Water brewery into brewing stardom. To the west is the **Cotswold Lion Brewery** at Cheltenham and **Goff's Brewery** in Winchcombe and, further south, the towns of Uley, Stroud and Bath all have their own breweries. With the exception of Bath Ales (which was sold to Cornish brewers St Austell Brewery in 2016), all the Cotswold breweries remain independent and are a far cry from the mass-produced conglomerates.

WHERE TO BUY & TASTE FOOD & DRINK

I've included my pick of places in which to buy or, indeed, taste Cotswold-produced food and drink within each chapter, including details for farmers' markets in Dursley, Malmesbury, Oxford, Stroud – considered one of the finest – Stow-on-the-Wold and Wotton-under-Edge. You'll also find farmers' markets in Bath, Cirencester, Cheltenham, Chipping Norton, Witney and Woodstock, generally held once a month except in Bath, the first farmers' market to be established in the UK in 1997, which is held every Saturday.

Farm shops can be an over-used ambiguous term these days, with much produce in so-named establishments imported from abroad, the shops themselves often not associated with any particular farm. The Cotswolds is fortunate to have numerous farm shops that genuinely sell produce from,

---

◀ **1** Try lavender shortbread while looking over the fields of purple at Cotswold Lavender (page 108). **2** The weekly farmers' market in Stroud is excellent (page 309). **3** Stock up on local produce at Jolly Nice Farm Shop & Kitchen (page 295). **4** The Cotswold lion sheep breed is known for its handsome looks and tasty meat (page 16).

in many instances, its own large farmland estate, the most notable being Daylesford (page 245), which has developed significantly over the years to encompass all things food-related and more, from a cookery school to Green Michelin-starred restaurant. Daylesford is not the only cookery school in the Cotswolds, with others gaining a prominent reputation for their enthusiasm about just-picked, seasonal and local (I mean a couple of miles, not 40) produce – Thyme at Southrop (page 224) and Foodworks Cookery School (page 233) in Colesbourne. For something extraordinary, there are baking courses, such as the outdoor wood-fired baking and heritage flour day at Shipton Mill (⌀ shipton-mill.com), organic flour millers near Tetbury. There has been a mill here since (at least) 1086!

LET SOMEONE ELSE DO THE COOKING

It's refreshing to see Cotswold born-and-bred chefs returning to their roots to cook up the countryside; chefs like Richard Craven at the **Royal Oak** in Whatcote (page 124) who walked the fields surrounding Chipping Campden as a child and, in his Michelin-starred gastro-pub, uses produce from friends on neighbouring farms.

One of my favourite places to eat is **StarBistro** (page 188), the epitome of the Slow Movement, where food not only nourishes the body but also the soul and the mind, as it provides work experience for young people with disabilities.

A COTSWOLD MENU

If I could create a menu from the Cotswolds, I'd choose fresh, in-season asparagus from the Vale of Evesham (page 91) to start, Gloucester Old Spot Pork from Todenham Manor Farm (page 150) or Cotswold lamb (the breed, rather than meat simply from the region) served with, well actually, vegetables from my garden, and for dessert? Ice cream from Winstones (page 330), Gorsehill Abbey Farm (page 103), Marshfield (page 350) or Quince & Clover (page 127) to accompany a bowl of fresh-picked fruit from Hayles Fruit Farm (page 180). Not forgetting the Cotswold cheeses and ale, or a glass of fizz from Woodchester Valley Vineyard!

HOW TO USE THIS BOOK

Despite going into some detail, *Slow Travel Cotswolds* is really a collection of choice pickings to inspire your own exciting exploration;

getting out there is by far the best bit. I've lived in the Cotswolds all my life and yet, although I hope to have given a good insight into the area, I feel as if I have so much still to learn about it myself.

I've touched upon much of the terrain within the boundaries of the National Landscape, but I've also added in a few gems on the fringes – some of my favourite places that I feel are worth exploring too and that, in my eyes, deserve to be included as part of the Cotswolds. For many years I've watched as tourists have flown in from all over the globe, 'done' Stratford-upon-Avon, hopped on a coach to take a photograph of Bibury (from the coach door) *en route* to Bath before 'doing' Oxford, then climbed back into an aeroplane to tell friends and family that they've been to 'the Cotswolds'. I'm not knocking this approach to travel (entirely) but I really hope that you can see a little more and get under the skin of what the Cotswolds are all about, meeting the communities that live and work here. Hence, I've broken the area down into more manageable pieces – or 'locales'. As it is such a rural region, I've included Stratford-upon-Avon, Oxford and Bath as those essential urban gateways to the Cotswolds.

Of course, there's only so much that you can include within the restrictions of word counts and numbers of pages. I've reluctantly had to remove some content in order to replace it with fresh material I desperately wanted to include for this third edition and, even so, still left out little nuggets.

To really appreciate the area in detail, I thoroughly recommend getting hold of a good, detailed **map**; I find the OS 1:25,000 Explorer series the most useful. Those covering the areas in this book are: OL45 *The Cotswolds*, 155 *Bristol & Bath*, 156 *Chippenham & Bradford-on-Avon*, 167 *Thornbury, Dursley & Yate*, 168 *Stroud, Tetbury & Malmesbury*, 169 *Cirencester & Swindon*, 179 *Gloucester, Cheltenham & Stroud*, 180 *Oxford*, 190 *Malvern Hills* (covers Bredon Hill in the Cotswolds), 191 *Banbury (Bicester) & Chipping Norton* and 205 *Stratford-upon-Avon*. Perhaps better for car touring or on-road cycling is the OS 1:50,000 Landranger series. Try: 172 *Bath & Bristol*, 164 *Oxford*, 163 *Cheltenham & Cirencester* and 151 *Stratford & Banbury*.

MAPS

The **double-page map** at the front of this book shows which area falls within each chapter. Each chapter then begins with a map featuring numbered stopping points that correspond to numbered headings in the text. The ♥ symbol on these maps indicates that there is a **walk** in that area, and featured walks are also given simple sketch maps. References are given to relevant **OS Explorer** or **Landranger** maps in the walk boxes, indicated by a ✤ symbol.

ACCOMMODATION, FOOD & DRINK

Throughout this book, I've listed a snapshot selection of recommended B&Bs, camping and glamping sites, unique self-catering cottages that are not second homes or bought specifically to run as holiday accommodation, lodges and a few boutique hotels: welcoming, heart-warming and occasionally quirky places. Those featured are my personal choice – the kinds of places I'd like to stay when visiting the region; no place has asked or paid to be in the guide. The hotels and B&Bs featured in this section are indicated by 🏠 under the heading for the town or village in which they are located. Self-catering options are indicated by 🏠, campsites by ⚊ and glamping ⚊. Descriptions of these properties appear at the end of the relevant section.

Also included throughout the book are suggestions of places to **eat and drink**. These can be a delightful tea room that serves extraordinarily good cakes, or a pub with something special to offer whether in its menu, its use of local or seasonal produce, or its exceptional location. There's also the odd fine-dining establishment – a hotel restaurant, for example, that offers extra special surroundings coupled with an excellent menu. Of course, places can change with exceedingly rapid speed; a change of ownership can make a place decline as fast as another gains an outstanding reputation. So, while this is my pick of places at the time of going to press, it is unlikely to be the same selection another time!

GETTING THERE & AROUND

Slow favours public transport and leg power: not only are these methods of travel kinder to the environment but they also allow you to see and experience places at the right pace. The most rewarding journeys

---

1 Cycling, such as across Minchinhampton Common (page 328), is a great way to get around. **2** The Cotswold Way provides 102 miles of beautiful walking (page 82). **3** Horseriding is popular in the Cotswolds; here, riders make their way through Stanton village (page 112). ▶

SHEILA TALBOT

NICK TURNER/COTSWOLDS

YOLFRAN/D

through the Cotswolds are those spent on foot or in the saddle to see the minutiae of a locale. You won't see the rare rufous grasshopper, localised to Cranham Common, or the gorgeous Duke of Burgundy butterfly, found on Rodborough Common, from the comfort of your car driving at 50 miles an hour. And, indeed, many of the Cotswolds' best-kept secrets *are* secret, because you can only reach them on foot.

Public transport

An entirely car-less holiday is possible in the Cotswolds, but it will take some planning, and while we speak of going slow, you will need to factor in significantly greater chunks of time to reach off-beat places. A relatively large **rail** network, with direct links from London, Birmingham, the southwest and south Wales, will get you started: one of the most useful stretches of line, particularly for the north Cotswolds, is run by Great Western Railway (⊘ gwr.com) between Oxford and Worcester with eight small-scale stations getting you into the heart of the countryside. Otherwise, mainline stations at Oxford, Banbury, Stratford-upon-Avon, Cheltenham Spa, Gloucester, Swindon and Bath Spa will help you on your way.

I've given **bus routes** where available under each place of interest, but changes to routes, route numbers, stops and timetables are frequent so it's advisable to check local council websites for Oxfordshire, Warwickshire, Gloucestershire, Wiltshire plus Bath and North East Somerset before travelling to avoid getting stranded. Each has a web page dedicated to current bus services.

Walking

It's as if the Cotswolds were made for walking, with the option to admire the views from the hills or stick to the riverside paths in the valleys. And for solitude, there are plenty of hidden valleys and wide expanses of hilltops to escape the crowds. That said, the most popular walk – and one of the most well-loved walking routes in the British Isles – is the **Cotswold Way**, the 102-mile National Trail between Chipping Campden and Bath. Indeed, Hilary Bradt, founder of Bradt Guides, declares it to be her favourite long-distance trail in Britain. Says Hilary, who hiked the full Cotswold Way with friends one May, 'We were lucky with unbroken sunshine, but it was the variety that made it so special, and the fact that the trail is so well maintained. At times we'd be walking through beech woods full of bluebells, then up to the escarpment for the views, then down to characteristic Cotswold villages. Also, nothing is too strenuous. I was nearly 82 when I did it (and did cut some days short) so I was relieved that it was manageable. If pushed to choose the best bit, I think it would be the extraordinary drop-off views around Leckhampton Hill (page 189) and the Devil's Chimney. I never expected the Cotswolds to deliver this sort of drama.'

There are many other named trails that criss-cross the Cotswolds including the **Monarch's Way**, **Macmillan Way**, **Thames Path**, **Shakespeare's Way** plus more localised trails such as the **Windrush Way** or **Kenelm's Way** that will help you to explore a locale in detail.

The Cotswolds has six **Walkers are Welcome** towns, which means each has joined a national initiative (walkersarewelcome.org.uk) to ensure their locales are attractive for walking, offering information on nearby walks and keeping footpaths and signposts well maintained. You'll find many pubs and cafés bearing the Walkers are Welcome window sticker: feel confident that they will not mind your muddy boots and wet-weather gear.

Cycling

For seasoned cyclists, the Cotswold hills are an exciting challenge; for those who last hopped on a bike some years ago, they can be daunting. However, there is sufficient diversity to please every type of cyclist with quiet, relatively flat, lanes to allow you to potter from village to village and traffic-free routes such as the Kennet and Avon Canal Path as well as regular inclines.

I've given tips on Sustrans' National Cycle Network routes and other trails under the *Cycling* heading in each chapter and listed reputable places for hiring and buying bikes – including electric bikes for those who like the idea of some assistance on the hills – and accessories or getting repairs. Guided cycle tours are thriving in the Cotswolds and I've included details of these too.

JOIN

THE TRAVEL CLUB

THE MEMBERSHIP CLUB FOR SERIOUS TRAVELLERS
FROM BRADT GUIDES

Be inspired
Free books and exclusive
insider travel tips
and inspiration

Save money
Special offers and
discounts from our
favourite travel brands

Plan the trip
of a lifetime
Access our exclusive concierge
service and have a bespoke
itinerary created for you
by a Bradt author

Join here:
bradtguides.com/travelclub

Membership levels to suit all budgets

Bradt GUIDES

TRAVEL TAKEN SERIOUSLY

1
COTSWOLD GATEWAYS

The Cotswolds is blessed by having on its doorstep three of England's most handsome and photogenic towns and cities: Stratford-upon-Avon in the north, Oxford to the east and Bath at the southern tip of the National Landscape. Hence, a visit to the Cotswolds doesn't need to involve a public-transport arrival in some grotty city locale followed by a hurried escape to your ultimate destination.

All three locations have been written about ad infinitum. Rather than regurgitate much of the same, I thought I'd introduce you to some of my favourite places to visit. Some are, indeed, world famous anyway – such as the magnificent Royal Shakespeare Theatres in Stratford-upon-Avon or the Royal Crescent in Bath. Others are less well known, like Shotover Country Park or the tiny village suburb of Iffley in Oxford. And some provide an alternative look at a famous location – the interior of Bath Abbey, for example, or Christ Church Meadow in Oxford, from where Britain's first ever hot-air balloon took off in 1784.

However you access the Cotswolds, do stay a while in one of these Cotswold gateways. They will not disappoint.

STRATFORD-UPON-AVON

🏠 Arden Hotel

As the birthplace of Shakespeare, this market town has been written about for centuries, 'done' by coachloads of ocean-hopping sightseers on wearying whistle-stop tours of Britain, and is arguably more famous than capital cities ten times its size. And yet, despite it being so celebrated, how many visitors *really* get to know Stratford?

I once overheard a tourist, clearly having been on one of those 'Britain-in-a-week' kind of holidays, respond to his wife, 'Stratford-upon-Avon? Now which one was that?' Stratford must surely leave a more lasting

TOURIST INFORMATION

Stratford-upon-Avon Bridgefoot CV37 6GW ✐ 01789 264293
⊘ shakespeares-england.co.uk

impression. And yet, where would Stratford be without Shakespeare? There are some who believe the town would be considerably better off if he'd been born somewhere else. Financially, I doubt that very much. I'm in the camp that's thrilled he was born in Stratford. Given my upbringing nearby, I consider myself extremely fortunate to live in close proximity to his legacies. Indeed, there's a gaping hole in Stratford's make-up if you don't at least acknowledge Shakespeare's importance to the town. So, rather than divide Stratford into geographical areas, I've split this section into two: Shakespeare's Stratford and – because there is more to Stratford than the literary man – the alternative side.

GETTING THERE & AROUND

Stratford is on a spur of the railway line from Birmingham Moor Street to Leamington Spa so all trains must pass through one or other of these stations to get there. It means that, despite the town being so famous, trains are not as frequent as you might think, the journey can be painfully slow and changing trains (from London) is inevitable. **Chiltern Railways** (⊘ chilternrailways.co.uk) runs a service from London Marylebone, changing at Leamington Spa while West Midlands Railway (⊘ westmidlandsrailway.co.uk) operates a direct route from Birmingham Moor Street. There are a couple of late evening trains back to Birmingham (none to London) to cater for theatregoers, but don't expect to squeeze in a post-theatre dinner. The station is a 15-minute walk from the town centre.

There is no specific **bus** station in Stratford. Bus stops line one side of Bridge Street and Wood Street; from there, buses depart for outlying villages within the Cotswolds plus Warwick, Leamington Spa, Evesham and Birmingham. You can access a timetable and service numbers at ⊘ warwickshire.gov.uk. **National Express** (⊘ nationalexpress.com) coaches from London Victoria stop at the Riverside coach park on Bridgeway (next to the leisure centre).

A hop-on, hop-off open-top **City Sightseeing Tour** (⊘ city-sightseeing.com) operates from Bridgefoot between April and October. It's a good way of reaching the few attractions away from the town centre, including Anne Hathaway's Cottage (though you can walk here, too – page 34), otherwise all sites mentioned in this chapter are within walking distance of one another.

The town has plenty of green spaces to take a quiet walk (page 40) rather than pounding the main shopping streets. Or you can take a guided **Stratford Town Walk** (⌖ stratfordtownwalk.co.uk) either during the day (including Christmas Day) or at night for the Stratford Town Ghost Walk, run by the same organisation.

The long-distance **Shakespeare's Way** is described by its founder Peter Titchmarsh (who also created the Macmillan Way) as 'a journey

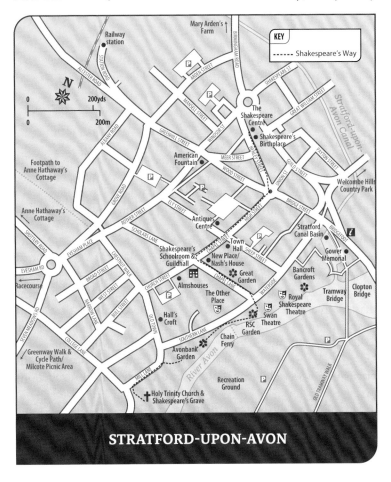

STRATFORD-UPON-AVON

of imagination'. Imaginary it certainly is, for it can only replicate by thought the route that William Shakespeare may have taken on his journeys between Stratford and London. The entire 146-mile route is fully waymarked and there's a complete map on ⊘ shakespearesway.org. The route starts at the poet's birthplace in Stratford and cuts across town before wheedling its way through some of the areas covered elsewhere in this book. It continues until reaching its destination, Shakespeare's Globe Theatre in London.

The Sustrans **National Cycle Network Route 5** runs through Stratford, including along the **Greenway** (page 41), a traffic-free cyclepath/footpath that uses an old railway line just to the west of Stratford.

BIKE HIRE, CYCLE SALES & REPAIRS
Stratford Bike Hire The Stratford Greenway, Seven Meadows Rd ⊘ 07711 776340 ⊘ stratfordbikehire.com. This place offers mountain bikes, touring bikes, children's bikes, tandems and trailer bikes, plus tricycles for the very youngest. Collect from the hire centre or they will deliver to your accommodation or starting point.

SHAKESPEARE'S STRATFORD

Stratford-upon-Avon is a relatively small town so there is no need, for the purposes of this guide, to split it up into areas. The town is growing considerably and fast, however, and you need to penetrate some unremarkable outskirts that give no hint of the attractive old centre.

The Royal Shakespeare Theatres
Royal Shakespeare Company Waterside ⊘ rsc.org.uk

If the reason you're going to Stratford is for its connection to Shakespeare then the places, more than any other, that I recommend visiting are the theatres, the home of the **Royal Shakespeare Company (RSC)**. Just saying or writing the words gives me tingles down the spine. Ben Jonson, a friend and contemporary playwright of Shakespeare, once wrote about his work: 'He was not of an age, but for all time!' The theatres are the place to connect with the man and his work; they are where his efforts live on for all time.

You don't have to watch a production just because it's the thing to do in Stratford, though I'd thoroughly recommend it. Visit one of the theatres, look around the foyer and free exhibitions, climb the RSC Tower connected to the theatre for views over the town or take a backstage tour and feel the energy and excitement that the buildings create. The chances are that as you discover more about his work and how it fits the modern world, the more you will want to watch a production. The RSC is, after all, the master craftsman at Shakespeare's plays.

Three performance spaces used by the RSC in Stratford are currently open to the public: the **Royal Shakespeare Theatre (RST)**, the **Swan Theatre** and **The Other Place**. My favourite is still the beautiful Swan. Its intimacy and warm brick and timber structure is worthy of a visit regardless of whether you enjoy watching a production there. Years back in my days as a young drama student dreaming of becoming a stage manager at the RSC, I would carry out work experience at the Swan, working alongside eminent lighting designers and technicians to change filters and watch productions from the lighting box. Even now, I feel energised as I enter the theatre and the first thing I do as I take my seat is to look up towards the lights – and as they fade and focus, drink in the creative vitality of the space.

However, there are other ways to enjoy the theatres and make the most of the Royal Shakespeare Company's presence. Look out for open days and special events, which may include visits behind the scenes, or a hands-on demo. Themed theatre tours are frequently available – including Touch Tours for visually impaired visitors – and there are regular talks by directors and actors about shows in production and

SHAKESPEARE'S BIRTHDAY

The date 23 April may be St George's Day, but in Stratford-upon-Avon it is Shakespeare's birthday (and the day of his death). There are always celebrations happening on that day in town, especially at his birthplace and at the Royal Shakespeare Theatre. You'll usually find a piece of birthday cake somewhere, and a colourful, flag-waving pageant and procession from his birthplace to 'Shakespeare's Church', where he was baptised and where he's buried, takes place every year on the Saturday closest to his birthday. The procession is led by boys from King Edward VI Grammar School, where he was a pupil, and includes representatives from organisations in the town, other schoolchildren, foreign dignitaries and members of the RSC. The procession files through the church, offering a new writing quill and placing flowers upon Shakespeare's grave to the ringing of the church bells. Members of the public are also invited to join the end of the procession and lay flowers.

events for families and children. No age group is left out – the RSC is adamant that Shakespeare is accessible to all.

I can vouch for that. My first visit to the RST was a production of *Henry V* at the age of four. I don't remember every detail, but I still have some enjoyable memories of the show. And that is where the strength of Stratford lies – in connecting with the powerful words of Shakespeare, watching a sublime performance of a play in an iconic setting and holding onto those memories forever.

Shakespeare's houses & gardens

Shakespeare Birthplace Trust Henley St (main office) ✆ 01789 204016
🖮 shakespeare.org.uk

So many places in Stratford enjoy celebrating a Shakespeare connection that you half expect a plaque on the wall of a building exclaiming excitedly that the great man 'may' have been troubled by flatulence there. Every Tudor building in the town has the possibility of some sideways association. However, five houses are genuinely linked to the man. They include **Shakespeare's Birthplace** and properties once owned by him (**New Place**) and his family (**Mary Arden's Farm, Anne Hathaway's Cottage, Hall's Croft**). As some of the few remaining wattle-and-daub buildings left in the town, they tend to sit prominently along the street frontages. Four of the houses (Hall's Croft is not currently open to the public) have events taking place throughout the year, from readings of the sonnets to outdoor plays, Tudor living history and children's activities.

There's no need for me to go into detail here about all five houses; you'll find plenty of information on the website of the Shakespeare Birthplace Trust (who own and care for the properties), which will help you gauge which of the properties you'd like to visit. I've simply expressed my reasons for visiting here. Note, however, that a combined ticket for the three properties open routinely to the public represents excellent value for money.

Shakespeare's Birthplace is noticeably out of keeping with the remainder of the properties in Henley Street. Its long road frontage

STRATFORD: Walk in Shakespeare's footsteps by visiting Anne Hathaway's Cottage (**1**) and his home at New Place (**2**). **3** A colourful pageant processes through Stratford to celebrate Shakespeare's birthday. **4** There's plenty of information and demonstrations at Shakespeare's Schoolroom. **5** Enjoy a performance of the Royal Shakespeare Company. ▶

SS

SHAKESPEARE BIRTHPLACE TRUST

SARA BEAUMONT PHOTOGRAPHY

DAVID TETT/RSC

SHAKESPEARE BIRTHPLACE TRUST

woos many a foreign visitor for whom this moment might be the first time they have ever seen such a quaint-looking house. Indeed, it is extremely striking for its antiquity both inside and out, and the garden in which it sits is kept beautifully.

For me, however, the most interesting aspect is not the room in which Shakespeare was born in 1564, but the exhibition through which you pass to reach the house. Located in the adjacent Shakespeare Centre, it gives a quick run-down of Shakespeare's life and, far from elevating him to dizzying heights beyond our grasp, proves him to be a human being. One who had to get married at the age of 18 (though this was quite usual in the period) because he'd got his older girlfriend pregnant, one who was caught poaching deer in nearby Charlecote Park, one who was fined for hoarding corn and one who was twice listed for tax evasion! There are poignant moments to pick up on too, such as the timing of his writing of *Twelfth Night*, a play about reuniting lost, believed dead, twins, shortly after the tragic death of one of his own children – also a twin. With a copy of the first folio of his plays from 1623 – now 400 years old – the exhibition explains how Shakespeare has helped to shape us into who we are, illustrating some of the many phrases and words from his plays that remain in common usage today.

Tucked into a quiet lane in a little offshoot village of Stratford known as Shottery is **Anne Hathaway's Cottage**, the childhood home of Shakespeare's wife, Anne Hathaway. Considered one of the most romantic of the Shakespeare houses, this is of course noted for being the place where the young and virile William wooed his future wife. One can understand how Shakespeare would have easily been seduced by the

WALK TO ANNE HATHAWAY'S COTTAGE

You can walk from the town centre along a pleasant, well-signposted, one-mile footpath to Anne Hathaway's Cottage. The footpath entrance is at Evesham Place next to the Woodstock Guest House. Follow it straight on, crossing minor residential roads, to a large open playing field (Shottery Fields) and continue to the sign on the opposite side, pointing left or right to the cottage.

The right-hand route is slightly more direct, but turn left (signposted Anne Hathaway's Cottage via Shottery). Turn right on Shottery Road and follow it round, past thatched cottages and The Bell public house to a mini roundabout. Turn left into Cottage Lane and walk a short distance to the cottage on the left-hand side. You'll find the house gable-end on to the road.

timber and thatched property alone, for it is the setting of the house and its gardens that is so eye-catching. Old orchards surround the house, providing the perfect opportunity for a gentle walk through the dappled shade. Ponder a while in a living willow cabin, or read a sonnet or two on a bench beneath the apple blossom and among the cowslips. Of particular note are the cottage gardens brimming with traditional floral scents and the allotment, which is based on Anne Hathaway's vegetable patch and features a range of fruit and vegetables, the varieties of which date back to the 16th century.

Perhaps of all the Shakespeare houses, **Shakespeare's New Place** has the closest connection, it being the property that the playwright bought from his earnings, and where he died in 1616. But there's a problem: New Place was bulldozed several centuries ago. Hence, like magic, visitors enter the 'property' as if walking through the front wall, on Chapel Street and into the courtyard; archaeological digs discovered the foundations that have allowed a reimagination of the grounds.

"Ponder a while in a living willow cabin, or read a sonnet or two on a bench beneath the apple blossom and among the cowslips."

There are permanent and temporary exhibitions in the neighbouring property, Nash's House, once belonging to Thomas Nash, the husband of Shakespeare's grand-daughter Elizabeth.

But the beauty of New Place, for me, lies not in the exhibitions but in the Great Garden behind. This is one of Stratford's loveliest green spaces with lawns, the flowing lines of bulbous yew hedges cossetting it from Chapel Lane. There are glorious views of the Royal Shakespeare Theatre buildings, The Guild Chapel, and the soft-pink gable-ends of Nash's House. The gardens are filled with colour, and an aging mulberry tree with connections to Shakespeare. It's a peaceful place to sit and contemplate Shakespeare enjoying the same view.

Holy Trinity Church

The spindly spire of what is known as 'Shakespeare's Church' dominates the skyline of the southwest side of Stratford. This is where William Shakespeare was baptised in 1564 and where he is buried, though you'll find a hunt around the grounds for his gravestone fruitless. His final resting place is inside the church and you have to pay a small fee to view it and the memorial bust that sits above (although entrance to the church is free). His wife Anne, daughter Susanna, son-in-law John Hall and grandson-in-law Thomas Nash are all buried in the chancel alongside him. His twin children Hamnet and Judith are buried in the churchyard with no known grave; two rowan trees have been planted along the North Walk to acknowledge and commemorate their lives.

That William is granted a grave free from the ravages of weather is not owing to his status as the greatest playwright that ever lived. He paid for the privilege! Keen not to have his bones dug up and placed in a charnel house to make way for other incumbents, he placed a curse upon his grave to ensure he could lay there in peace for eternity. To date no-one has dared to test this curse.

The church sits in a peaceful part of town, its spire towering above the banks of the River Avon. There's a pleasant riverside walk – and pilgrimage route – from the RSC theatres to the church.

Shakespeare's Schoolroom & Guildhall
Church St ⏿ shakespearesschoolroom.org

Few schools today can boast of possessing such historical buildings as King Edward VI Grammar School. But the long, low building that

THE SHAKESPEARE CENTRE LIBRARY & ARCHIVE
Henley St ⏿ shakespeare.org.uk. Access to the Reading Room is free of charge.

Archives can sound like stuffy places full of decaying books gathering dust. Not so the Shakespeare Centre Library, where the staff's enthusiasm for Shakespeare rubs off on anyone who wanders through the door of the Reading Room. The Shakespeare Birthplace Trust holds the world's largest and most important collection of material relating to Shakespeare, including early printed books, the sources of his plays, records and documents relating to Shakespeare's life and to Stratford in his lifetime as well as performance collections. The Trust looks after the entire archive of the Royal Shakespeare Company too, plus Shakespeare-related ephemera from all periods such as playbills and programmes, newspaper articles, manuscripts, original artworks, engravings, photographs and videos.

Says Paul Taylor, Head of Communications for the SBT, 'The whole purpose of the Trust is that we make Shakespeare engaging and fun. While there are scholars undertaking academic research, Shakespeare doesn't have to be intellectual. It can be emotional. After all, the best bit about Shakespeare is the stories, including his own; a smalltown boy made good.' It's important that visitors are not intimidated to come in through the doors of the Reading Room. All that's dominates Church Street is a heady mix of ancient timbers and the mirror-like sparkles of ageing leaded windows. In some respects it's 'just another' extraordinarily lovely building, but it's everything that this building represents that fires the imagination. For this is where William Shakespeare spent his formative years, 12 hours a day, six days a week for seven years. It's where, on the ageing floorboards and back-aching wooden forms, he sat and listened to Greek tragedies, learnt Latin and watched the performances of professional theatre troupes scuttling around a tiny room.

While the interior remains relatively bare, there's plenty of information to digest here about Shakespeare's education and there are numerous activities for children (and adults – try writing with a quill!) to do as they sit at sturdy wooden desks carved with the ancient graffiti of pupils distracted from their Latin verbs. But what I like about this building is not so much the knowledge that Master Shakespeare sat in this room for seven years but that it is still in use by the school; gold-inscribed boards hang on the wall with the names of the school's Head Boys and Girls and a morning meeting may well have taken place in the room before the tourist visitors arrive. It's a living, breathing space.

asked is that visitors arrive with some kind of preconceived interest. Rather than arriving and saying, 'I want to find out about Shakespeare,' visitors may have an interest in a particular play, a certain actor's involvement with the RSC or a particular aspect in relation to Shakespeare.

It is the RSC archives that are likely to be of interest to the casual visitor. These include prompt books and production notes including set and costume designs for all their plays and the shooting script for renowned stage performances that have been turned into films. Stage management recordings and professionally filmed cinematic recordings for live shows are all accessible, too.

Says Paul, 'It's really interesting to see how theatre has evolved, or otherwise. The prompt books for today's productions still arrive in ring binders with sticky notes and pencil markings all over them. You'd think these would be on an iPad now, but they're still pen and paper – and in the archives for anyone that wants to look at them.'

Look out, too, for leisure learning courses developed by the Trust (details in the 'What's On' section of the website). These can be between one and three days in Stratford and are usually in relation to a current RSC production at the theatre. They include a theatre ticket plus talks and activities by people involved with that production.

STRATFORD WITHOUT SHAKESPEARE

It is almost impossible to avoid a reference to Shakespeare surreptitiously creeping into the notes about other places in town. He is omnipresent. Without the poet, Stratford-upon-Avon would be an ordinary market town. Its name is a literal translation of 'the street at the ford on the river', the town having been an important crossing point over the Avon. Medieval town planners drew up Stratford on a grid system and the centre remains very similar today. The architecture has changed, however, with each street becoming a hotchpotch of styles including the few remaining half-timbered properties, Georgian townhouses and glass shopping malls. It's a compact town so you can easily walk the main streets within a morning to gather your bearings before deciding where you might like to visit. My preference is for the green spaces and a wander around **Old Town**, to the west of the town centre. There are no visitor attractions as such, but it provides an interesting and quiet change away from the fray. To see the best of Stratford's buildings, the following short, self-guided walk takes in some of the town's prettiest streets: from Shakespeare's Birthplace on Henley Street to High Street, Sheep Street, Waterside, Southern Lane, Old Town, College Street, College Lane, Bull Street, Narrow Lane, West Street, Chestnut Walk, Church Street, Chapel Street, and back to High Street.

The River Avon

After the Bard, it is the River Avon that is the biggest draw, for some the fun being to watch inexperienced rowers steer their hire boat – and its passengers – into the overhanging trees before fighting with an uncooperative oar to get them out of strife.

Despite its 85-mile length from Naseby in Northamptonshire to Tewkesbury, where it joins the Severn, the Avon is barely navigable before it reaches Stratford, and only then by a couple of locks downstream does it allow larger boats. Therefore the two-mile stretch from **Alveston**, a small village east of Stratford, to Holy Trinity Church (page 35) is virtually reserved for day-tripping rowers.

You can hire either traditional wooden rowing boats or engine-propelled craft – all named after a Shakespeare character of course –

1 See a different side of Stratford by boating or kayaking on the River Avon. **2** The Greenway, starting on the edge of Stratford, is a pleasant route for walkers and cyclists. ▶

CLAUDIO DIVIZIA/S

DAVIDMARTYN/D

from the boathouse by **Clopton Bridge** and next to the **chain ferry** southwest of the theatres.

Clopton Bridge is the main thoroughfare over the river in Stratford; the next crossing upstream is not for several miles. Built in 1480 by Hugh Clopton, later Lord Mayor of London, the bridge spans the entire width of the river with 14 arches, plus a ten-sided tollhouse at its northern end. It is one of Stratford's most enduring images.

To my mind, with only a small stretch of waterway available to rowing boats southwest of the bridge, which is also used by narrowboats and guided tours, the nicest option for **rowing** is to travel upstream underneath Clopton Bridge. You'll pass private gardens on one side of the river and open space on the other bank. Half a mile upstream is a picnic area where you can moor up and stretch your legs.

"Watch inexperienced rowers steer their hire boat – and its passengers – into the overhanging trees before fighting with an uncooperative oar."

The alternative to your own muscle power is to take a sightseeing cruise. **Avon Boating** (⊘ avon-boating.co.uk) runs half-hour cruises leaving from the Bancroft Gardens in a fleet of vintage boats. Alternatively, between April and October, there's an hour-long cruise with a tutored gin-tasting, partnering with **Shakespeare Distillery** (⊘ shakespearedistillery.com). Located in the town, the distillery makes multi-award-winning gins and is certified as a carbon-neutral business. You can also book a tour of the distillery, and take part in its gin school.

Green spaces & gardens

Stratford's abundance of green spaces is certainly one of the town's special points. The gardens around the Shakespeare properties are, surprisingly, some of the most peaceful, and colourful (page 32). They're not so much for sunbathing but they do provide a pleasant place to sit and read a book and enjoy the riot of colour from the flower borders.

Of the public parks, the **Bancroft Gardens** are the best known and most used owing to their location next to the River Avon and between the Royal Shakespeare Theatre and marina. There's usually a street artist performing and boats in the marina serving ice cream and snacks. On the Bridgefoot side of the marina, around the Gower Memorial – the most significant of many memorials to Shakespeare in the town – the gardens incorporate floral displays and a rose garden. The Bancroft

Gardens are the place to watch the world go by – and often the entire world does indeed seem to be there; don't expect solitude.

On the other side of the river to the Bancroft Gardens and the theatres is the **Recreation Ground** (or 'The Rec'). Occupying a large area running right the way along the river from Tramway Bridge (a pedestrian-only bridge adjacent to Clopton Bridge) to beyond Holy Trinity Church, this is one of the best areas for picnics with plenty of space to play and run around. There's a large playground here, too. On the north bank, to the west of the theatres are the connected **Avonbank and Swan gardens**. The Swan Garden, nearest to the town centre, looks over the Swan Theatre and is where the RSC puts on occasional events. Despite its proximity to the Bancroft Gardens – only the theatre stands between the two – it is considerably quieter and exudes a different atmosphere. The Avonbank Garden, also owned by the RSC, is quieter still, except on days when open-air productions are performed. Sitting between the Swan Garden and the Holy Trinity Church, it is leafier than any of the other open spaces. The 'pilgrimage' footpath from the theatres to Shakespeare's Church also runs through these two gardens.

The Greenway

A railway until 1976, the Greenway forms a traffic-free route for walkers, cyclists and horseriders. The route, which overlooks Stratford Racecourse for the first half-mile, begins from a car park and picnic area off Seven Meadows Road on the southwest outskirts of the town and continues for five miles to the village of Long Marston, where there is parking for horseboxes to allow riders to use the recreational route. Along the way are further picnic stops, one by Stannels Bridge on the banks of the Avon three-quarters of a mile from the start, the other at Milcote tucked away in a garden on the site of an old railway station.

"The Bancroft Gardens are the place to watch the world go by – and often the entire world does indeed seem to be there; don't expect solitude."

You can take a 3½-mile circular walk starting at either the Seven Meadows Road or the Milcote picnic area entrances and using the Greenway together with the Avon Valley Footpath or the **Monarch's Way** (for the best views of Holy Trinity Church) on the banks of the Avon. It's a pleasant out-of-town stroll that can be accessed from the centre of town when the crowds become too much. The Greenway suits wheelchairs and pushchairs; but anticipate that the Monarch's Way, here, gets very muddy in winter.

🧳 SPECIAL STAYS

Arden Hotel Waterside CV37 6BA ✆ 01789 298682 ⊘ theardenhotelstratford.com. Short of bunking down in the wings, this is as close to the Royal Shakespeare Theatre as you can stay. It's a boutique hotel that's won multiple awards, with very comfortable king-size beds and large bathrooms. A brasserie, champagne bar, lounge and beautiful terrace with knot garden overlooking the theatre complete the package.

🍴 FOOD & DRINK

Stratford has a huge number of places to eat and drink; however the town has somewhat lost its culinary way in recent years, gobbled up by the endless chain restaurants found in any town and with few establishments that have much to say about using local produce or sustainability. However, because of the theatres you'll get food well into the evening. Pre-theatre menus usually begin around 17.00, there's then a second sitting for those not going to the theatre followed by post-show dinners. These are my pick of the best in town.

Bobby's The Greenway, Seven Meadows Rd ⊘ bobbysstratford.co.uk. Light bites (toasties, breakfast baps) and excellent homemade cakes and coffee in a converted railway carriage overlooking Stratford Racecourse. Weekend evenings includes a bar. Very pleasant spot.
Dirty Duck Southern Lane ✆ 01789 297312 ⊘ greeneking-pubs.co.uk. Also, but rarely, known as the Black Swan – look at the pub sign hanging over the door. The Dirty Duck is a Stratford institution for being the place where actors from the RSC hang out after a show, it being 2 minutes' walk from the theatre. There are much better places to eat in town but come here to drink in the Actors' Bar, which is covered with signed photos of past thespian customers, or sit outside on the terrace overlooking the river and the theatres.
Green Intentions The Antiques Centre, off Ely St. A tiny (six tables) coffee shop with a cosy ambience in a corner of the Antiques Centre, this is a useful place to pick up knick-knacks. It serves light lunches (homemade soup, smoked salmon and ricotta quiche), excellent homemade cakes and the best coffee in Stratford, using local Monsoon Estates fresh-ground beans. The first zero-waste coffee shop in town, where 90% of waste is reused, repurposed, recycled or composted.
RSC Rooftop Restaurant Royal Shakespeare Theatre ✆ 01789 403449 ⊘ rsc.org.uk. Restaurant on the third floor of the Royal Shakespeare Theatre providing commanding views over the river and Bancroft Gardens. Pre-theatre menus, using local produce, are available along with light lunches (one of the nicest places in town for lunch), afternoon tea, dinner, cocktails and Sunday brunch.

The Woodsman Chapel St ℰ 01789 331535 ⬧ thewoodsmanrestaurant.co.uk. A theatre-style restaurant, cooking over wood and charcoal, where you can watch the chefs at work. Using the best, sustainably sourced British ingredients, including wild food harvested by the restaurant team and the restaurant's own deer larder, with nothing wasted. 'We know the story of everything on the menu.'

OXFORD

🏠 **Malmaison Oxford**

It was the poet Matthew Arnold who first described Oxford as the 'city of dreaming spires' in 1865, and the epithet has stuck ever since. Arnold was a professor of poetry at the university when he penned it, depicting the panorama of turrets and pinnacles seen from Boars Hill, southwest of the city. Seen from here (and it's well worth the walk; page 54) or any one of the other viewpoints around the outskirts of the city, or by climbing a tower in the centre, the skyline has a magical quality that makes even the most hurried tourist stand still for a moment. It's like seeing the Duomo in Florence for the first time or the plan of Paris from the Arc de Triomphe.

But I like the notion that in this university town, Arnold's 'dreaming spires' are all about the hopes and aspirations of the thousands of

THE UNIVERSITY OF OXFORD

Oxford University is an umbrella institution for 38 self-governing colleges and students are affiliated to one of these for the duration of their studies. Consequently, there is no campus as such but endless college halls and, in among them, the buildings of the various faculties – Music, History, Engineering, and so on. Many colleges, such as Balliol and Christ Church, are centuries old. They began as religious institutions and their ornamented cloistered buildings reflect this: quadrangles, chapels, formal gardens, gatehouses and porters' lodges are frequent features.

Tourists may visit the grounds of some university colleges and go inside some halls.

The best known – Christ Church, Magdalen and New College, for example – charge nominal fees (with the opportunity to visit free of charge during the annual Open Doors event), but there are several colleges that you may enter free of charge. Of these, take a look at St John's, All Souls and Keble colleges in particular for architectural interest and a view of college traditions. Dates and times of entry for visitors vary between colleges and seasons; most display a board outside the gatehouse indicating whether they accept visitors and when, or you can visit the university website ⬧ ox.ac.uk, which provides opening hours and costs for each college.

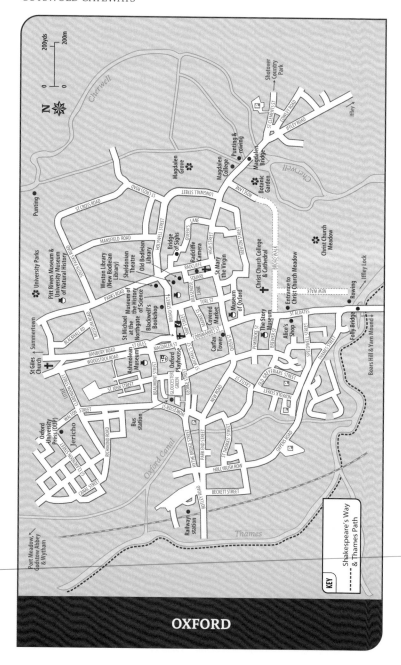

OXFORD

students that pass through the halls, passageways and courtyards every year. For there is no doubt that the architecture and the traditions embedded within the walls of the Oxford colleges make the city an inspirational place to study. Watching the scholars chatting in the cafés takes me back to my own student days, poring over reams of literary notes, a novel several inches thick open on the table, while trying to make one coffee last several hours.

The city may be rooted in tradition, but it's not stuck in the past, the romantic scholarly buildings merely the backdrop upon which to create an exciting stay.

GETTING THERE & AROUND

Oxford is remarkably easy to get to and has excellent connections. Traffic in Oxford is, however, a problem and the cost of car parking is extortionate. The city has introduced a Zero Emission Zone; relatively small at the moment, covering a handful of streets, but with plans to extend following public consultation. I strongly recommend using one of the five park-and-ride sites on the outskirts if you are driving to the city.

Frequent direct **train** services operate between Oxford and London Paddington and Birmingham New Street. Services from the north are via Birmingham, from the south via Reading and from the west via Didcot.

A very frequent **coach** service, the **Oxford Tube** (⊘ oxfordtube.com), operates every few minutes between central London and Oxford 24 hours a day. The journey takes approximately an hour and 40 minutes, terminating at the coach station at **Gloucester Green**. It's relatively efficient (traffic permitting) and comfortable, and considerably cheaper than rail. Services from elsewhere in the country are available by **National Express** (⊘ nationalexpress.com) and **Megabus** (⊘ megabus.com). The Oxford Bus Company also runs a frequent service, **the airline**, between the city and Heathrow and Gatwick airports.

There are frequent bus services between Oxford and the outlying villages too, mostly operated by Stagecoach and the Oxford Bus Company, as are the services around the city centre.

The best way to see Oxford is **on foot**, with several of the streets in the city centre pedestrianised. **Walking tours** are big business in Oxford, departing daily from Broad Street; tours should be pre-booked with Oxford Official Walking Tours (⊘ oxfordofficialwalkingtours.org). Pick your theme; there are six, from simple tours of the colleges to specific themes such as Inspector Morse, Ghosts, or Harry Potter Highlights.

"Oxford's streets rival Beijing's for the concentration of bicycles, and cycling is the preferred mode of transport for the city student."

There are plenty of opportunities to get away from the city streets for a quieter amble too. Both Shakespeare's Way and the Thames Path pass through the centre of Oxford and places such as **Port Meadow** to the northwest provide acres of peace. My choice every time would be to visit **Christ Church Meadow**. It's right in the very centre, so you can combine bustling city sightseeing with quiet riverside contemplation without having to travel too far to reach it.

Oxford's streets rival Beijing's for the concentration of bicycles, and **cycling** is the preferred mode of transport for the city student. Racks of bikes are a familiar sight, so you won't look out of place parking up against a lamp post. Just make sure you have a sturdy lock and chain though – bikes are desirable items in Oxford.

There's traffic-free cycling alongside the **Oxford Canal**, which travels right into the centre of Oxford from the north, though you should observe the 'No Cycling' signs in places. Sustrans **National Cycle Network Route 5** provides an alternative from Birmingham. A short section of the **Thames Path** also offers traffic-free cycling from Folly Bridge to Kennington.

If you'd prefer someone else to take charge, **Bainton Bikes** (see below) offer the **Official Oxford Cycle Tour** alongside various other theme-specific cycle tours.

BIKE HIRE & REPAIR

Bainton Bikes 78 Walton St ✆ 01865 311610 ⊘ baintonbikes.com. Bainton Bikes offers bicycle hire, including children's bikes (though, frankly, I wouldn't recommend children cycling around the busier streets), together with free puncture repair and breakdown support. Courtesy bikes are provided while they work on any repairs. 24/7 hire available from city locations using a phone app. They also offer various guided and self-guided tours around Oxford. Bikes can be delivered to your accommodation as required.

Bike Zone 28-32 St Michael's St ☏ 01865 728877 ⬦ bike-zone.co.uk. Bike hire, repairs and sales are provided here. Head upstairs to the Handle Bar Kitchen for eats.

A PERSONAL TOUR OF OXFORD

Oxford can easily be cut into four segments, with the **Carfax Tower** right in the city centre being the midpoint. Four roads, running almost due north to south and east to west, conveniently converge here – **St Aldates** to **Cornmarket Street** (running north towards **St Giles**) and the **High Street** to **Queen Street**. These I use as borderlines. The ethos of slow travel is not about cherry picking but here, I select the places I would take you to first if I was personally showing you around the city. I don't include, as you might imagine, all the major sights such as the Sheldonian Theatre or major museums, rather choice pickings of favourite haunts.

North of Queen Street & west of Cornmarket Street

My starting point is the **Carfax Tower**, at the crossroads of the four main streets in Oxford. Its name is derived from the French for crossroads, carrefour, and it's worth climbing the tower's 99 steps to get some bearings. There are so many 'dreaming spires' that they tend to blend into a confusing mishmash until you begin to recognise certain landmarks – the slender cupola of Tom Tower of Christ Church, the dome of the Radcliffe Camera, the spire of St Aldates Church or the pinnacled tower of Merton College Chapel.

The Carfax Tower is all that remains of St Martin's Church, the main body having been demolished to make way for road widening at the end of the 19th century. On its east façade, facing the High Street, is the church clock, accompanied by two 'quarter boys' who chime the bells every quarter-hour.

St Giles is the widest boulevard-like street in the city, adorned by magnificent university college buildings built with those dream-like qualities referred to by Matthew Arnold – St John's College on the east side and Blackfriars, on the west, home to a community of Dominican friars. St Giles, the patron saint of the poor, has a church dedicated to him at the northern end of the road where the Woodstock and Banbury roads converge. St Giles provides the eastern edge for an area of Oxford known as **Jericho**. Formerly the quarter where print workers lived, this has always had a unique character and in recent years has become a

CHRIS DORNEY/D

EXPERIENCE OXFORDSHIRE

NIELS VAN GIJN/AWL

OXFORD UNIVERSITY MUSEUM OF NATURAL HISTORY/EXPERIENCE OXFORDSHIRE

trendy part of town, occupied by chic eating houses such as Raymond Blanc's Brasserie Blanc on **Walton Street**. Neighbouring Great Clarendon Street is home to the enormous – in both square footage and stature – **Oxford University Press** and the world's most famous dictionary, the *Oxford English Dictionary* (OED). You can visit, by appointment, the OUP museum to see displays of, among historic printing equipment, *Alice's Adventures in Wonderland* and the OED.

Just off Walton Street, tucked around the corner on Beaumont Street, is a plaque that marks the Norman Beaumont Palace. No longer standing, it was once a significant structure and the birthplace of two of England's most notable kings, brothers King John and Richard the Lionheart.

North of High Street & east of St Giles

To Oxonians, the High Street is simply known as **The High**, a street bordered by shops for the first few yards from the Carfax Tower before being lined with the silk of smooth, honey-stoned college buildings. The area north of the High Street is one of the most concentrated university areas in Oxford, with some of the best-known colleges, such as Brasenose, Jesus, Queen's, New College, Balliol, Trinity and All Souls, along with the most familiar university landmarks – the Radcliffe Camera, the Bodleian Library and the Sheldonian Theatre.

This is the best quarter for walking, with plenty of car-free streets, where you can glance at the magnificent architecture, craning your neck to look at the numerous grotesques and gargoyles that hang from the walls like impious schoolboys. One of the narrowest streets to wander in this area is the winding Queen's Lane that leads to New College Lane and Catte Street. Crossing the two is the **Bridge of Sighs** joining the old and new quadrangles of Hertford College. So called because of its supposed similarity to the Venetian Bridge of Sighs (it actually resembles the Rialto Bridge more closely), its official title is Hertford Bridge.

To me, nowhere more epitomises how special learning in Oxford is than **Radcliffe Square**, with the well-dressed entrance to Brasenose College on the west side, the ornamented gilt gates entering the other world of All Souls College to the east, the University Church spreading

◀OXFORD: **1** Spot the 'quarter boys' who chime every quarter-hour on the Carfax Tower clock. **2** The iconic Palladian Radcliffe Camera. **3** The Covered Market is full of independent boutiques. **4** The awe-inspiring interior of the University Museum of Natural History.

itself between the square and The High, the mesmeric matter of the Bodleian Library to the north and, in the centre, encompassed by iron fences, the **Radcliffe Camera**. This Palladian building is one of the most iconic landmarks of Oxford and is now used as a part of the **Bodleian Library** (⥢ visit.bodleian.ox.ac.uk).

One of the greatest research libraries in the world, the Bodleian is also one of a handful entitled to receive a copy of every book published in the UK; it now stores over eight million volumes on 110 miles of shelving, much underground. Visitors are allowed to visit the Old Bodleian Library, which includes the Divinity School, the university's oldest teaching and examination room, dating back to 1427. Entrance to the Schools Quadrangle, the courtyard in the centre of the Old Bodleian Library and the Exhibition Room, where regular displays are held, is free but you can take a behind-the-scenes guided tour of other areas within the library, worth every penny just to see the vaulted ceiling, as intricate as a lady's lace fan, in the Divinity School as well as the Camera. My most recent visit was to the Weston Library (a part of the Bodleian), on Broad Street. The building itself is a work of art that has won many architectural prizes, but I was there to look at *Oxfordshire*, one of the set of **Sheldon Tapestry Maps** (page 142) on display. Showcased in the vast entrance hall, the mezzanine above lined with ancient volumes, the tapestry is grand in scale and distinguished in quality, though limited chunks of it remain. Despite its patchy existence (parts of the Cotswolds are on view and labelled so within the stitching), it is, quite simply, one of the most beautiful things that you will see in Oxford.

> "The Museum of Natural History is a fabulous building. Internally, the roof and ribs of the building are as skeleton-like as the exhibits it shelters."

Two of the best museums owned by the university are in this quarter: the **University Museum of Natural History** (⥢ oumnh. ox.ac.uk) and the **Pitt Rivers Museum** (⥢ prm.ox.ac.uk). Both are free to enter and a big hit with children. The Museum of Natural History is a fabulous building. Internally, the roof and ribs of the building are as skeleton-like as the exhibits it shelters. Marble busts and figures of eminent scientists such as Darwin, Aristotle, Galileo and Newton peer down upon you from among the arches as if to say, 'Don't you know anything?' There's a portrait of the Oxford dodo within the museum, information about the pigeon-like bird, where it came from and how one came to be in Oxford – and how European explorers and settlers aided its extinction.

The Pitt Rivers Museum provides a dramatic change from the light and lofty natural history museum, through which it's accessed. Very dark, it is like entering Granny's attic, and is likeably old-fashioned. Three floors are stuffed full with over half a million artefacts and objects from around the world – anything from a totem pole to an ivory salt spoon, a knuckleduster to an old typewriter. Visitors are provided with torches to peer in the cabinets and anywhere else that objects from the anthropological collection are crammed. Children love the whole feel of the museum and there are many family events and activities planned throughout the year. But there is far too much to take in over one visit, so it's an idea to explore a couple of themes at a time.

South of High Street & east of St Aldates

Along **St Aldates** you'll see the vast expanse of **Christ Church College**, the slender cupola of the Tom Tower a giveaway to its presence. The tower is named after Great Tom, the bell within that resonates across Oxford 101 times every night at 21.05. The timing is significant, as the five-minute time delay is equivalent to 21.00 'Oxford Time', being west of the Greenwich meridian.

Built by Sir Christopher Wren, the Tom Tower hangs over Tom Gate, the main entrance to Christ Church College. The entrance for visitors to the college is through the wide decorative gates just to the south of

THE FIRST ENGLISH AERONAUT

James Sadler might not be a familiar name today but 200 years ago all of England knew his name. He was a lowly pastry chef who had an eye for science. He began to experiment with gas-filled balloons, was the first to use heat (a fire in the basket) to 'control' a balloon's altitude and on 4 October 1784 he became the first Englishman to fly, taking off from Christ Church Meadow in a balloon that he'd made himself. The balloon rose to approximately 3,500ft before coming down near Woodeaton, four miles away. He returned to the city 'an absolute hero', balloon fever gripped the nation and 30 years later Sadler had the patronage of the royal family for balloon flights in Hyde Park at the 1814 Jubilee.

All that remains to mark one of England's greatest achievements is a commemorative plaque along Dead Man's Walk, close to the spot where Sadler took off. He is buried within the grounds of St Edmund Hall, Oxford.

the college, from where you can access the Great Hall, which provided inspiration for the set of Hogwarts Hall in the Harry Potter films, Christ Church Cathedral and the Christ Church Picture Gallery with its collection of Old Masters.

These gates take you into **Christ Church Meadow**, one I would single out above all others in Oxford – an Arcadian idyll in the centre of a bustling city. From the gates are the most famous views of Christ Church across the carefully tended and colourful Memorial Garden. The Broad Walk cuts a straight line between the meadow and Merton Field to the River Cherwell. Linking up with the Broad Walk is the Dead Man's Walk that skirts Christ Church, Corpus Christi and Merton colleges, so named because it was the route taken by coffins to the Jewish cemetery – now the Botanic Garden – in the 13th century. But take the time to turn off the Broad Walk down the New Walk, another avenue of shady trees, past the longhorn cattle that graze the meadow towards the Thames, and you'll come to a more peaceful world.

One of the vintage views of Oxford is from the top of the little bridge that crosses the Cherwell to the Oxford University boathouses. With the cattle of Christ Church Meadow grazing the foreground, the spires of numerous colleges and churches and the dome of the Radcliffe Camera prick the skyline. A favourite spot of mine is a quiet bend in the River Cherwell just behind the boathouses at the very tip of Christ Church Meadow, where you hear the bells of the cathedral melodiously ringing in the distance and watch the whispery seed heads from the thistles that line the meadow floating away downstream.

"Watch the whispery seed heads from the thistles that line the meadow floating away downstream."

The meadow path along the banks of the Cherwell, being the furthest from the entrance gates at St Aldates, is one of the most pleasant places in Oxford for a summer picnic or a winter walk. Your lunchtime entertainment might be the hilarity of watching punts slide sideways as the inexperienced try to grasp the knack of punting, frequently finishing up with their pole stretched between two branches of a riverside tree. A leisurely punt along the Cherwell is as much a part of river life in Oxford as serious rowing. You can hire punts – or rowing boats – from the boathouse at Magdalen Bridge (⊘ oxfordpunting.co.uk), accessed off the High Street. Punts can also be hired from the **Cherwell Boathouse** (⊘ cherwellboathouse.co.uk), just north of University Parks, with a pleasant punt north to the 'rural' Victoria Arms, where you can moor your punt and have a drink in the pub garden before drifting back along the Cherwell.

I'd also really recommend a walk along the Thames Path to **Iffley**, 1½ miles downstream from Christ Church Meadow. One of the village suburbs that make up Oxford (Old Marston, Headington Quarry and Wolvercote are also notable and worth a detour), Iffley is filled with pretty houses and unexpected rural cottages and the stretch of river here is particularly attractive beside the lock. You can stop for a drink at the quirky Isis Farmhouse (⌀ theisisfarmhouse.co.uk), which has a huge grassy riverside garden.

Butting up to the Cherwell is the university's **Botanic Garden** (⌀ obga. ox.ac.uk), fit for any season and open all year round. Botanical family collections are grouped in large, rectangular borders and there are collections grouped by geography too. With over 7,000 different types of plant concentrated in just over four acres, it's the most compactly diverse collection of plants in the world, as well as being Britain's oldest botanic garden. One thing you'll not fail to miss is the impressive specimen *Pinus nigra* (black pine) tree with its stubby trunk and branches that

LEWIS CARROLL & ALICE IN WONDERLAND

No author was actually called Lewis Carroll: this is the pseudonym of Charles Lutwidge Dodgson. The Latin for Charles is Carolus, thereby Carroll, while Lutwidge translates as Ludovic, or Lewis when anglicised, hence Lewis Carroll.

Charles Dogdson both attended and, later, taught mathematics at Christ Church College. The college was also significant in the life of Alice Liddell, upon whom his celebrated book is based; Alice's father was Dean of Christ Church and a very good friend of Charles Dodgson. The mathematician would take Alice and her siblings for frequent rowing trips and picnics on the Isis, telling bizarre stories as they travelled. *Alice's Adventures Under Ground*

was born from this, and was later published as *Alice's Adventures in Wonderland*.

There are many places and features around Oxford that crop up in Lewis Carroll's books, one of which is the Oxford dodo. The Great Hall in Christ Church College houses portraits of Henry Liddell, Alice's father, and Charles Dodgson plus an 'Alice' window depicting Alice Liddell, the dodo and other Wonderland characters. The St Catherine Window in Christ Church Cathedral is dedicated to Alice's sister, Edith.

Alice's Shop, opposite the entrance to Christ Church Meadow on St Aldates, stuffed with Alice memorabilia today, was the sweet shop where the little girl would buy her favourite barley sugars.

twist and curl their way to the heavens. However, it's the second half of the garden, through the giant stone pillars, that I find more exciting. Less formal, it has paths curving around orchards and beanpoles, water features and borders exploding with colour from spring to autumn. And ferns, alpines, palms and tropical lilies the size of tractor tyres shelter from Britain's unpredictable weather in the greenhouses close to the river.

OXFORD'S OUTSKIRTS

Sometimes the world of academia and streets filled with ancient institutions can feel slightly claustrophobic and the need to escape bombards the mind. **Summertown** is a vibrant suburb to the north of Oxford with its own community feel and collection of shops and restaurants. It still retains the buzz of city life but without the glut of historic buildings. Alternatively, visit the multi-cultural **Cowley Road** and head off to the Mini Plant at Cowley where the bodywork of the Mini car is manufactured, a 'sample' decorating the factory roof as if perched ready for some kind of *Italian Job* stunt. You can take a tour of the Oxford plant by pre-booking via ⌀ visit-bmwgroup.com.

To the east of the city is **Shotover Country Park**, where 289 acres of hillside can be explored. With views over the city from the hilltop, bracken-covered slopes sit side by side with ancient woods – it was once part of the royal forest of Shotover – flowery meadows, marshes and ponds. Celandines, bluebells and ox-eye daisies swathe slopes frequented by butterflies, song thrushes and muntjac deer. The three waymarked trails all begin from Mary Sadler's Field, near the free car park at the hilltop entrance, plus an extensive network of other paths. A 20-station orienteering course is marked out around the park too.

The other high point, to the southwest of Oxford, is **Boars Hill**, where Matthew Arnold wrote about Oxford's dreaming spires. His poem attracted many people who built houses there to take advantage of the view he described, and the view disappeared. **Jarn Mound** was built by hand to retrieve the vista across the land on the north side of the hill, which is now owned by the Oxford Preservation Trust, an organisation

OXFORD: **1** Christ Church Meadow is an idyllic spot in the heart of the city. **2** The Botanic Garden features borders bursting with colour. **3** A punt along the River Cherwell is a quintessential Oxford experience. ▶

PAUL MURRAY/A

OXFORD BOTANIC GARDEN & ARBORETUM

EXPERIENCE OXFORDSHIRE

similar to the National Trust, but specifically for Oxford. Walking here, among the grass meadows, is magnificent.

Perhaps Oxford's most celebrated outlying area is the low-lying **Port Meadow**, adjoining Wolvercote Common. The 300 acres of riverside common land is a popular strolling ground, accessed at its southern end from Jericho close to the city centre and at its northern end from Wolvercote, where the popular Trout Inn tucks up against a spur of the River Isis (Thames). The Thames Path gives distant views of Oxford's roofline to the south and the remains of **Godstow Abbey** to the north. The 12th-century abbey was built for an order of Benedictine nuns, but was closed down during Henry VIII's Dissolution of the Monasteries. A nunnery noted for scandalous events including regular 'hospitality' for local monks, it was here that Henry VIII's royal ancestor Henry II met his long-term mistress Rosamund Clifford, with whom he had a son. Considered one of the most beautiful women of the time, she is depicted in many works of art and literature. The shallow spur of the river by the Airmen's Bridge just west of Lower Wolvercote makes this part of the water meadow a popular place for bathing, especially as it has a picnic area and a car park.

"The Thames Path gives distant views of Oxford's roofline to the south and the remains of Godstow Abbey to the north."

It was this section of the Isis, alongside Port Meadow, that Lewis Carroll and his young companions – Alice Liddell and her sisters – rowed one summer's day. During the trip the story that would become *Alice's Adventures in Wonderland* was created. Oxford River Cruises (⌀ oxfordrivercruises.com) run boat trips along this stretch of the river, including a three-hour Picnic Cruise. Afternoon tea trips and straightforward sightseeing trips on the stretch of river past Christ Church Meadow (page 52) are offered, too.

One final hideaway, only a mile west of Port Meadow is the tiny village of **Wytham**. It was a tradition before the age of the car for residents of Oxford to drive out from the city with a pony and cart for strawberry teas at Wytham. The University of Oxford owns most of the village today – Wytham Great Wood, on the hill behind, is a large ecological research 'laboratory' for the study of birds. Tucked over the little Wytham stream with its handsome manor house and church, the village is worlds apart from city life. The little village shop includes a tea garden where the tradition of having a strawberry tea continues. You can walk to the village from the city using the Thames Path or by crossing Port Meadow and walking the last few yards along the quiet road from the Trout Inn.

SPECIAL STAYS

Malmaison Oxford Oxford Castle, 3 New Rd, OX1 1AY ☏ 01865 689944 ☖ malmaison. com. Your chance to 'do time' in what was once the Norman castle, later adapted into Oxford Prison. The beds are more comfortable these days, and the bathrooms considerably more than a bucket in the corner, but you still get to stay in the same cells. The original features of the prison are retained: the main 'hall' is extraordinary while the al fresco terrace was once the exercise yard. Expect the food to be a good deal more pleasurable than it was as a prison.

FOOD & DRINK

Oxford is a cosmopolitan city and you can buy sushi or tapas just as easily as you can bangers and mash. The **Cowley Road** is where you'll find an eclectic mix of restaurants from many nations while small enclaves such as **Summertown** and **Jericho** each have their own collection of restaurants and bars. Afternoon tea in the Randolph, an Oxford institution, sits equally with intellectual chat in one of the many town pubs.

Cafés & restaurants

Gatineau 209 Banbury Rd ☏ 01865 311779 ☖ gatineau.uk.com. My guilty pleasure in Summertown – a French-owned and -run pâtisserie that's better than many in France! Come here for morning pastries, baguettes, amazing quiches, gateaux and desserts handmade (you can watch) on the premises.

G & D's Ice Cream ☖ gdcafe.com. Oxford's own small chain of boutique ice-cream parlours. George & Davis in Little Clarendon Street is where it's all made. Then there is also George & Danver in St Aldates and George & Delila on the Cowley Road. High-quality ice cream made in Oxford using natural ingredients.

THE COVERED MARKET

Oxford's Covered Market is special. Accessed off The High, Cornmarket Street and Market Street, it's full of cosy cafés and tiny independent boutiques selling interesting things. There is, still, a food market with a traditional butcher, fish counter and greengrocer. You can find products such as Oxford Blue cheese, Oxford Sauce with a kick that will send you flying over college roofs and Oxford Marmalade, sadly the only one now outsourced from other parts of the country. Look out for the market's famous Cake Shop too, where cake artists shape and decorate the cakes in the window.

Joe's Bar & Grill 260 Banbury Rd ✆ 01865 554484 🖥 joesrestaurants.co.uk. One of my other favourites. Inviting and very popular 'local' bistro restaurant with cosy, circular booths, outside tables and bar stools. Fabulous, freshly prepared food from breakfast to dinner, or you can enjoy a drink and nibbles. Joe's homemade burgers (beef, chicken, pulled pork or veggie) with a choice of toppings and homemade sauces); grilled goat's cheese salad.

Pierre Victoire Bistrot 9 Little Clarendon St ✆ 01865 316616 🖥 pierrevictoire.co.uk. Tiny, authentic, French-owned bistro serving classic, hearty dishes such as *moules marinière* and *cassoulet*. Set menus are good value with plenty of choice.

Vaults and Garden Café University Church of St Mary the Virgin, Radcliffe Sq ✆ 07814 264828 🖥 thevaultsandgarden.com. Come here just for the location – a quiet garden overlooking the Radcliffe Camera – or tuck down in the vaults of the University Church. Wholesome food made using organic and Fairtrade produce, much of it sourced from nearby farms.

Pubs

Cherwell Boathouse Bardwell Rd, OX2 6ST ✆ 01865 552746 🖥 cherwellboathouse. co.uk. On the banks of the River Cherwell, this is more restaurant than pub with wholesome, seasonal menus (coconut curried dauphinoise with sweetcorn, lime, chilli, mint and coriander; skate wing with garlic and caper butter). Not the cheapest in town but offers excellent quality. Hire of punts also available.

Lamb and Flag 12 St Giles ✆ 01865 515787. A literary institution that has been popular with students for decades. Thomas Hardy's *Jude the Obscure* was reputedly written here. Owned by St John's College and run by a community-interest company. Come here for a drink (real ale) but go elsewhere for food.

Perch Inn Binsey Lane ✆ 01865 728891 🖥 the-perch.co.uk. A 17th-century thatched pub in Binsey combining traditional Englishness with one of the best pub gardens I know. Dishes include braised pork shoulder, apple and grain-mustard suet-crust pie; and spinach, leek and tarragon cakes with goat's cheese cream .

Rusty Bicycle 28 Magdalen Rd ✆ 01865 435298 🖥 dodopubs.com/locations/the-rusty-bicycle. A quirky, sociable, community pub located between the Iffley and Cowley roads. Serves its own home brew alongside well-known ales, cocktails and an extensive wine list. Specialises in homemade burgers (the best in town) and slow-rise pizzas. A real find. You could also try its sister pub, **The Rickety Press** in Jericho, should you find yourself on the other side of town.

Trout Inn 195 Godstow Rd, Wolvercote OX2 6PN ✆ 01865 510930 🖥 thetroutoxford.co.uk. It takes a little effort to get here, but it's worth it for the superb location alone, and is my pick of the pubs. Frequented by many authors over the years including Lewis Carroll, C S Lewis and Colin Dexter, it has a large terrace on the banks of the Thames. Extensive vegan menu alongside popular gastro-pub favourites.

BATH

🏠 **Broad Street Townhouse**

As the birthplace of my mother and the city that launched my grandfather's career in music, I have affection for Bath. But then who doesn't? Its remarkable UNESCO World Heritage Site architecture and town planning, green spaces and attractive location, and associations with the Romans, Jane Austen, civilised living and restoring health maintain its draw as a fashionable city just as much now as it did in historical times.

In the legend recorded in Geoffrey of Monmouth's *Historia Regum Britanniae* in the 12th century, the story of Bath begins not with the Romans but with **King Bladud** in around 863BC. As a young prince he spent time in Greece where he contracted leprosy. Shunned and cast out when he returned home to England, he took a job as a swineherd in the marshy Avon Valley and drove his pigs across the Avon in search of acorns. The herd contracted his disease but seemed to be miraculously cured when they rolled around in the foul-smelling mud where hot springs bubbled from the earth's surface. Amazed by what he saw, Bladud bathed in the hot mud too and was cured in turn.

"Amazed by what he saw, Bladud bathed in the hot mud too and was cured in turn."

Free from stigma, Bladud returned home and became King of the Britons (and later father to King Lear, the very one immortalised by Shakespeare). Grateful for his cure, he founded the city of Bath and dedicated the thermal springs to the Celtic goddess Sul. Some 900 years later the **Romans**, hearing of the powers of the waters at Bath, came to worship the goddess and named the city Aquae Sulis, or 'Waters of Sul'. A statue of Bladud and one of his pigs stands in the **Parade Gardens**, next to the river. So, if you see pigs around the city, wooden or otherwise, you'll know why.

Like Oxford and Stratford-upon-Avon, I've selected my personal favourites here – the places I would choose to take you to if I were showing you around the city, or indeed the places I tend to gravitate towards myself. I haven't included popular attractions like the famous **Roman Baths**, the **Jane Austen Centre** or Mary Shelley's **House of Frankenstein** (the book was written in Bath); you can pick up oodles of

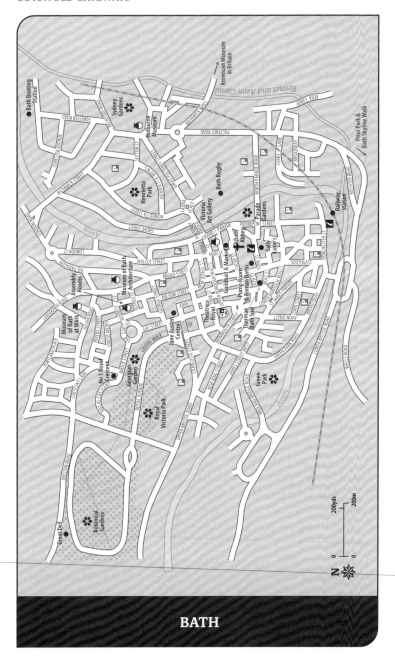

BATH

ⓘ TOURIST INFORMATION

Bath (no physical TIC exists so if you need a map, it's worth downloading prior to your visit)
⊘ visitbath.co.uk

---

information about these sights on their own websites. Though, naturally, I recommend visits to these, too!

GETTING THERE & AROUND

Great Western Railway (⊘ gwr.com) operates **train** services from London Paddington to Bath Spa and from the West Country and south Wales. Services also operate from London Waterloo and the southeast with, incongruously, **South Western Railway** ⊘ southwesternrailway. com). From the north, a change is likely at Bristol Temple Meads. Bath Spa station is next to the Southgate shopping centre and a ten-minute walk from the Roman Baths.

Coaches operate to Bath from most major towns in the UK, with frequent services from London Victoria coach station and direct from major airports. Regular **bus** services operate around the city, especially from Bath Spa station, and these are useful for reaching the outskirts. However, there is no substitute for walking in the city centre – indeed it's necessary, with many streets pedestrianised; it would be worth allowing an extra day in Bath to provide time to walk to all the attractions.

Those travelling by **car** are encouraged to park at one of the three park-and-ride sites on the outskirts of the city – use Lansdown from the north and east; Newbridge from the west or Odd Down from the south; just follow the 'P&R' signs – and catch the bus into the centre. Bath has introduced a Clean Air Zone through the centre; you can check if you need to pay for your vehicle at ⊘ beta.bathnes.gov.uk/ bath-clean-air-zone.

A **hop-on, hop-off sightseeing tour** operates in Bath, with 37 stops or a 45-minute non-stop journey if you use it as an initial introduction to the city in order to gather your bearings. Two routes operate, one around the main city centre, although you will need to walk to most attractions, but more useful is the 'Skyline Tour', which takes passengers east of the river and is particularly good for getting to the American Museum in Britain and Prior Park. There's no need to book, as buses run every few minutes from Bath Abbey (City Centre Tour) and Bath Spa station (Skyline Tour).

Despite its hilly tendencies, Bath is a delight for **walking**. The city – or the abbey to be precise – is of course the end, or beginning, of the **Cotswold Way** and as such makes it something of a modern-day pilgrimage site. For those who don't wish to trek the full 102 miles, a six-mile 'circular' walk has been devised whereby you can catch a bus from the city centre to the Lansdown park-and-ride site, walk across Bath Racecourse and then pick up the last few miles of the long-distance trail. On the way you'll get superb views of the city from **Kelston Round Hill** before descending towards the abbey. Full instructions for the 'Journey's End' walk can be downloaded from ∂ nationaltrail.co.uk/en_GB/trails/cotswold-way/circular-linear-walks-2.

Bath also has many options for **themed walking trails**, either guided or self-guided. You can pick up a 'City Trail' leaflet from the World Heritage Centre on York Street (beside the Roman Baths) to take yourself on a self-guided walk of all the sites in Bath that make it a UNESCO World Heritage Site.

You really do get something for nothing in Bath, in the form of **free walking tours**. Operating every day of the year, regardless of the weather, they begin at the Abbey churchyard entrance to the Pump Rooms and are taken by the Mayor of Bath's fully trained honorary guides. Tours last approximately 2 hours. An alternative stroll is the **Bizarre Bath Comedy Walk** (∂ bizarrebath.co.uk), which has now been running for more than 20 years. It's more street theatre than guided walk, and you'll find the evening flies by discovering stories of Bath that stretch the traditional image of the city. Running every evening from April to October, there is no need to pre-book; simply turn up at the Huntsman Inn (on North Parade Passage) at 20.00. Walks take place regardless of weather or dark evenings. Other options include Jane Austen's Bath, Bridgerton film locations, food and drink (∂ savouringbath.com), or a photo tour, led by a professional photographer.

"It's more street theatre than guided walk, and you'll find the evening flies by discovering stories of Bath that stretch the traditional image of the city."

For views over the centre of Bath and some of the idyllic surrounding countryside from the city, take the waymarked **Bath Skyline Walk**. The six-mile circular route gives you the chance to explore the area around

Claverton Down and **Bathampton Down** to the east of the city centre. You'll pass by an Iron Age hillfort, Roman settlements and Sham Castle, an 18th-century folly, as well as taking in wooded valleys and wildlife meadows owned by the National Trust. Take bus 410 or 418 from the bus station (next to Bath Spa railway station) to the University of Bath, where you can pick up the trail, signposted 'Bath Skyline' from Bathwick Fields.

For **cyclists**, the National Cycle Network Route 4 runs through the city, connecting Bath with Bristol to the west and Bradford-upon-Avon to the east. Much of the route is traffic-free, either using the very picturesque Kennet and Avon Canal Path, or the Bristol to Bath Cycle Path, along a disused railway west of the city.

 BIKE HIRE

Bath Bike Hire Bath Narrowboats, Sydney Wharf, Bathwick Hill BA2 4EL ✆ 01225 447276 🖉 bath-narrowboats.co.uk. Adults' and children's bikes for full-day hire plus trailers and tag-a-longs. Situated by the Kennet and Avon Canal, a 20-minute walk from Pulteney Bridge, and at Brassknocker Wharf; you can cycle straight from the hire centre onto the traffic-free cycle route along the towpath. Helmets are not provided.

Green Park Bike Station Green Park Road, Bath, BA1 1JB ✆ 01225 920148 🖉 greenparkbikestation.com. Twenty-four-hour and multiple-day hire of bikes and e-bikes. Helmets are not provided or available for hire. Bike sales, repairs and maintenance, too.

OLD BATH – AROUND BATH ABBEY

Before Bath reinvented itself in the 18th century by creating wide, fashionable avenues, it had a network of small alleyways and streets. There's little truly medieval in Bath such was its sweeping out of the past, but a few streets close to Bath Abbey give an impression of life in the city before its reincarnation. With tiny shopfronts and not-so-high buildings, they provide a fascinating change to the Palladian style of Georgian Bath. Many of the streets around Bath Abbey are pedestrianised, so make the most of this walking territory and spend a morning ambling from shop to shop.

The Pump Room

The 43 minerals within the water, which apparently cured Bladud, were deemed to have healing properties and new medical ideas in the late 17th century made 'taking the water' extremely fashionable. For this purpose, a Pump Room was opened in 1706 and **Beau Nash**, Bath's master of ceremonies, turned the building into a fashion icon. The vast, high-ceilinged room that you see today is the work of massive alterations in 1796 to accommodate all the new residents – Bath's population exploded from 2,000 to 38,000 during the late 18th century.

Taking afternoon tea in the Pump Room is an attraction in its own right, but this is still *the* place to take the waters and if you've paid to visit the Roman Baths then you are entitled to a free glass of spa water. It's pumped direct from the bubbling King's Spring below into an elegant urn placed reverently in the bow of a giant window. 'Do I have to drink it all?' I asked the waitress meekly. Memories came flooding back of struggling with a glass of the very same hot, sulphurous-cum-ferrous-tasting liquor in a show of macho Britishness to a French exchange student years before. 'Not if you don't want to, but it's good for you!' replied the matronly figure. It may not be the most elegant approach to drinking a glass of water in such an esteemed location, but my best advice is to 'down it' so that the drink barely touches the sides – the water has an undeniably revolting taste.

The alternative is to 'dine' in the Pump Room, where a glass of fizz can be ordered to disguise the taste of the water. Or do as I did and eat a Bath bun, designed for the very job of hiding the taste of the spring water. (A Bath bun is a little like a toasted teacake with currants and crystallised sugar on the top, served with cinnamon butter.)

Elegance is the word to sum up the Pump Room. Its very nature makes you sit up straight. The giant chandelier – taller than the height of most people's living rooms – sparkles across the hall, while the dashing figure of Beau Nash, holding his set of etiquette rules, peers down from the wall as if to make sure that you are holding your teacup correctly and keeping your elbows off the table. I cast an ear to the bow-tied Pump Room Trio, feeling some sense of connection in the room; this was where my grandfather held one of his first jobs as a conductor in the 1930s, leading the Pump Room Orchestra, allegedly one of the oldest established ensembles in the British Empire, founded by Beau Nash.

Thermae Bath Spa
Hot Bath St 𝒥 01225 331234 🖉 thermaebathspa.com

It's all very well looking at where the Romans enjoyed a bathe, but the spa waters still hold their therapeutic properties and Bath retains its

A HISTORY OF BATHING IN BATH

There are three naturally hot springs in Bath; one is the **King's Spring**, upon which the Roman Baths and the temple to Sulis Minerva were built. The other two are the **Cross Spring** and the **Hetling Spring**, close to one another in Hot Bath Street. Although Bath is principally known as a Roman and Georgian city, many people came in the intervening centuries to make use of the natural waters.

While the Georgians made 'taking the water' and bathing particularly fashionable, it was previous generations who paved the way, creating greater interest in Bath and its springs. Charles II, desperate for an heir and unable to produce a legitimate son, came to Bath to take the waters in the hope that their mystical powers would do something. He may have been suffering from syphilis, as was his brother James II, many of whose children conceived with his second wife, Mary of Modena, did not survive. Desperate

for a male heir, James and Mary both came to Bath and soon after produced a son, which caused many conspiracy theories about the paternity of the offspring. Regardless, the 'miracle' created something of a boom in tourism for Bath and once Queen Anne had paid a visit in 1702, sealing it as the place to be, Georgian Britain came to the city.

Following the Georgian period the spas in Bath continued to wave in and out of fashion for more than 150 years until they closed completely. In 2006 the **Thermae Bath Spa**, or New Royal Bath, opened to continue Bath's bathing traditions while in 2023, Cleveland Pools, reputedly Britain's oldest lido, reopened for the first time in 40 years following a restoration programme, saved from being demolished by the community. Though not spa water, the Grade II-listed heritage site is a welcome place for an open-air bathe.

fashionable status as a spa town. From the Roman baths, wander down Bath Street (the only double-colonnaded street in Britain) and at the far end, directly in front of you, you'll come to the Cross Bath and, to your left, the modern-day, glass-caged Thermae Bath Spa, promoting itself as 'Britain's original natural thermal spa'.

The open-air Cross Bath, opposite the spa's main entrance, is an intimate thermal pool enclosed by a World Heritage Site Georgian shell, where bathers can book the entire facility for private use. It's particularly popular with brides before a wedding and ideal for groups of friends looking for a special treat as nibbles and drinks can be served as part of a hire package. Inside the main glass-fronted spa building, numerous pools, steam rooms and treatment rooms all use the healing powers of the naturally heated waters to send visitors into a trance-like state of relaxation. The smell, by the way, is sweet-scented and nothing like that of the spa water drunk previously. But of all the alluring hot pools, massage jets, frankincense-infused steam rooms and body-wraps, the most inviting must be the open-air rooftop pool. 'Beauty heals,' said my guide, and the views of the city, abbey and green pastures beyond, which can all be seen while lying back in the steaming pool, are certainly stunning. It may be all in the mind rather than the water, but bathing here for an afternoon, or an evening as the sun goes down with the lights illuminating the abbey, has to be one of the best ways to enjoy the Cotswolds slowly.

Bath Abbey
🖮 bathabbey.org

The history of Bath Abbey is described in an extensive exhibition in the Discovery Centre beneath this illustrious building, so I don't feel the need to repeat it here. Instead, I'd prefer to focus on something that really caught my eye in a building that's so immense in scale and craftsmanship that you need to concentrate on selected aspects of it so as not to become punch-drunk.

It's the stone carving behind the high altar, beneath the dazzling east window. The carving is mind-blowing in detail and fragility, like a fine lace or ivory crochet. Knitting-needle columns progress to fan-shaped arches of graceful proportions, Gothic arches frame intimately carved reliefs and above are borders of leaves and flowers so soft and delicate they can't possibly be created from something as hard as stone. It made me look closer to seek out an accidental slip of the chisel that needed to be covered up, and wonder how much the stone carver swore and groaned at the prospect of a job so intricate, where tiny birds hidden among the leaves are carved so that you can see the eye and the tip of the beak.

"Tiny birds hidden among the leaves are carved so that you can see the eye and the tip of the beak."

While the fan-vaulted ceiling of Bath Abbey is a thing of extraordinary beauty, too, I'm inclined to watch my step crossing over the many dedications to the departed in the ledgerstones. One such grabbed my attention in the South Aisle. Dated 1742, it's to 'The Very Ingenious Mr Harvey'. No further detail, and we're left wondering why Mr Harvey was so very ingenious.

NEW BATH – 18TH-CENTURY BATH

No area of Bath was left untouched by the architect's pen when the city was remodelled: even the older streets close to Bath Abbey were tinkered with. But it is as the city moves north, away from the river, that we see the most profound effects. To appreciate the Bath that we see today is to understand something of 18th-century town planning when the city was transformed beyond recognition, and of the four men who were largely responsible for the changes (page 71): Ralph Allen (the man with the money), John Wood the Elder and his son John Wood the Younger (the architects), and 'Beau' Nash (the dandy).

Queen Square, The Circus & the Royal Crescent

These three addresses, some of the most fashionable in Bath, are linked by their architects, John Wood the Elder and Younger. The first to be built, in 1730, was **Queen Square**, an area of Bath that was badly damaged during World War II in the Baedeker Blitz, when the Luftwaffe targeted places of cultural interest by picking them out from Baedeker guidebooks. On the west side of Queen Square is the **Bath Royal Literary and Scientific Institution** (𝒥 01225 312084 𝄞 brlsi. org). The cultural centre provides a focal point for talks, discussions and debates, plus exhibitions throughout the year; you do not need to be a member to join events. A list of forthcoming activities, many

SYMBOLISM IN BATH'S ARCHITECTURE

Shape is crucial to Queen Square, The Circus and the Royal Crescent, and it's believed that the Woods had connections with the **Freemasons**. Much as he was obsessed with Palladian architecture, John Wood the Elder was also very interested in ancient monuments and druid activity, believing that there had been druid temples worshipping the sun and moon on Lansdown Hill in Bath. The Circus is partly inspired by Stonehenge (as well as the Colosseum in Rome) and supposedly represents the sun, while the Royal Crescent is a symbol of the moon.

Queen Square, supposedly representing the earth, is also aligned in such a way that it follows the Masonic path of the sun. There are many symbols associated with Freemasonry on the buildings themselves, particularly in The Circus, where you'll find a band of symbols such as set squares, compasses and shapes surrounding the circular 'street'. A **Masonic Hall** still operates in Bath, in Old Orchard Street. The original Theatre Royal building (𝄞 oldtheatreroyal.com), which you can visit, has a museum and collection of Masonic artefacts.

VISIT BATH

VISIT BATH

JENIFOTO406/D

RICH HOWMAN

SALLY LUNN'S

presented by eminent speakers and lecturers, is shown on the BRLSI website and in the foyer.

Just north of Queen Square, at the top of Gay Street, is **The Circus**. Begun in 1754 by John Wood the Elder, it was the first circular terrace in modern Europe but Wood died soon after the first stone was laid and his son (the Younger) completed the project. The terrace was originally called King's Circus after King Bladud and the acorns that adorn the tops of the buildings are a reference to the king and his swine herd.

Wander along **Gravel Walk**, between Gay Street and Royal Avenue, and you'll see the backs of the properties that introspectively look to The Circus. The backs reveal so much more and are by no means as elegant as the façades. Accessed through a half-hidden doorway off Gravel Walk is a **Georgian Garden**, recreated following excavations that revealed three garden plans. Formal box hedges, bulbs, roses, herbs and hardy perennials, all historically correct, fill this little-frequented space with colour.

To the west of The Circus, connected by Brock Street, is the **Royal Crescent**, designed by both John Wood the Elder and his son, the latter building the famous street between 1767 and 1775. Like The Circus, its shape was a first in modern European architecture. The builder effectively sold the façades and owners would then create a house behind so that, while there is elegant uniformity from the front, the rear of the property is a mix of rooflines and styles.

Number 1 Royal Crescent (✆ 01225 428126 ♂ no1royalcrescent. co.uk) is the most fashionable address of the street. Now a museum, the property is decorated and furnished as it might have been during the period 1776 to 1796. But there's more to the museum than accurate wallpaper designs and period furniture. This highly engaging immersive museum follows a day in the life of its resident family as you wander from room to room. You're soon drawn into sibling squabbles and parental concerns, and find yourself rooting for sisters Charlotte and Alice to 'find a good match' at the Assembly Rooms ball while giving brother Richard a stern talking to for being so insolent to his father.

◀ BATH: **1** Thermae Bath Spa's rooftop pool offers beautiful views across the city. **2** Royal Victoria Park is the launch site for hot-air balloons. **3** Bath is famous for its Georgian architecture, including the striking Royal Crescent. **4** The magnificent interior of Bath Abbey. **5** Sally Lunn's tea room is a Bath institution.

Royal Victoria Park & the Botanical Gardens

You'd think, by its very name, that Bath's largest green space is Victorian. To some extent it is, but it was created during the Regency period and named the **Royal Victoria Park** by a perhaps rather bumptious Princess Victoria when in 1830, at the age of 11, she opened the new park. A park of many parts, it extends over 57 acres; the Royal Crescent overlooks the section closest to the city centre. From there it spreads out north and west to incorporate large greens filled with numerous specimen trees for summer shelter, formal flower borders in town-park style, a vast playground, a duck pond, two golf courses and the Botanical Gardens.

In the northwest corner, the **Botanical Gardens** are the furthest to reach from the city centre but are my pick of the green spaces in Bath, with lots of distinct areas to give colour throughout the year. Winding pathways draw you from one to another, a rose walk to a magnolia lawn, heather borders to a butterfly garden, and a lovable garden within a bath, created and maintained by Bath Womens' Institute. Pockets of lawn offer restful places to sit and enjoy the surrounding scents. The main entrance is off Royal Avenue, which curves around the floral part of the garden; to the north, on the opposite side of the road, is the **Great Dell**, an undulating tree garden, where the heady scent of pine rises above you and cyclamen sprout at the roots of trees. It's a restful place, and a world apart from the crowds that gather in front of the Royal Crescent, just ten minutes' walk away. If you wish to give a helping hand during a visit to Bath, there are fortnightly volunteering sessions in the Botanical Gardens, led by the Parks Team (⊘ beta.bathnes.gov.uk/volunteer-gardening-botanical-gardens). There's no need to book, tools are provided, training is given, and you get to learn about the gardens while you work.

Gravel paths criss-cross the vast lawns of the park for winter promenading but they are also the launch site for **hot-air balloons** that drift off early morning and evening to give passengers a stunning view of Bath from above. **Virgin Balloon Flights** (⊘ 01225 435505 ⊘ virginballoonflights.co.uk/location/bath) take off from the Royal Victoria Park three to four times per week; bookings are essential.

Museums of Bath

For something a little grittier, the **Museum of Bath at Work** (⊘ 01225 318348 ⊘ bath-at-work.org.uk) off Julian Road illustrates

A MAN'S WORLD – BATH'S BIG FOUR

As a teenager **Ralph Allen** was a post office clerk and postmaster in Bath, but over his lifetime he totally reformed the British postal system and earned himself large sums of money. With his wealth he bought quarries at Combe Down and Bathampton Down, providing much of the Bath stone that was used to create Georgian Bath. He worked closely with John Wood the Elder, who built Prior Park on the edge of the city in 1742 for him. You can see Allen's town house and office, with its ornate columns and parapet above, in North Parade Passage. Mayor of Bath as well as a philanthropist, he donated the money and stone to build the Mineral Water Hospital and is still revered in the city.

An ardent follower of the designs of the 16th-century Italian architect Andrea Palladio, **John Wood the Elder** ensured that Georgian architecture in Bath is essentially Palladian in style. He was responsible for requesting that Ralph Allen quarry the stone in smooth, giant blocks rather than rough rubble; hence Wood could achieve the clean lines necessary to create the architectural effects he had in mind. On his death in 1754, his son, **John Wood the Younger**, took on his architectural projects. The Woods' legacy to town planning is huge, as their ideas in Bath became the model for towns and cities worldwide.

While John Wood the Elder created the buildings, **Richard 'Beau' Nash** filled them with parties, dances, concerts and gamblers (he was a prolific gambler himself) and turned Bath into the most fashionable place to be seen. A dandy and a fashion icon, Nash's ideas on fashion and how the social classes were expected to behave were followed closely; he even drew up a set of 'Rules to be observ'd at Bath' on etiquette and behaviour. As master of ceremonies he was at the centre of society life and, like Allen, is very much a hallowed name in Bath. He lived in a house where the sumptuous Theatre Royal now stands, at the west end of Upper Borough Walls.

2,000 years of earning a living in the city. The museum is housed in an impressive building that was built as a Real Tennis court in 1777. The bulk of the displays are from J B Bowler's workshops, opened in 1872, an old engineering and brass foundry where nothing that looked vaguely useful was ever thrown away. Consequently the contents are all there. Changing with the times, the company moved into fizzy-pop manufacture, so it contains plenty of machines, bottles and drinks labels too.

It's a fascinating collection of social history, with rooms and tools laid out just as they were when the last shift bell rang, where belts, pulleys, cogs and levers vie for attention. You purchase your ticket at a solid wooden counter in the old stores, packed with brass this and iron that.

The furniture-making workshops of Keevil and Son, renowned in Bath from the 18th century for cabinet making and later for fitting out department stores and ocean liners, were dismantled and reconstructed here too. The quarrying of Bath stone is, of course, highlighted, as well as Plasticine, which was invented and made in Bath. There's also the Bath Chair, the Bath Oliver biscuit and numerous other products developed off the back of the high-class 'medical' tourist industry. Providing interest for hours, to my mind it's one of the most absorbing museums in the city.

However, it's closely rivalled by the **Museum of Bath Architecture** (The Paragon museumofbatharchitecture.org.uk), where visitors can discover how the city was transformed during Georgian times. It amply fleshes out the background to the rebuilding, with information on the principles of Palladian architecture and the ideologies of John Wood the Elder and his son. The construction of a Georgian house and street are illustrated through original materials, with masonry, street signs, ironmongery, railings, street lighting, plasterwork, tiling and architectural decoration featuring throughout the museum. A giant scale model gives an insight into the layout of the city.

"It's a fascinating collection of social history, with rooms and tools laid out just as they were when the last shift bell rang."

EAST OF THE RIVER

Much of the city centre sits in a pocket, tucked into a narrow loop of the Avon. But there's plenty to see east of the river.

The River Avon in Bath

One of Bath's great landmarks, **Pulteney Bridge** was completed in 1773 to the designs of Robert Adam. Like the Ponte Vecchio in Florence that inspired it, it is one of the few European bridges with buildings on it. The bridge, with its row of shops, has a front and back – the front, facing south, is relatively decorative, while the back is somewhat plain.

Beneath the bridge by the Pulteney Weir and sluice gate (the latter is not particularly pretty but it helps to stop Bath from flooding) is the entrance to **Bath Rugby Ground** and starting points for **river cruisers** (pulteneycruisers.com), which make for an idyllic trip, as you sit on board and let the buildings drift past. The urban views don't last for long; as the boat weaves around the overhanging trees, the snaking river becomes quite rural and intriguing. The sycamore, ash and chestnuts overhang so much that you can't see the next stretch of river. The blue flash of a kingfisher is quite likely as the valley suddenly opens out to river meadows and views of Little Solsbury Hill and Bathampton Down.

"The blue flash of a kingfisher is quite likely as the valley suddenly opens out to river meadows and views of Little Solsbury Hill and Bathampton Down."

The boat turns at Bathampton Weir, manmade 600 years ago and a rural outpost of the city. On the return trip you can stop off at the **Bath Boating Station** (⌀ bathboating.co.uk), an attractive black-and-white timber boathouse where you can hire wooden rowing skiffs, punts and canoes, all handmade on the premises by the fourth generation of a boat-building family. Alternatively laze on the very attractive riverside lawns of the **Bathwick Boatman** (✆ 01225 428844 ⌀ bathwickboatman.com) pub, where you can enjoy a meal as the boats come and go.

Boats cannot access the river west of Pulteney Bridge, so to explore the river here, walk or cycle a section of the **River Avon Trail** (⌀ riveravontrail.org.uk), beginning at Pulteney Bridge and leading 23 miles out of Bath into Somerset.

Great Pulteney Street

Great Pulteney Street is the grandest, straightest road in Bath at 1,000ft long and 100ft wide. Its understated elegance rivals that of the Champs-Elysées in Paris. Not the work of the usual architectural suspects in Bath, the street, built in 1789, was designed by Thomas Baldwin, who was also responsible for the Guildhall west of the river and numerous other streets east of the river. But like so many other streets in Bath, the architect designed only the façades in Great Pulteney Street, with the rear of each property differing from the one next door. At the eastern end of Great Pulteney Street is the **Holburne Museum** (✆ 01225 388569 ⌀ holburne.org), situated in the Sydney Gardens, with the fine arts represented in both permanent collections and regular exhibitions.

Kennet & Avon Canal

Large villas and town houses line the broad avenue that is **Bathwick Hill**, climbing out of Bath towards **Claverton Down**. Turn to face the city and the whole centre is laid out in front of you. Bathwick Hill, and indeed the Sydney Gardens, cross over the Kennet and Avon Canal, which begins in Bath, connected to the River Avon in **Widcombe**, a small, delightful Georgian suburb rarely explored by tourists.

Like its disused counterpart, the Thames and Severn Canal further north in the Cotswolds, the Kennet and Avon links the Severn with the Thames. But the section through Bath is truly historic: a mile-long stretch north from the canal's junction with the Avon, known as the Widcombe Lock Flight, includes 19 listed structures along its length, such as giant chimney stacks (used for steam pumps to help boats through the series of locks), and old lock-keepers' cottages. A walk along the towpath here is magical, with the sharply rising escarpment to Claverton Down terraced with smart Bath stone town houses to one side, and commanding views over the centre of Bath to the other, together with the odd splash of colour from a passing narrowboat. At the Bathwick Hill entrance to the canal, you can hire day boats from **Bath Narrowboats** (𝒮 01225 447276 𝒹 bath-narrowboats.co.uk) to take a gentle cruise out of Bath towards the Limpley Stoke Valley and the Dundas Aqueduct. Making the most of the canal is a must, either walking the towpath or working the locks with a boat.

Prior Park Landscape Garden

Ralph Allen Drive 𝒮 01225 833977; National Trust

Completed in 1764 by John Wood the Elder, Prior Park was commissioned by Ralph Allen, the postmaster and owner of the Bath stone quarries, as a home for himself from which he could 'see all of Bath and for all of Bath to see'. The vast house and buildings have been used as a private school for the last 150 years but couldn't manage the upkeep of the 28-acre garden so gave it to the National Trust in 1993.

Far removed from formal parterres and topiary statues, Prior Park is entirely naturalistic in style, making the most of the sharp descent from the house down towards Widcombe. While the view of Bath is the key component, one of the most attractive parts of the garden is at the bottom of the hill (though, confusingly, being north of the house,

---

BATH: **1** The delightful American Museum and Gardens. **2** Pulteney Bridge is one of the city's landmarks. **3** Enjoy the towpaths alongside the Kennet and Avon Canal. **4** The Holburne Museum has excellent displays of fine arts. ▶

CAROLINE MILLS

DAVID BARFOOT/D

1000 WORDS/S

regarded as the top of the park), the Wilderness Area where you can sit by the Serpentine Lake and gaze into the waters from the Palladian Bridge. It is a wonderful place to stretch your legs, and stretched they will be, as the climb back to the exit is punishing unless you take it slowly. To break the return climb I spent half an hour watching a not-very-nocturnal badger snuffling among and rooting out carefully planted bulbs and rhizomes from a woodland bank.

Prior Park is considered a green tourism site by the National Trust. There is no parking on site and visitors are encouraged to catch a bus (Bath to Combe Down) from Dorchester Street in the city centre; the bus stops outside the entrance to Prior Park. Alternatively Prior Park is one of the Skyline Tour stops on the city sightseeing bus. And from here you can pick up the six-mile circular Bath Skyline walk (page 62).

American Museum & Gardens

Claverton Manor BA2 7BD ⌀ 01225 460503 ⌀ americanmuseum.org

It takes a little effort to reach (page 61), but the American Museum & Gardens on Claverton Down is a delight; indeed I'll go as far to say it's (probably) my top attraction in Bath. Tranquilly set away from the city centre in the handsome Claverton Manor, it has 125 acres of magnificent gardens, and views over Limpley Stoke Valley. The American-themed gardens include the New American Garden, Mount Vernon, which is a replica of the gardens from George Washington's house outside Washington, DC. On my last summer visit, the gardens were so striking, I rated them as some of the finest to view in Europe.

The museum is dedicated to exhibiting and educating about colonial America. The only one of its kind outside the United States, it gives a fascinating insight into the 'quiet' America, even if the history it's portraying isn't so. Period rooms such as Conkey's Tavern bring the history to life, with most of the furnishings coming from colonial homes in the States. The museum focuses on the discovery and colonisation of America, as well as encounters with Native Americans; it has a strong emphasis on the crafts of both natives and colonials.

The museum holds one of the finest textile collections in the world, and I particularly like the Textile Room, where antique quilts, hooked rugs, tapestries and samplers hang. It's an inspiring room and there are various talks held daily, not only about the quilts on display but practical talks such as getting started in quilt-making.

The American Garden Deli serves delicious homemade American fare (try the snicker doodles!) and there are monthly 'All American BBQs' throughout the summer. Numerous courses, events and family activities take place, including important temporary exhibitions staged in the purpose-built exhibition gallery.

📎 SPECIAL STAYS

Broad Street Townhouse 32 Broad St, BA1 5LP ✆ 01225 330190 ⌖ butcombe.com/ broad-street-townhouse-bath. What a superb location! Two-minutes' walk to Bath Abbey and Pulteney Bridge, slap-bang in the city centre. There are eleven en-suite rooms in this Grade II traditional Georgian townhouse, beautifully decorated and with extremely comfortable beds. Organic Bramley toiletries, minibar with local goodies and plenty of choice at breakfast, served in the downstairs coffee shop (once an old pharmacy with its features retained), with bucket seats and sofas.

🍴 FOOD & DRINK

One of the big attractions of Bath is making the most of its remarkable selection of places to eat and drink. The city is one of the places in Britain that made drinking tea fashionable and there are plenty of options for experiencing a civilised afternoon tea. Beware, though, as many tea rooms are either closed or stop serving tea by 16.00 in preparation for dinner service. The city also has numerous very hospitable pubs and excellent restaurants. You won't go hungry in Bath!

There's a farmers' market held every Saturday morning at Green Park station. If you're self-catering, or want a goody bag to take home, you can pre-order from **Taste of Bath** (⌖ taste-of.co.uk), who source all its artisan produce from within ten miles of the city. And if you want to learn new baking skills, at **The Bertinet Kitchen** (12 St Andrew's Tce ✆ 01225 445531 ⌖ thebertinetkitchen.com) you can learn to make your own pâtisserie, bread and other fantastic *viennoisserie* with world-renowned Richard Bertinet.

Tea rooms & cafés

Green Park Station Green Park Rd ✆ 01225 787910 ⌖ greenparkstation.co.uk. Housed beneath the arches where trains once pulled into Bath, you'll find a delightful complex of ethical eateries alongside the market in Green Park Station. From wood-fired pizzas and Mediterranean street food to crêpes and a decent cup of coffee, plus Green Park Brasserie, a good place for brunch.

The Green Rocket 1 Pierrepont St ✆ 01225 420084 ⌖ thegreenrocket.co.uk. A vegetarian café that also offers vegan and gluten-free options, along with organic coffee, freshly squeezed juices, wine and beer. Dishes include gnocchi *trapenesi* with almond, tomato, basil and mint pesto, cashew cream and parmesan, or warm root-vegetable salad served with puy lentils, marinated tofu and tarragon tahini dressing .

The Pump Room Abbey Churchyard ⊘ thepumproombath.co.uk. The elegant Pump Room is an attraction in its own right and was considered one of the most socially desirable places to 'be seen' for well over 200 years. Morning brunch and an elegant afternoon tea is a speciality. The restaurant opens for dinner in July and August, when booking is essential. Come here to try the spa water and the distinctive Bath bun. Listen to the Pump Room Trio or the resident pianist perform while you eat.

Sally Lunn's The renowned tea room is featured below.

Pubs & restaurants

Clayton's Kitchen 15A George St ✆ 01225 724386 ⊘ claytonskitchen.com. Fine dining from local Michelin-star chef Robert Clayton. Slow-cooked pork bonbons or goat's curd with heritage tomatoes to start, roast rack of Somerset lamb or pea and shitake mushroom risotto with Wyfe of Bath cheese (from the Bath Soft Cheese Co) for a main, and vanilla panna cotta with strawberries for dessert. There's also a dedicated vegan menu and a children's menu of 'proper food for little people'.

Hall & Woodhouse 1 Old King St ✆ 01225 469259 ⊘ hall-woodhousebath.co.uk. Owned by the famous Hall & Woodhouse Brewery (Badger Original, Fursty Ferret, Tanglefoot, etc), this is a very large and magnificent bar-cum-restaurant. It offers superb food and drink and attentive service, but visit for the surroundings alone – choose from several areas, each with its own ambience, over four floors. Or head to the Manhattan-style rooftop terrace for views of the city. A place to take time and relax.

Sally Lunn's 4 North Parade Passage ✆ 01225 461634 ⊘ sallylunns.co.uk. A Bath institution, I've categorised this under restaurants rather than tea rooms because, while Sally Lunn's is celebrated as a place for morning coffee and afternoon tea, it's less known for its quiet candlelit dinners, and yet I've eaten extremely well here. In the quaint terraced tea shop, full of ambience and friendly staff, you'll find very good, hearty food. Try the 'trencher' meals, served on the famous **Sally Lunn Bun**, a brioche-like bun from the 17th century; meat and gravy on a bun may not sound right but it really works. This is the only place in the world to buy the Sally Lunn Bun.

The Star Inn Vineyards ✆ 01225 425072 ⊘ abbeyinnsbath.co.uk/#the-star-inn-bath. Oozing character (and people), The Star Inn is listed on the National Inventory of Heritage Pubs. Beer (that's Abbey Ales beer, The Star being the brewery's flagship pub and tap room) is still served from jugs, and you can sup in one of the four bars while playing cribbage or shove ha-penny. The Star won CAMRA Pub of the Year 2022 for the Bath area.

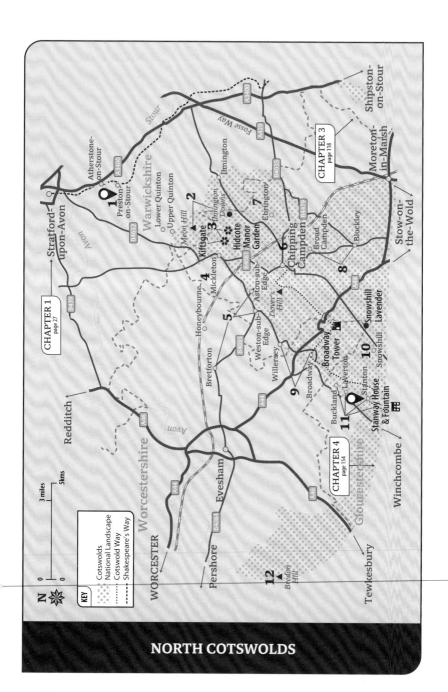

NORTH COTSWOLDS

2
NORTH COTSWOLDS

This chapter covers the northwest tip of the Cotswolds, the very fringes where the rocks and the stone peter out – or begin. Within my locale's entirely hand-drawn boundaries lie four very distinct and different areas – the northern fringe of villages running along the River Stour in south Warwickshire and the tiny part of the Cotswolds that flows into Worcestershire around the Vale of Evesham and Bredon Hill, all of which frame the start of the Cotswolds National Landscape near the Hidcotes and Chipping Campden. Further south, more familiar names start to crop up such as Broadway and Snowshill, by which time we are well and truly immersed into the Cotswolds. This is bolt-hole territory for me, just a few miles from home and where I can spend a few hours enjoying a view or taking a walk; Ilmington Downs and Dover's Hill will always be special simply for their views, but I love the simplicity of an off-the-beaten-track walk in the Stour Valley too (page 84).

GETTING THERE & AROUND

Your best option for this locale by **train** is the **Cotswold Line** operated by **Great Western Railway**. The closest stations are at Moreton-in-Marsh (page 150), approximately five to eight miles from Chipping Campden by road (less on foot across the fields) and Honeybourne, four miles from Broadway. An alternative train service is to Stratford-upon-Avon (page 28) from Birmingham Moor Street or Leamington Spa.

There is a reasonable **bus** service from Stratford-upon-Avon (Bridge Street) to Chipping Campden and Broadway from Monday to Saturday. It stops at several of the villages in this locale including the Quintons, Mickleton, Broad Campden, Weston-sub-Edge, Willersey and Blockley. More frequent services tend to run during school term times. You can access a current timetable at ⬧ warwickshire.gov.uk/buses.

THE COTSWOLD WAY

Beginning or ending in Chipping Campden, the Cotswold Way is a National Trail and runs along the western escarpment of the National Landscape. A plaque in the town, beside the historic Market Hall, marks the official start. Along its 102 miles, walkers will see a noticeable variation in landscape between the start and the end, finishing at Bath Abbey. The views from the trail are amply rewarding for just about the whole way, mainly because you're on the high Cotswold escarpment, though you do need to be prepared for some steep climbs. For the purposes of this book, I refer to the Cotswold Way as it's walked north to south, roughly in line with the chapters, which begin in the north Cotswolds and finish in the south.

The Cotswold Way is so well signposted and well-trodden that you barely need a map to follow the route. However, you can download and print digital National Trail maps or purchase an iPhone app from the National Trail website (nationaltrail.co.uk). The latest information about the trail, including sections that might be temporarily closed or rerouted, is also on the website.

I particularly like the series of circular walks created using sections of the Cotswold Way. They're a great way to explore a particular part of the Cotswolds and, over time, you'll cover most of the National Trail. There are currently 27 waymarked routes available, the directions downloadable from the National Trail website.

If you'd like to walk the entire length of this National Trail, but don't fancy backpacking, there are many companies offering walking holidays on the Cotswold Way, both guided and self-guided, and several that will simply carry your luggage ahead for you. All of the following companies will arrange accommodation, luggage transfer and route planning:

Cotswold Luggage Transfers 01386 840688 luggage-transfers.co.uk
Cotswold Walks 01386 833799 cotswoldwalks.com
Sherpa Van Project 01748 826917 sherpavan.com

The Cotswolds were made for **walking**, and this area is no exception. Chipping Campden is, after all, where the **Cotswold Way** begins (or finishes). One of my favourite sections of the route, for a simple afternoon stroll, is at **Dover's Hill**, just outside Chipping Campden and soon after the long-distance path begins. It's fabulous in autumn when the rosehips have ripened and give bursts of vibrant reds and oranges against the big skies, over far-reaching views. Perhaps the views with the greatest 'wow factor' as seen from the Cotswold Way are those at **Broadway Tower**.

Besides the Cotswold Way, there are several other long-distance footpaths through this area. **Shakespeare's Way** turns south out of

ⓘ TOURIST INFORMATION

Broadway Russell Sq ☏ 01386 852937
Chipping Campden High St ☏ 01386 841206

Stratford-upon-Avon, following the River Stour, while the **Monarch's Way**, **Diamond Way** and **Heart of England Way** all play their part in a walker's paradise. The **Wychavon Way** cuts through the Worcestershire countryside and over **Bredon Hill**, the anomalous Cotswold peninsula that juts into the **Vale of Evesham**.

You can find endless possibilities by making round walks up from the OS map. The villages snuggled beneath the escarpment make rewarding objectives, such as walking through the fields from Stanton to Buckland via Laverton, climbing up onto the top and joining the Cotswold Way back to Stanton, a superb circular walk of about five miles.

For **cyclists**, the National Cycle Network Route 5 runs through this area, starting from Stratford-upon-Avon, and travels along both roads and traffic-free cycleways, such as The Greenway recreational route (page 41) out of Stratford. It then continues using B-roads through the villages of Lower Quinton and Ilmington and on towards Shipston-on-Stour. The Cotswold Line (NCN Route 442) links Honeybourne in the west with Moreton-in-Marsh, utilising quiet roads close to the railway for easy access via public transport.

For those without their own bicycles, there are e-bikes to hire by the day (6hrs) from Tower Barn at Broadway Tower (☏ 01386 572284 ⌂ broadwaytower.co.uk). Cotswold Electric Bike Tours (page 206) offer guided e-bike tours around Broadway and Chipping Campden within this locale.

SOUTH WARWICKSHIRE

The Cotswolds National Landscape peeks over the county boundary into Warwickshire in two places: along a northwest-facing ridge (known as Edgehill; page 122) following the border with Oxfordshire and a tiny parcel south of Stratford-upon-Avon that hooks itself onto Gloucestershire around the villages of Ilmington and the Quintons. There's nothing significant to tell that you're in either county; indeed, these small village parishes of south Warwickshire were part of

Gloucestershire until the early 20th century. But you are right on the very fringe of the Cotswolds, the land merging with the Vale of Evesham.

1 THE STOUR VILLAGES

Due south of Stratford the **River Stour**, a 'provincial' river not much wider than a stream, pushes its way into the larger River Avon. A skinny little thing, the Stour looks quiet and innocent enough but locals will tell you that it has been known to make a nuisance of itself occasionally, its rising water magnetically drawn towards residents' living rooms in times of heavy rain. It is only 15 miles long with its source near Wigginton Heath (page 127) in Oxfordshire, but by the time it nears its journey's end, it has passed through seven tiny villages: Newbold-on-Stour, Crimscote, Alderminster, Wimpstone, Preston-on-Stour, Atherstone-on-Stour and finally Clifford Chambers.

"The land, particularly around Preston- and Atherstone-on-Stour, is relatively flat though both villages enjoy the shelter from a western hummock."

These seven riverside villages are also linked by **Shakespeare's Way**, a 146-mile path from Stratford-upon-Avon to the Globe Theatre in London. The waymarked path uses existing footpaths and bridleways before entering the village of Alderminster, where it's worth stopping to top up at the **Bell Inn** (page 85).

The land, particularly around Preston- and Atherstone-on-Stour, is relatively flat though both villages enjoy the shelter from a western hummock. The road that connects the two is deserted save for farm traffic and if you arrive by car you can park close to the weir on Preston Lane (off the A3400) and walk through Preston to Atherstone along the quiet road – with magnificent views of the most northerly Cotswold hills, including Ilmington Downs and Meon Hill, and the Malvern hills – and back across the fields along a footpath before filling up with tea and cake at Preston's traditional tea garden, adjoining the village shop.

As you walk over the fields along the footpath between the two villages, you'll notice a rather splendid house just across the river. It's Alscot Park (⌀ alscot.co.uk), a most perfectly proportioned Rococo Gothic house with a crenellated roof. It can also be seen from the A3400. The house, grounds and gardens are not routinely open to the public but do open on occasion for specific events. If you happen to be in the area on such an occasion, I recommend a visit. These gardens, filled with colourful borders, formal parterres, topiary and a traditional potager, and the parkland filled with fallow deer and giant cedars, make Alscot Park truly magnificent.

FOOD & DRINK

Bell Inn Alderminster ✆ 01789 335671 ♦ brunningandprice.co.uk/bell. This has been a popular haunt, particularly for food, for many years, with 'regulars' travelling some distance to eat. The gastro-pub has a two-floor restaurant with a glass balcony offering wonderful views overlooking the Alscot Estate. Accommodation available.

Preston-on-Stour Village Shop & Traditional Tea Garden Preston-on-Stour ✆ 01789 450180. Tiny shop selling local produce including bread, milk, cakes, jams and honey, plus a small café and summer tea garden serving cakes and cream teas plus delicious coffee from Monsoon Estates (♦ monsoonestates.co.uk), artisan coffee roasters located on the Alscot Park estate.

2 MEON HILL & ILMINGTON DOWNS

Meon Hill is the very beginning of the Cotswold ridge sitting beside the Avon Valley. By comparison with the sharp escarpments further south, Meon Hill is merely a mound, said to have been put there by the devil throwing a clod of earth in irritation at the building of nearby Evesham Abbey. An Iron Age fort once sat on the top of this flat-topped hill, which puts paid to the devil's handiwork theory, given that Evesham Abbey was built in the 8th century.

"Meon Hill is merely a mound, said to have been put there by the devil throwing a clod of earth in irritation at the building of nearby Evesham Abbey."

Walking along the Centenary Way across the lower slopes of Meon Hill, you come to the village of **Ilmington**. The houses are built more from ironstone, still a Jurassic limestone but much darker in colour than all other Cotswold stones, having the iron deposits scattered throughout. Middle Street, right in the centre and lined by a particularly unspoilt group of cottages, is one of the prettier roads in the village, which leads to St Mary's Church – look for the carved church mice and a tapestry illustrating the old apple orchards in the village. At the core of the village is the **Howard Arms** (page 87), one of the best pubs in the area both for food and atmosphere and where, during the summer months, you can catch the **Traditional Ilmington Morris Dancers** (♦ ilmingtonmorrismen.org.uk) dancing over a pint. You can also watch the side, established more than 400 years ago and

MORRIS DANCING IN THE COTSWOLDS

'Are we dancing this in D or G?' echoes across the silent hilltop. 'In Ilmington!' accords a reply with a band of hailing laughter. Though still in the parish, a half-dozen members from the **Traditional Ilmington Morris Dancers** and a handful of supporters are not actually in the village, yet. It's May Day and the softness of the dawn brushes over 'The Summit' of Ilmington Downs, the highest point in Warwickshire. The lime greens of fresh-feathered barley fields, the lusciousness of dewy grass and the stillness of the dawn – where mist still lingers in the valley below – make the 04.30 start worthwhile.

'We've been doing this for 450 years, but there are no original dancers left!' pipes up The Bagman, otherwise known as Paul Bryan, a retired air traffic controller, as one or two of the dancers limber up (two squats) on the single-track lane that crosses the top of the hill. The dancers are costumed in grey cord trousers, with a royal blue and yellow baldric (a crossbelt that would have held a sword or powder for cannon in days of old) over a casual white shirt. With bells and rosettes gently tinkling against the still dawn, they tip their top hats, swallow a nip of whisky to welcome the month of May, then fall into line as Rob, the local GP, strikes up on the melodeon.

Eight bars in and Peter, the Squire, calls 'This time', and the dancing begins. Wooden sticks are tapped and white handkerchiefs twirl as the dancers frolic. But the sun is shy to rise. The side and its supporters move on, into the village and the next stopping point on the annual May Day tour of Ilmington, when the morris dancers tour the village. It's not long after 06.00. Curtains twitch as bank-holiday slumberers are woken to the sound of bells buckled around ankles.

At The Howard Arms, I catch up with the Bagman over morning coffee. Paul explains, 'Every village has its own dances and movements of hands, feet, handkerchiefs and sticks. The Traditional Ilmington Morris Dancers perform dances from many different villages, mainly from the shires. But particular to Ilmington is "The Keeper".

now Warwickshire's last-surviving traditional village morris dancers, see in the May Day sunrise on **Ilmington Downs**.

Ilmington Downs is not one hill but a group of hills, the highest of which, at 860ft, is the highest point in Warwickshire. What makes it so prominent as a landmark is the sharpness of the gradient on the village side. A footpath climbs the slope from the village to the top of Knowlands Hill and Windmill Hill but for the best views, climb Stoke Hill to the southwest. On a clear day, when the visibility is limitless, you can easily see the high-rise buildings of Coventry and Birmingham to the north; with binoculars you can even make out the Bull Ring rotunda in the

Tradition and the history of morris dancing in Ilmington is extremely important.

'Most dances are performed by six or eight men together with musicians (melodeon, pipe, tabour and fiddle) and a "fool" who helps to entertain the crowd. Sometimes a beast, usually a horse, will also become involved. These characters evolved from the old mummers' plays, the beast being an animal that villagers would have been accustomed to seeing in the fields.'

I look on as the 'Fool' – today performed by Paul - with multi-coloured socks and flowers on his hat, goads the dancers and supporters with a traditional sheep's bladder balloon. It sounds ludicrous – and it is – but it's entertaining.

These athletes from the seven ages of man – many sides will have father and son dancing alongside each other – have just as nifty footwork as any expensively paid footballer, the steps intricate and complex to coincide with the hand movements and shake of a bell. One wrong move and a hurdle over a long stick could be excruciatingly painful.

With a wander to the final stop of the May Day tour – past the church and grazing sheep in a village meadow – the morris dancers offer one last dance. Then the tapping sticks fall silent, the jollity ends. A skylark can be heard overhead. Summer has arrived.

Morris dancing can be seen throughout the Cotswolds, usually in pub gardens but also at various festivals. Far from being stereotypically daft, it is the most fabulous rural entertainment that you can have over a pint of local brew and a bag of crisps.

Traditional Ilmington Morris Dancers ⌁ ilmingtonmorrismen.org.uk. You may also come across the **Gloucestershire Morris** ⌁ glosmorris.uk and the **Chipping Campden Morris** ⌁ chippingcampdenmorrismen.org, who also perform regularly around the north Cotswolds. Also look out for the trio of morris-dancing sides at Bampton (page 283).

centre of the latter city. There are also nearby views of neighbouring villages such as the Hidcotes, Mickleton and the sub-Edges, to the west from the top of Ebrington Hill (look for the marker stone hidden behind an oak tree, beside the transmission mast station).

¶¶ FOOD & DRINK

Howard Arms Lower Green, Ilmington ✆ 01608 682226 ⌁ howardarms.com. A great gastro-pub with cosy fireside armchairs and snugs in winter and an attractive garden in summer. Sunday roasts are legendary. A three-course vegan menu available with 48hrs notice. Eight attractive bedrooms too, suitable for families.

TOWARDS THE VALE OF EVESHAM

The Vale of Evesham is renowned as a market garden, filled with mineral-rich soils growing vegetables and fruits; Evesham asparagus is a particular speciality, as are plums. As the Cotswolds drop away to this flat vale, Cotswold stone merges with red brick, the influence of the West Midlands, but old orchards remain evident on the hillsides too.

3 HIDCOTE MANOR GARDEN & KIFTSGATE COURT GARDENS

Hidcote Manor Garden ✆ 01386 438333; National Trust; **Kiftsgate Court Gardens** ✆ 01386 438777 ⬧ kiftsgate.co.uk

Hidcote Bartrim and, half a mile to the south, **Hidcote Boyce** both lie on a ridge that is the edge of Ilmington Downs. Residents enjoy some of the loveliest views in the north Cotswolds over the lower slopes of Baker's Hill and the Vale of Evesham beyond. But the name 'Hidcote' is better known as the location of **Hidcote Manor Garden**, designed in an Arts and Crafts style by American-born Major Lawrence Johnston at the start of the 20th century. What's so stimulating about Hidcote and its garden 'rooms' is that Johnston's gardening skills were entirely self-taught, so you can visit and wander from 'room' to 'room' with the belief that, 'if he can do it, so can I'.

Tall hedges of beech and yew provide both the walls and the wallpaper for each little garden room, and every individual garden has its own character, some tranquil and calm, others raging with vibrancy. My personal favourite – I use the garden as a bolthole when I'm in need of time off – is to walk to the end of the Long Walk, sit beneath the magnificent holm oak tree and soak up the views across the cornfields; when Johnston's mother bought the house in 1907, these fields were all that existed before her novice gardener son set to work. Owned by the National Trust, it has a tea room, but with such an idyllic location, I recommend taking a picnic and keeping the sheep on the hillside company over lunch.

If you're going to visit one garden, you may as well visit two, as **Kiftsgate Court Gardens** lies opposite the entrance to Hidcote Manor

1 Kiftsgate Court Gardens is the home of the rambling Kiftsgate rose. **2** There's lovely walking on the flat land around the River Stour. **3** The Traditional Ilmington Morris Dancers perform a range of local dances. ▶

KIFTSGATE COURT GARDENS

ANDREW ROLAND/D

JULIA LINDOP

Garden. They are both so very different that it is impossible to select a favourite, although Kiftsgate perhaps wins on its position. On the very edge of the escarpment, the garden runs down the steep hillside (and is not recommended for those with limited mobility or young children). It's the home of the rambling Kiftsgate rose (Hidcote gives its name to an electric-blue lavender) and of Anne Chambers, whose mother and grandmother tended the garden before her.

"Take some time to sit and reflect in the Lower Garden, where the soaring pine trees shelter you as you look out across wooded hillsides and the Vale of Evesham."

Kiftsgate really is a plantswoman's garden, with unusual species throughout and an exceptional collection of roses besides the Kiftsgate rose – Anne is extremely knowledgeable on the plants growing in her family's little bit of escarpment – but take some time to sit and reflect in the Lower Garden, where the soaring pine trees shelter you as you look out across wooded hillsides and the Vale of Evesham. The views do make you stop in your tracks. Kiftsgate is my pick of the two tea rooms in these neighbouring gardens, with good homemade cakes and scones, and a decent-sized pot of tea.

4 MICKLETON

The village of Mickleton is where the Cotswolds and the Vale of Evesham come together. It sits at the foot of the Cotswold escarpment with Kiftsgate and Hidcote on the ridge of hills to the east, Meon Hill to the north and the Vale stretching out to the west. With the Vale renowned for its fruit and vegetable production, clusters of glasshouses and orchards begin to appear in the area.

Mickleton is a village of two halves, with an uninteresting collection of modern housing estates to the northeast yet with a pretty group of timeless houses spanning the roads towards Broadway and Chipping Campden. The Heart of England Way passes through.

¶¶ FOOD & DRINK

David Moore Family Butcher High St, Mickleton ✆ 01386 438288
⌂ davidmoorefamilybutcher.com. Useful to know if you're self-catering, this is one of the best butchers in the area; all kinds of game including venison, pheasant and fresh duck.
The King's Arms High St, Mickleton ✆ 01386 438257 ⌂ kingsarmsmickleton.co.uk. The northernmost pub in Gloucestershire, housed in an attractive 18th-century building of block

stone, with an attractive garden and traditional pub fare. A useful stopping point for those on the Heart of England Way.

Lower Clopton Farm Shop Lower Clopton CV37 8LQ ✆ 01386 438236 ⟠ lowerclopton. co.uk. Cracking farm shop selling meat and poultry direct from the farm together with seasonal PYO fruit and veg, and a café too. Beneath Meon Hill, midway between Mickleton and Upper Quinton on the road towards Stratford-upon-Avon. Beautiful Victorian brick buildings – look out for the giant clock tower. Farm trail and picnic area on Meon Hill.

5 BRETFORTON & THE SUB-EDGES

Strictly speaking, you're out of the Cotswolds and into the Vale of Evesham by the time you've moved a couple of miles west of Mickleton. But there is something in Bretforton worth a small detour. Here, amid the near-ubiquitous red brick and multiple nurseries, is the famous timber-framed **Fleece Inn**, a pub of tiny, irregular proportions (with a huge orchard for a garden) and walls that defy gravity. Owned by the National Trust, it is the leading venue for the annual **British Asparagus Festival**, with the surrounding area renowned for growing this delicious vegetable.

Taking the road from Bretforton to Chipping Campden (the B4035), you'll come to the two villages of **Weston-sub-Edge** and **Aston-sub-Edge**. As their name implies, both sit below the edge of the Cotswolds escarpment, the same ridge that runs northeast on towards Mickleton and the Hidcotes. Both are tiny hamlets really, each a ribbon development of houses built from the deep golden northern Cotswold stone, with a

THE BRITISH ASPARAGUS FESTIVAL

⟠ britishasparagusfestival.co.uk

Forget supermarket sales of a vegetable that has travelled all the way from Peru; Evesham asparagus is simply the best. Thought of as an aphrodisiac (consider its shape) and given to 19th-century bridegrooms because of its reputed powers, asparagus is celebrated all around the Vale of Evesham and the north Cotswolds through many events. The most famous is perhaps the annual Asparagus Auction, which takes place at the Fleece Inn, Bretforton, followed by a Festival Day.

The festival takes place each year from St George's Day (23 April) to Midsummer's Day (21 June). The auction and main festival day happen over the late May bank-holiday weekend. You'll also find fresh Evesham asparagus on many pub and restaurant menus during asparagus season.

THE COTSWOLD OLIMPICKS

⊘ olimpickgames.co.uk

Dover's Hill is named after a 17th-century lawyer, Robert Dover who, in 1612, organised a sports festival here. The festival was a huge fixture in the calendar, acknowledged by contemporary writers such as Ben Jonson and Thomas Heywood. It has continued on and off ever since and is now an annual event known as the **Robert Dover's Cotswold Olimpick Games**. While the sports festival is recognised by the British Olympic Association as being a part of the Olympic history, the participating sports are very different.

The Games (held at the beginning of June) are opened in front of Dover's Castle, a giant, temporary stage prop replicating that used in the original festival to kick off proceedings. Events include shin-kicking, tug of war and a traditional sack race, with teams and athletes competing for the Championship/ Champion of the Hill. A torchlight procession from the competition grounds to the centre of Chipping Campden is rounded off with dancing and pageantry to befit a medieval games festival.

I've watched these games and they are extraordinarily fun. Shin-kicking sounds medievally brutal – and it is – but you do get a bundle of straw to tuck down your trousers as shin pads. There are, of course, some competitors that are determined to be world champion; others entering simply to discover what it's all about. More fun is the Championship of the Hill, a team event. The winning team is the one that has collected the most water, while having buckets of water hurled at them. Not so easy when a bottle of washing-up liquid has been squeezed out onto the already slippery surface.

central manor house. A public footpath connects the two villages along the foot of the escarpment. Burnt Norton, the manor house and garden once visited by the poet T S Eliot, gives its name to the first poem of his work, *Four Quartets*. Though not open to the public, the gardens frequently appear in the imagery of the poem. For a pacey work of fiction, based upon the unfortunate history of the house and its past owners, pick up a copy of *Burnt Norton* by Caroline Sandon, the present owner of the manor house.

This part of the ridge, sat between the two villages, is known as **Dover's Hill**. Owned by the National Trust, it is a massively famous landmark in the area, and with free access for walkers. It was one of the first places that, as toddlers, my children would go for a 'long' walk, complete with backpack and picnic. What's so special about the hill is the diversity of the landscape within such a small area.

At the very top are the incredible views over the Vale of Evesham – a pictorial map pinpoints notable landmarks. Along this flat ridge run the very beginnings of the Cotswold Way, a curious dog-leg from its starting point in Chipping Campden before walking southwest. The hill then falls dramatically away, yet only for a few feet before this undulating landscape creates watering holes, small pockets of woodland and warm patches in the sunlight of the open field. Further down the ridge lies the Lynches Wood, still part of the National Trust-owned landscape, where a circular footpath (with steep steps back up the hillside) takes you on a journey under the canopy. My children nicknamed it 'the Gruffalo Wood' – and the name has stuck to this day. It's where we would go in search of gruffalos (the frighteningly lovable character created by Julia Donaldson in her famous children's book), establishing evidence that the beast had been there; dens were found along with gruffalo wool hooked to fences – it's really sheep wool, but please don't tell my children that!

"The hill then falls dramatically away, yet only for a few feet before this undulating landscape creates watering holes, small pockets of woodland and warm patches in the sunlight of the open field."

FOOD & DRINK

Fleece Inn Bretforton ✆ 01386 831173 🖱 thefleeceinn.co.uk. Tiny bar plus restaurant all tucked into a 14th-century timber-framed longhouse. Delicious food from local produce and, keen to keep local traditions alive, lots of events throughout the year. Idyllic orchard used for the pub garden. Stay over in the quaint Master's Bedchamber; you'll be the guests of honour – it's the only room available, in addition to a traditional glamping caravan in the orchard.

Seagrave Arms Friday St, Weston-sub-Edge ✆ 01386 840192 🖱 seagravearms.com. Superb pub and restaurant housed in a listed Georgian building. Produce sourced from local farms and suppliers to create upmarket British comfort food. Accommodation available.

CHIPPING CAMPDEN & AROUND

To reach the top of Dover's Hill from the Vale of Evesham in the northwest, it is a sharp incline; there is nothing gradual about it, the hill prominent and sudden. But Dover's Hill is equally as steep to reach from its southeastern side. The town of Chipping Campden, sometimes deemed the epitome of the Cotswold town, lies in a bowl at its foot along with that of Westington Hill to the south and Ebrington Hill to the north. Around the town's southeastern perimeter lie the catchment villages of Ebrington, Charingworth, Paxford, Draycott, Blockley and Broad Campden.

6 CHIPPING CAMPDEN

🏠 East/West Banqueting House

Chipping Campden has the prerequisites to be the most exceptional of all the Cotswold towns, and its warm character makes it difficult not to be charmed. Yet I'm sorry to say that Chipping Campden is one of those towns I was referring to when writing the introduction to this book; I reluctantly take it for granted.

Firstly, I recommend arriving on foot or by public transport if you can. The Heart of England Way, Monarch's Way, Diamond Way and Cotswold Way all converge in the town centre – a stone pillar close to the town hall indicates 'the beginning and the end' of the Cotswold Way, with a reminder that Bath (the other beginning and end) is 102 miles away. Unless you arrive very early in the morning, parking is

ERNEST WILSON – PLANT-COLLECTOR

Wander along the High Street away from all the shops towards Mickleton (where the High Street becomes 'Leysbourne') and you'll come across a tiny archway in the wall that leads to the **Ernest Wilson Memorial Garden**, just before Cidermill Lane. The garden, dedicated to a Chipping Campden-born botanist and explorer, is a little haven of tranquillity away from the bustle of the High Street shops. Ernest 'Chinese' Wilson (or E H Wilson) was a renowned plant-collector to whom many 21st-century gardeners are indebted. Born in a house on the Lower High Street in Chipping Campden (a plaque on the wall indicates the building) in 1876, he began his employment with a local nursery as a gardener before working at the Birmingham Botanic Gardens and later the Royal Botanic Gardens at Kew.

Posted to China as a plant-collector for an English nursery, he explored much of Asia over several years, returning with the seed for hundreds of species that were then unknown to Western gardeners. In all he is attributed with introducing over 1,200 species of plant into Western horticulture – more than any other botanist – including many garden favourites such as varieties of clematis, rhododendron, Japanese cherry, the handkerchief tree and the regal lily. He was awarded the Victoria Medal of Honour by the Royal Horticultural Society for his work.

Keep a look out for the large-leaved lime tree at the entrance that all but grows into the wall. Tree-huggers will struggle to wrap their arms around this huge beauty.

notoriously difficult. However, if you do decide to arrive by car with the intention of walking the early stages of the long-distance footpaths, the recommended parking is at **Back Ends**, which runs parallel with the High Street.

And it's the **High Street** that I wish to begin with – an S-shaped ribbon that lures the visitor around each bend. It's this winding street that may well make Chipping Campden one of the cosiest of all Cotswold towns, simply because there is no long and elegant straight avenue. The stone is among the darkest of the Cotswold stones, almost ginger in colour, the houses redolent of historic wealth and mellow grandeur.

This wealth, like that of most other Cotswold towns, was derived from wool. William Grevel, considered one of England's most successful wool merchants, built his 14th-century house in the High Street. **Grevel House** (almost opposite the entrance to Church Street) still stands and remains one of the most prominent buildings in the town. On the other side of the High Street, **Woolstaplers Hall** is equally impressive, a symbol of importance for the town as a collecting point for fleece, which was later sold to Flemish and Italian clothiers.

"It's this winding street that may well make Chipping Campden one of the cosiest of all Cotswold towns, simply because there is no long and elegant straight avenue."

Other wool-related locations include the **Noel Arms** on the southern side of the High Street, the archway of which leads to George Lane, once a packhorse track for transporting wool from the town to Bristol and Southampton. The Noel Arms (originally known as the George) was an important coaching inn and stopping point for the horses. The open-sided **Market Hall**, in the centre of the High Street and close to the Noel Arms, was used by other traders for selling food. It is still used occasionally, but spends most of its time as photographic fodder for tourists and is one of the most photographed market halls in the Cotswolds.

What is refreshing about the High Street is that, while it retains several shops selling gifty items and expensive jumpers, there are still some ordinary (in the best sense) shops too – a butcher and greengrocer, delicatessen and wine shop, and post office. These are interspersed with tea rooms, pubs, hotels and restaurants all eager to continue the rich trading traditions that the town became accustomed to centuries ago. On the whole, these are of the cosy variety with log fires and snugs. The

High Street is indeed alluring and it can be easy to remain locked to this one thoroughfare, but if you do, you'll miss out on some treats.

Continue from the High Street up Cidermill Lane and you'll come across the parish church of St James, built upon the prosperity of the wool trade. Next to it you'll see an imposing set of lodge gates through which to have a nose at the remains of **Old Campden House**. It was once a fantastically grand and ornate pad that was struck by fire only 25 years after its excruciatingly expensive build in 1613. It's the banqueting houses, with its spiralling chimneys, that are still intact and now let out as holiday homes (page 97) by the Landmark Trust. If you fancy a clearer view of the remains, you can see much more from the Shipston road (around the corner past the church).

Close by the lodge gates of Old Campden House and opposite the gabled row of almshouses is **Court Barn Museum** ($\mathscr{D}$ 01386 841951 $\mathring{O}$ courtbarn.org.uk), celebrating a hundred years or so of the Arts and Crafts Movement in and around Chipping Campden. In 1902 the architect and designer C R Ashbee moved his Guild of Handicraft from the East End of London to Chipping Campden. With him he brought cabinetmakers, blacksmiths, silversmiths and jewellers to set up workshops in an old silk mill in **Sheep Street** (at the western end of the High Street). It was a turning point in the fortunes of the otherwise declining town, with artists and designers attracted to the rural idyll, keen to follow traditional skills. The museum celebrates this history in a magnificent 18th-century stone barn.

"It was once a fantastically grand and ornate pad that was struck by fire only 25 years after its excruciatingly expensive build in 1613."

For contemporary artistry, the attractive **Old Silk Mill** in Sheep Street is the place to visit. Many of Ashbee's guild returned to the industrial towns but some of the best craftsmen remained at the mill, including the silversmith George Hart. The Hart silversmith workshop, run by the same family, is still working today at the mill, along with other artists, craftsmen and women working with paint, wood, textiles and pottery. One particular artist's work caught my eye on my most recent visit: that of David Birch, a one-time farmer turned professional artist whose ancestry in Chipping Campden goes back 400 years. David's studio has been in the town for more than 50 years and his paintings offer vibrant scenes of local vistas. The whole enterprise is known as **The Gallery at** the Guild; you can wander around the studios, watching the artists at work and purchase their wares. The renowned silversmith and designer Robert Welch also had his workshop in the Old Silk Mill. His family continue to sell his designs from the nearby Robert Welch Shop.

You'll also find, dotted around the town, members of **Creative Campden** (⌖ creativecampden.co.uk) – an organisation of artists, designers, craftsmen and musicians. The annual **Chipping Campden Literature Festival** and the **Chipping Campden Music Festival** are also ever-popular cultural events within the town.

🛍 SHOPPING

The Gallery at the Guild Old Silk Mill, Sheep St ✆ 01386 840345 ⌖ thegalleryattheguild. co.uk. Contemporary arts and crafts including Hart Gold and Silversmiths.
Little Oak Vineyard Paxford Rd ✆ 01386 840079 ⌖ littleoakvineyard.com. First planted in 2006, this one-hectare vineyard produces still and sparkling white wine. Visitors are welcome to call in and purchase a truly Cotswold wine. Tours and tastings, too.
Robert Welch Lower High St ✆ 01386 840522 ⌖ robertwelch.com. Selling goods from the designs of the late Robert Welch, including a vast collection of cutlery. Though designed in the Cotswolds, note that products are not necessarily manufactured in the UK.

🧳 SPECIAL STAYS

East/West Banqueting House GL55 6LN ✆ 01628 825925 ⌖ landmarktrust.org.uk. Two extraordinary houses that are regarded as two of the most important Jacobean sites in England; both are Scheduled Ancient Monuments. The pair, saved and restored by The Landmark Trust, are on the outskirts of town, overlooking meadows and the ruins of Old Campden House (which was razed to the ground by Royalists during the English Civil War). East sleeps six while West sleeps four. No dogs.

🍴 FOOD & DRINK

Chipping Campden caters for every kind of eating and drinking, from tiny tea rooms to fine dining.

Bantam Tearooms High St ✆ 01386 840386 ⌖ bantamtea-rooms.co.uk. The large bay window stuffed full of homemade cakes, giant meringues and treats tempts you down the steps to sit by a roaring log fire. Enjoy the courtyard garden in summer. Excellent B&B accommodation, too.
Michael's at Woolmarket House High St ✆ 01386 840826 ⌖ michaelsmediterranean. co.uk. This restaurant has been a part of the Chipping Campden scene for as long as I can

remember and is always busy. Menus are full of Mediterranean flavours but with produce from the Vale of Evesham and surrounding Cotswolds. B&B accommodation available.

Toke's Food & Drink High St ✆ 01386 849345 tokesfoodanddrink.co.uk. Popular deli, used by many of the local restaurateurs, run by a born-and-bred Chipping Campden resident. Impressive cheese and wine lists plus food, including main dish meals, made on the premises.

7 EBRINGTON

As with so much of the Cotswolds, agriculture and horticulture are still major sources of income for the area, and the north Cotswolds are no different. Taking the road out of Chipping Campden towards Ebrington, you'll pass Campden BRI, a research institute for food and drink and the largest employer in the community. The large complex includes laboratories and food-processing halls to test and research a vast range of issues connected with the science and technology of the food and drink industry. Continue on up the hill into Ebrington and you'll come across the other end of the food spectrum – a lookout point over fields of vegetables and crops, fruit farms and cattle.

Travelling through the village recently, my husband commented, 'This is about as good as it gets.' I don't need to add any further poetic description. Do go and visit! The Diamond Way long-distance footpath passes through Ebrington and you can make a very good short, circular walk climbing north out of the village up the southwestern slope of Ebrington Hill on the Diamond Way (worth stopping for views west here). You then turn southwest, staying on the Diamond Way to cross the Hidcote road, then south through the Campden BRI research centre to join a field footpath travelling east, which takes you back to the village.

FOOD & DRINK

Ebrington Arms GL55 6NH ✆ 01386 593223 theebringtonarms.co.uk. Fine 17th-century village pub with superb views. Considered one of the prettiest pubs in one of the prettiest villages in the Cotswolds. Very much a foodie pub with locally sourced produce though it still has the heart and soul of a traditional community venue. Accommodation, too.

◀**1** The Cotswold Olimpicks are held on Dover's Hill. **2** & **3** Chipping Campden has some wonderful shops, as well as members of Creative Campden such as the Hart silversmiths **4** The beautiful village of Ebrington. **5** Broad Campden is a useful base for walking and cycling.

8 BROAD CAMPDEN & BLOCKLEY

Southeast of Chipping Campden lies a cluster of villages, the closest to the town being **Broad Campden**. It's a useful focus for walks, with the Diamond Way, Monarch's Way and Heart of England Way all converging conveniently near to the Baker's Arms, the hub of the village. These long-distance routes give plenty of opportunities for circular walks using other footpaths and quiet lanes, in particular around the Sedgecombe Plantation and Wood to the southeast.

Sedgecombe Wood is a part of the **Northwick Park Estate**, which lies between the villages of Broad Campden and **Blockley**. Once belonging to the Spencer-Churchill family (relations of Sir Winston Churchill), the estate was taken over as an American field hospital during World War II. However, from 1947 until the end of the 1960s it became one of several camps in Gloucestershire used to house displaced Polish people. Several

"To my mind, the village of Blockley is one of the most compelling destinations within the north Cotswolds."

thousand Poles lived with their families in small Nissen huts, which they decorated with climbing flowers and where they planted gardens. In 1952 General Wladyslaw Anders, the leader of Free Poland, visited the camp, a major event during their lives.

Northwick Park is the only one of the Polish camps to survive intact; with the manor house turned into flats, the remainder is now a business park. These businesses run from the very same Nissen huts that were used as residences and in 2007 a monument was erected on the site to commemorate all those who lived at Northwick Park and the importance of this and other camps for displaced people. At the back of the business park is a plaque on a grotto built by the Polish people during their residency.

I've been to this business park several times over the years, unaware of its former life until I was researching this book. A fascinating website (⊘ northwickparkpolishdpcamp.co.uk) created by Zosia Biegus Hartman describes her life growing up at Northwick Park, and what it felt like having arrived with her parents at the age of five. Before going, do have a look at the website, which is full of remarkable photographs of the era, and which for me made the visit particularly poignant.

I then went on to visit the cemetery in Blockley where, I discovered, there are over a hundred graves of Polish residents from Northwick

Park who once dreamt of returning to their homeland but were never able to do so. Up on a hillside in the centre of the village, they have a beautiful landscape to look upon but I couldn't help feeling that, however picturesque their final resting place, it's not exactly where they wanted to be.

To my mind, the village of **Blockley** is one of the most compelling destinations within the north Cotswolds. It certainly catches the attention of location scouts; the village has been used for the long-running TV series *Father Brown*, adapted from the books by G K Chesterton and set in the fictional village of Kembleford. Lying on the side of a steep hill and running into a small valley carrying Blockley Brook, it has all the classic Cotswold village elements – a charming collection of houses to look at, a few places to stay, plenty of good, scenic walks (providing you don't mind beginning and/or ending with a hill), a reasonable pub, and a cracking village shop and café.

⅋ FOOD & DRINK

Baker's Arms Broad Campden ✆ 01386 840515 ⊘ bakersarmscampden.com. Small and rustic village pub with a good atmosphere and reasonable garden. Hearty, staple meals: cheesy-topped cottage pie, sausage, egg and chips, steak and ale pie.

Blockley Village Shop & Café Bell Ln, Blockley ✆ 01386 701411 (shop); 01386 701054 (café). A community-owned shop selling lots of local produce including honey, ales, fruit and veg and meat from local farms. The village **café** (⊘ blockleycafe.co.uk) next door punches well above its weight with dishes you'd expect to find in a four-star hotel. Proprietor and head-chef Craig Stanley is Blockley born-and-bred, and knows where to source the best local ingredients for his breakfasts, lunches and seasonal dinners; most within 12 miles of the village.

Churchill Arms Paxford ✆ 01386 593159 ⊘ churchillarms.co. The more upmarket of the two village pubs selected here by a long way (TV chef Nick Deverell-Smith is at the helm), with accommodation also available. Sunday lunch is popular. Very limited parking, so come on foot or by bike if you can.

BROADWAY & ITS VILLAGES

Broadway is one of the best known and most popular of the Cotswold villages. It is extraordinarily pretty (though no more pretty than other Cotswold villages that don't see anything like the same number of tourists) but it does have an exceptional history, too. It's a centre for smaller satellite villages too – **Willersey** to the north, **Snowshill** and its famous manor to the south together with lesser-known settlements like **Stanway** and **Stanton**. It's around here that you start to get some of the more dramatic views of the north Cotswolds, obtained from **Broadway Tower**.

9 WILLERSEY & BROADWAY

🏠 **Abbots Grange Guest House**

The village of **Willersey** is worth a mention because of its boulevard-like main street, not dissimilar to that in Broadway. The outskirts include some undistinguished modern houses, but the centre is truly lovely. Unusually, the stone houses along the High Street do not butt up to the road but sit well back with wide, grass verges that give the village an appearance of space. A central village pond finishes off the picture, while drinkers at the Bell Inn can make the most of the views along the High Street by sitting outside overlooking the duck pond. A mile outside the

THE WANDERER

There can be few slower ways to travel than by touring caravan pulled by a horse. When Dr William Gordon Stables retired as a surgeon from the Royal Navy in his thirties due to ill health, he commissioned the building of a caravan (inspired by the Romany way of life) in 1885, in which he could undertake a tour of the UK.

Constructed from mahogany, lined with maple and adorned with gold mouldings, the two-ton 'house-on-wheels' became the first ever custom-built leisure caravan. Inside are cooking and washing facilities, and a salon with sofa that turned into a bedroom at night.

Upon completion, Stables embarked on a 1,300-mile tour of the UK from his home in Berkshire. It took two months to reach his destination, Inverness in Scotland, travelling at an average of two miles an hour. Stables wrote about the journey as he travelled – the first caravan road trip that inspired others to take up caravanning.

The Wanderer is a beautiful beast. Now owned by The Caravan and Motorhome Club, it resides behind glass – alongside a caravan once owned by HRH The Duke of Edinburgh – in Broadway, housed in the former railway Goods Shed of the Great Western Railway (now the Gloucestershire and Warwickshire Steam Railway). Visitors can view the first ever leisure caravan, and find out more about Stables and his slow travels, in the old Goods Shed at Broadway Caravan & Motorhome Club Site (Station Rd, WR12 7DH); you do not need to be staying at the campsite to view The Wanderer, but do call into the reception upon arrival.

village, you can pick up a pint of organic milk, a milkshake or some of the area's finest homemade ice cream at Gorsehill Abbey Farm.

One of the few Cotswold settlements that fall into Worcestershire, **Broadway** is another of those gateway villages, providing the link between the Cotswolds and the Vale of Evesham. Situated in the district of Wychavon – a not very ancient (1974) local government renaming of the area – Broadway nods towards the west and the towns of Evesham and Pershore, and yet has all the hallmarks of a Cotswold destination, its broad way (the High Street) attracting coachloads of visitors to the numerous cafés

"Drinkers at the Bell Inn can make the most of the views along the High Street by sitting outside overlooking the duck pond."

and restaurants. There are few 'everyday' shops; those that are there play to the tourist's wallet, but there is a notable collection of interior design and antique shops, drawn by Broadway's connection to the Arts and Crafts Movement and the American colony of artists that lived and worked here at the turn of the 19th to 20th centuries (page 106).

Within Broadway's centre is the **Gordon Russell Design Museum** (*🕾* 01386 854695 *🖱* gordonrussellmuseum.org), housed in the restored workshops of his furniture company. Much like the Arts and Crafts Movement within Chipping Campden at the turn of the 20th century, Sir Gordon Russell enthused a new crowd of craftsworkers in Broadway to design and make furniture, having been asked to restore antiques to furnish a hotel run by his father. The hotel became one of the most famous in the country, the Lygon Arms; Russell went on to be appointed head of the Design Council and was knighted for his services. His workshop and museum lie just behind the hotel, away from the main street.

Visitors have a second museum to admire, on the High Street. The **Broadway Museum and Art Gallery** (*🕾* 01386 859047 *🖱* broadwaymuseum.org.uk) combines an important historic 17th-century former coaching inn with displays of period furniture, plus ceramics, curiosities and paintings from, and curated by, the formidable Ashmolean Museum in Oxford. There's always a special exhibition on at this community-funded museum together with an eclectic mix of monthly lectures.

I love this museum, not only for its enthusiastic volunteer-led workforce (the wonderful building was provided to the community on the proviso that it was used for community purposes) but because what you think may be a quick glance around a little museum draws you in, until you find you've stayed far longer than you anticipated.

Visit for the building alone – the pine panelling and the Tudor room of the one-time Angel Inn are worthy distractions from Broadway's supply of modern-day eateries. But you'll find you're pulled through the immersive experience of what Broadway was like from the traveller's perspective, arriving at the inn during the height of the coaching industry when the village was on the main coaching route from London to Holyhead, in far-away Anglesey, and acted as a service station for passengers, horses and coachmen. Also here is an excellent exhibition adding colour to the story of Broadway when it was filled with American artists in the 1880s, and of the famous artworks painted here.

Broadway sits in a hollow, tucked up against the foot of the Cotswolds. The escarpment on its eastern side is known as Fish Hill. Its name is something of a mystery (though it could be something to do with monks storing fish). Along the ridge from Fish Hill and south of the main road stands the landmark **Broadway Tower** (⌀ 01386 852390 ⊘ broadwaytower.co.uk), a crenellated folly built in 1798 for the Earl of Coventry based upon an idea by the landscape designer Capability Brown.

There are few superlatives to match the view from the top on a gin-clear day, along the bumpy ridge and out across the Vale of Evesham to Bredon Hill. If heights are not your thing, the views are equally spectacular from the ground. Inside there's an exhibition on the history of the folly, including its holiday-home status to the likes of the artist William Morris and his Pre-Raphaelite chums (page 279). Unexpectedly, close by is an underground **Nuclear Bunker** (open to visitors and with tickets available from Broadway Tower) that was used by the Royal Observer Corps during the Cold War. Below the tower is a deer park with a particularly good café, Morris and Brown, though I give a thumbs-up to the designated picnic area as one of the best places to eat outdoors in the Cotswolds on a sunny, wind-free day.

One of my favourite approaches to the Tower is along the Cotswold Way from Dover's Hill. You'll then wander through the beautiful Clump Farm, which is National Trust-owned land, an important site for wild

1 The landmark Broadway Tower offers spectacular views of the countryside. **2** The beautiful town of Broadway is one of the best known in the Cotswolds. ▶

PHOTO:ECCLES/S

CARON BADKIN/S

BROADWAY – AN AMERICAN ARTISTS' COLONY

Broadway's High Street – and its side streets for that matter – is a disordered, jumbled collection of ochre-coloured houses that are so attractive they're all consuming on the eye. So, too, the lure of the shop selling upmarket cushions and scented candles for the home, the chocolate shop and the whiff of coffee coming from one of many barista-created cafés, or the sight of guests dining beneath giant umbrellas.

One can easily walk up High Street along one pavement and down the other, ogling at the architecture, oblivious to the Anglo-American artistic history of the place.

At the centre of the story is Francis Millet and his family who arrived here in the 1880s, introduced to the decaying village by artist William Morris and their mutual friend, the American critic Laurence Hutton. Many others, such as John Singer Sargent, joined Millet, creating an artistic hotbed of talent who enjoyed the cheap rents and the bucolic countryside. American actress Mary Anderson arrived, too, with a host of literary greats as visitors (George Bernard Shaw, J M Barrie, Robert Browning and Victor Hugo).

In the gardens of Farnham House (on the corner of High and Church streets), Sargent worked on his famous painting – *Carnation, Lily, Lily Rose* (now exhibited in London's Tate Britain). Francis Millet, meanwhile, purchased and renovated Abbots Grange (see below) as an artists' studio, saving the derelict building with the assistance of William Morris. Here, in the Great Hall, he painted his most famous work, *Between Two Fires* (also exhibited in Tate Britain). Guests such as artist Claude Monet and writers Henry James and Oscar Wilde visited and Sargent joined, too.

Millet left his family in Broadway for a brief visit to New York, on *Titanic*. The artists' colony in Broadway was never the same after he perished, gradually disbanding after his wife and children returned to live in America. A lychgate with inscription was erected by his friends at the entrance to the cemetery on the Snowshill Road, just beyond St Eadburgha's Church.

orchids, cowslips and other rare wildflowers, and an idyllic sunken valley, lined with hawthorn bushes. It is one of the best sights in the Cotswolds in late spring when the blossom erupts.

📖 SPECIAL STAYS

Abbots Grange Guest House Church St, Broadway WR12 7AE ☎ 02081 338698 ⌂ abbotsgrange.com. An amazing medieval monastic manor house full of period features such as Gothic archways and cruck-framed ceilings. It's believed to be the oldest dwelling in Broadway and stands in eight acres of gardens as a wonderful, secluded retreat, yet within 20yds of Broadway's High Street. Sit beside the fire in the medieval Great Hall (where Francis Millet's famous *Between Two Fires* was painted) for cream tea and cake, or take the outstanding breakfast in the wood-panelled dining room following your stay in one of the nine exceptional rooms and suites (the Elizabethan Suite or Bishop's Suite are my personal choice). Past visitors to Abbots Grange, once owned by Francis Millet, apparently included Henry James, Oscar Wilde, John Singer Sargent, Claude Monet and William Morris. In my humble opinion, this is the most charming of all places to stay in the Cotswolds.

¶¶ FOOD & DRINK

As is to be expected, Broadway has a large range of places to eat and drink, including the historic Lygon Arms Hotel, where dining in the Great Hall, complete with its 17th-century minstrels' gallery, is all about the ambience. It's not a cheap experience, though. The Swan, at the foot of the High Street, offers a full vegan menu. I've selected my favourites.

Broadway Deli High St ☏ 01386 853040 ⊘ broadwaydeli.co.uk. If we all had a shop like this on our doorsteps, we would not go to the supermarket at all. The range of local produce includes a comprehensive selection of cheeses, Vale of Evesham-grown fruit and veg attractively displayed outside, home-cooked pies fresh from the oven and a daily homemade soup and salad. Visit here and you will not want to eat out – other than with the picnic goodies you've bought, although there is a snug café and beautiful garden with tables at the rear.

Morris & Brown Café Broadway Tower ☏ 01386 852945 ⊘ broadwaytower.co.uk. Delicious food home-cooked on the premises, from coffee and cake to appetising lunches. Sit inside beside the fire in a William Morris-decorated snug or take in the views from the terrace outside. Arrive on foot or by bike; be aware that car-parking charges apply with a minimum of four hours parking; fine if you're off for a walk, or visiting Broadway Tower, but pricey added onto the cost of a coffee.

Russell's of Broadway High St ☏ 01386 853555 ⊘ russellsofbroadway.co.uk. Beautifully presented and delicious British fine-dining, specialising in local Cotswold produce. Fixed-price menu (two courses £30/three courses £35). To the side of the building is **Russell's Fish & Chips** – an upmarket fish-and-chip dine-in or take-away restaurant with arguably the best fish and chips in the Cotswolds.

10 SNOWSHILL

Though any route to (or from) Snowshill is scenic, I recommend arriving along Snowshill Road from Broadway. The country lane, which runs along a valley before climbing towards Snowshill, is particularly lovely, with charming views of Broadway Hill and Broadway Tower in one direction and Laverton Hill the other. Along the way is the photogenic 15th-century St Eadburgha's Church. The building is no more or less pretty than any other Cotswold church but its proportions, coupled with its lichen-mottled stone churchyard make the prospect just-so in its outlying landscape. And, when the cherry blossom is on display at the entrance, the totality of the scene is complete.

So much has already been written about Snowshill being the epitome of an English village, with its narrow, hillside lanes and 'quaint' gable-windowed houses. The village does attract lots of tourists for all the reasons above and, not least, to visit the National Trust property, **Snowshill Manor** (✆ 01386 852410; National Trust), which houses a bizarre collection of toys and knick-knacks. Charles Wade's appetite for 'stuff' was clearly insatiable and he used the house as an exhibition space to display his bits and pieces from around the world rather than as a place to live. Indeed, Wade, an architect and craftsman living at the turn of the 20th century, bought the semi-derelict old farmhouse specifically for his adored collection. He would spend hours there tinkering with the objects (all 22,000 of them) while he lived in the Priest's House, a much smaller property in the farmyard, with his wife

COTSWOLD LAVENDER

Hill Barn Farm, Snowshill WR12 7JY ✆ 01386 854821 ⌂ cotswoldlavender.co.uk

A couple of miles east of Snowshill, Hill Barn Farm is the home of Cotswold Lavender, where on summer days, a hazy purple hue smothers the stony soil.

With 420 acres of farmland covered with brashy, shaley limestone and a microclimate that sees average temperatures 3°C lower than nearby Broadway, Charlie Byrd decided he needed to look for alternative crops to cover the diminishing returns he and his family were receiving from growing the usual British fare. He noticed that lavender in his garden was growing well, so at the turn of the millennium, he bought 500 lavender plants, dotted them into the ground and waited to see what would happen.

The plants survived the climatic conditions of a Cotswold hillside, so Charlie bought 30,000 more, planting up 55 acres with 40 different varieties of lavender. The diversification of a small part of the farm had begun, intended merely as a helpful addition to the farm income.

Almost 25 years on, Cotswold Lavender produces scent on a commercial scale for the perfume industry, keeping 30% for its own use. The lavender is harvested over a fortnight in July and August, using a specially adapted machine that only snips the heads off the plants. The flowers must be distilled within three to four hours of cutting, so the process is completed on site to create a lavender oil.

in an even pokier room. It's not something a wife might put up with in modern society but as one of the volunteer guides quoted, 'It's not called Snowshill for nothing. The Priest's House is much warmer than the manor. Even relegated to a smaller room, I know which building I'd rather live in'.

The manor house is filled to the rafters with anything and everything – historic children's toys, costumes, primitive bicycles and even Samurai armour. Little is behind glass or in showcases but displayed as Wade intended, on the floor, on tables, stacked on shelves, hanging from ceilings and leaning

"So much has already been written about Snowshill being the epitome of an English village, with its narrow, hillside lanes and 'quaint' gable-windowed houses."

against walls. The Wade family motto was 'Let nothing perish', a mantra Charles took to heart, but what's astonishing is that you would perhaps expect his objects to have been collected on expeditions to the colonies and trips around the world. Not a bit of it; most items were acquired from antique shops and dealers in the UK.

The farm grows two species of lavender for commercial purposes: the higher-quality *Lavandula augustifolia* (well-known varieties such as 'Hidcote' and 'Munstead') and *L. intermedia*, a higher-yielding but lower-quality variety that is used in products such as room fragrances. Many other types are also grown, providing a collage of colour over the fields for visitors. The peak season, when the lavender is at its best for viewing, is from June until early August with the puffed indigo rows and the green of the surrounding hills a magnificent sight, especially with the wafts of fragrance that lift the air as you brush past a lavender bush.

Charlie has now added three acres of wildflowers through which mown paths allow visitors to wander, and you're encouraged to take a picnic to enjoy amid the flowers. A woodland trail in a former quarry allows children to play and explore. Says Charlie, 'Woodland and hedges have grown up and matured in the three generations since my family moved to Hill Barn Farm, but the places where we played and trees we climbed as kids are still here. I am now lucky enough to be able to watch my children playing in the same fields that I did as a child. I hope that by opening up the Beechwood Trail, others will be able to enjoy some of these same experiences with their families.'

As well as wandering and picnicking in the colourful fields, you can buy Cotswold lavender toiletries and fragrances, plus lavender ice cream and lavender scones — and the lavender shortbread is to die for.

The gardens and orchards at Snowshill Manor are an extension of the property, rambling with a collection of cottage garden perennials and roses, ancient apple trees and lawnmower sheep. The gardens are therapeutic and offer fine views over otherwise hidden valleys and Cotswold folds.

Wander around the village midweek and you can find life returned to something akin to normality, with residents tending to the roses that climb the cottage walls. Their charming appearance also owes something to their roofs, which are made from a single kind of Cotswold slate. Look on an Ordnance Survey map and you'll find the area around Snowshill littered with centuries-old slate pits and quarries. They are no longer working quarries and are now a natural part of the up-and-down landscape. Names like Upper Slatepits, Scarborough Pits and Hornsleasow Quarry give the game away.

11 STANWAY, STANTON, LAVERTON & BUCKLAND

From Broadway the Cotswold ridge runs north to south dividing Snowshill from a quartet of villages linked by the Cotswold Way. Each one tucks itself close to the base of the hill for shelter, using the natural folds of the land for added protection. **Buckland** and **Laverton** are furthest north, each one only accessible by road along a no-through route, though a bridleway and several footpaths bring the two together. Their tucked-away character makes them particularly restful.

The furthest south of the four, just as the sharper inclines of the ridge slow down a touch, the hamlet of Stanway is little more than a house and a church, but it is some house. **Stanway House and Fountain** (✆ 01386 584469 ⌀ stanwayfountain.co.uk) offers sumptuous Jacobean architecture, full of knobs and furbelows, while in the grounds Britain's tallest fountain (and the highest gravity-fed fountain in the world at 300ft) erupts from a Cotswold water garden like an Icelandic geyser. I'd argue that Stanway House and Fountain is one of the most underrated places to visit in the Cotswolds. Take the time to climb through the parkland estate to the Pyramid, an 18th-century folly. The views of the

1 Bredon Hill, which is criss-crossed with footpaths, is a National Nature Reserve. **2** The quirky living room in the Priest's House at Snowshill Manor. **3** Stanway House is home to the highest gravity-fed fountain in the world. **4** Stanton Guildhouse offers workshops in arts and crafts, including pottery. ▶

DAVIDMARTYN/D

STUART ANDREWS/D

STANTON GUILDHOUSE

CAROLINE MILLS

house, the church and the hills beyond – turned miniature by the height of the fountain – are well worth the effort.

Stanway House is very much a private family home. Entering the dining room, I was told, 'Do go and have a look at the kitchen while you can. The Lord will come down for his tea soon and we'll close the doors then.' I peeked inside to see a lived-in look; the kettle ready and waiting for Lord Neidpath, the 13th Earl of Weymyss to arrive and make his afternoon cup.

The remainder of the house is in similar voyeuristic detail. Scouring the bookshelves for what the owners read, looking at portraits of family members past and present, and even peering into bedrooms in daily use. A sign on one open door read 'The Library. Please come in'. I did, so too a small group of Canadian tourists. There, at work with papers scattered, was the owner, and a conversation ensued about the Great Lakes.

J M Barrie, author of *Peter Pan*, was a regular summer visitor here in the 1920s and would host many of his literary friends. He organised cricket matches, with his team including George Bernard Shaw, A A Milne, Rudyard Kipling and Jerome K Jerome, among others. He also donated the village cricket pavilion, an endearing thatched timber structure that, unusually, rests on staddlestones.

My favourite of the quartet of villages – indeed possibly my favourite Cotswold village for its aesthetics – **Stanton** sits just north of Stanway and pushes its way up the ridge. As with the others, the Cotswold Way passes through (Laverton has a spur), straight along the main street past many pretty cottages and slightly grander manor houses. At the far end of the village, high on the hill (just like the other four villages, Stanton has no

"At other times of the year, there are 'quiet days' where you can simply sit, relax and reflect in a conducive environment."

through route) is **Stanton Guildhouse** (⌂ stantonguildhouse.org.uk) a manor house serving as a venue for summer schools and workshops in arts and crafts, including woodwork, pottery and textiles. At other times of the year, there are 'quiet days' where you can simply sit, relax and reflect in a conducive environment, away from everything but the countryside. The Mount Inn (page 114) sits just below, with some of the finest views of any Cotswold pub.

Within the village is **Cotswolds Riding** (☎ 01386 584250 ⌂ cotswoldsriding.co.uk), run by Jill Carenza. Jill has more than 50

A walk above Stanton

✿ OS Explorer map OL45; start: Stanton village, ♀ SP072342; 3 miles; one strenuous uphill section

The delectably varied escarpment here makes for some of the choicest short circular walks in the Cotswolds. For a three-mile taster from Stanton, follow the well-marked Cotswold Way up to Shenberrow Hill, and look down over the Vale of Evesham towards the jagged outline of the Malverns. Carry on northwards, and return to Stanton by the track that once served local quarries. As you drop back into the village you pass the Mount Inn, very handily sited as a final reward.

You could extend this route to five miles by turning right at Shenberrow Buildings, then dropping past Parks Farm, through Lidcombe Wood and down to the B4077, then branching off past the grand gates to Stanway House. If it's open, I recommend you visit. The road and the Cotswold Way bear round to the left and, just past the church, to the right. Out of the village, the route is wonderful. With parkland and the escarpment on your right and passing the cricket ground (with J M Barrie's pavilion) and flower-strewn pastures on your left, you can choose to wander the quiet road, lined with 'ornamental' trees in estate-like fashion, or through the parkland and open fields along the Cotswold Way; both will take you back to Stanton. Past the cricket ground you'll also see views of the long Stanway Viaduct and, if you're lucky, you may catch a glimpse of one of the steam trains on the Gloucestershire Warwickshire Steam Railway (page 180) that now uses this once-disused line.

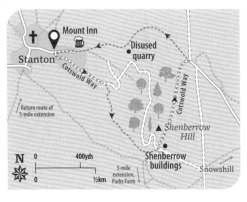

horses and ponies to suit any level of ability, with the opportunity for visitors, from beginners to experienced riders, to take a one-hour hack into the hills above Stanton or enjoy a day's riding with a pub lunch. Countryside hacks can be as a group or private. And, if you wish to make a weekend or longer riding holiday, Jill also runs The Vine B&B (website as for Cotswolds Riding) in Stanton.

🍴 FOOD & DRINK

Buckland Manor Hotel and Restaurant Buckland ✆ 01386 852626 🖉 bucklandmanor. co.uk. Exquisite dining in a beautiful manor-house hotel within large private grounds. Enjoy a champagne afternoon tea in the garden or order a picnic hamper to share in the ten-acre grounds.

Mount Inn Stanton ✆ 01386 584316 🖉 themountinn.co.uk. Locally sourced wines, food and Donnington ales (page 165). A steep walk up, at the top of the village, within 100yds of the Cotswold Way and just below the Guildhouse. The views over the Vale of Evesham and Malvern Hills reward the effort. The small patio is the place to savour them, or you can look out through the pub windows over the rooftops of Stanton and beyond. Arguably the finest views from any Cotswold pub.

12 BREDON HILL

Bredon Hill is a Cotswold anomalous lump, an island of Cotswold stone sticking out from the flatness of the Vale of Evesham and the river plains of the Avon.

A long and wide hill, it is circumnavigated by endless footpaths and bridleways accessed from a ring of base-camp villages, including one that runs around the rim of the steepest part of the escarpment – on the northern side.

"Much of the architecture in the nine villages that circle the base of the hill bears little resemblance to the typical Cotswold village."

It's here that you'll come across the outline of an Iron Age fort, **Parson's Folly** and the Banbury Stone, just below, also known as the Elephant Stone because of its shape. Parson's Folly is the highest point, bringing the total hill height to just over 1,000ft. The hill is a National Nature Reserve for its great importance to wildlife, which includes rare beetles.

Depending on which side of the hill you walk along, there are views to Broadway Tower, Ilmington Down, Tewkesbury and the Severn Valley, the Malverns and Cleeve Hill. However, my choice walking route is from **Elmley Castle**, along the foot of the hill before climbing through Cames Wood to Even Hill and past Doctor's Wood to the summit. Then follow Long Plantation before descending past Castle Hill and through the Deer Park back to the village.

Much of the architecture in the nine villages that circle the base of the hill bears little resemblance to the typical Cotswold village, with brick and the odd black-and-white half-timbered structure in the villages on the north side of the hill, which looks towards the vale. At Deer Park

Wines (Woollas Farm, WR10 3DN ✆ 01386 750267 ⏃ deerparkwines. co.uk), near **Great Comberton**, it's possible to book a tour (with tasting) of the new vineyard that's planted on the lower slopes of Bredon Hill. It's a very pleasant spot to enjoy the views of the vale and the steeper slopes above, with interesting creases and folds.

Overbury and **Conderton**, on the south side of the hill are by far the prettiest villages and with the most Cotswold stone on display, the pair worthy of a walk. The slopes of Bredon Hill are much gentler here than the north-facing side, filled with old orchards. For a short two-mile circular walk, you can follow the quiet, paved lanes north through Overbury (the churchyard, which sits beside a tiny stream, has a collection of flowering, low-growing cherry trees, a real treat to see in spring) along Pigeon Lane then south to Conderton, returning west to Overbury. Or, to extend, there are footpaths and bridleways that head up to the ridge of Bredon Hill, through Overbury Park, offering very pleasant estate parkland.

In Conderton, where it's possible to stop for refreshments at The Yew Tree, do make time to visit **Conderton Pottery** (✆ 01386 725387 ⏃ toffmilway.co.uk) owned by Toff Milway. It's a very restful spot that's a nice place to simply be at the foot of Bredon Hill and, in spring, the blossom from the surrounding pear orchards with resident sheep nibbling beneath is a delight. Toff specialises in salt-glaze slipware, and his pottery, every piece unique owing to the techniques, is beautiful. Says Toff, 'I've lived in the village for 38 years. I don't make artwork to sit on plinths. I like making cooking pots, pie dishes and plates that you can put on the table and sit around with friends to thrash out the world over a good meal.' Housed in a centuries-old Cotswolds stone byre is the studio – and Toff is delighted to show you into his studio to see where all the pottery is made – beside

"A wonderful place full of creativity, there are pots, plates, dishes and mugs everywhere, all over old pine dressers, in drawers, against stone walls and across the floor."

which is the showroom. A wonderful place full of creativity, there are pots, plates, dishes and mugs everywhere, all over old pine dressers, in drawers, against stone walls and across the floor.

Conderton is not the only place filled with creativity. In the neighbouring village of Beckford is **Beckford Silk** (✆ 01386 881507 ⏃ beckfordsilk.co.uk), where the Gardner family has been dying and printing silk for customers such as the V&A, The National Trust and the Royal Academy of Arts since 1975. The business is now run by the second generation of the family. It's possible to visit, with a small exhibition on how silk is made and the history of silk-making in Britain. They sell a huge selection of dyed and printed silk fabrics, including offcuts, plus silk clothes, ties, scarves and craftwork.

FOOD & DRINK

The Crown Inn Kemerton ✆ 01386 725030 ⌂ thecrownkemerton.co.uk. Attractive Cotswold-stone pub on the village high street with outdoor seating for watching the world go by. Real ales, local cider, and a menu that includes meat reared in the neighbouring village and own-grown vegetables whenever possible.

The Old Post Office Beckford. Lovely place for tea, coffee, cake and light lunch bites, with a sunny garden that's filled with fragrance in summer.

The award-winning Slow Travel series from Bradt Guides

Over 20 regional guides across Britain.
See the full list at bradtguides.com/slowtravel.

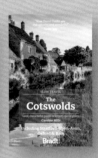

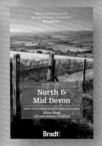

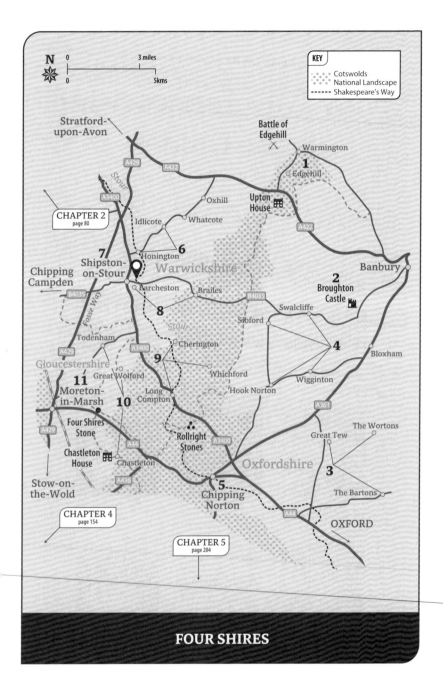

FOUR SHIRES

3
FOUR SHIRES

This was, until the last few years, the hidden part of the Cotswolds, the forgotten part. It has been discovered of late and is in danger of losing that hidden charm. Not as dramatic in appearance as the western escarpment, it's cosier and has just three small towns – **Shipston-on-Stour**, **Moreton-in-Marsh** and **Chipping Norton**.

Strictly speaking, there are only three shires within this chapter – Warwickshire and Oxfordshire, plus a tiny scrap of Gloucestershire. The 'four shires' refers to the Four Shires Stone, not far from Moreton-in-Marsh. It marks the point where four counties once met – Warwickshire, Oxfordshire, Gloucestershire and an enclave of Worcestershire. The borders have changed and now Worcestershire begins several miles away.

Within these boundaries, the areas become even more localised. We're at the very southern tip of Warwickshire, and the most northern part of Oxfordshire. Residents in these borderlands will feel much more akin to one another than they will to the remaining parts of their respective counties. Even the term '**Banburyshire**' (referring to the market town of Banbury just east of this locale) is still used today, demonstrating the closeness of the two counties at this point.

The bond between south Warwickshire and north Oxfordshire is perhaps because of their shared heritage and style of architecture. This is still the Cotswolds – just. We are on the very fringe here and, though there are still plenty of rolling hills, it is the flattest part of the Cotswolds overall, leaving the sharp western escarpment behind.

The B4035 from Shipston-on-Stour to Banbury cuts the area in two (it's almost the county boundary) and then a line from Oxhill in the north to Chipping Norton in the south divides it further still, utilising another county boundary. This is a very localised area, and if you've lived here for many years, you'll understand.

GETTING THERE & AROUND

You can access the locale by **train**: Banbury, to the east, is a mainline station, with direct trains from London Marylebone (Chiltern Railways), and from London Paddington (GWR) via Oxford. Trains to Banbury from the southwest stop at Reading (Cross Country) or Oxford (GWR), where a change needs to be made; trains from the north are via Birmingham (Cross Country or Chiltern Railways). In the west of this locale, Moreton-in-Marsh is the main station on the **Cotswold Line** (part of GWR), with stations at Charlbury, Finstock and Kingham, a few miles to the south.

It must be said that **buses** are extremely sporadic throughout the district. Some routes to the villages operate only once a week to reach market days in the nearby towns of Moreton-in-Marsh (Tuesdays) and Banbury (Thursdays and Saturdays). A Monday to Saturday service operates (by Stagecoach) between Banbury, Stratford-upon-Avon and Shipston-on-Stour, calling at some of the villages in the very north of Oxfordshire. Similarly, there are multi-hour daily services between Chipping Norton and Stratford, via Shipston-on-Stour. The only bus route in the area that operates every hour is from Chipping Norton to Banbury. This is operated by Stagecoach Oxfordshire. Pulhams Coaches can get you to Chipping Norton from the railway stations at Kingham and Finstock respectively. Unless you are prepared to do lots of walking and waiting (or cycling), a car is pretty much essential in this part of the Cotswolds.

In terms of **walking**, the area is too far east of the main Cotswold escarpment to pick up the Cotswold Way. However, **Shakespeare's Way** (page 29) continues its journey from Stratford-upon-Avon to London through this area from Shipston-upon-Stour to Chipping Norton. The **Cross Cotswold Pathway**, which follows much of the Macmillan Way through the Cotswolds, passes through the locale.

This being predominantly rural territory, the local footpaths accrue a handsome mileage and because the terrain is hilly but not dramatically

---

i **TOURIST INFORMATION**

Banbury Spiceball Park Rd ☎ 01295 236165
Moreton-in-Marsh High St ☎ 01608 650881

so, the walking is attractive without being harsh on the legs. This makes it easy to create any length of walk that you like to suit the abilities of the walkers concerned, from a short and gentle stroll through the woods picking up acorns with children to a grand-scale pub-to-pub walk.

There is a real fashion for **horseriding** in these parts, and livery yards, stables, riding schools and training are big business. You will inevitably see some horses wherever you go, particularly on the quiet lanes. There are also bridleways aplenty and much of the 63-mile Claude Duval Bridle Route crosses this area.

The **National Cycle Network Route 5** from Stratford-upon-Avon to Oxford via Banbury continues through the area. Two short sections of this are traffic-free. There are few other designated traffic-free cycle routes, but plenty of tiny lanes. A good option is the 75-mile **Cotswold Line Cycle Route**, which follows the Cotswold Line railway so you can cycle as far as you like, then catch the train back. It uses quiet roads and the odd off-road track between Oxford and Worcester, passing through Moreton-in-Marsh. Also of note are 20 downloadable cycle rides from the Cotswolds National Landscape website, including the **Ancient Stones and Manors** 19-mile circular cycle route from Kingham station or Chipping Norton. Many of these fall within the Four Shires locale covered by this chapter, and those of the Thames tributaries (page 205).

BIKE HIRE/REPAIR

Shipston Spokes 9 Church St, Shipston-on-Stour CV36 4AP ☏ 01608 664588
⌖ shipstonspokes.com. Bike and equipment sales, as well as parts, servicing and repairs.
TY Cycles Worcester Rd Trading Park, Chipping Norton OX7 5XW ☏ 01608 238150
⌖ tycycles.co.uk. High-quality hybrid and e-bikes for hire including helmets, locks, panniers, maps and routes, and an on-call breakdown service. Delivery of bikes within a 15-mile radius of Chipping Norton (which covers most of this locale and some of Chapter 5). Bike repairs too.

SOUTHERNMOST WARWICKSHIRE & NORTHERNMOST OXFORDSHIRE

Other than a county sign on the roadside there is little to distinguish Warwickshire from Oxfordshire, at least not at first glance. But talk to an elderly person who has lived in one county all their life – and whose ancestors have preceded them in the same manner for generations – and they will fiercely proclaim to be in one camp or the other. And yet the boundaries are becoming more blurred: Edgehill has an Oxfordshire postal address but is physically in Warwickshire. Other boundaries exist in this area; the traditional hedges that were installed during the Enclosure Act of the 18th and 19th centuries are very evident in these parts. The traditional, native 'Saxon Mix' (so called because the Anglo-Saxons were prominent hedge-planters) includes hawthorn and blackthorn interspersed with field maple, ash, hazel and elm; the elm of course all but gone. You'll occasionally come across a hedge-laying competition; the contenders are works of art when compared with their machine-slashed counterparts.

1 EDGEHILL

♠ Castle at Edgehill

As the Cotswold hills formed, two ridges appeared to the west: the more dramatic Cotswold escarpment that ends with Meon Hill (page 85) just south of Stratford-upon-Avon and, slightly further east, a thinner spine that now forms the Warwickshire/Oxfordshire county boundary. It is this more easterly line of Jurassic limestone that stop-starts its way further northeast towards Lincolnshire.

However, the Cotswold ridge dramatically stops at a place inevitably called Edgehill. Known to locals for its castle-shaped pub, the **Castle at Edgehill**, and for the beautifully named Sunrising Hill that drops down the ridge to the plains below, Edgehill hosted a raging battle that took place 350 years or so ago. This whole area is big English Civil War territory and almost every village, major house or

"The village green complete with duck pond amid the square of houses makes the village just-so."

stately home and even field has something to say about its connection with that period; many local families became involved, their ancestors still living in the area today. The 1642 Battle of Edgehill was the first pitched battle of that war, and one that ended inconclusively. The October battle involved approximately 28,000 men (3,000 of whom perished), with the Royalist camp set up on the top of the escarpment, where the pub now stands, and the Parliamentarians on the plain below. It was the Royalists who made the first move, charging down the escarpment.

The battlefield is now inaccessible – covered, ironically, by the UK's main ammunition depot – and much of the escarpment is covered with trees. But there are good vantage points of the battlefield (especially from the Royalist viewpoint) from the Castle at Edgehill pub. The Macmillan Way and Centenary Way run along the top of the ridge, generally through the trees, but a stone obelisk just below the pub and alongside the footpath gives good views.

The unusual Castle inn has an octagonal tower, the building of which was begun in 1742 to commemorate the 100th anniversary of the battle. It opened in 1750, on the anniversary of the death of Oliver Cromwell.

Not surprisingly, there are other pubs in the area connected to the Civil War. In **Whatcote**, one of those villages that take a bit of seeking out, just like neighbouring **Oxhill** (which really is worth finding), the pub sign of the **Royal Oak** depicts two pikemen, a crown and an oak tree. The pub was reputedly used by Parliamentarian officers following the battle at Edgehill. However, its name is derived from the hollow oak tree that Charles II hid in during his escape from the 1651 Battle of Worcester in part two of the English Civil War. The pub has good views of the Edgehill escarpment.

Just south of the village of Edgehill and close to Sunrising Hill is **Upton House** (OX15 6HT ✆ 01295 670266; National Trust). Its history is a little more modern, the grand ironstone house being the one-time home of Lord Bearsted, the first chairman of Shell, a company that his father had founded. It is the 1930s décor that is the real eye-opener (sadly the sumptuous pink and silver Art Deco bathroom was off-limits when I last visited; do ask to see it!) although the house is best known for Lord Bearsted's remarkable fine-art collection, which includes works by Canaletto, Hogarth, El Greco, Stubbs and Bosch, plus notable porcelain and tapestry collections.

HORNTON STONE

Across this most northern ridge are former quarries where great lumps of rock were once dug out. It's known locally as Hornton ironstone, getting its name from the village of **Hornton**, though the quarries reach out towards Radway, Alkerton and Wroxton, where a stone-processing quarry remains. It's a ferruginous limestone with colours ranging from deep brown to golden brown and even tinges of grey and blue, the harder, veined blue stone used mostly for stonemasonry. Many of the houses in the surrounding villages are built from this material, though the colour and size of the stone varies depending upon where it was quarried. The only remaining quarry of similar ironstone in the area is at Great Tew (page 126).

To the north of the escarpment, at its foot, is **Radway**, a village with nothing noteworthy to pay money to visit. There's no visitor attractions, there's not even a pub (you can see the Castle at Edgehill from the village). But it is particularly pretty, and well worth some time spent enjoying its beauty. So too, neighbouring Arlescote and, further east, **Warmington**. You're right at the farthest outpost of the Cotswolds National Landscape here. And it feels like a very different Cotswolds to that of the south. The characteristics of Hornton stone and village green complete with duck pond amid the square of houses makes the village just-so. Stop here and set up a picnic by the village bench and enjoy the enclosed view.

SPECIAL STAYS

Castle at Edgehill OX15 6DJ ✆ 01295 670255 ⌂ castleatedgehill.co.uk. There are few rooms in the Cotswolds that are on higher ground than this. Right on the Oxfordshire/ Warwickshire border (you'll stay in the former but look over the latter). Overlooking the battlefield from the English Civil War; the views are outstanding. Stay in one of two castle towers (five en-suite rooms) at this foodie pub. Weekends are best when a cooked breakfast is included in the price. Inside the public rooms, there's plenty of Civil War history on show with muskets, breastplates, halberds, maps and relevant paintings adorning the walls. Unique architecture (including wood-panelled rooms, Gothic arched windows and a restaurant with floor-to ceiling windows to take advantage of the hilltop views) plus a beautiful pub garden that also has good views. Food is excellent. A great base for exploring the most northern tip of the Cotswolds.

FOOD & DRINK

In addition to the **Castle at Edgehill** (see above):
Royal Oak Whatcote ✆ 01295 688100 ⌂ theroyaloakwhatcote.co.uk. Chef-owner Richard Craven is a child of the Cotswolds, hailing originally from Chipping Campden, and has, with his wife Solanche, created a Michelin-starred gastro-pub. Richard is dedicated to using produce grown or made in the Cotswolds (eggs, vegetables and rare-breed meats from a farm a mile away) and cooks British dishes showcasing those local ingredients.

2 BROUGHTON CASTLE

Broughton, Banbury ✆ 01295 276070 ⌂ broughtoncastle.com

Seven miles southeast of Upton House is another remarkable property. While the fan-shaped village of Broughton is mostly modern, Broughton Castle is anything but. Of all the castles (it's actually a fortified manor house) in Britain, this is the one I love most for its sheer visual impact, and the one I would recommend others to visit more than any other. I'm not the first to say it sums up England, but it certainly does. As it is just about on my doorstep, I've visited the house on many occasions and driven by hundreds of times and yet I never tire of the sight of it, especially towards dusk when the fading sunshine lights up the soft brown walls until they glow a pumpkin orange. These colours are reflected in the square moat, the sweet little gatehouse and bridge.

The owner is Baron Saye and Sele, a part of the Fiennes family – the very same one as the explorer Sir Ranulph Fiennes, a distant relative, and the actors Ralph and Joseph.

You may find the house, and in particular the Great Hall, strangely familiar, as Broughton Castle has been used on many occasions as a location for films, advertisements and television programmes, including Hollywood movies and television dramas.

Cannonballs dredged from the moat, now on display, show its direct link with the English Civil War, along with hiding holes, secret doors and tiny passageways, making it the stuff of children's storybooks. But the Great Hall is particularly striking, filled with displays of shiny armour, as are the gardens, especially the Ladies' Garden with its fleur-de-lys box hedging stamped on the ground and abundance of scented roses, sublime in summer. Climb to the roof for an overhead inspection of the garden and the moat.

"I've driven by hundreds of times and yet I never tire of the sight of it, especially towards dusk when the fading sunshine lights up the soft brown walls until they glow a pumpkin orange."

You can also wander through Broughton Park, north of the house, at any time of year (several footpaths cross it); the views of the house from here are magnificent.

3 THE BARTONS, THE WORTONS & THE TEWS

As you move south, a strange landscape unfolds, or rather folds. One of the least-populated parts of Oxfordshire, it encompasses a beautiful valley and series of hummocky hills that makes you feel in the middle of nowhere; a strange sensation given the increasing population in the area. The National Cycle Network Route 5 runs right through it, and it's on a bike that I'd recommend exploring if you can cope with the ups and downs, for while there are numerous footpaths, they are somewhat random and don't necessarily take you from A to B.

A string of tiny villages and even smaller hamlets on the edge of the National Landscape are scattered in among the hills and valleys. There is nothing particularly distinguishing about any of them in terms of visitor attractions or even a local pub, but it's this seclusion from society that provides the charm, simply a few clusters of comely looking houses in restful countryside. Furthest south are Steeple and Westcote Barton (ignoring much of Middle Barton, which is unremarkable) and **Sandford St Martin**, unusually for the area not paired with another village of a similar name. Next come Ledwell and the Wortons, **Over Worton** first and then **Nether Worton**, barely a hamlet with one beautiful manor house and a couple of additional dwellings.

"A string of tiny villages and even smaller hamlets on the edge of the National Landscape are scattered in among the hills and valleys."

To either side of you now, the hummocks intensify as a ridge creases the landscape, the folds flowing in and out of each other. One has been named Steepness Hill, its title justifiable. Spinneys, copses and traditional hedges break up the pastures and leys, and there are numerous bubbling springs with many tiny streamlets.

Furthest west are the Tews – Little Tew and Great Tew. Slightly larger than all the other villages, **Great Tew** has already made a name for itself and is regularly described, unfortunately, as chocolate boxy owing to its numerous thatched cottages. Visitors have been arriving for decades to sit on the grass and sup a pint from the minute bar at the Falkland Arms. Despite its seemingly fossilised qualities – properties were not connected to mains facilities until the latter part of the 20th century – Great Tew is a thriving village with most of the houses and land still owned by the Great Tew Estate. A bridleway leads through the park, itself clutching to the twists and folds of the land and there are three short circular walks permitted through the estate, all beginning and ending at the Falkland Arms.

For a gentle 11-mile circular cycle ride linking these villages, begin in Great Tew (where there is a car park at the northwest entrance to the village), travel east along Ledwell Lane then north to Nether Worton. Head east past Manor Farm, then take the turning for Over Worton (NB: this is a gated road). Travel south to Middle Barton; at the crossroads in the village, turn east along the B4030 (taking care; this road can get busy on weekdays) then take the turning southwest for Steeple Barton. At the church, turn northwest on to Church Lane towards Middle Barton (the prettiest road within the village); at the crossroads in the village, continue onto Fox Lane. Turn left onto the B5040 and, within 200yds, turn right to Sandford St Martin. Half a mile beyond the village, turn right to take a short detour to see Ledwell (which is along a no-through-road). Return to Great Tew along the Ledwell Road on which you began the cycle tour.

ⴵ FOOD & DRINK

Falkland Arms Great Tew OX7 4DB ℘ 01608 683653 ⌀ falklandarms.co.uk. Owned by Wadworths, a not-so-local brewery, but the charms of this widely admired pub have something of a cult following. Cosy bar and restaurant with log fire. Also open for breakfast. Accommodation available.

Quince & Clover Great Tew OX7 4DB ℘ 01608 683225 ⌀ quinceandclover.co.uk. Outstanding café with homemade everything, from breakfast pastries and brunch pancakes to wholesome seasonal salad bowls and stew pots for lunch, and its own ice cream, made using cream from North Cotswold Dairy. Eat in (the café is located right in the centre of the strikingly handsome village) or take away for picnic treats.

4 WIGGINTON, SWALCLIFFE, SIBFORD & HOOK NORTON

Wigginton might well be considered sleepy. It has no distinct village centre – the church is on one edge of the village, the pub is on the other. However, Wigginton grabbed the headlines worldwide some years ago when rumours sprang up that actually quite a lot had been going on back in 1940 with the apparent temporary residency of Unity Mitford at a hush-hush maternity home for the gentry. Unity, one of the Mitford sisters, who lived a few miles away at both Swinbrook (page 213) and Batsford (page 213), was allegedly in residence to give birth to Adolf Hitler's love-child. The story remains the kind of tittle-tattle that makes it into the script of a village soap opera, but it did drag Wigginton into the limelight for its 15 minutes of fame, however truthful the story is.

Climb the hill northwards from Wigginton towards **Sibford**, and you'll come to an area known as Wigginton Heath and Tadmarton Heath. It's home to one of England's most esteemed provincial golf clubs, **Tadmarton Heath Golf Club**, which has a reputation for having a rather special heathland course. Visiting golfers are welcome, particularly on weekdays, although it is recommended that arrangements to play are made in advance. Standing at Wigginton Heath, you might feel that the east-west ridge has no traits to make it significant. There is one: it is a notable watershed. Rivers running north of the ridge ultimately flow into the Severn, while rivers to the south flow towards the Thames.

Continue along the single-track road towards **Swalcliffe** and **Sibford** and you'll cut across what is known to locals as the Prairie. It's a most inviting strolling ground, with some fabulous views west along the valley of the **River Stour**, which rises at Wigginton Heath (and eventually runs into the Severn). In the distance is **Brailes Hill** with its clump of trees on the top, a notable landmark for miles around (page 143), and **Oatley Hill**, the top of which is the county boundary between Oxfordshire and

HOOK NORTON BREWERY

Brewery Visitors' Centre & Museum 🕿 01608 730384 🖉 hooky.co.uk

As I approach my local brewery along the narrow, twisting lane, it suddenly appears like a giant friend, the sun lightening the dark brown ironstone, the familiar black-and-white timber latticework decorating the skyline. It has been a while since I visited last and I had forgotten how beautiful this listed industrial construction is at close quarters. I say a 'giant friend' because the building, though tucked away in the west end of this thriving north Oxfordshire village, is a landmark for locals approaching Hook Norton.

Inside and out, there is a buzz of activity, the detail of the original painted timbers on the tower and decorative brickwork on the malthouse matched to that of brewing award-winning ales. As I step inside, the smell of brewing hops pervades the air on the first floor, the sweetness of malted barley on the second, with a maze of staircases, huge timber barrels, giant copper cauldrons and steel tanks, old wooden floors that would be the envy of any house renovation and the sunlight throwing shafts of warmth across the cool brick floor of the racking room. And at the very top of this traditional six-storey tower brewery is the architectural gem, for it provides some of the most spectacular views in the county over north Oxfordshire, south Warwickshire and Northamptonshire.

To say that Hook Norton Brewery is old-fashioned would totally misrepresent its 175-year history. Forward-thinking, it celebrates and embraces its traditions, while keeping ahead of the competition. Its director, James Clarke, is an old primary-school acquaintance of mine. In the playground the 'What do you want to be when you grow up?' line was never really discussed but I guess 'brewer' would have been an automatic answer. James followed his father into the family business, one that was set up by his great-great-grandfather John Harris in 1849, each generation

Warwickshire. Swalcliffe offers an impressive 15th-century half-cruck tithe barn. Built by New College, Oxford, the barn houses agricultural vehicles from the County Museum Collection along with a display of Romano-British artefacts.

Sibford is made up of three villages: **Sibford Ferris** and **Sibford Gower** combined with **Burdrop**. The two enclaves are divided by a steep river valley (the Sib) and some worthwhile village walks will take you past beautiful houses made both of Hornton ironstone and the paler Cotswold stone.

A couple of miles to the west of Sibford is **Traitor's Ford**. This beautiful ford hidden in the trees is a well-known spot for local children

handing down the secrets to the masterful art of brewing.

James is of the firm belief that, while developing regulations and consumer demands require the brewery to keep up with change, not all aspects need to. The steam engine, installed over a hundred years ago to run the brewery, is still in use (it's fired up once a month and many visitors make a point of coming then). Hook Norton is one of only two breweries left in the country transporting its beer by the traditional shire horse-drawn dray wherever possible, a magnificent sight on the roads around the village. This usually happens Wednesday to Friday, but it's worth checking with the brewery if this is your main reason for visiting.

Energy-saving beliefs run through the heart of the brewing process. Solar panels account for supplying much of the energy, the water (obtained direct from the brewery's own well) used in the brewing process is re-used as much as possible and the surplus spent grains and yeast are sent to local farmers for animal feed. The pigs it feeds return as sausages and bacon for the Malthouse Kitchen restaurant on-site that serves a daily cooked breakfast.

The range of beers has grown significantly over the past 20 years to more than 14 beer styles. 'Our four core beers account for 80% of our production,' says James. 'Old Hooky is the beer we are best known for but Hooky Best has the greatest output and is very drinkable. Then there's Hooky Mild, a chestnut-coloured ale, and Off the Hook, a pale IPA. We then have a seasonal programme with a different beer released every two months.'

Like the Clarkes, generations of families have worked at the brewery. Rob, one of the current brewers, was preceded by his father. Many staff have worked at the brewery for more than 20 years and retired former employees return each year for a Christmas lunch. There's a true community vibe to the place; I say hello to several I know.

Many of the 35 Hooky-owned pubs can be found across the Cotswolds.

EXPERIENCE OXFORDSHIRE

CAROLINE MILLS

MARTIN FOWLER/S

NICK TURNER/COTSWOLDS.COM

keen to dip their feet in the cool waters of the River Stour (though the base is very slippery) and play Pooh-sticks from the bridge. Apparently the name has nothing to do with traitors but the grisly tale that I was told as a child is that a headless horseman – a traitor from the English Civil War – rides through the ford every night at midnight. It's worth following the Macmillan Way a few yards north along the footpath next to the ford (it's known as Ditchedge Lane) and up the hill. Turn around and you will see gentle views of an undulating landscape of small hills and valleys, with **Whichford Wood** (page 145) in the distance over to your right. Whatever time of year, the colours here never fail to please, be it the blood-red poppies in the wheatfields, the chameleon hues of autumn or skeletal winter trees brushed with frost against a blue sky.

"Some worthwhile village walks will take you past beautiful houses made both of Hornton ironstone and the paler Cotswold stone."

By far the largest of the four villages is **Hook Norton**, of a sufficient size to warrant named parts: Scotland End (in the west), Down End, East End and Southrop. It has had extensive housing built since World War II, but its centre remains very attractive. Once upon a time Hook Norton (or 'Hooky', as it is known) boasted seven pubs – two of them next door to one another – not a bad ratio for a village. You'd think that all the residents would have been permanently pickled but the high proportion (there are now only three pubs) is owing to the celebrated **Hook Norton Brewery**.

Hook Norton was once on the railway that ran from Chipping Norton to Banbury, and, other than the brewery, one of Hooky's most distinguishing landmarks is the **Hook Norton Viaduct**. At the time of building, in 1887, the 85ft-high viaduct was the tallest in Britain. Closed to passengers in 1951 and freight after a landslide in 1958, much of the railway route is still evident in the area through broken bridges that cross roads and parallel lines of trees. Originally there were two iron viaducts and a lengthy tunnel; only the piers of the more southerly viaduct survive and the area south, the Hook Norton Cutting, is now a Wildlife Trust nature reserve, renowned for its butterflies and the sighting of oolitic limestone fossils and a pleasant spot for a walk. Access

◀ **1** The remarkable Broughton Castle. **2** The Castle at Edgehill pub. **3** Chipping Norton's striking Bliss Tweed Mill. **4** Hook Norton Brewery still delivers by shire horse-drawn dray.

is off the Swerford Road (Cow Lane), a quarter-mile south of the village. Alternatively, there are lovely views of the village – and the viaduct – as you approach along the D'Arcy Dalton Way from the southwest.

¶¶ FOOD & DRINK

Pear Tree Inn Scotland End, Hook Norton ✆ 01608 737482 ⌂ peartreeinnhooknorton. co.uk. The closest Hook Norton Brewery-owned pub to the brewery itself, about 150yds away. Basic pub food is served but it doesn't present itself as a gastro-pub – think '80s standard fare with chips. Wednesday night is a traditional games night – darts, dominoes, cards and chess. Turn up to have fun.

Wykham Arms Sibford Gower ✆ 01295 788808 ⌂ wykhamarms.co.uk. Comfortable bar and restaurant areas. Log fires in winter. Try the seared pigeon breast with apple compote, confit of Warwickshire pork belly with bubble and squeak or chocolate latte with coconut macaroons.

5 CHIPPING NORTON

🏠 **The Crown Inn,** 🏡 **Heath Farm Holiday Cottages**

Chipping Norton is one of those places that I ashamedly take for granted, visiting frequently but usually with too much to do. Every so often, I have a few moments to sit and look up. Then comes the comment at how pretty the town is. Known as 'Chippy', this is the highest town in Oxfordshire, and has particularly good views. As you enter the town from the east along the Banbury road, there are glimpses across the rooftops to the Cotswold hills beyond; catch the light at just the right moment, especially with a grey-blue thundering sky, and the whole place glows. The town, along with its environs, also has the envied status of being one of the best places in the UK to live, regularly receiving the thumbs up from property pundits. Judging by the number of celebs who have chosen to make it their home in recent years, there must be something in it.

"Catch the light at just the right moment, especially with a grey-blue thundering sky, and the whole place glows."

The Georgian façade belies the town's age, having been granted a charter by King John to hold a market (hence its name Chipping, from Old English *éping*) in 1205. The town is even older than that, with evidence of Saxon history and the earthworks of a Norman castle.

The 'new' market town was built on the hillside above the village and evidence of the thin burgage plots east of the High Street are still there, in the form of thin strips and narrow alleyways, quite apparent if you walk along Albion Street behind the High Street. The market flourished and wool was traded, bringing prosperity to the town, hence the 'new' Georgian façades that were added to buildings. A new town hall was built to show off the town's wealth too.

The most striking building in the town – or rather just on the edge surrounded by Chipping Norton Common – is the **Bliss Tweed Mill**, its slender chimney reaching for the clouds. Having begun as a small cottage industry, Chipping Norton tweed gained a reputation for its quality. The mill closed in 1980 and was converted into flats but there are fine views of it to be had with a walk across the common.

More recent history includes the **Chipping Norton Recording Studios** in New Street, which was responsible for lots of '70s, '80s and '90s hits from bands like the Bay City Rollers (*Bye Bye Baby*), Duran Duran, Gerry Rafferty (*Baker Street*), Status Quo, Level 42 and The Proclaimers (*I'm Gonna Be (500 Miles)*). The studios closed in 1999 but there's a blue plaque on the building.

The **museum** (opposite the town hall) on the High Street gives a community-eyed view of the town's history from its earliest roots, the industries that have come and gone, the railway that came and went and the town's brush with fame as the inventor of baseball, long before the Pilgrim Fathers sailed to America. Do make a point of taking a wander along **Distons Lane**, built by William Bliss for workers at the nearby tweed mill, parallel with the High Street, to Castle Banks, the site of an old Norman castle, and **Church Street** with its row of almshouses close to the amenable St Mary's Church.

The **High Street** and large **Market Square** sit on a hillside that has slipped up many a shopper on an icy morning. And it's really here that everything happens in this compact town. A few high-street names in small-branch sizes mingle with plenty of independent shops, all clustered around the central town hall. Look out for the artistic endeavours of the Chippy Yarnbomber too, who mysteriously decorates the town overnight! Along

"Look out for the artistic endeavours of the Chippy Yarnbomber too, who mysteriously decorates the town overnight!"

Market Street is **The Theatre Chipping Norton** (📞 01608 642350 🖥 chippingnortontheatre.com). The building alone is worth a look, as the theatre is one of the smallest that you will find (just over 200 seats)

and yet it's also one of the loveliest with its iconic cream and bottle-green façade (the building was once a Salvation Army citadel) and the sweetest of interiors, too. But it also has a superb reputation; many well-known faces come to the theatre, often at the start of a run to try out a show, with live theatre, music, films and workshops adding to the attraction. A gallery also holds art and photography exhibitions. You can even get married here.

Chipping Norton is brimming with independent shops, from boutique children's clothes and art galleries to an excellent bookshop, homewares and gifts. My favourite is **The Fibreworks** (𝒜 01608 645970), not just for the retail space, where colourful yarns, threads and fabrics adorn the shelves, but also for its community spirit. Upstairs is an inspirational social studio where workshops in numerous textile crafts are run including day courses for newcomers and social groups for creative projects.

Southeast of the High Street (with access off Albion Street) is the **lido** (Fox Cl 𝒜 01608 643188 𝒸 chippylido.co.uk). The outdoor pool, heated by solar energy, is a well-loved friend to the town (I learnt to swim here); an annual auction of promises has been held for years to help keep the pool open. It's a lovely place to be for both an early morning swim or a family splash. Generations of families have enjoyed basking in the sunshine for an afternoon on the lido's grassy picnic area and taking a dip to cool off.

🧳 SPECIAL STAYS

The Crown Inn Church Enstone OX7 4NN 𝒜 01608 677262 𝒸 crowninnenstone.co.uk. A traditional country pub in a charming Cotswold-stone village with flagstone floors, low beams, rustic tables and a conservatory to dine in that's flooded with light. Excellent food with changing, seasonal menus of pub classics and innovative alternatives (such as beer soup and cheddar beignets). Seven bedrooms each individually decorated with soft muted colours and en-suite washrooms that provide a very comfortable stay. The Cottage/Studio can be booked together to create a self-catering cottage as it has a self-contained kitchen.

Heath Farm Holiday Cottages Swerford OX7 4BN 𝒜 01608 683270 𝒸 heathfarm. com. Six cottages converted from old stone farm buildings, set within 70 acres of meadow and woodland. Owners David and Nena Barbour converted the buildings using natural materials 30 years ago and, where possible, commissioning local craftsmen and stonemasons to do much of the work; furniture and fittings within the cottages were made at the small joinery they set up on the farm for the purpose. Enjoy the extensive grounds and wildlife habitats, including David's nuttery planted with hazelnuts, walnuts and chestnuts, and the small collection of livestock. This is a Green Tourism member with Gold status, and part of the Caring for the Cotswolds scheme (⌂ cotswolds-nl.org.uk/looking-after/caring-for-the-cotswolds).

¶¶ FOOD & DRINK

There are several pubs in and around the Market Square and High Street including **The Fox**, a Hooky pub (page 128), and **Bitter and Twisted**, though **The Chequers**, next door to the theatre, has the edge for character. My preferred choice is **The Crown Inn** (see opposite), three miles from town. All serve food. Two miles from the centre is **Diddly Squat Farm Shop**, on the road to Chadlington and Burford, for picking up locally grown and made produce.

Jaffé and Neale Bookshop & Café Middle Row (in the Market Pl) ✆ 01608 641033 ⌂ jaffeandneale.co.uk. A superb independent bookshop, run by Patrick and Polly, with some of the best coffee I've ever come across, and homemade bakes. It's a very pleasant place to sit – indoors or out – and view the world. Book events are held regularly.
The Living Room Cinema High St ⌂ thelivingroomcinemachippy.co.uk. Modern community cinema with an all-day café that becomes a cosy, sparkling cocktail bar serving light bites in the evening.
Mor Bakery West St ⌂ morbakery.co.uk. Baked goods including morning Danish pastries, cinnamon buns and sourdough, plus coffee from Monsoon Estates, near Stratford-upon-Avon. Everything is baked in the Mor Bakery in nearby Chipping Campden.

FELDON & THE STOUR VALLEY

We have moved northwest now to the top-left quarter of our locale. This is very definitely south Warwickshire – no blurring of the sacred county boundaries here courtesy of Royal Mail. Except that once upon a time this quarter was in Worcestershire – an enclave surrounded by Warwickshire.

On the very edge of the Cotswolds, the **Stour Valley** falls between the two northern Cotswold escarpments, with Chipping Campden, Dover's Hill and Meon Hill in the west and the Edgehill escarpment in the east. The **River Stour** (one of five River Stours in England as well as one in New Zealand) rises at Wigginton Heath (page 127) and flows west until it reaches **Shipston-on-Stour** and then north before joining the Avon at Stratford. And yet it is really the central part, around Shipston, that is considered the Stour Valley.

Warwickshire was also, centuries ago, split into locales. Most famous is Arden, or more specifically the Forest of Arden, north of Stratford and the Avon. The particular part of south Warwickshire around Shipston, Honington and Idlicote is known as Feldon, a 'feld' being an Old English term for 'open, cleared land'. Parkland and agriculture are clearly evident in the area.

6 IDLICOTE & HONINGTON

Ordinarily there is no reason to go to **Idlicote**. It is a couple of miles from the main road along twisting narrow lanes and the few houses that are there do not offer grand visitor attractions. But it's worth coming this way to look out towards the Edgehill escarpment, the ridge so prominent all the way around to the village of Shenington. It's also more evident from here just how tree-smothered the hill is now, though not so in the days when Cavalier soldiers marched (or slid?) down to battle.

Take the quiet road to **Honington** and you'll appreciate how agricultural this area is – and has been, with noticeable ridge and furrow fields demonstrating the ancient art of ploughing. You'll cross through open parkland meadows with views west over Ilmington Downs and the slender spire of Todenham's church, a well-known landmark when travelling in these parts. Climb Idlicote Hill on foot – there's a footpath from Idlicote and the **Centenary Way** passes straight over the top – and you'll be able to see even further across several counties.

The village of Honington is particularly attractive. A blend of Cotswold stone, ironstone, brick and rendered houses, where the obligatory climbing rose and cottage garden sit alongside village greens and open spaces; no wonder that it has won numerous 'Best Kept Village' awards. On the banks of the River Stour, behind lofty metal gates – you can't help but notice them – sits **Honington Hall**. A symmetrically precise mellow brick manor house from the 1680s, it has been described as the perfect model for a doll's house. Unfortunately, it's not open to individual visitors, but make up a group of ten people and you're allowed in if you book in advance (✐ 01608 661434).

Shakespeare's Way passes through Honington, having come from the north, following much of the River Stour. It uses the footpaths

1 Grade II-listed Honington Bridge crosses the River Stour. **2** There is excellent shopping in Shipston. **3** St George's Church in Brailes stands out among the fields. ▶

STEPHEN SYKES/A

BEN MOLYNEUX/D

BEN NICHOLSON/A

and quieter back roads to reach **Shipston-on-Stour** rather than the busy A3400 as most travellers do. While in Honington, take a look at **Honington Bridge**, which crosses the Stour close to the main road. It's a pretty little thing with Grade II-listed status and the river is at its loveliest around here running along towards Tredington.

7 SHIPSTON-ON-STOUR

🏠 The Old Kiln House

By its very name, Shipston – or 'Sheep Wash Town' as it was called, translated from the Old English *Scepwaeisctune* – lies on the west side of the River Stour, with only one bridge crossing on the road to Brailes, close to the Old Mill.

A part of the Kingdom of Mercia during Saxon times, Shipston became an enclave of Worcestershire, surrounded by Warwickshire, until a change of county boundaries in 1931 when Warwickshire swallowed it up. Granted a charter for a weekly market and an annual fair, Shipston prospered as a centre of trade, mainly in sheep given the lie of the land around it, and later in spinning and weaving, and became an important stopping point on a drovers' route, along which cattle were transported from Wales to the markets in London. The town became well known for a woollen velvet known as 'shag' during the 17th century. The annual **Shipston Wool Fair** is held on the late May bank holiday to commemorate this heritage.

"It's perhaps their old-fashioned approach to customer service that keeps them going, but they have many loyal followers."

Shipston is a thoroughly appealing town for **shopping**. The town has been developed over the decades so its borders are sprawling out, but its shopping heart remains focused around the High Street and Market Place and a few other roads that extend from these – Sheep Street, New Street and The Bury. The town has some charmingly traditional shops, whether it's clothes and shoes or housekeeping; in fact, most of these purveyors of goods have survived for decades. It's perhaps their old-fashioned approach to customer service that keeps them going, but they have many loyal followers.

The absolute gem of Shipston is the quality of its food stores, with a fresh fish shop, greengrocers mainly selling produce from the nearby Vale of Evesham, **Taste of the Country**, a terrific local produce store, and **Edward Sheldon**, one of the most respected independent wine merchants in the country. Gourmets are truly spoilt. On the corner of **New Street** and **West Street**, Edward Sheldon has been supplying wine in Shipston since 1842 and is a Warwickshire institution. It gained a reputation for the quality of its wine, vintage port, sherry and Madeira, supplying affluent country gents and university colleges in its early days. The brick building is interesting enough at ground level, with a wine cellar kind of smell inside that will never leave you. But it is below ground that the building becomes really interesting, having over 12,000 square feet of labyrinth cellars to store wines at just the right temperatures. A guided tour (held once a month) of the cellars, followed by an underground tutored wine tasting, is worthwhile.

🛍 SHOPPING

Edward Sheldon New St ✆ 01608 661409 🖉 sheldonswines.com. Wine merchants in a superb and historic building and a great range of wine from inexpensive plonk to Château Pétrus.

Taste of the Country Market Pl ✆ 01608 665064 🖉 tasteofthecountry.com. Fabulous bakery and deli selling local everything plus homemade bread and cakes.

🧳 SPECIAL STAYS

The Old Kiln House 8 West St ✆ 07850 435408 🖉 theoldkilnhouse.co.uk. Tucked away behind a high stone wall with a hidden entrance and a rambling rose is this townhouse B&B. Attention to detail is outstanding from the furnishings the interior design, the service and the food. The atmosphere is calm, quiet and relaxed.

🍴 FOOD & DRINK

The Bower House Market Place ✆ 01608 663333 🖉 bower.house. Behind the charming Georgian bay windows is a vibrant interior serving bistro food all day, from breakfast and brunch, morning coffee and cake to lunch and afternoon tea, cocktails and evening dinner with small plates and charcoal grills. Weekend brunch is particularly fine. Using genuinely local produce (Cacklebean eggs from Stow; homemade granola; coffee from Monsoon Estates). Accommodation, too.

George Townhouse High St ✆ 01608 661453 🖉 thegeorgeshipston.co.uk. The grandest façade on the High Street, a hotel with no fewer than six individually decorated spaces (wood panelling, flag floors, exposed stone and brick walls, roaring fires and summer terraces) in which to dine as non-residents. Breakfast, lunch and dinner; excellent value set lunch menu with choice of three starters, mains and desserts (smoked harissa hummus with grilled flatbread; mini steak and ale pie with red wine jus; treacle tart with crème fraîche).

8 BARCHESTON & BRAILES

Just east of Shipston, a matter of a few hundred yards away over the River Stour, is **Barcheston**. It is a tiny rural hamlet among the fields and yet for its size, its importance has been mammoth.

William Sheldon established England's first tapestry-weaving enterprise in the manor house at Barcheston in the second half of the 16th century. Living in Weston Park (page 144) a few miles south, he acquired the village and, keen to utilise the wool trade in Shipston, set up workshops and installed looms in the manor house.

A cycle ride around Feldon

✳ OS Explorer map OL45; start: Mill Bridge car park, Shipston-on-Stour, ♀ SP259404; 14 miles; easy

The Cotswold and Feldon Cycle Route has been created from Shipston-on-Stour around the Feldon area. With Feldon being open lowland, this is an easy, signposted cycle ride around quiet country lanes without too much strenuous effort. A 14-mile-long circular route (although there is an additional, more challenging seven-mile section), it provides the perfect chance to pass through villages and countryside that you might not otherwise visit. Details of the route can be downloaded from ⌕ warwickshire.gov.uk.

From Shipston-on-Stour, follow the road towards Banbury, over the River Stour. Take the first right (opposite the recycling centre) towards Barcheston and follow the road on to Willington then Cherington. Continue past the Cherington Arms pub to Stourton, and at a T-junction turn left for Sutton-under-Brailes.

In Sutton follow the road round towards Lower and Upper Brailes. At the T-junction with the main B4035 turn left (take care as this is a busier road) and within a few yards turn right off the main road towards Whatcote (down Castle Hill Lane), next to the village hall and playing field. Prior to this, you could take a quick detour by turning right at the T-junction in Brailes to visit St George's Church, known as the Cathedral of the Feldon.

Continue along Castle Hill Lane towards Whatcote. Pass a turning for Winderton on your right and Aylesmore Farm on your left. At the next crossroads turn left signposted for St Dennis, past fields of ridge and furrow, the legacy of ancient ploughing techniques with a shire horse, and return to Shipston.

There are **places to eat** in Shipston-on-Stour but if you want to stop for refreshments en route, I'd recommend the Cherington Arms in Cherington, the Cotswolds Distillery in Stourton or The Kitchen at Feldon Valley, Lower Brailes.

A local man, Richard Hyckes, was employed to oversee things and he and his team of weavers were responsible for creating the finest Tudor tapestries – indeed some of the finest ever made. Their initial output was mostly of commonplace items (though still spectacular in quality) – bed valances, cushion covers and cuffs for gloves. But pictorial wall hangings were soon created, commissioned for country houses as the workshop's fame grew for the quality of work. When William Sheldon died his son Ralph Sheldon acquired Weston Park and he commissioned Hyckes to create a series of pictorial maps to hang in his house. These are known

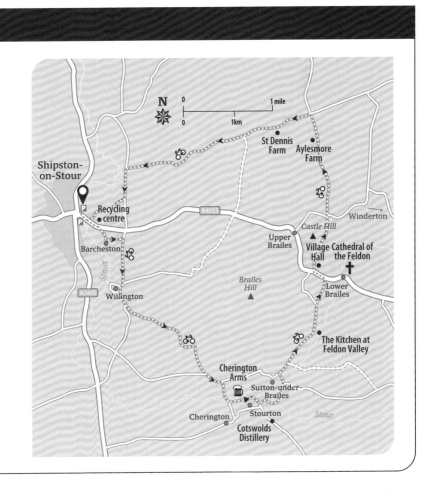

THE SHELDON TAPESTRY MAPS

All the tapestry work that survived from the looms at Barcheston is notable – there are examples that hang in the Victoria and Albert Museum in London – but none more so than the Sheldon Tapestry Maps. Created in the 1580s and 1590s by Richard Hyckes for his employer and landlord Ralph Sheldon, the tapestries form a set of four maps that illustrate the four counties of Warwickshire, Oxfordshire, Gloucestershire and Worcestershire.

Woven in wool and silk, the tapestries are absolutely exquisite, technically unrivalled, with the landscape, rivers and towns depicted in vibrant colours and immaculate weft. Some are decorated with flowers and mythological motifs too. However, these are more than just decorative masterpieces. The four tapestries are of major cartographic importance.

Three of the impressive-sized tapestries – those of Oxfordshire, Gloucestershire and Worcestershire – are held at the Bodleian Library in Oxford. The Oxfordshire map is on permanent display within the Weston Library (a part of the Bodleian) and is a must-see on a visit to Oxford (page 50). The fourth, Warwickshire, measuring 13ft by 8ft, is held at the County Museum in Warwick.

as the **Sheldon Tapestries**, though other tapestries from the same workshop are also known under this guise. It's believed that he went on to receive commissions from Queen Elizabeth I.

Richard Hyckes died in 1621 aged 97 and is buried at Barcheston. The tapestry industry at Barcheston survived for only 90 years, with work ending abruptly at the outbreak of the Civil War in 1642.

Being such a tiny hamlet – barely more than two houses – there is little to look at in Barcheston except to appreciate its location. However, little **St Martin's Church** is a gem. The tiny 12th-century church, sunbathing in a grassy garden accompanied by yew trees and past residents, is known as the Pisa of Warwickshire. Its castellated tower, rebuilt in the 15th century, leans precariously from the remainder of the building. It's a quirky feature that is, somewhat surprisingly, relatively stable. The church is home to a fine organ, and recitals are given on the first Sunday of every month from May to December, with a series of distinguished guest organists. Barcheston is also on the long-distance footpath of Shakespeare's Way.

There are three Brailes villages – **Upper Brailes**, **Lower Brailes** and **Sutton-under-Brailes**. Of the three, my favourite is Sutton, a quiet village set on its own with some really pretty houses around a large village green and the odd ancient oak tree to picnic under. Lower and

Upper Brailes are barely indistinguishable from one another (though residents may correct me on that), the ribbon development along the Banbury to Shipston road linking the two. Upper Brailes lays claim to a motte and bailey castle, though its only evidence is a mound on the top of Castle Hill. It's easily seen from the perimeter roads and there are numerous footpaths to it from the village. Lower Brailes is home to St George's Church, the 'Cathedral of the Feldon', grand in size and stature by comparison to most other churches in the area. Once upon a time, Lower Brailes was larger than Birmingham, would you believe! The scale of the church intimates the village's importance during the Middle Ages.

In terms of renown, all three villages are overshadowed by their neighbour, **Brailes Hill**. A Cotswold outcrop, at 760ft high it is a landmark for miles around. Its distinguishing feature is Highwall Spinney, which from a distance appears like a line of trees on the top of the hill. Unfortunately there are no public footpaths to the top, but you can climb the first slopes from Gillett's Hill Lane in Upper Brailes. One of the finest views of Brailes Hill is from the top of Whichford Hill (page 145).

¶¶ FOOD & DRINK

The Kitchen at Feldon Valley Lower Brailes ✆ 01608 685633 ⊘ feldonvalley.co.uk. Serving modern British cuisine with a farm-to-table ethos. Dishes include meat from nearby Paddock Farm (which has a butcher's shop in the village), eggs from Sibford and bread from Chipping Norton.

AROUND THE FOUR SHIRES STONE

The final quarter, in the far southwest of this locale, is, I think, the prettiest of the four that make up this chapter. Around the Four Shires Stone, charming villages create a fan shape converging on Moreton-in-Marsh, the Gloucestershire town. Naturally, with Worcestershire gone, the stone pinpoints the coming together of the other three counties, Oxon, Warks and Glos – using their abbreviated names.

9 CHERINGTON, WHICHFORD & LONG COMPTON

Swinging round to the southwest from Brailes, **Cherington** and its conjoined partner **Stourton** lie at the southern foot of Brailes Hill and, below that, Cherington Hill. They are beautiful villages, with very little modern infill to detract from the many Cotswold stone cottages and elegant Georgian façades. It's a pastoral community. I remember going to one of the village-centre farms every Christmas as a child for preposterously ancient spinster sisters (as they seemed to me) to despatch, pluck and dress our goose. I always returned home with a plate of meltingly light shortbread biscuits, the likes of which I have never tasted so good since.

"The estate is a hidden slice of the Cotswolds, with gentle parkland views that warrant gazing at over a quiet roadside picnic."

The two villages provide an ideal afternoon strolling ground after a lunchtime drink at the Cherington Arms, either along the River Stour, or across the fields from Stourton to Sutton-under-Brailes. But, if you're looking for additional entertainment, take a tour of the **Cotswolds Distillery** (⌂ cotswoldsdistillery.com). Established in 2014, the distillery is filled with gleaming copper where the world-renowned Cotswolds Single Malt Whisky and Cotswolds Gin are crafted. You can book guided tours or sit beside the log fire in the café (page 148) and tasting room for cheese and charcuterie boards.

Southwest of Cherington is the **Weston Park Estate**. A narrow, gated road runs straight through the centre where you'll usually see some sheep or cattle grazing beneath the many oak and ash trees. Weston Park was the seat of the Sheldon family in Tudor and Elizabethan times, the name synonymous with the Sheldon Tapestries from Barcheston. What an amazing house this must have been, in such magnificent grounds. But it was pulled down in 1827, the site now covered in trees close to the Cherington road. Legend has it that the Sheldon family could drive a coach from Weston Park to Coventry (some 35 miles away) while staying on their own land. A new Weston House was built in 1830, designed by the architect Edward Blore who also drew up Buckingham Palace. Weston House too has now gone but old photographs show it to be an overtly ornate neo-Gothic palace.

The estate is a hidden slice of the Cotswolds, with gentle parkland views that warrant gazing at over a quiet roadside picnic. If you happen to be wandering down Hack Lane and past Little Wolford Heath – on the western edge of Weston Park – during May, glance into the trees for a stunning sea of bluebells, one of the best woodland floral displays in the area.

South of Cherington is the Cotswold-fringe village of **Whichford**, with its little tag-on, Ascott. Spread around a large village green, it has significant Norman roots, evident in the names of some of the roads, the Norman Knight pub, and the fact that some of the villagers still have the French names inherited from their French forebears. Hummocky remains exist of a moated Norman castle (the moat is still there too, though privately owned). The tiny church of St Michael's, also of Norman origins, is of mellow moss-strewn stone, with its castellated tower, and is one of the prettiest in England. But then I am biased – I got married there! Its calm interior houses the De Mohun Chapel, a reference to the Norman knight who was given the village by William the Conqueror, and includes a 15th-century tomb with a pair of spectacles carved on the side – one of the earliest references to glasses.

Yet it is the exterior that is so joyful to look at. One of my favourite views in the country is from the road that comes into the village from Weston Park. Turn a corner, and the church is there sitting so comfortably in its landscape. Take some time to listen to the church bells if you can; it's one of the few churches in the district to have a full octave.

Whichford lies in a bowl, the surrounding hillsides once lined with sheep, although less so now. To the west of the village is **Whichford Wood**, a sizeable landmark woodland on a hillside of mixed evergreen and native trees that put on a colourful display in autumn. It's a well-known spot for walkers and the Macmillan Way runs along the southern perimeter of the wood with some fine views of the neighbouring valley, though for the best views, you need to climb either Ford Hill (the Macmillan Way utilises the hilltop) or the tree-lined avenue to the top of Whichford Hill. At 775ft high, it's second only to Ilmington Downs in the area, with a notable panorama from the top.

"One of my favourite views in the country is from the road that comes into the village from Weston Park."

The Normans may have got things started here but Whichford is now more synonymous with clay. **Whichford Pottery** (☏ 01608 684416 ⌂ whichfordpottery.com) is run by Jim and Dominque Keeling and their son Adam; their pots are renowned – and sold – worldwide and there are numerous trophies in the cabinet awarded for their displays at the Chelsea Flower Show. It is truly a local business, with an evident community atmosphere – most of the staff commute a few paces from their doorsteps in the village. The pottery's buildings are beautiful, the gardens inspirational and the craftsmanship the quintessence of quality. Best known are the terracotta garden pots – all of which are available to purchase from the outdoor showroom, but Jim and Dominique also make their unique sgraffito earthenware pottery for the home. Visit the Octagon Gallery to see more and look out for their extremely popular pottery sales, events, often including well-known garden designers, and open days when you can visit the workshops. And don't miss a stop-off at **The Straw Kitchen**, within the grounds of the pottery and run by the Keelings' daughter and her partner.

"The village was allegedly home to no fewer than 17 witches in the late 19th century – with one of them murdered in 1875 for bewitching a man."

At the most southerly tip of Warwickshire, the village of **Long Compton** stretches nearly three-quarters of a mile along the main A3400 Oxford to Stratford road, beneath a ridge of Cotswold limestone. The village was allegedly home to no fewer than 17 witches in the late 19th century – with one of them murdered in 1875 for bewitching a man.

There's no evidence of covens now though their earlier presence is thought likely owing to the proximity of the Neolithic **Rollright Stones** that stand on the Cotswold ridge south of the village. These might not have the grandeur of Stonehenge but they have some fun stories worth mulling over. There are three sets of stones: on one side of the road that divides them is a circle of stones known as the King's Men and, some yards from these, another group of stones huddled together and known as the Whispering Knights. Then, opposite the King's Men is the slender, yet crooked figure of the lonely King Stone.

Some 5,000 years old, the Whispering Knights is a burial chamber of a long barrow, and some claim the stone circle and King Stone are astrologically aligned standing on a prehistoric path. Whatever the reality and the reasoning behind the presence of these Neolithic stones, the myths particularly stir the imagination. The legend goes that a would-be king of England reached this particular spot on his travels when a witch challenged the king with the words, 'Seven long strides thou shalt take and if Long Compton thou canst see, King of England thou shalt be.'

---

1 Chastleton House is a fine example of Jacobean architecture. **2** The King's Men section of the Neolithic Rollright Stones. **3** Cotswolds Distillery is full of gleaming copper. **4** Cotswold lion sheep are judged in a contest at the Moreton Show. ▶

CHRISATPPS/S

JASON SALMON/S

JACQUI MARTIN/S

CAROLINE MILLS

Whether the ground rose up in front of him upon his seventh stride or he simply misjudged the lie of the land, he didn't make it. The witch responded, 'As Long Compton thou canst not see, King of England thou shalt not be. Rise up stick and stand still stone, For King of England thou shalt be none. Thou and thy men hoar stones shall be, and I myself an eldern tree.'

Hence the would-be king, his men and the conspirators across the field were all turned to stone. The witch, in the hedge along the road, is meant to bleed if cut when in blossom. Every child likes to have a go at taking the seven strides and they can also attempt to count the number of king's men in the stone circle. Two myths exist, one somewhat more pleasant than the other: one is that if you count the stones in the circle three times and reach the same number every time, you won't live; the other is that the person that you love will be yours.

"Despite the ambitious king's fruitless efforts, there are actually some sweeping views from the top of the ridge over Long Compton and south Warwickshire."

Despite the ambitious king's fruitless efforts, there are actually some sweeping views from the top of the ridge over Long Compton and south Warwickshire. But head to the Whispering Knights and you look out far over Oxfordshire, Chipping Norton and yet more Cotswold hills.

¶¶ FOOD & DRINK

Cotswolds Distillery Stourton ✆ 01608 238533 ⟨⟩ cotswoldsdistillery.com. Brunch, light lunches (charcuterie/cheese boards, quiche, croque monsieur, wood-fired pizzas) and homemade cakes. Excellent setting plus comfy sofas beside the log burner in winter; outdoor tables overlooking the copper stills in summer.

Red Lion Main St, Long Compton ✆ 01608 684221 ⟨⟩ redlion-longcompton.co.uk. Cotswold stone pub with cosy flagstones-and-rugs bar. Excellent food, using local produce. Regularly included in beer and pub guides. Good accommodation. Very dog friendly. My go-to for birthdays.

Straw Kitchen Whichford Pottery ✆ 01608 684416. Based in the grounds of Whichford Pottery, as its name implies, the building is made of straw and lime plaster, using traditional building techniques. The furniture doesn't match, the flowers are from the garden and hedgerows, the vases are jam jars, the artwork includes old 'masters' drawn by the Keeling children when they were young and you'll find old wine bottles pressed into the walls. It's a refreshing change from today's squeaky-clean image. Oh, and the food is divine – watch it being prepared fresh in front of you.

10 TODENHAM, GREAT WOLFORD & CHASTLETON

It would take appreciable effort to cover every village in this small pocket of south Warwickshire but virtually every one is worth taking the time to explore and there's a string of villages that warrant a short north-to-south cycle tour. **Todenham** has a fine church, its spire a landmark for miles around. **Great Wolford** offers the prettiest of Cotswold cottages and Barton-on-the-Heath has Barton House, a fine Elizabethan manor house (redesigned by Inigo Jones in 1636) that stands opposite the village green. **Little Compton** offers one of the cosiest pubs of the villages and then **Chastleton** is the secret gem, tucked across the border in an oddly jutting corner of Oxfordshire, with Warwickshire and Gloucestershire extremely close by. The Diamond Way and Macmillan Way converge at Chastleton, with a bridleway taking you on a spur to Chastleton Barrow, an Iron Age hillfort.

However, the architectural masterpiece is **Chastleton House** (✆ 01608 674355; National Trust), a fine example of Jacobean architecture. It is simply a cosy home and one that remained in the same family from 1612 (when Walter Jones built the house having bought the estate from Gunpowder plotter Robert Catesby) until 1991.

The family lost their money in the English Civil War by staying loyal to the wrong side (the Royalists) – there was much plotting that took place in the secret rooms – and the house gradually decayed because of the cost of the upkeep. Without the trappings of modern life it has remained virtually unchanged for 400 years, with the bits and pieces collected over time lying as they did when the family left. The Long Gallery at the very top of the house, with its creaky floorboards and cracking plasterwork on the barrelled ceiling, is a delight; one wonders how many mischievous children have, over the centuries, made the most of the room length and slippery floorboards as a socked skating venue. In the rooms below pewter plates sit side by side with equally historic tins of beans, golden syrup and some kind of liniment, while ageing tennis rackets are juxtaposed with Civil War 'memorabilia'. The National Trust, which has conserved rather than restored the house, owns Chastleton.

"If you're an artist of any kind, take your watercolours or pencils with you when you visit; the house and its surroundings have a bewitching effect."

I remember visiting the house as a young child, when it was still lived in by the Jones family, long before the National Trust took over or it was widely known. Even at such a tender age I recall being mesmerised by the beauty of the architecture, sitting on the lawn to paint a picture of the house. If you're an artist of any kind, take your watercolours or pencils with you when you visit; the house and its surroundings have a bewitching effect. You can spend an afternoon playing croquet in the garden too; and this is very much the place for it, being the exact spot where the rules of lawn croquet were first laid down in 1865.

¶ FOOD & DRINK

Red Lion Little Compton ⌀ 01608 674397 ⊘ redlionlittlecompton.com. Pretty Cotswold stone pub with large garden. Authentic, cosy interior with plenty of character. Basic menu that seems not to have changed since the 1980s (prawn cocktail; scampi and chips), but then you're coming here for the five-star Cask Marque-rated Donnington Ales. Accommodation too.

Todenham Manor Farm Todenham GL56 9PQ ⌀ 01608 654341 ⊘ todenhammanorfarm. co.uk. Producing high-quality outdoor-reared pork and beef from rare-breed pigs, Aberdeen Angus and South Devon cattle that are reared using ethical farming practices and the highest welfare. Visit the butchery, farm shop and Moo's Café, serving bacon and sausage baps and homemade cakes in a safari tent with views.

11 MORETON-IN-MARSH

Receiving its charter in 1227 to hold a market, Moreton-in-Marsh is still one of the Cotswolds' main market towns today, with the district's largest market held every Tuesday. It's a busy day, with shoppers bussed in from the surrounding area. It's not a high-quality or classy market, and not the place for a quiet browse among the dozens of stalls, but there is a certain buzz in the town centre on market day.

With an extraordinarily broad High Street, Moreton does give off a sense of space and offers the visitor a good selection of shops, from cheeses to chocolates, candles to carpets, all sold behind the elegant pale stone façades and beneath the rooflines of the 18th-century town houses. The Queen Victoria Gardens, at the north end of the town, offers an inviting place to picnic once you've purchased your wares. Art lovers shouldn't miss the **John Davies Gallery** (⌀ 01608 652255 ⊘ johndaviesgallery.com) with exhibitions and artworks for sale celebrating Impressionist, Modern and Contemporary art.

The town has long been important to travellers, with the Roman **Fosse Way** passing through the town and crossing the main A44 Oxford to Worcester road; a list of tolls charged in 1905 is still marked up on the side of the town hall today. In fact, no fewer than seven roads converge on the town. Moreton also received one of the country's first ever railway stations in 1826 when the Moreton to Stratford tramway was built. The railway line is still considered one of the most important today cutting across the north Cotswolds (though heading for Worcester these days, not Stratford).

"With an extraordinarily broad High Street, Moreton does give off a sense of space and offers the visitor a good selection of shops, from cheeses to chocolates."

Unusually for a Cotswold town, Moreton is neither built on top of a hill nor in a river valley, but sits in the centre of a relatively flat and large bowl. On the outskirts is the old airfield that was once RAF Moreton-in-Marsh. During World War II, bomber crews were trained here to fly Wellington aircraft, a number of which crashed in the district. There's a quirky museum in the town centre dedicated to those who trained at the base. With its tiny façade and propeller blades guiding you in, the **Wellington Aviation Museum** (𝒔 01608 650323 𝒶 wellingtonaviation.org) reveals itself Tardis-like inside, stuffed full of thousands of artefacts.

The old aerodrome (inaccessible to the general public) is still in use for training purposes, though for a different personnel. Laid out on the old runways are full-size models of every construction you can imagine

MORETON SHOW

Moreton Showground 𝒔 01608 651908 𝒶 moretonshow.co.uk ☉ first Sat in Sep

One of the highlights of the Cotswold calendar, Moreton Show is among the largest one-day rural shows in the country, with 20,000 visitors enjoying the sights each year. More than half a century since the first show, Moreton remains ever-more important to those who live off the land to retain a sense of rural identity and as an annual meeting place to catch up, alongside showcasing the best in farming. It is an all-family attraction with country pursuits and all-round entertainment on offer, but agriculture and rural life are still at its heart. Cattle, sheep and goats are still judged to determine 'Best in Show' and everything from vintage tractors to giant onions and gladioli is displayed. Many of the region's finest food producers come together, selling everything from grass-fed beef to local ice cream. Horseriders compete in the showjumping ring and sheep shearers compete to be the best. It's also the main showcase for the Cotswold Sheep Society.

required for firefighters to train – it is now home to the world's leading fire service training college. It includes the M96, the only motorway in Britain that you're not allowed to drive on!

FOOD & DRINK

Grouch Coffee 3 New Rd ⟲ grouchcoffee.co.uk. Peel off the High Street to find this little gem, which only does coffee (plus hot chocs and tea) and traybakes, made on the premises. Coffee and cake, done very well.

Henne High St ✆ 01608 544603 ⟲ restauranthenne.com. 'Local. Seasonal. Ethical' is Henne's motto, run by chef patron Darren Brown and FOH Nick Fenton. A 14-cover restaurant, it offers a tasting menu using produce sourced from in and around Moreton and championing ethical and sustainable food production.

Huffkins High St ✆ 01608 238090 ⟲ huffkins.com. The most recent café tea room to join the Huffkins brand, serving morning treats, light lunchtime bites and afternoon tea, with products made in the Huffkins craft bakery (page 218).

No 1 Cotswolds High St ✆ 01608 654444 ⟲ no1cotswolds.co.uk. Breakfast, brunch (bacon & maple pancakes), lunch and dinner (beef brisket burger with chipotle relish) using local produce, served in a shop setting selling homewares, also locally produced.

White Hart Royal Hotel High St ✆ 01608 650731 ⟲ whitehartroyal.co.uk. A refurbished 17th-century coaching inn where King Charles I reputedly stayed; the entrance hall has a copy of his unpaid bill. Choice of three eating venues – the restaurant, alfresco in the courtyard or by the fire in the Snug Bar. Afternoon tea, including a children's version with a teapot of squash.

Adventures in Britain

LIZZIE CARR

PADDLING BRITAIN

50 BEST PLACES TO EXPLORE BY SUP, KAYAK & CANOE

CAROLINE MILLS

CAMPING ROAD TRIPS UK

30 ADVENTURES WITH YOUR CAMPERVAN, MOTORHOME OR TENT

Bradt

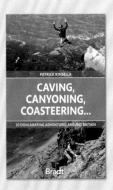

PATRICK KINSELLA

CAVING, CANYONING, COASTEERING...

30 EXHILARATING ADVENTURES AROUND BRITAIN

Bradt

LOTTIE GROSS

DOG-FRIENDLY WEEKENDS

50 BREAKS IN BRITAIN FOR YOU AND YOUR DOG

Bradt

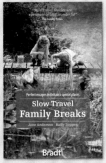

"Slow Travel Guides are a pleasure and wonderful"
The Sunday Times

Perfect escapes in Britain's special places

Slow Travel Family Breaks

Jane Anderson   Holly Tuppen

Bradt

WILLIAM GRAY

FAMILY WILDLIFE ADVENTURES

50 BREAKS IN SEARCH OF BRITAIN'S WILDLIFE

Bradt

Bradt GUIDES

TRAVEL TAKEN SERIOUSLY

bradtguides.com/shop

 BradtGuides   @BradtGuides  @bradtguides

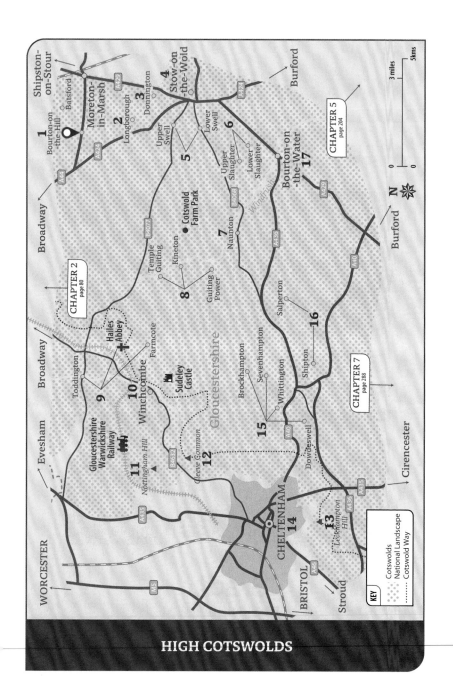

HIGH COTSWOLDS

4
HIGH COTSWOLDS

There's a little bit of everything in this area. In the east, the curvy hills remain with interlocking valleys and vistas that make you feel a part of the landscape. Some of the most visited villages and towns are here: the Swells, the terrifying-sounding Slaughters and the hyphenated beauties of Stow-on-the-Wold and Bourton-on-the-Water. I've also slipped in some lesser-known jewels that rarely make it onto the tourist trail itinerary, such as Salperton and Longborough, Kineton and Hampnett.

In the north, the town of Winchcombe has established itself as a base for walkers and is proud of its image as a working tourist town without the trappings of being 'too pretty'.

Further west, you begin to see the more aggressive side to the Cotswold Hills, rugged escarpments that on a windy day make walking on the edge feel somewhat threatening. Places such as Cleeve Common, the highest point in the Cotswolds, and Leckhampton Hill – alternately sublimely calm or alarmingly volatile when a storm approaches and the air is thick with deep mauve thunderclouds.

These hills envelop the spa town of Cheltenham, struggling to cling onto the glory days of its former life as a fashionable health resort yet still retaining that charisma in places.

My heart lies somewhere between them all – the high points in the west and those mellower pastures in the east, striped with flourishing hedgerows and guarded by stone walls, standing defiant whatever the weather throws at them.

GETTING THERE & AROUND

Cheltenham is served well by **rail** with three mainline routes. **Great Western Railway** (⊘ gwr.com) runs direct from London Paddington and from the West Country. The town sits midway on the **Cross**

Country Trains (⊘ crosscountrytrains.co.uk) route from the southwest and the northeast plus East Anglia via Birmingham. Services also run from Cardiff and Gloucester, again using **Cross Country Trains**.

The **Cotswold Line** (a part of GWR) from London to Worcester serves the eastern side of the locale, the closest stations being at Kingham and Moreton-in-Marsh (five and four miles respectively from Stow-on-the-Wold).

A special **steam train** (page 180) also runs from Broadway (page 101) and Toddington, in the north of the locale, to Cheltenham Racecourse via Winchcombe, operated by the **Gloucestershire Warwickshire Steam Railway** (⊘ gwsr.com). The timetable is irregular and the train does not run every day, so check the website before travelling.

National Express coaches travel countrywide to Cheltenham, stopping in the Royal Crescent, right in the centre of town. **Local buses** run daily between Moreton-in-Marsh and Cheltenham via Stow and Bourton-on-the-Water. A further route runs between Cheltenham and Winchcombe.

Of particular use to visitors is **Pulhams'** (⊘ pulhamscoaches.com) Explorer ticket, available for single days. This allows unlimited hop-on, hop-off travel on Pulhams routes in and around Gloucestershire and Oxfordshire, and especially covers the area in this chapter.

Long-distance **walkers** are spoilt here with so many longer routes criss-crossing the area in addition to local footpaths. These include the Heart of England Way, Monarch's Way, Macmillan Way, Gloucestershire Way, Diamond Way and Kenelm's Way in addition to the Cotswold Way.

Of note, two footpaths that cross the locale are the **Warden's Way** and the **Windrush Way**. Both take separate journeys beginning and ending in the same two places – Winchcombe and Bourton-on-the-Water. The Warden's Way, travelling slightly further north than the Windrush Way, is the one to pick for good stopping-off points, including Guiting Power, Naunton and Upper and Lower Slaughter. The 13-mile route sticks mainly to the valleys. The 14-mile Windrush Way travels much more through open countryside over the hills and, but for the tiny hamlet of Aylworth, doesn't pass through a settlement at all. Remember to pack a picnic.

Winchcombe has declared itself the 'walking capital of the Cotswolds', with the town awarded 'Walkers are Welcome' status. This

TOURIST INFORMATION

Bourton-on-the-Water Victoria St ✆ 01451 820211
Cheltenham ⌂ visitcheltenham.com
Stow-on-the-Wold St Edward's Hall ✆ 01451 870998
Winchcombe High St ✆ 01242 602925

honour is given to towns and villages that have something special to offer walkers. Information on walking in and around Winchcombe, including full details of its annual walking festival, is available at ⌂ winchcombewelcomeswalkers.com.

Cycling is one of the best ways of seeing this part of the Cotswolds, with idyllic country lanes and small villages providing numerous rewarding stop-off points. The roads may undulate gently but apart from the main A40 and A416 in the south of the area the large tract of rural land in the middle is excellent for cycling.

In the east, a good straight north-to-south-ish route (an old Roman road known as Buckle Street) with fine rural views and few undulations begins at Cutsdean Hill, just east of the village of Cutsdean, ending at Bourton-on-the-Water. It gives ample opportunity for taking short detours to small villages to the right and left such as the Guitings and the Slaughters.

The Cotswolds National Landscape has devised a circular cycle route within the eastern area of this locale. Titled 'Bourton, Bulls and Beer', the 26-mile ride encircles Stow-on-the-Wold and takes in sites such as Adam Henson's Cotswold Farm Park, Bourton-on-the-Water, Donnington Brewery and several pubs along the way. A map and details of the route can be downloaded from ⌂ cotswoldsaonb.org.uk.

BIKE HIRE & CYCLING HOLIDAYS

Cheltenham Bike Hire & Compass Holidays Cheltenham Spa railway station ✆ 01242 250642 ⌂ cheltenhambikes.co.uk, compass-holidays.com. Bike hire including road, electric and mountain bikes, kids' bikes, tandems and tagalongs for self-guided trips. Packaged cycling holidays including accommodation, bikes and luggage transfers around the Cotswolds.
Hartwells Cotswold Cycle Hire High St, Bourton-on-the-Water ✆ 01451 820405 ⌂ hartwellscotswoldcyclehire.uk. Choice of mountain bikes, hybrid and touring bikes plus tandems and tagalongs. Servicing & minor repairs.

BETWEEN MORETON & STOW – A TRIANGLE OF VILLAGES

Between Moreton-in-Marsh and Stow-on-the-Wold, the Roman Fosse Way, now followed by the A429, stretches south. The main A44, meanwhile, heads due west from Moreton before peeling off towards Broadway. And the stubby A424, known as Five Mile Drive for obvious reasons, forms a triangle that also connects with Stow. This creates a triangular frame in which sit three villages: **Bourton-on-the-Hill**, **Longborough** and **Donnington**. Together the villages form a pretext to explore this small pocket of countryside.

1 BOURTON-ON-THE-HILL

On the northern edge of the triangle is Bourton-on-the-Hill, its suffix added in the 15th century to distinguish it from nearby Bourton-on-the-Water. As its name implies, it sits on an (east-facing) escarpment with some spectacular views over the bowl in which Moreton-in-Marsh lies and beyond to the eastern edge of the Cotswolds.

Bourton-on-the-Hill's 17th- and 18th-century roadside cottages are very good looking with mullioned windows and Cotswold dormers, but unfortunately the busy A44 splits the village in two, with the cabs of articulated lorries at roof height to the houses. Hence most people simply see this particular Bourton from the comfort of their car, en route between Moreton and Broadway.

Since the 18th century Bourton has been well known for training racehorses – there are still several stud farms on Bourton Down west of the village – and, up until the middle of the 19th century, for being the location of a gibbet on which the bodies of highwaymen were hung. But the village has happier associations today, with a fine gastro-pub and three great sights on its doorstep in the form of Bourton House Garden, Batsford Arboretum and Sezincote.

Bourton House Garden

Bourton-on-the-Hill GL56 9AE ♪ 01386 700754 ⌂ bourtonhouse.com

Surrounding a fine neo-classical manor house made from large slabs of smooth cream-cheese stone and perfectly proportioned sash windows are the accompanying gardens, awash with light and colour. Ten interlinked areas of the garden provide different views of the house and

A walk along Bourton Hill

✸ OS Explorer map OL45; start: Bourton-on-the-Hill, ♀ SP176324; 5 miles; easy

With your back to the church, walk right for 100yds before turning right at the signpost for the Heart of England Way. Passing through the village, you'll follow this route along Bourton Hill to the village of Longborough. As you go, you'll pass through the grounds of Sezincote (page 161) and its spring-fed lakes.

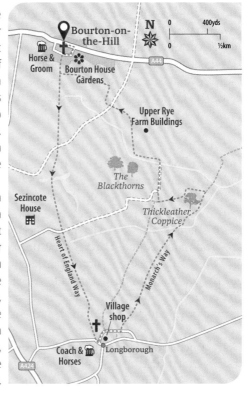

Upon reaching Ganborough road in Longborough, the Coach and Horses Inn will be in front of you where you can stop for refreshments (alternatively, you could visit Longborough Village Shop, which is on your left, down the hill, just beyond the turning for High Street). Turn left and immediately left again, along Charlesway, passing the village church, also on your left. In 250yds turn left along the Monarch's Way, following the footpath for just under a mile. Leaving the Monarch's Way behind, turn left to skirt the northern edge of Thickleather Coppice before crossing to Upper Rye Farm.

Turn right and walk north for a quarter of a mile before tracking left to the corner of another coppice, The Blackthorns. Turning right, you'll follow the route of an ancient ditch, crossing the track to Sezincote before arriving back in Bourton-on-the-Hill. There you can either enjoy a wander around the gardens of Bourton House, which serves tea and cake, or enjoy a drink at the Horse and Groom, at the western end of the village.

Note, there are a lot of stiles on this walk, offering a good workout, but it's not suitable for those with mobility issues.

exhilarating changes of mood. Of the ten, my favourites are the long borders full of riotous colours, the raised walk facing the house, where a gentle brush against the shrubs erupts amazing scents into the air, and, by contrast, the White Garden, where monochrome shades mingle with green foliage, against immaculately clipped box hedges and lichen-covered stone pillars. At the far end of the White Garden are scrolled-iron gates through which you can look over the hillside.

You enter the garden through a most impressive tithe barn. One of the largest in Gloucestershire, it retains its 16th-century timbers, under which you can sit to sip tea and devour homemade cakes.

Batsford Arboretum

GL56 9AT (for sat nav) ✆ 01386 701441 ⊘ batsarb.co.uk

A hundred yards east of Bourton-on-the-Hill, towards Moreton-in-Marsh, is the entrance to Batsford Arboretum, the largest private collection of trees in the UK with over 63 acres and 3,300 labelled specimens. The arboretum holds the national collection of Japanese flowering village cherries and an extensive collection of acers, making spring and autumn obvious seasons to visit. Having said that, in winter aconites and snowdrops carpet the floor of this south-facing hillside, followed by drifts of daffodils and later summer bulbs.

"In winter aconites and snowdrops carpet the floor of this south-facing hillside, followed by drifts of daffodils and later summer bulbs."

Great American redwoods tower above swathes of flowers in winter, the largest handkerchief tree in Britain displays its tissue-like bracts in May and the 'cathedral' lime offers respite from the sun in summer – stand beneath it and gaze skywards; you will feel as though you're in an enormous church. Autumn, of course, is the time to experience bursts of glistening gold, firework reds and shiny copper.

In among the glades are features such as a hermit's cave, bog garden and Japanese resthouse, installed by Algernon Freeman Mitford, grandfather to the famous Mitford sisters, in the late 19th century. He designed the arboretum with a restful, informal layout around the grand neo-Tudor house (not open to the public) that stands within the grounds of Batsford Park. From the top of the arboretum you look across to the house and the Evenlode Valley (page 242) beyond.

The **Mitford sisters** continued to live in the park until 1916, when the house and estate were sold. The eldest sister, Nancy, based the early part of her novel *Love in a Cold Climate* on the family's time at Batsford. Algernon and other Mitford family members are buried in the tiny church of St Mary's on the far northeast edge of the arboretum. This church, with its unusual apsidal-ended chancel reminiscent more of the French countryside than the Cotswolds, is accessible from the arboretum – although you cannot enter the arboretum from this side.

Today the arboretum is owned by the Batsford Foundation, a charitable trust that ploughs any profits back into maintaining the park and awarding gifts to other charities such as the Gardeners Royal Benevolent Society in addition to local schools and churches.

Sezincote

Moreton-in-Marsh GL56 9AW ⊘ sezincote.co.uk

Opposite the entrance to Batsford Arboretum, on the other side of the A44, is an unassuming gate. Continue along the lengthy driveway and you'd be forgiven for forgetting that you're in the Cotswolds at all.

Sezincote is a poetic word. The 'cote' or shelter is obvious enough but Sezin- is derived from *la chêne*, the French for oak tree, hence 'home of the oaks'. Such an unusual name should prepare you for something extraordinary, as instead of a grand manor house with classic Cotswold architectural styles, Sezincote is Indian-inspired.

"Sezincote is a startling, but nonetheless very appealing and elegant, incongruity in the cosy uniformity of the area."

Built in 1810 by Charles Cockerell to a design by his brother, Samuel Pepys Cockerell (the pair were related to the diarist Samuel Pepys), Sezincote is in the Mogul style of Rajasthan, with a central dome, minarets, peacock-tail windows, jali-work railings and pavilions. A long, sleek orangery curves around the Persian Garden of Paradise with its fountain and canals. In 1812 the Prince Regent visited Sezincote and, inspired so much by the architecture, adapted a farmhouse into the Royal Pavilion in Brighton. Sir John Betjeman described 'exotic Sezincote' in his autobiographical poem, *Summoned by Bells*.

Sezincote is a startling, but nonetheless very appealing and elegant, incongruity in the cosy uniformity of the area. Its golden Cotswold stone – quarried from Bourton-on-the-Hill but allegedly dyed – contrasts

JULIAN CIVIERO

NAGELESTOCK.COM/A

NICK TURNER/COTSWOLDS.COM

DONALD COOPER/A

with the copper-blue onion domes and metalwork railings. The Indian theme disappears inside, where conventional classical style takes over. Outside, however, the exotic theme continues with water gardens, an Indian bridge and a temple to the Hindu sun god – all within a very English parkland setting of oak trees.

2 LONGBOROUGH

From Bourton-on-the-Hill, the Heart of England Way runs due south along the east-facing escarpment, past Sezincote and on to the village of Longborough. This footpath meets up with the Monarch's Way from Moreton-in-Marsh, conveniently a few yards from the Coach and Horses public house.

The village, clinging to the side of Bourton Hill, remains a peaceful oasis of calm for most of the year – Longborough is off the general tourist trail, though there's no reason it should be – and if I had to pick a 'top ten villages in the Cotswolds', this would be one of them. The two footpaths converge and then divide again, offering many options, combined with additional footpaths for circular walks. Longborough is indeed a great base from which to explore the hills and valleys of this small parish. If you need a picnic to take with you, the community-owned village shop can supply you with everything you need for lunch on the go.

¶¶ FOOD & DRINK

Coach and Horses Longborough ✆ 01451 830325 ⊗ coachandhorseslongborough.co.uk. Traditional village pub serving classic bar meals (gammon, egg and chips) alongside specials (such as sherry & chorizo braised pig cheeks) and local Donnington ales (page 165). Pub garden with good views; as the pub states, 'you'll be transported back 100 years – the village cross, cottages and church look like something out of a period film drama.'

Longborough Village Shop & Café Moreton Rd ✆ 01451 833534 ⊗ longboroughvillageshop.co.uk. A community-owned shop run by a team of volunteers. Lots of locally produced food and drinks on sale in the shop and a café menu including hot sausage rolls, wraps and pasties cooked on the premises, sandwiches and homemade cakes. A useful stop-off when on a walk.

◀ **1** The striking 19th-century Sezincote was built in the Mogul style. **2** Donnington Brewery is housed in a 16th-century watermill. **3** Singers performing at Longborough Festival Opera. **4** Bourton House Garden has colourful borders.

LONGBOROUGH FESTIVAL OPERA

Longborough GL56 0QF ✆ 01451 830292 ⌖ lfo.org.uk

As with so many of the settlements around here, Longborough could easily be the film set for a period drama, but it is opera for which the village has made a name.

The Cotswolds unleash a few surprises. Arriving at the home of Longborough Festival Opera on selected dates from mid-June to the beginning of August is one of them, not least because there is a permanent opera house, with glistening chandeliers and all the glamour of a London-based outfit, deep in the Cotswolds countryside.

Longborough Festival Opera sits on a hillside – the same east-facing escarpment as Bourton-on-the-Hill and Sezincote. The views from the 'picnic field' – more on that later – and the opera house terrace are part of its very special character and certainly something that the Royal Opera House couldn't possibly compete with. They scan a full 180 degrees of the surrounding countryside including the Evenlode Valley and a variety of landmarks such as Brailes Hill and Ilmington Downs even though, from this position, they appear to be ironed out to a uniform plain.

The opera house was set up in the grounds of an extremely handsome house owned by Martin and Lizzie Graham. Martin grew up in Longborough and from an early age was inspired by listening to music, in particular Wagner. He began to organise charity performances using a travelling opera company and eventually his idea to create a permanent opera house came to fruition when an old cattle barn next door to his house was transformed. Today you'd never guess the building's former use, given its striking, salmon-orange-tinged classical façade topped

3 DONNINGTON

That east-facing slope upon which Bourton-on-the-Hill, Sezincote and Longborough sit suddenly turns a corner and creates a short, stumpy ridge of hills sandwiched between the A424 and the Fosse Way as they begin to meet at Stow-on-the-Wold. The ridge drops off and then dramatically climbs higher again as it approaches Stow, but on this particular ledge is the village of Donnington.

Donnington is known around Gloucestershire for its eponymous brewery, though this is some way from the village in about as picturesque a location as you could possibly find (it's closer to the village of Upper Swell). You can walk to the brewery from the village by heading west across the ridge using a local footpath before joining up with the Heart of England Way – it's approximately 1½ miles on foot. In fact, Donnington is at a crossroads of footpaths, so you could head northwest to Longborough (page 163) along the Monarch's Way to with figures of Wagner, Puccini and Mozart – sculpted by the local potter, Jim Keeling of Whichford Pottery (page 145) – and elegant reception rooms awaiting the arrival of guests.

Martin's daughter, Polly Graham, an acclaimed opera director, is artistic director, creating an imaginative programme that almost always includes something from Wagner. Far from amateur, the live orchestra is made up of instrumentalists from the top orchestras in London, Birmingham and elsewhere in the Midlands, who enjoy performing for a season in the Cotswolds, with professional singers, and backstage and production crews.

Community spirit is evident elsewhere too, the opera house providing education programmes in local schools and giving emerging professional singers stage experience, despite the opera house being completely unsubsidised by Arts Council grants.

Perhaps the most appealing aspect of visiting Longborough Festival Opera is complementing a sublime performance with a truly memorable meal. Guests are invited to picnic anywhere in the grounds of the opera house, or dine in the purpose-built festival restaurant, a convivial, typically Cotswold atmosphere. A lengthy mid-performance interval allows guests to dine and after the curtain goes down, visitors may sit around for as long as they wish by candlelight to soak in the sunset, eat and drink while chatting about the performance. It's all part of a highly civilised and magical experience.

For those who want to enjoy a private party before or after the show, guests may book the use of House Tower, a folly that Martin built in the grounds of his home.

create a triangular circuit , returning via the Heart of England Way and then the footpath (heading east to return to the village) that otherwise leads to the brewery.

Donnington Brewery

Donnington GL54 1EP ℰ 01451 830603 ⊘ donnington-brewery.com

For the first time in its 158-year history, Donnington Brewery opened its doors to visitors in 2023 for tours of the tower brewery. Do spend time enjoying its position, tucked away from the modern world. It's housed in a striking 16th-century Cotswold stone watermill – the millwheel is still used to drive some of the machinery – that bridges the barely known River Dikler. To one side is the millpond, an attractive pool for the resident ducks, geese, moorhens, coots and even black swans. The Dikler flows through the pond, ultimately sidling by Upper and Lower Swell towards Bourton-on-the-Water in a steep-sided valley.

Donnington Brewery was set up by Richard Arkell in 1865 and it's still run by a branch of the Arkell family (also known for Arkell's Brewery in Swindon) today. Its beers are produced in much the same way as they were back then, using spring water from the spring beside the millpond. On my tour, it was Phil, the head brewer, that guided a small group around. He's been working at the brewery for 44 years – and he's not the longest-serving member of staff! 'I was born [and still live] two fields away,' he commented, as if his commute to work is too far. This is a brewery of customary informality. If you want to buy beer, there's a sign at the door that says to speak to Roger, or place your money in the honesty box.

Stepping inside the brewery, it's a refreshing change to see a business that clearly takes the 'don't fix what ain't broke' motto to heart. Giant cogs made of apple and holly wood, belts and pulleys and simple but effective pieces of chunky iron machinery that, in many businesses would have been scrapped long ago through modernisation schemes, are used to drive the equipment, as well, of course, as the two water wheels.

"Stepping inside the brewery, it's a refreshing change to see a business that clearly takes the 'don't fix what ain't broke' motto to heart."

Nineteen pubs are tied to the brewery, all of them within a few miles of the watermill. For the ultimate of pub crawls, drinkers can walk the **Donnington Way**, a 62-mile circular route that links 15 of these pubs and wanders through some of the most iconic and gentle Cotswold scenery. All the pubs are listed on the brewery's website, though ironically the village of Donnington doesn't have a pub of its own.

HILLS & VALLEYS – STOW & ITS WESTERN NEIGHBOURS

Stow's full name – **Stow-on-the-Wold** – offers some clue to its location. It sits on a high hill, the slender tower of the parish church providing a beacon for miles around – every approach road must climb to reach the town. That there are eight approach roads illustrates the town's prominence as an important meeting point.

To the west is the Dikler Valley, where **Lower Swell** and **Upper Swell** lie on two arteries into Stow, the villages themselves linked by the river, a quiet country lane and the Heart of England Way.

Further west again, in the next parallel valley are **Upper** and **Lower Slaughter**, this time lying on the tiny River Eye. Finally, as the landscape shifts and pivots, the village of **Naunton** lies on a river valley running west to east, at least for a few moments. In this area the valleys, escarpments and interconnecting roads twist and turn, accommodating the changing folds in the rock beds. Many quarries, disused and working, are in evidence.

4 STOW-ON-THE-WOLD

On a hill 800ft above sea level, Stow has the enviable status of being the highest town in the Cotswolds. That in theory should make it one of the chilliest or windiest too. However, somehow it feels far from bleak, particularly thanks to the **Market Square**, at the heart of the town, being sheltered by the tall buildings that surround it, providing something of a microclimate.

Stow as a settlement dates from the Iron Age, and witnessed one of the last skirmishes of the English Civil War in 1646, the Battle of Stow, in which Royalist troops were driven back from the outskirts of the town to fight in the Market Square. It has been a trading place since Norman times; the sheep that were so instrumental to the town's prosperity were grazed on The Green, once considerably larger than it is now, at the northern end of the Market Square.

Today the trade is in antiques and horses, the two standing uncomfortably cheek by jowl twice a year in May and October when the Stow Horse Fair takes place on the edge of town and thousands of Romany Gypsies from across Europe descend. During the remainder of the year, the antiques shops and increasing collections of sellers offering products for the home, attract thousands of visitors to browse and enjoy the charm of the town.

The notoriously abrasive restaurant critic A A Gill once remarked of Stow that it was 'catastrophically ghastly'. The hordes of tourists who flock to the town each year would clearly disagree. And every one of the numerous restaurants, pubs and hotels that string along Sheep Street in between the antiques dealers look inviting, particularly as lights begin to twinkle at dusk. One such shop that never fails to draw my attention (it's right beside the main junction with a set of traffic lights) is **Christopher Clarke Antiques** (∂ campaignfurniture.com). The shop has been there for as long as I can remember and specialises in military

STOW ART GROUP

☎ 01451 798845 ⊘ cotswoldartclass.com

Aside from art galleries selling both antique and contemporary art in Stow, the area attracts many artists, craftsmen and -women who offer opportunities for visitors to make the most of their rural surroundings for inspiration through workshops and courses.

One such, for those living relatively close to Stow or taking an extended break in the Cotswolds, **Jill Jarvis** runs half-day classes over a ten-week term in drawing and painting at all levels, including beginners. And for short-stay visitors to the area, Jill runs open art sessions during the summer, usually on Saturdays at Oddington Village Hall, Lower Oddington (page 246).

Jill is the inspiration behind the **Stow Art Group**, which presents an annual exhibition in Lower Slaughter (page 170) every summer. The standard of work is high and most of the paintings and artwork on show are for sale, giving visitors the opportunity to discover affordable work by local artists and take away a piece of artwork as a souvenir of the Cotswolds (I've come away with some beautiful paintings). Exhibition dates are promoted on the group's website.

campaign and travel furniture, with a veritable collection of wooden campaign chests, travel cases, tables, chairs and globes all appearing to come from a period when any kind of travel would be classed as an adventure.

Digbeth Street is the place to visit to put a picnic together, with a great butcher's selling local Gloucester Old Spot pork, several competing delis offering superb goodies and a chocolate shop where the chocolates are made on the premises. Add in the farmers' market, held on the second Thursday of every month (and twice monthly from May to September), and you will have a feast.

If it's the history of Stow rather than the window-shopping that interests you, a visit to St Edward's Church is a necessity – as it is for photographers, to take a snap of the north door, guarded by two gargantuan, gnarled yew trees. It is rumoured to be the 'Doors of Durin' in Tolkien's *The Lord of the Rings* – and many a visitor photographs it for this reason, though the claim has never been verified.

 SHOPPING

Borzoi Bookshop 1 Digbeth Court ☎ 01451 830268 ⊘ borzoibookshop.co.uk. Long-standing bookshop in Stow (more than 40 years) with a lovely vibe and a wonderful selection of books on the countryside.

Cotswold Chocolate Company Digbeth St ✆ 01451 798082
⌖ cotswoldchocolatecompany.com. Delicious chocolates handmade on the premises (though Rob is a retained firefighter so you may just see him disappearing out the door, fast). You can watch the chocolates being made while you browse.

D'Ambrosi Digbeth St ✆ 01451 833888 ⌖ dambrosi.co.uk. Upmarket deli serving restaurant-quality food-to-go from American expats Andrew and Jesse d'Ambrosi. Racks of ribs, pork belly, shrimp rolls and slaw. Collect in-store or delivery within five miles of Stow.

Lambourne's Butchers Digbeth St ✆ 01451 830630 ⌖ lambournesbutchers.co.uk. Fine traditional butchers with most of the produce reared on farms within a few miles. Includes game in season.

⑂ FOOD & DRINK

There is no shortage of delicious places to eat and drink in Stow, from brewery-owned pubs like Brakspear's **The Porch House** (reputedly the oldest pub in England) or Arkell's **The Stag** (check out 'Feast Food' for parties) to **Stow Town Coffee** (reputedly the smallest roastery in the UK). Far too many to mention here, but this is my selection:

Little Stocks Coffee Shop Market Square ✆ 01451 83066 ⌖ oldstocksinn.com. The antithesis to the snug New England Coffee House (see below), this one offers a bright and airy contemporary Scandi design. Great coffee and excellent treats. Accommodation within neighbouring Old Stocks Inn, too.

New England Coffee House Digbeth St ✆ 01451 831171 ⌖ newenglandcoffeehouse. co.uk. Charming 'nooks and crannies' coffee house serving speciality teas and coffees, all with coffee beans freshly roasted on the premises and using milk from a local dairy. Homemade cakes and biscuits. Head upstairs for the snug with old wooden floorboards, wooden beams, comfy sofas and soft lighting.

The Old Butchers Park St ✆ 01451 831700 ⌖ theoldbutchers.squarespace.com. Family-run restaurant owned by Peter and Louise Robinson. Pete does the cooking; Louise is restaurant manager. Lots of Cornish fish and seafood on the menu.

5 UPPER & LOWER SWELL

There's nothing to suggest a height difference between these two villages, the pair sitting comfortably in the narrow Dikler Valley with sharpish inclines either side. If anything, Lower Swell is slightly higher up the hillside than its neighbour, but it's simply that Upper Swell lies north of Lower Swell.

Sadly, both villages are strung along their own twisting roads with cars that go far too fast and this does hamper their likeability even if the buildings are aesthetically perfect. My recommendation is to explore the village's neighbourhood off the main road by walking the mile-long footpath between the two, along the valley floor; it's part of the Heart of England Way. Indeed, a good circular walk from Stow-on-the-Wold visits both villages, utilising the Gloucestershire Way (Stow to Upper Swell), the Heart of England Way between the villages and returning to Stow from Lower Swell along the Monarch's Way.

6 UPPER & LOWER SLAUGHTER

Few villages in the Cotswolds are better known or attract more visitors than the Slaughters. Their name sounds as if they hide some grisly past and yet 'slaughter' comes from the Old English 'slohtre', which simply means 'muddy'. Where this mud comes from, I've not been able to establish but I can only presume that it must have some link to their location on the tiny River Eye.

The pair of villages are approximately a mile apart by narrow lanes, but less so if you take the Warden's Way (page 156) that runs through and between them. The Eye, of course, connects them too, and it's the water that seems to make them all the more idyllic – and all the more attractive to visitors. North of Upper Slaughter the river runs through a series of lakes. The most northerly of these is inaccessible, on private land, but the one nearest to the village is in line with the Warden's Way. This and the lake are sandwiched by a line of trees and it makes a pleasant short walk out of the village.

Upper Slaughter proves less popular with visitors than Lower Slaughter, but take the trouble to wander around the village, attractively tucked as it is between steep-sided hills and with a quintessential Cotswolds quaintness, and a small ford. It's considered a 'thankful' village, a name given to the very few settlements in Britain that did not receive any fatalities among its volunteer servicemen during World War I. Indeed, Upper Slaughter can be even more thankful that this feat was repeated in World War II. Despite the lack, thankfully, of a war memorial there is, however, a roll of honour in the village hall that commemorates the lives of all those villagers who did their duty.

If you're not partaking in afternoon tea at the celebrated **Lords of the Manor Hotel** (⏚ lordsofthemanor.com) – it's considered one of the best places to do so, even if it does lighten your wallet substantially – you can catch a glimpse of the building at least by taking a wander up the hill towards Lower Swell and turning right into the field just past the last house.

Or else visit Simon Weaver's **Cotswold Organic Dairy** (⊘ simonweaverorganic.co.uk), which makes a very tasty organic Cotswold brie at Kirkham Farm, on the road to Lower Swell. You can buy the cheese direct from the creamery.

The River Eye is much more noticeable in Lower Slaughter, running past cottages and miniature gardens. Tucked against the river is the **Old Mill**, its square brick chimney rising above the Cotswold slate roofs. But the greatest lure for me is sitting by the river, while your toes play in the shallow waters. It's one of the ultimate pleasures of summertime visits here.

The village hall, on the other side of the narrow river, is also well known for putting on art exhibitions throughout the year, usually with work for sale.

One of my favourite local views is from the little road that runs just to the right of the villages, turning off the B4068 Stow to Naunton road. Head down this road and you'll see both villages tucked among the trees, with the church spire of St Mary's in Lower Slaughter peeking above.

7 NAUNTON

Naunton is to one side of the road that passes high above from Stow to Cheltenham. It's very easy simply to pass by, but the village amply repays the small diversion, lying at the bottom of a steep-sided valley, with the River Windrush gushing through on its way to Bourton-on-the-Water and beyond. From the Stow road that passes up above the village there are three prominent buildings: St Andrew's Church on the west side of the village, the Baptist chapel in the form of a long, low building perched on the hillside and a dovecote below it.

In front of **St Andrew's Church** is a wooden bench with an apt inscription from *Ailce's Adventures in Wonderland*. The Reverend Edward Litton, a friend of Lewis Carroll (real name Charles Dodgson) lived in the fine old vicarage during the latter part of the 19th century, where the author would come and stay.

The **Baptist chapel**, I think, makes Naunton. It is certainly the building, with its long, arched windows, that draws one's eye from a distance, along with the **dovecote** below and to one side. That this 15th-century dovecote was built in a valley right next to a river is unusual itself,

MO WU/S

IAN LITTLEWOOD/A

ROBERT TALBOT

ANDREW S/S

as these shelters are usually built on higher, more prominent ground. Owing to its unusual position, it was converted to a mill for grinding corn. The village community bought the four-gabled building in 1997 to save it being turned into a guesthouse. Take a look inside: the odd dove and pigeon still enjoys their own bed and breakfast accommodation but beware of the deposits that these visitors leave behind. The Naunton Dovecote Trust is keen to raise funds to maintain this listed Grade II Ancient Monument, so buying a postcard or tea towel helps the coffers, or indeed sponsoring a 'nest hole' within the dovecote. Whenever my family and I go for a walk here, we end up munching on a sandwich while dangling our legs over the neighbouring bridge above the River Windrush. It's a therapeutic stop-off along the Warden's or Windrush ways. There's also an annual summer Duck Race on the Windrush, with money raised supporting the dovecote.

Another alternative way to enjoy Naunton and the Slaughters is by taking a **Treasure Trail** (treasuretrails.co.uk). I took my children on the 'murder mystery' trail, solving clues by looking at the village environment as we walked to discover a 'culprit'. The children loved the game and it encouraged us to look more closely at the villages. A little booklet with all the directions and clues is available to download from the website.

Look at an Ordnance Survey map and you'll see that the area around Naunton is full of disused quarries. Much of the stone used for the historic buildings in the area came from these (quarrying at Naunton is referred to in the *Domesday Book* of 1086) but many of the quarries also dug out the kind of stone used to make the traditional Cotswold roofing slates, many of which made their way onto some of the finest buildings in Oxford.

¶¶ FOOD & DRINK

Black Horse Inn Naunton 01451 850565 donnington-brewery.com/the_black_horse_naunton.htm. On the main street is this thriving village pub connected to Donnington Brewery. It's a popular stop-off for walkers on the Warden's Way, or a small detour for those on the Windrush Way. Traditional pub food.

◄**1** The River Eye flows right past cottages in Lower Slaughter. **2** The 15th-century dovecote in Naunton. **3** St Mary's Church in Temple Guiting. **4** Two huge yew trees guard an entrance to St Edward's Church in Stow-on-the-Wold.

THE GUITINGS & KINETON – THE QUIET CORE

By comparison with other places in Britain, the area around the Guiting villages is far from remote. And yet, when you're there you get a delicious sense of isolation, finding secluded pockets of countryside that provide blissful, pastoral scenes just right for a morning's stomp, yet with the odd tiny village to remind you that civilisation is never very far away. And you're still only within a few miles of Stow, Bourton-on-the-Water, Broadway or Winchcombe.

WITNESSING THE BIRTH OF NEW LIFE AT ADAM HENSON'S COTSWOLD FARM PARK

Bemborough Farm, Kineton GL54 5UG ✆ 01451 850307 ⌂ cotswoldfarmpark.co.uk.

Where else is better suited to witnessing the birth of a lamb than in the Cotswolds? After all, the entire area looks the way it does because of sheep. That's what I had the privilege of witnessing on a visit to **Adam Henson's Cotswold Farm Park**, a mile or so east of Guiting Power and the home of BBC *Countryfile* presenter Adam Henson.

Watching a ewe give birth, one can't help feeling slightly indecorous, as if I and fellow visitors should turn away to provide this clever lady with some privacy. How many other mothers were 'sensing' every contraction and acknowledging the discomfort of this ewe's labour?

Onlookers – and there were many sat upon straw bales in the lambing barn, ranging from those still in nappies to grandparents – were put at ease by Rory, the shepherd keeping a watchful eye on the flock. He provided explanations and a respectful running commentary on the process, from detecting the early signs of labour to

bonding. That included the fact that the ewe, who kept looking me in the eye during the early stages of her labour, would not be aware of our presence once focussed on the birth. Thank goodness.

And so it was that we witnessed the birth of twins and watched their very first, tentative, rising on to all fours. Three lambs had already been born earlier and there was evidence of further arrivals later. That was just one morning – lambing begins on the farm in February and continues through until the end of April.

That said, there are so many lambs, calves, chicks and kids (baby goats, not little humans) at the farm, that the spring and summer months are a delight, with plenty of youthful creatures to cuddle, stroke and handle. Experienced animal handlers are around to assist as children sit with overly cute fluffy bundles on knees while a widescreen TV offers live footage of chicks emerging from eggs within incubators.

The valleys are unpredictable as the folds of the earth dart this way and that, with tiny streams that bubble along. It's what makes the landscape here so interesting. I prefer this area to that around the Slaughters, as it does not attract visitors in anything like the same numbers.

8 THE GUITINGS & KINETON

As the crow flies, or indeed if you're travelling along the Warden's Way, the village of **Guiting Power** lies approximately 1½ miles northwest of Naunton. By a narrow and twisting country lane, it's somewhat further. Preposterously photogenic, the heart of the village lies around a small

Kate Lord, Farm Park Manager, explained to me how the farm came into being. 'It was Adam's father, Joe Henson, who set the farm park up, together with his business partner, John Neave. Joe had a passion for rare-breed animals and having taken over the tenancy of Bemborough Farm [where the farm park is based] in the 1960s, he wanted livestock, so bought his daughter some Cotswold sheep. Then came other breeds – Gloucester Old Spot pigs and Gloucester cattle – and he and John decided to show their collection to the public.'

Joe was becoming increasingly concerned about the number of native breeds of livestock that the country was losing, so in the early 1970s he helped to found the Rare Breed Survival Trust in what was the world's first farm park.

The park is now run by Joe's son Adam and his business partner and friend from agricultural college, Duncan Andrews. Said Kate, 'The farm park has changed over the years and will hopefully continue to develop for many more, but at its core it will always be a rare-breeds centre.'

There are now over 50 breeds of farm animal at the park – sheep, cattle, pigs, poultry and horses. These are positioned around an informative rare breeds trail, giving visitors a chance to meet them all. People can see how farmers have changed and adapted to meet demand. And aside from these animals Adam and Duncan continue to run the 1,600-acre Bemborough Farm, which also includes a commercial flock of sheep and mixed arable crops.

In addition to visiting the farm park, visitors are free to wander a two-mile waymarked Wildlife Walk around the farm and view a farming landscape that has been shaped over 6,000 years. There are butterflies and birds, and over a hundred species of wild flowers and grasses on the walk, including typical limestone-loving flowers and some unusual species as well as the very rare Cotswold pennycress.

There's on-site camping and glamping, too.

green and its war memorial, overlooked by a compendium of Cotswold architecture. Large stone barns, a mix of houses that anyone would be eager to live in and the Norman church of St Michael, which has one of the most pleasing exteriors of any church in the area, complete the picture.

Foresight is a wonderful thing. In the 1930s village resident Moya Davidson purchased 12 dilapidated properties to ensure they continued to be rented to local people. Over the decades, this morphed into the Guiting Manor Amenity Trust, which owns and manages about 50% of the village's residential properties with, as in the 1930s, a policy of choosing tenants from local families and people working in or near the village. It has allowed the village to retain its true Cotswold character, full of community spirit. That includes the **Guiting Music Festival** (⌀ guitingfestival.org), with its series of classical-music concerts, open-air folk and jazz, which runs every summer.

Temple Guiting lies two to three miles north. Unlike the clustered Guiting Power, Temple Guiting is stretched out, crossing the River Windrush. The Diamond Way links the two villages. Considered a hideaway, Temple Guiting was once owned by the Knights Templar (hence the prefix). Head to St Mary's Church and you'll find a Templar Cross on the stonemasonry. If you sit on a rise overlooking the river, the churchyard provides a particularly gentile and soothing view. Meanwhile, **Temple Guiting Manor** (⌀ templeguitingmanor. co.uk), which now provides luxurious holiday accommodation, is one of the most graceful Tudor manor houses you're likely to see.

"If you can stomach the constantly undulating landscape, cycling the quiet lanes is a good way to appreciate the beauty of the area."

In between the two villages is the hamlet of **Kineton**, which slopes down a steep hillside to rest at two fords and the even tinier **Barton**, merely a couple of large houses and a tiny river crossing.

If you can stomach the constantly undulating landscape, cycling the quiet lanes is a good way to appreciate the beauty of the area. One of my favourite lanes to cycle or wander along here, **Critchford Lane,** runs west of Kineton. Approaching from the west, the gated road begins by cutting through a very steep-sided valley. The landscape then opens out and sheep nibble the pastures down to the next, perpendicular-running valley. The Diamond and Warden's ways both run through this valley, just to one side of a tiny riverlet and the site of a medieval village. There is a ford that is perfect for paddling and a tiny car park for walkers. From here, look west for views of a superb manor house, behind which is the vast expanse of **Guiting Wood**. Both aforementioned footpaths lead you into the woodland, though for a truly lovely walk, follow the Warden's Way from the car park, through Guiting Power to Naunton, enjoying a picnic by the Windrush or a pub lunch before returning by the same route.

¶¶ FOOD & DRINK

The Cotswold Guy Guiting Power ✆ 01451 851955 ⬦ thecotswoldguy.co.uk. Small but excellent 'farm' shop in the centre of the village with meat, veg, bakery, dairy and cooking ingredients. Also sells cookery kits including a Cotswold Full English Breakfast kit.

Halfway House Kineton ✆ 07425 970507 ⬦ thehalfwayatkineton.com. A 17th-century pub tied to the Donnington Brewery. Traditional pub food using much local produce, including Donnington ale rarebit and Cacklebean egg scotch egg with pickled walnut purée. Accommodation, too.

Hollow Bottom Guiting Power ✆ 01451539890 ⬦ hollowbottom.com. A 17th-century pub with a horseracing theme owing to the number of top racehorse stables in the vicinity (renowned racehorse trainer and former jockey Nigel Twiston-Davies's race stables are a few hundred yards up the road). Very popular during Cheltenham Festival.

Old Post Office Guiting Power ✆ 01451 850701 ⬦ oldpostofficeguiting.co.uk. Very pretty house right in the centre of the village opposite the green, with a couple of tables inside and out serving exemplary coffee, homemade cakes and a few savouries (such as 'summer on a plate': creamy feta, roast peaches, confit onions, grilled courgettes, mixed leaves with apricot dressing). Also sells country interiors and gifts.

THE SEAT OF MERCIA – WINCHCOMBE & ITS VILLAGES

As we head further west towards **Winchcombe**, the ridges of the Cotswold hills become greater, higher, steeper and then suddenly plunge into the flat lands of Tewkesbury and the Severn Vale, where the M5 motorway thunders along. Then there's just the odd isolated hill or hummock, such as Alderton Hill and Oxenton Hill close by and Dumbleton Hill followed by Bredon Hill in the distance.

Mercian kings made it this far and declared the town of Winchcombe as a capital. Nearby **Sudeley Castle** has royal connections too, though of a different era, while the remains of **Beckbury Camp**, northeast of Winchcombe, and **Belas Knap**, due south, show signs of an age long before any kings stamped their mark on the area.

9 FARMCOTE, HAILES ABBEY & TODDINGTON

⌂ **North Farmcote B&B**

I find that if you drive towards this part of the Cotswolds from the east – from Stow and through Ford – you don't really appreciate the lie of the land and how it has been getting steeper, because the car's engine has ironed out all the ups and downs. But walk or cycle around these parts and you appreciate that you are now on the western Cotswold escarpment. By the time you've reached the hills just west of Ford you're standing roughly 930ft above sea level and with some captivating views of the Severn Vale and the Malverns.

"It looms large and anyone making an ascent on foot via the Salt Way will really feel the calf muscles working hard."

We're now sufficiently far west to pick up the Cotswold Way again; having come from Stanton and Stanway (page 110) north of this locale, the route runs along an old sheep-drove road known as Campden Lane and then to one side of **Beckbury Camp**, an Iron Age hillfort that teeters on the edge of the escarpment. It's a particularly picturesque stretch of the long-distance trail. There's evidence too, on the hillside, of the 'strip lynchets' or long parallel terraces that were created by centuries of ploughing with oxen.

A few yards south of the camp is the minutest of hamlets, **Farmcote**. It comprises little more than a farm, a tiny Saxon church, bed and breakfast (page 180) and a half-dozen other dwellings but these fortunate residents have, arguably, one of the best locations in the Cotswolds, with a sharply rising hill behind for shelter from the cold northeasterly winds and views out to the west beyond compare as the land drops away below. To add to the idyllic setting, the settlement is only accessible via a tiny lane that runs along the top of the escarpment from the south, or a footpath that links up with the Cotswold Way to the north.

Within this cluster of dwellings, in what would seem the unlikeliest of settings for passing trade, is **Farmcote Herbs and Chilli Peppers** (⌂ farmcoteherbs.co.uk), a little nursery specialising, as the name gives away, in growing and selling dozens of different kinds of herbs and numerous varieties of chilli peppers. The setting is under the shade of giant walnut trees on the edge of the escarpment; plant selection takes some considerable time as you gaze at the views. In addition, the owners Tim and Jane sell chilli chutneys, chilli chocolate and chilli sausages and burgers. Opening times are variable throughout the year, so check on the website.

To the west of Farmcote, the land falls away sharply into a short steep-sided valley, the open ends of the V folding out at right angles to itself to create further escarpments. Running parallel with the road to Farmcote, on the other side of the valley, is the **Salt Way**, an ancient route that crosses **Salter's Hill**, used for transporting salt from the Midlands to London. From its foot, Salter's Hill is frighteningly prominent. It looms large and anyone making an ascent on foot via the Salt Way will really feel the calf muscles working hard. But the views from the top are amply rewarding.

At the point where the aforementioned valley opens out, tucked at the foot of Salter's Hill, **Hayles Fruit Farm** has made the most of the mineral-rich soils (there are no fewer than six springs bursting out from the surrounding hillsides, all heading for the farm) and planted acres of fruit trees and soft-fruit bushes. Accessible along a quiet no-through road – which becomes the Cotswold Way up the hill towards Farmcote – it's a most bucolic fruit-picking location with a scenically placed campsite getting views of Salter's Hill and Hailes Wood.

"One wonders what was going through his mind as he looked upon the destruction of such a majestic building in such a glorious location."

Just below the fruit farm are the remains of **Hailes Abbey**. It's run by English Heritage and the National Trust now, but until its dissolution in 1539 housed a small group of Cistercian monks. The abbey became a place of worldwide pilgrimage after it was alleged that a phial of Christ's blood was held there, even referenced in Chaucer's *Canterbury Tales*. Benefiting from perhaps one of the greatest scams of the Middle Ages, the abbey grew rich off the proceeds from the religious tourists, and the phial turned out to be nothing but some coloured honey! A group of beech trees on the hill above, close to Beckbury Camp, is known as **Cromwell's Clump**, believed to be the place where Thomas Cromwell, Henry VIII's commissioner, watched the dismantling. One wonders what was going through his mind as he looked upon the destruction of such a majestic building in such a glorious location. Atmospheric ruins, draped with ivy and fighting against large horse chestnut trees, are all that remain today in this peaceful spot.

Approaching Hailes Abbey from the northwest, you'll cross over a railway line, which carries the **Gloucestershire Warwickshire Steam Railway** (✆ 01242 621405 ⌂ gwsr.com). The railway uses a part of the old Great Western Railway's main line from Birmingham to Cheltenham via Stratford-upon-Avon. Steam trains now run for 14 miles between the village of Broadway and Cheltenham Racecourse, no mean feat given that the track and the stations have been restored entirely by volunteers and enthusiasts. The station at **Toddington** is home to the Locomotive Departments and there are guided tours of the loco sheds, a loco yard viewing area and a demonstration signal box. The route from Broadway and Toddington to Cheltenham passes through some pleasant Cotswold countryside with views of the surrounding hills and further afield to Tewkesbury Abbey and the Malverns on a clear day. Trains run from March to December with numerous special events. There's also the opportunity to step on the footplate and learn how to drive a steam or diesel locomotive or try your hand at being a signalman. Afternoon tea in a first-class carriage and fish and chip specials are very popular.

🧳 SPECIAL STAYS

North Farmcote B&B North Farmcote GL54 5AU ✆ 01242 602304 ⌂ northfarmcote.co.uk. One of the finest and most remote locations in the Cotswolds, as one of only six handsome properties along a lengthy no-through road. Perched on a steep escarpment with wide-ranging views over the Cotswolds and as far as Bredon Hill, the Malverns and the Welsh hills. The mellow Cotswold stone farmhouse has been lived in by David Eayrs for 60 years; it is cosy and the gardens, with superb mature walnut trees, are inspirational. There's a magnificent terrace for sunny breakfasts and afternoon tea, or you can relax in front of the log fire. The Cotswold Way passes within a few yards of the front door.

🍴 FOOD & DRINK

Hayles Fruit Farm Hailes GL54 5PB ✆ 01242 602123 ⌂ haylesfruitfarm.co.uk. Pick-your-own fruit sales plus farm shop. Sales of their own totally natural apple juice and cider – lots of varieties from which to select. Small campsite with great views.

1 The Gloucestershire Way passes Winchcombe. **2** The beautiful manor and formal gardens of Sudeley Castle. **3** Look out for the gargoyles on St Peter's Church in Winchcombe. **4** The atmospheric ruins of Hailes Abbey. ▶

SHEILA TALBOT

STOCKER1970/S

CAROLINE MILLS

JO JONES/S

10 WINCHCOMBE

When I spoke to Carole Price, the visitor assistant in the tourist information centre at Winchcombe, she described the town as 'rustic'. She commented, 'Winchcombe is not pretty like Broadway but it has its own kind of prettiness as a self-contained, working town. You can buy everything and anything from the shops here.'

I agree with Carole. With over 60 shops crammed into the three main roads in the town centre, every one independent from those giant national retailers, Winchcombe is a pleasure to visit. Combine this with its architectural diversity and a good choice of places to eat – it abounds in special qualities.

Sat in the middle of a horseshoe of steep escarpments, the town has been a crossroads, a meeting place and a focal point for travellers, traders and religious pilgrims over hundreds of years. Its origins go back approximately 3,000 years, although it wasn't until the 8th and 9th centuries that the town became really important, when Offa, the Anglo-Saxon king of Mercia, made it his capital. His successor, Kenulf, had a son, Kenelm, who as a young boy was murdered at the request of his envious sister. Many miracles were then attributed to Kenelm as a result and the town became a place of pilgrimage; St Kenelm's Well on the escarpment to the east of Winchcombe is believed to be one of the miracle locations and the water is reputed to have healing properties. Coupled with the pilgrims who began descending on nearby Hailes Abbey in later years, Winchcombe became a busy and prosperous place.

Now walkers with alternative motives descend on the town, with seven long-distance paths converging on the High Street: the Cotswold, Warden's, Windrush, Salt, Wychavon, Gloucestershire and St Kenelm's ways. Winchcombe has promoted itself in recent years as a town for walkers and has been awarded 'Walkers are Welcome' status as having something special to offer those travelling on two feet.

"Coupled with the pilgrims who began descending on nearby Hailes Abbey in later years, Winchcombe became a busy and prosperous place."

Don't assume the beauty or the grandness of Chipping Campden or Broadway, but take time to explore its streets and alleyways (not forgetting the renowned collection of gargoyles hanging from St Peter's Church). The view from the Corner Cupboard Inn into town along Gloucester Street, and Vineyard Street, which descends to a little bridge across the

River Isbourne particularly deserves seeking out, as does Dents Terrace, a row of almshouses built by Emma Dent, the owner of Sudeley Castle in Victorian times and a relative of the present owners.

Vineyard Street also takes you to the entrance for Sudeley Castle and the start of the Windrush Way. From this you can take a quick detour to Spoonley Wood to see the stark remains of **Spoonley Villa** together with its small mosaic. It was one of three Roman villas situated around Winchcombe, indicating the importance the Romans placed on the area prior to King Offa.

Lovers of classic stoneware should also take the time to visit **Winchcombe Pottery** (✆ 01242 602462 ⊘ winchcombepottery. co.uk), half a mile north of the town on the Broadway Road. One of the longest-running craft potteries in the UK, the pottery is approaching its centenary and continues to use its wood-fired kiln to create a collection of rustic, sturdy, domestic ware that befits any kitchen.

Sudeley Castle & Gardens
Winchcombe GL54 5JD ✆ 01242 604244 ⊘ sudeleycastle.co.uk

When Henry VIII died in 1547 his widow, Catherine Parr, married Sir Thomas Seymour, the brother of Henry's earlier wife, Jane Seymour. They moved to Sudeley Castle, where Catherine gave birth to a daughter and died shortly after. She was buried in the chapel of St Mary within the castle grounds. Her husband was later executed for treason and, among other things, lascivious acts towards the young Queen Elizabeth.

Sudeley has had many other royal connections throughout its thousand-year history, including an attack by Parliamentary forces when Charles I used it as his headquarters during 1643. The battle scars are still evident on the castle walls today.

I love visiting Sudeley. The atmospheric ruins of the old banqueting hall with rampant plants escaping through the rooftop and the cannonball-shot window frames are inspirational. The knot garden with its design based upon a dress worn by Elizabeth I and the dilapidated ruins of the vast tithe barn, now filled with ornamental colour, the unusual octagonal tower and the formal Queens' Garden, with its old English roses, are all masterpieces. So, too, is the extensive view from the southernmost point of the gardens over the surrounding hills.

The interior of the castle is filled with interesting exhibitions about its history and relevant themes, from Roman finds to exquisite textiles,

Tudor queens to personal World War I recollections. And, with an extended route around the castle, don't miss the Tudor Document Room. There, amid the red and gold opulence, you'll find Catherine Parr's handwritten books and a love letter to Sir Thomas Seymour accepting his proposal of marriage.

Some rooms within the original 15th-century west wing of the family-owned and lived-in castle are also open to the public. Here you'll see the historic library with a copy of a book by Erasmus and a 16th-century Sheldon tapestry (page 142). So, too, a portrait of Rubens by Van Dyck and, in the neighbouring Morning Room, a J M W Turner painting of Stourhead in Wiltshire.

The wider grounds offer perfect strolls, with picnics in the large parkland meadow car park (though the Pavilion café offers a good spread), and there's an excellent fortress adventure playground for children. Both the Warden's Way and Windrush Way pass through the estate, so you can still catch a glimpse of the castle even if you're not visiting.

¶¶ FOOD & DRINK

There's no shortage of places to eat and drink in Winchcombe, with a good selection of pubs (Corner Cupboard Inn on Gloucester St is 15th century), plus cafés like The Tipsy Egg, and a deli, butcher and bakery all in town. Here's my pick.

Lion Inn North St ✆ 01242 603300 ⌖ butcombe.com/the-lion-inn-gloucestershire. A 15th-century inn with plenty of welcoming charm and character; beautiful interior decoration and an even prettier garden. Breakfast, lunch and dinner menus (crisp lamb-belly scrumpets; hot smoked chalk-stream trout with Niçoise salad and lemon dressing). Lovely accommodation, too.

The Old Bakery High St ✆ 01242 437632 ⌖ theoldbakerywinchcombe.com. Welcoming and cosy café and wine bar serving simple but tasty fare, all freshly prepared. From homemade cakes and frothy coffees to wine, beer and gin with charcuterie/cheese boards and pork pies from Vale & Hills butcher opposite. Run by Austin and Sally, two ex-teachers who fancied a career change – and they're doing a good job of it. Come to look at the 200-year-old-vine growing in the garden conservatory, too.

Williams of Winchcombe Delicatessen & Coffee Shop 12 North St ✆ 01242 604466 Notable deli selling tasty picnic goodies including homemade breads, pies and pastries, cheese, salads, bottles of wine etc, plus plenty of regional foods. Hot and cold light bites and drinks in the coffee shop.

THE COTSWOLDS' HIGHEST POINT – CHELTENHAM & ITS HIGH COMMONS

Leaving Winchcombe via the Cotswold Way heading south, the land becomes dramatically steeper quite quickly. For walkers it's a punishing climb, although the views make it worthwhile. Within a few short yards, the hill ascends to almost 1,000ft above sea level. Close to the top is **Belas Knap**, a very fine Neolithic long barrow, which, when excavated in the mid 19th century, was found to hold the remains of 31 people.

To the west of Winchcombe are first Langley Hill then **Nottingham Hill**, home to the Bugatti Owners' Club and the celebrated Prescott Hill Climb. And cutting a diagonal line across a map, splitting Winchcombe from **Cheltenham**, are Cleeve Hill and **Cleeve Common**, the highest point in the Cotswolds. These are serious hills now, the escarpment really making itself noticeable as it continues around the eastern and southern sides of Cheltenham to **Leckhampton Hill**.

11 NOTTINGHAM HILL

Nottingham Hill is less well known than its neighbour Cleeve Hill. Like a spur or growth, it juts out of the main line of the escarpment, its southern edge wrapping itself around **Woodmancote**, a village split from **Bishop's Cleeve** by the Gloucestershire Warwickshire Steam Railway. Both villages have attractive historical centres, but the latter has grown dramatically over the last century.

"Anyone who enjoys a picnic in the fresh air and a wander through the woods will like it here."

The southwest-facing side of Nottingham Hill holds the steepest slopes, while the north side periodically hums to the tune of burning rubber on the hillside racetrack. The Bugatti Owners' Club has the 60-acre Prescott Estate as its headquarters and built the **Prescott Hill Climb** (🖰 prescotthillclimb.co.uk). It's considered one of the world's greatest motor-racing venues where visitors can watch as vintage, classic and modern racing cars and bikes make their way up the 1,127yd course.

While the Hill Climb may be considered the prerogative solely of those who love the smell of engine oil, the countryside is scenic in the extreme and the events are invariably exciting. Anyone who enjoys a picnic in

RUSSELL BURTON/COTSWOLDS.COM

ANTHONY PAUL PHOTOGRAPHY/COTSWOLDS.COM

1

2

the fresh air and a wander through the woods will like it here. I've visited in spring for the British and Midland Hill Climb Championships, when bluebells cover the ground. It's possible to walk beside the racetrack; views from the top are wholesome. Alternatively, you can take your own car up the hill-climb track under the tutelage of an instructor.

More ancient still is the fort on top of the hill. It is the largest of all the Cotswold hillforts but not a lot is known about its origins, although there are some magnificent Bronze Age swords dug up while ploughing that are exhibited occasionally in The Wilson: Cheltenham Museum and Art Gallery (page 191). The whole of the hilltop is fortified and you can walk – or ride a horse – straight across the middle of it on the Sabrina Way, the long-distance bridle route. From the top you get 360-degree views that reach as far as the north Cotswolds in one direction and across Cheltenham to Leckhampton Hill and the continuing Cotswold escarpment in the south.

If you don't fancy walking the full distance to the top, a very steep road leads to a car park close to the top near Longwood Farm.

12 CLEEVE COMMON

Three masts close to the highest point on Cleeve Common make this hill an obvious beacon for miles. To the west are huge views over Cheltenham, with Prestbury Park, the home of the Cheltenham Gold Cup, looking to be just a few furlongs away from the foot of the hill. Take a set of binoculars and you may have the best seat in the house on Gold Cup day. The Severn Vale and the Black Mountains in Wales are clearly evident too – at least on a day when the wind is not blowing the rain sideways. To the east are views over Winchcombe and Sudeley Castle; you realise from here just how undulating that area of the Cotswolds is.

With little shelter, the vast expanse of limestone grassland blows cold in winter, but summers here are divine. In geology terms this has some of the thickest sections of oolitic limestone in the country – there's evidence of numerous quarry workings on the slopes – and that creates an amazing display of wildflowers and grasses throughout the spring and summer months, with harebells, field scabious and perennial cornflowers making a regular appearance.

◄ **1** The Neolithic long barrow, Belas Knap. **2** Cleeve Common sits atop a steep escarpment.

The Cotswold Way passes along the very western edge of the escarpment, precariously so in places. Yet, if you can stomach the sheer drops below that appear just west of the three masts, this is where some of the finest displays of wildflowers are. This area is known as the **Prestbury Hill Reserve**, owned by Butterfly Conservation. It has some of the best unimproved grassland on Cleeve Common, with steep, stony slopes rich with butterflies such as the chalkhill blue and Duke of Burgundy feeding off the flowers.

Plenty of other footpaths in addition to the Cotswold Way cross Cleeve Common to create lots of circular walks. And with the land undulating so much, the parts of the common change abruptly in character, from gorse bushes one moment, immaculate lawns of the Cleeve Hill Golf Club the next and then sheep-grazed pastures, making it a spectacular place to spend a few hours.

Numerous paths climb the common from the surrounding area but there are two car parks close to the top, one by the golf club off the Winchcombe to Cheltenham road (B4632) and one by the masts, accessed along a narrow country lane from the village of Whittington.

CHELTENHAM'S STAR ATTRACTION

StarBistro Ullenwood, National Star College ✆ 01242 339988 ⊘ nationalstar.org

Two miles south of Cheltenham, National Star College, as its website states, 'is a provider of specialist further education, training, personal development and residential services for people with physical and learning difficulties and acquired brain injuries'. It's a wonderful place, offering world-class facilities and allowing those with such difficulties to realise their potential and lead active, positive lives over which they take control. What's more, the college is a lively place, buzzing with energy, bursting with floral displays and gardens, and filled with the most welcoming of people, both staff and students.

On a recent visit to StarBistro, the college restaurant open to the public, my children and I were given the warmest of welcomes from a front-of-house team leader and her assistant, a smiley young lady in a wheelchair who showed us to our table. Offering us menus, she moved off to make coffee for us while we admired the feathery cosmos amid the floral borders outside through the picture windows. Had the weather been as vibrant as the welcome, we could have sat outside.

We watched as, in the open-plan kitchen, a group of young people with varying disabilities gained work experience within a professional hospitality environment as they prepared our

13 LECKHAMPTON HILL

⚐ StarGlamping

With the escarpment swinging round the eastern side of Cheltenham, Leckhampton Hill and its conjoined twin Hartley Hill, far from facing west, faces north to enclose the town. The Leckhampton Hill Local Nature Reserve close to its summit incorporates Charlton Kings Common and creates an upturned horseshoe shape pushing towards the town. The area is designated as a Site of Special Scientific Interest (SSSI) for its diverse flora and fauna. Roe deer, badgers and wood mice coexist with adders, lizards and slow worms as well as Roman snails, rare butterflies and glow worms. Wild thyme, vetch and everlasting peas colour these rich grasslands too.

The Cotswold Way runs along this escarpment, through a strangely shattered landscape, variously quarried and thrust up by natural forces within the earth – it's a good place for fossil browsing. Park at the southern tip of the reserve in the disued quarries and you can see the thick bands of limestone strata. Look out for the **Devil's Chimney** too, a limestone pinnacle that, legend says, is the chimney to the devil's underground home.

food. The work surfaces can be raised and lowered accordingly. This is a professionally run bistro with a menu that serves in-season dishes (some of the seasonal vegetables are grown in the college's horticultural department) with ingredients sourced from the Cotswolds. Think confit duck and fennel salad, or National Star grown tomatoes and basil with roasted peppers, mozzarella and croutons, dressed in a pumpkin seed and watercress pesto.

Says Simon, StarBistro and Catering Manager, 'Our students are fully involved in everything within the bistro. They work the tills, meet and greet, provide service and make dishes within the kitchen. The students are always the priority, their needs, wishes and aspirations. While 80% of our students are on a work outcomes programme, where they spend a year in college then look for work placements, the most important thing here is learning life skills.'

So, should you visit to support these students? Well, yes. As Simon explains, 'For the students, the life skills of meeting new people, maybe from a different country or who speak a different language is so important. For some, simply being able to talk to someone they've never met before could be the biggest achievement of their day.' The students are the priority – and, as a guest, you're receiving some of the tastiest food you can get in the Cotswolds. It's a win-win.

 **SPECIAL STAYS**

StarGlamping National Star College, Ullenwood GL53 9QU ✆ 01242 527631
⌀ nationalstar.org. Three camping pods and The Shire House, an oak-timber 'hobbit' house, sited in a peaceful field on the grounds of the National Star College (page 188), the entrance to which is located on the Cotswold Way. Sleeps two to four people. Delicious food, including breakfast, is possible in the StarBistro while you can play a round of golf at the neighbouring 18-hole StarGolf. Your accommodation fees go towards helping young people with physical and learning disabilities that study at the college.

14 CHELTENHAM

The self-proclaimed 'Cultural Centre for the Cotswolds', Cheltenham is certainly a hotbed of culture, but don't be confused by its geographical reference. To the west of the Cotswolds AONB, the town is a useful gateway for those travelling from the west and important for making travel connections.

To give it its official title, Cheltenham Spa, its heyday was in Regency times when bold, classical architecture and wide tree-lined avenues were the fashion. Like any large town, parts of Cheltenham have lost their sparkle, having been invaded by architectural anomalies and the odd run-down shopping centre. Similarly, as is the norm, prominent

CHELTENHAM FESTIVALS

Cheltenham was once *the* place to take the waters. Now it's the place to celebrate, wherever your interests lie. Folk, jazz, science, food, travel, wine – they all have a festival. But the two for which Cheltenham has truly made a name are literature and horseracing.

The **Cheltenham Literature Festival** (⌀ cheltenhamfestivals.com) is one of the most important events in the literary calendar worldwide. It's when big-name authors sign copies of their latest tome, make speeches, read poetry and draw illustrations (or the illustrators do). Held every October, over 500 events usually take place, with plenty to interest children and young adults.

Meanwhile, spring sees the area around Cheltenham explode with bookies and punters as millions of pounds are won or lost on the National Hunt Festival Cheltenham Racecourse, at Prestbury Park. The four days of utter madness culminate in the **Cheltenham Gold Cup** (⌀ thejockeyclub. co.uk/cheltenham-festival), one of the most prestigious horseraces in the world at one of the most scenic courses in the country, with its backdrop of Cleeve Common and Nottingham Hill. Do be prepared for a serious drought of accommodation during the festival week; rooms around this area get booked up months in advance.

thoroughfares such as the Regent Arcade, *the* place to shop in the 1980s, are filled with find-them-anywhere brands. The **Promenade** is also filled with recognised 'high street' shops but more upmarket. However, regardless of shopping credentials, don't miss a visit inside the Regent Arcade if only for one thing – to see the **Wishing Fish Clock**, especially if you have children with you. The magic timepiece, hanging 45ft tall, is the work of celebrated artist Kit Williams (creator of the sumptuously illustrated book *Masquerade*) and includes allusions to nursery rhymes, a duck that lays golden eggs and a fish that blows bubbles every half-hour.

To find the best of Cheltenham, however, you need to move away from the High Street to areas such as the **Montpellier Quarter** and the **Suffolks** (my preference), where small independent shops, boutiques, restaurants and a good, artisan Sunday market (⏀ thesuffolks.co.uk/markets) blend with magnificent architecture, quiet, gentile residential squares (Suffolk Square is not to be missed) and, in the Suffolks, peaceful terraces of pastel-coloured houses. The Montpellier Gardens with their towering lime trees provide a pleasant place to sit when the sun is shining, as does **Sandford Park**, full of ornamental water features and a large summer lido. A riot of colour, even if it is from bedding plants out of tune with the town's Regency heritage, the **Imperial Gardens** provide a home to a statue of Gustav Holst, the classical composer who was born in the town.

The **Holst Victorian House** (⏀ holstvictorianhouse.org.uk) is one of the most interesting places to visit in Cheltenham. As Gustav Holst's birthplace and childhood home, the house and period rooms provide a good glimpse into the Victorian age, when Holst grew up here. His working years were spent elsewhere but Holst composed considerably more than his most famous work, *The Planets*, and the museum provides plenty of opportunities to discover his other music.

Elsewhere in the town, particularly if you're looking for somewhere with free admission, **The Wilson: Cheltenham Museum and Art Gallery** (⏀ cheltenhammuseum.org.uk) is extraordinarily good. With its grand glass-fronted atrium, it provides changing exhibitions and displays on local history and archaeology, paintings plus an internationally significant collection from the Arts and Crafts Movement, especially pieces associated with the Cotswolds. Browsing the furniture, pottery, textiles and manuscripts, you'll come across recognisable names of

A WALK AROUND CHELTENHAM

The sky was summer blue as I arrived in Cheltenham. No cloud dared to drift by and the outdoor pool at Sandford Parks was a tempting proposition as I wandered through the sprawling 'countryside-meets-town' park.

Crossing Montpellier Gardens, another of Cheltenham's notable green spaces, the celestial greatness forced my gaze to look up and I inadvertently made a wrong turn – thank goodness. For I discovered a street, Lansdown Terrace, I'd not walked along before but realised, owing to its splendour, that I really should have done.

Cheltenham is lined with lacy balconies adorning the façades of its grand Regency terraces. But there would appear to be no terrace grander than Lansdown Terrace, a little spur off the Malvern Road. Here, in place of lace, columns to rival the finest Greek temples ascend to the Gods, holding up pediments to frame the grandest of Georgian windows. The sheer scale, the height, the length of the Grade II-listed terrace is quite remarkable.

But it was to the very heart of Cheltenham that I intended to wander before my inadvertent diversion to Lansdown Terrace and I ultimately passed an anthology of ever more opulent-sized properties along Promenade, tempted but never swayed by the parade of boutiques that line the pedestrianised boulevard, instead drawn towards Cheltenham's most famous son, **Edward Wilson**. His statue, in thermals, fur-lined wellies and galoshes are more coastal than Cotswold and therein lies the clue to his departure from his native town.

villages and associated craftsmen mentioned elsewhere in this guide and, suddenly, the Cotswolds and its notable connection to the Arts and Crafts Movement falls into place.

I'm torn between the Arts and Crafts Museum within The Wilson and another exhibition here, dedicated to the scientist and artist from which the building bears its name, Edward Wilson. As an accomplished artist, Wilson captured icy scenes and detailed drawings of Antarctic wildlife. In the museum's wonderful Paper Store archive are display drawers full of his artistic work. The museum holds too large a collection to show all at once, so there's likely to be something different on every visit. What really struck me on my last visit was a selection of paintings depicting the weather in the Antarctic; something so very topical more than a century on.

One other leading attraction in the town is the **Pittville Park**, a Regency 'village' estate, and **Pump Room**. The town's largest ornamental park, full of specimen trees, lakes and walkways to 'promenade', it is

Wilson, born only a couple of hundred yards away from his bronze lookalike, in Montpellier Terrace, was a physician, natural historian, painter and polar explorer. He accompanied Captain Scott on two British expeditions to Antarctica, the Discovery Expedition and the Terra Nova Expedition, the latter of which, in 1912, claimed the lives of Wilson and his fellow explorers. A detailed exhibition of his life and work, including artefacts recovered from the Antarctic, is displayed in The Wilson (page 191).

From The Wilson, I took the easy-to-miss footpath that runs along the side of the museum and leads into the peaceful haven of St Mary's Minster churchyard. The diminutive parish church is Cheltenham's oldest, dating from the 11th century. It is not grand in stature like the surrounding Georgian terraces but beautifully modest and unimposing. It's a sweet little thing.

The exit from the churchyard brought me on to the not so remarkable High Street but within a few yards I was back to The Promenade with a chance to enjoy the Imperial Gardens, where sunseekers sat around the statue of composer Gustav Holst (Cheltenham's other famous son), waving his conducting baton.

With a stroll up Montpellier Street, brimming with artisanal boutiques, bars and restaurants, I looked back to spy, in the distance, Cleeve Common (page 187), which boasts the highest point in the Cotswolds. If the Cotswold skies remained as happy as the present day, I knew where I would be going the following morning, walking boots laced up.

home to the town's most flamboyant Regency building, the Pittville Pump Room, full of pomp in its columns and domes. As a spa town and health resort, this was the focal point for social engagements, and a source of Cheltenham's spa water to rival that of others in Montpellier – though it's no longer possible to drink the spa water from the original fountain. The park is a 15-minute walk from the town centre, but you can take a circular route via Pittville Lawn, returning back along West Drive, passing both Wellington Square and Clarence Square, for more architectural elegance.

¶¶ FOOD & DRINK

You'll never go hungry in Cheltenham, though for an extensive selection of really good places to eat (or something to drink), I'd send you to the Suffolks and Montpellier Quarter. There's everything from coffee bars (**Clementine Café**) and afternoon tea to wine 'retreats' (**Montpellier Wine Bar**) and Michelin-starred restaurants (**Le Champignon Sauvage**); too many good places to mention here, unfortunately.

Baker & Graze 48 Suffolk Rd 𝒥 01242 702428 𝄃 bakerandgraze.com. Bakery and restaurant (breakfast, brunch and lunch plus little plates) in the Suffolk Quarter with an imaginative brunch menu (shaksuka baked eggs with dukkah, coriander and sourdough toast).

Huffkins 25 Promenade 𝒥 01242 513476. My pick of places to eat in the heart of Cheltenham, with one of the most prestigious addresses. The café-tea room is in a listed 18th-century Georgian building with a pavement terrace. Morning pastries, light lunches (such as the Cotswold Garden Salad) and a fine afternoon tea (page 218).

Royal Oak Prestbury GL52 3DL 𝒥 01242 522344 𝄃 butcombe.com/the-royal-oak-pub-gloucestershire. On the outskirts of town, close to the racecourse, this Cotswold stone 'village' pub has a snug bar and dining room. Well-kept ales and extensive menu serving pub classics using local produce (courgette, spinach, pea and green herb risotto with burrata or Severn & Wye smoked-haddock fishcakes).

EAST FROM CHELTENHAM

Heading east out of Cheltenham, cutting through the sharpest escarpments, you can deviate from the A436 and follow the little villages either side of the main road towards Bourton-on-the-Water. This itself is known beyond compare but some of the little villages *en route* are gems that barely make it onto a road map let alone the tourist brochures. There's no reasoning behind it. Villages like **Whittington** and **Salperton** are quite enchanting and the scenery in which they sit is quiet, out of the spotlight of tourism.

15 WHITTINGTON, DOWDESWELL, SEVENHAMPTON & BROCKHAMPTON

Leaving Cheltenham through the suburb of Charlton Kings, the A40 lies parallel with the River Chelt, which runs in the opposite direction towards the Severn. The river flows through the Dowdeswell Reservoir, a flood-defence mechanism to prevent Cheltenham from becoming awash. The reservoir and the massive dark green swathe of evergreen woodland on the steep slopes behind make up the **Dowdeswell Wood** and **Reservoir Nature Reserve**.

---

1 Shipton Solers' 13th-century church was once used as a cowshed. **2** Every August there is a football match in the River Windrush at Bourton. **3** Cheltenham holds an annual jazz festival. **4** The Holst Victorian House is an interesting spot in Cheltenham. **5** Enjoy the mix of fine architecture and independent shops in Cheltenham's Montpellier Quarter. ▶

ANGELA HAMPTON PICTURE LIBRARY/A

THE PICTURE TAKER/ COTSWOLDS

CHELTENHAM FESTIVALS/COTSWOLDS.COM

HOLST MUSEUM/COTSWOLDS.COM

MIKAL LUDLOW PHOTOGRAPHY/COTSWOLDS.COM

The reservoir sees many migrant birds overwinter on its waters and lays permanent home to other waterfowl including little grebes and great crested grebes. Perhaps of most significance to the reservoir is its population of common toads, for which the site is a major spawning ground. With many toads migrating to the reservoir and its surrounding watery grasslands from the south, special toad tunnels have been created underneath the A40. But many prefer to take the overland route; it's quite a sight to see dozens of toads crossing the road at any one time. Some clearly won't make it, but 'warning of toads' signs are put up each year for the migration season. The grasslands around support orchids and cowslips and the pine woods behind allow roe and muntjac deer to roam freely. The areas of mixed deciduous woodlands give bluebells the chance to bloom in spring. Waymarked paths thread Dowdeswell

"The grasslands around support orchids and cowslips and the pine woods behind allow roe and muntjac deer to roam freely."

WHITTINGTON COURT: CREATIVE VIBES

There are some places that merely to look at, you gain a sense of personality. So it is with Whittington Court, an Elizabethan manor house whose stone exterior has seen few alterations in 300 years. Step inside, and the vibe is filled with inspiration and creativity. Panelled rooms, ornamental mantels, large Tudor fireplaces; family photographs, trinkets from holidays or feathers and pine cones picked up on a walk. Plus books; many of them.

Climb the chunky oak staircase, as old as Queen Elizabeth I who visited Whittington Court in 1572 and, on the first floor, you'll find owner Jenny Stringer's work studio.

It's not an average workroom. As a block-print textile artist, Jenny needs space and light. With leaded light windows framed in a giant bay window, in which her printing table sits, it's ideal. A floor-to-ceiling bookshelf accommodates not only aging books but also a teapot with an egg in the top, a jam jar with dried flowers, miniature houses made of card, photographs curled at the edges, a roll of wrapping paper and a large button, presumably significant. There is personality here. So too within the vast collection of homemade printing blocks, organised slightly chaotically in hand-labelled boxes.

Jenny has been specialising in designing and creating block-printed textiles since she arrived at Whittington Court more than 30 years ago; her customers have included the prestigious Stroud-based interior design company Lewis and Wood. On my visit, she is in the process of her latest commission, a series of textiles to commemorate the centenary of Cheltenham's Quaker community.

Wood, but these are only accessible from the Cotswold Way, which skirts the western edge of the trees.

As the Cotswold Way crosses over the A40, it travels through another area of woodland owned by the Woodland Trust. **Lineover Wood** is totally different in character from Dowdeswell Wood. Sandwiched between the main A40 and A436 roads, the wood spreads up another steep escarpment and features some nationally scarce large-leaved limes. One of the limes dates back over a thousand years, making the reputedly second-oldest beech tree, also in the wood, a mere baby at 400 years old.

With wide tracks between the trees, the wood feels more open than Dowdeswell. In addition to the Cotswold Way it has two waymarked circular walks of different lengths. If you fancy getting your hands dirty, the Woodland Trust is always looking for volunteers to help maintain this wood.

There is space for a couple of cars at the northern entrance to Lineover Wood, but my recommendation is to first visit Dunkertons Cider (see

Says Jenny, 'I cut the blocks from lino or rubber and the colour, a pigment in a binding agent, is applied with a sponge or roller. The block is then reversed down onto the fabric and pressed with the hand. Ironing makes the design completely fast.

'I like upcycling; at the moment I'm printing onto upcycled French cotton sheeting. As I print the lengths of fabric, they're wound onto an old rod from a tractor!'

I ask Jenny about her fabric designs, many of which are laid about in scrapbooks and giant paper folders labelled 'Abstract', 'Foliage etc'. She says, 'What I do is very niche. I can't do large scale, though I'd quite like that to change. I'm 80 [years old] now, and I'd like something left to be remembered by.'

Despite her modesty, Jenny has already generated quite a legacy through the classes that she provides, handing down her knowledge to others. 'Block-printed textiles is an endangered art. We're on the red list,' she explains. That's why she's keen to pass on the techniques. 'Send me an email with the date you'd like for private tuition, and I'll do my best to accommodate.'

Separate to pre-booked tuition, the Elizabethan **Whittington Court** is open for a couple of weeks a year in April and August. (✆ 01242 820556 ⌖ whittingtoncourt. co.uk); do make a visit if you get the chance. Within the grounds is Nomad Letterpress/ Whittington Press, a charming, old-fashioned letterpress printing and publishing company (page 12). This has an annual open day, on the first weekend in September, when visitors can look around the printworks and learn about this historic way of printing books.

below), 100yds west, for a meal and a tour of the organic cidery (or even a cider-making masterclass) then request to leave your car in the car park for an extra half-hour. Alternatively, park in the layby at the southern entrance, beside the A436. Not least, the views along the Cotswold Way as you leave Lineover Wood out into the open of Ravensgate Hill are mesmerising, looking out over Cheltenham to Cleeve Common and, northwest, the Malvern Hills.

The tiny stone villages of **Lower** and **Upper Dowdeswell** just east of Lineover Wood are worth a quick look if you're passing by; the parish of Upper Dowdeswell is one of the highest villages in the Cotswolds, while in the Chelt Valley the estate village of **Whittington** is a must-see location. There are only a few houses strung out along a country road just off the A40 but, with the hills looming large behind, its location is pretty. More so, check out the Ordnance Survey map (OL45 The Cotswolds) for the area, and you'll notice a multitude of footpaths and bridleways on which to create a selection of circular walks, ranging from a mile long to a day's walking.

"There are only a few houses strung out along a country road just off the A40 but, with the hills looming large behind, its location is pretty."

You can take a footpath up and over the hill northeast from Whittington to the villages of **Sevenhampton** and **Brockhampton**. These two really do nestle, tucked into a very tight and tiny river valley, the cottages clinging to the hills either side and, between them they have over 40 listed buildings.

¶¶ FOOD & DRINK

Dunkertons Cider Dowdeswell Park, GL52 6UT ℘ 01242 650147 ⊘ dunkertonscider.co.uk. A destination venue with a tap-room bar that also includes a selection of street-food vendors (The Woozy Pig; Bella Mia Pizza; Bombay Street Food Co.; Humble Kusina), and a farm shop and deli that includes a cheese and charcuterie counter plus Daylesford outlet, Waghorne's artisan butchers, La Boulangerie Artisan and The Padstow Fish Co.

16 SHIPTON, SALPERTON & NEARBY VILLAGES

Where the A40 from Cheltenham meets the A436 to Bourton-on-the-Water, two tiny villages appear, once again on a valley floor with wavy lines of hills either side. This time the valley is the River Coln (page 225), at this point no more than a trickle emanating from numerous springs around the two **Shipton** villages. Based upon two separate manor houses, Shipton Solers (also known as Solars and Sollars) lies to the west of the larger Shipton Oliffe. The Gloucestershire Way runs through both.

Shipton Solers has an atmospheric 13th-century church, with little more than fields for company. Unbelievably, the tiny St Mary's was used as a cowshed in the 19th century. One wonders if the beasts learned

"The deeply rural landscape is free from hordes of visitors and the tree-studded parkland a joy to wander through."

anything from the fragments of medieval text that are painted on the walls. Now a Grade-I listed building, the church is cared for by the Churches Conservation Trust.

Continue along towards Bourton-on-the-Water and you cross over the ancient Salt Way, which heading north takes you over Salter's Hill near Winchcombe and south towards Bibury and Lechlade. I enjoy approaching **Salperton** off the Salt Way through the Salperton Park Estate.

The park is surrounded by a very long and high Cotswold stone wall; having taken a course on dry-stone walling I could much appreciate the effort that must have gone into its making. As you venture through the gates to the park and cross the open parkland, the grand Georgian façade of Salperton Park is directly ahead of you with the tiny All Saints' Church to its side. The village, some distance away, is barely visible until you turn a corner and drop into a tiny valley. The village name is clearly derived from its association with the Salt Way but Salperton is also on an old wool-trade route from Chipping Campden to the southern Cotswolds, and much of the agriculture around here was once sheep farming. The deeply rural landscape is free from hordes of visitors and the tree-studded parkland a joy to wander through. With desolate roads and farm tracks, it's perfect for a circular walk or longer trek across the fields.

The villages around here in these more open wolds – Salperton, the estate village of **Notgrove**, **Hampnett**, **Turkdean** and **Cold Aston** – are all inconspicuously stunning. Each one of these unassuming farming communities deserves a visit and between them they make a very worthwhile walk, with footpaths and bridleways connecting them or cycle rides (page 234) utilising the unhurried country lanes. Take a picnic though – eateries to stop off at are scarce.

¶¶ FOOD & DRINK

Plough Inn Cold Aston ✆ 01451 822602 ⌀ coldastonplough.com. Tiny 17th-century pub with plenty of character and period features – beams, original flagstones and inglenook fireplace. Beef is big on the menu, from Dexter cattle reared on the landlords' own family farm, less than a mile from the pub. Accommodation available.

17 BOURTON-ON-THE-WATER

Yes, it's very picturesque; yes, the shallow River Windrush flowing through straddled by miniature bridges adds greatly to the character of this most visited of Cotswold honeypots; yes, the architecture, from humble rose-clad cottages to elegant Georgian 'town' houses-cum-hotels is certainly special. But Bourton is not so idyllic when the coach parks fill up and the streets throng with tourists – and the grassy banks that border the river become a pleasure beach so cramped that the resident mallards' only respite is to stand on one leg on a protruding pebble in the river. Unfortunately, Bourton is a victim of its own quaintness. The shops are firmly aimed at the souvenir-seeking day-tripper while the plethora of olde worlde tea shoppes clatter to the merry ring of cash tills. At least, that's the picture on a summer's day. To appreciate Bourton at its best, visit midweek during the winter – especially if you can get there when it snows – or early spring before the masses have awoken once more to the village's charms. You may need to wrap up warm, but at least you'll find a seat on which to sit to admire the trees that dangle their shadows into the river without the selfie-takers blocking your view.

"To appreciate Bourton at its best, visit midweek during the winter – especially if you can get there when it snows."

Of all the many attractions in the village, the one I recommend the most is the **Cotswold Perfumery** (⌀ cotswold-perfumery.co.uk). Makers of fine fragrances on behalf of niche brands for over 50 years, you can book a beginners' one-day or an advanced four-/five-day perfumery course where you learn about the science of smell and scent, and the concepts of perfume creation before having a go at making your own perfume to take away. Courses are led by John Stephen, the 'nose' behind the perfumery and one of only six independent perfumers in the UK.

Alternatively, take one of the many footpaths leading from the centre of the village and get out of Bourton altogether – from the High Street,

A GAME OF TWO HALVES – FOOTBALL IN THE RIVER

The Cotswolds are known for odd antics and Bourton adds to the reputation with an annual football match. Nothing strange about that, except that members of Bourton Rovers Football Club divide every August bank holiday Monday to play against one another in a far-from friendly clash in the River Windrush.

Events begin when the real-life ducks take a swift exit to make way for the plastic variety swimming their way to the winning line in the annual duck race. Then makeshift goals are erected between two bridges and everything turns slightly serious.

How serious the pre-match training is taken is anyone's guess – team tactics are discussed around the bar. The crowd size is far greater than at an average Bourton Rovers weekend game; most spectators are wet before a ball is even kicked, with the prelim warm-up moving on from passing round cans of beer to jogging on the spot, sidesteps and press-ups, each stamp of the foot placed with gusto to create the biggest splash.

When I went along to watch, the referee arrived with the ball and declared the rules, with the Greens at one end and Reds at the other. 'No getting wet and no splashing.' It was a bit late for that. With the first blow of the whistle, 30 minutes of combat ensued with a comical gravity and some dubious tackles. A drench-inducing throw-in from the 'sidelines' was clearly designed to create maximum distress for the spectators – much to their delight given the evident screams and squeals. Those who escaped the pre-match soaking were certainly wet through now.

And then the referee produced a yellow card from his sock, sternly presenting it to a player for a harsh tackle. It mattered not. As the Greens hit the back of the net, goal celebrations involved diving into the watery depths and the crowd received a soaking once more.

The final score? Who really knows or cares? Everyone had a great time and as for anyone who went home dry, well, they didn't see the half of it.

the Oxfordshire and the Diamond ways reach the **Greystones Farm Nature Reserve** on the edge of the village. Summer evenings reveal potential sightings of barn owls gliding over the flower-rich water meadows and farmland, while spring heralds the arrival of traditional Cotswold wildflowers such as lady's smock and cowslips. Or several footpaths will take you among a series of both large and small lakes. Once gravel pits, these are now embedded in their surroundings, filled with fish and make a very pleasant focus for a short walk, with the wolds rising behind. Two self-guided walks are available to download from gloucestershirewildlifetrust.co.uk/greystones-farm-explore.

¶¶ FOOD & DRINK

Virtually every other property in Bourton-on-the-Water provides food and drink in some shape or form, but in general it's the standard fare of paninis, jacket potatoes, pub grub, ice cream and an average cream tea. However, there are exceptions.

Coffee Hub High St. Modern coffee shop serving delicious fresh roasted coffees, frappés and tea. Friendly, knowledgeable baristas and newspapers to browse. Tiny space though, so anticipate having to opt for a take-away and sitting beside the river.

Dial House Hotel and Restaurant High Street ℘ 01451 822244 ⌀ dialhousehotel.com. First-class fine dining with a creative menu of classical French/English cuisine in a 17th-century manor house. Or experience Maxi's Tipi Lounge in the walled garden for street-food inspired dishes (Korean fried chicken, sriracha and tahini mayo; crispy Moroccan spiced lamb & tabbouleh) and cocktails. Accommodation too.

Hawkstone College Farm, Stow Rd GL54 2HN ℘ 01451 824488 ⌀ hawkstone.co. Fifteen+-year-old 'micro' brewery specialising in creating additive- and preservative-free British lager solely using ingredients from the UK, alongside ales and cider using apples from three counties (Gloucestershire, Worcestershire, Herefordshire). Now under the influence of Jeremy Clarkson. The 3.8 Pils and the Hawkstone Premium Lager are among the best I've tasted, rivalling the top European varieties (and I thought that long before Clarkson took on the brewery!). A Cotswold vodka is the latest project. Guided tours and sampling available.

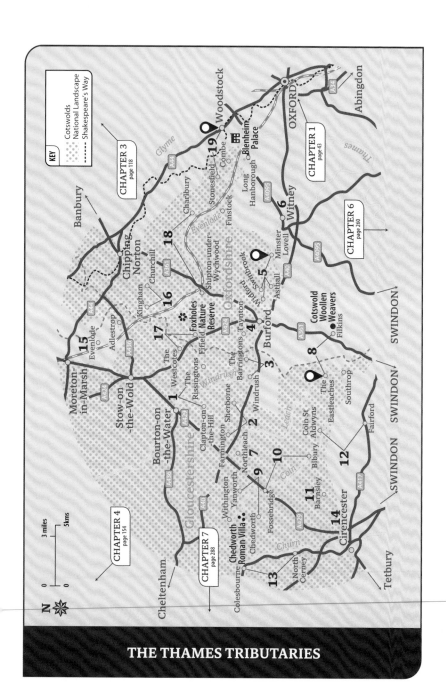

THE THAMES TRIBUTARIES

5
THE THAMES TRIBUTARIES

It might seem bizarre to be referring to both the Cotswolds and the River Thames within the same sentence, as the Thames Valley, London and Thames Estuary seem a different world. But the source of the Thames bubbles out of the Cotswold hills and a large swathe of the Cotswolds lies north of the Thames, within which are five small river valleys – the Churn, Coln, Leach, Windrush and Evenlode – each a tributary of Britain's most famous river.

Not one of the rivers here is particularly well known, but the villages and towns that they flow through are more acclaimed, such as **Cirencester** on the Churn, or **Burford** on the Windrush or the village of **Bibury** on the Coln. Yet each river valley very much has its own individual character.

Two counties fall into this chapter – Gloucestershire and a large chunk of Oxfordshire. Often referred to as the **Oxfordshire Cotswolds**, this is an area of the Cotswolds that is occasionally forgotten about – by visitors, at least.

GETTING THERE & AROUND

In terms of **train** services, the **Cotswold Line** (⬦ gwr.com) runs direct from London Paddington via Oxford to Worcester. There are small stations at Hanborough, Combe, Finstock, Charlbury, Ascott-under-Wychwood, Shipton and Kingham, *en route* to Moreton-in-Marsh. Be aware that most of these stations are away from the villages, so there may be a walk of some distance involved, in particular at Combe, Finstock and Kingham.

The Gloucestershire part of the locale is less well served by train. **First Great Western** travels from London Paddington to Gloucester, with the most convenient stations for this locale at Swindon (though still some distance away) and Kemble, only four miles from Cirencester. Travelling from the north or southwest requires a change at Gloucester.

There are multiple **bus** routes within this area – too many to mention in detail here – but Pulhams Coaches covers the area well, although some of the routes are not especially frequent, sometimes just one or two a day. The Pulhams website (♂ pulhamscoaches.com) provides all the details of bus routes, numbers and timetables. It is potentially worth visitors to this locale purchasing a Pulhams' **Explorer Ticket** for unlimited hop-on, hop-off travel. The day ticket represents a good-value way of seeing both this area and towns and villages further afield, such as Tetbury, Stow-on-the-Wold and Moreton-in-Marsh.

Gentle hills make for gentle **walking**. The views may not be quite so dramatic as those obtained from the 'extreme' heights of the Cotswold escarpment, but there are views nonetheless from the tops of hills such as **Habber Gallows Hill** near the Rissingtons. Woodland walks abound here too, in particular the great **Wychwood Forest**, one of the last-remaining centuries-old royal hunting forests, or **Foxholes**, an important nature reserve. But the main focus for walking in this chapter is a stroll alongside small, bubbly rivers.

As much of this area contains gentle, rolling hills, **cycling** is pleasurable without the strains of excessively steep slopes. Main roads such as the A40, A429 and A361 are fast and busy all day and generally to be avoided. The Sustrans **National Cycle Network Route 48** travels from Northleach to Cirencester; however, none of it is traffic-free. **Route 57** runs from Witney to Northleach, much of it using the quiet lanes along the Windrush Valley to create a 17-mile wiggly cycle ride through Burford and some pretty villages such as Minster Lovell and Great Barrington. **Route 45** runs south from Cirencester to Cricklade.

Many other interesting circular routes, including some direct from Kingham station, can be downloaded from ♂ cotswoldsaonb.org.uk.

Cotswold Electric Bike Tours (♂ cotswoldelectricbiketours.co.uk), based in Kingham, offers cycling holidays, mini breaks and short guided cycle tours of the Cotswolds on e-bikes.

ℹ TOURIST INFORMATION

Burford High St ☏ 01993 823558
Cirencester Corinium Museum, Park St ☏ 01285 654180

BIKE HIRE & REPAIR

Cotswold Woollen Weavers (page 224) Bike hire by the hour (minimum 3hrs). Location is useful for exploring the areas around the Rivers Leach, Coln and Windrush.

Ride 247 Apollo Court, Love Ln, Cirencester GL7 1ZR ☏ 01285 642247 ⌖ ride247.cc. On-site bicycle-repair workshop. Bike (and coffee) sales, too.

Windrush Bike Project Corn St ☏ 07554 363635 ⌖ windrushbikeproject.uk. Servicing and sales of secondhand road and mountain bikes plus accessories.

THE WINDRUSH VALLEY

The previous chapter on the High Cotswolds has several mentions of the River Windrush, the source of which is actually some way north of this locale, in the tiny village of Taddington. From there it flows southeast through the villages of Cutsdean, Temple Guiting, Kineton, Barton and Naunton as a racy little stream before being tamed by the formal stone-clad banks of Bourton-on-the-Water.

However, once past Bourton, the landscape seems to change as the river broadens. The Oxfordshire countryside through which the Windrush flows has different characteristics from those northern parts – shallower slopes and a more open look to the water meadows and pastures.

After leaving Bourton, the Windrush doesn't flow through any settlement until it reaches the town of **Witney** some 16 miles or so downstream. Villages such as **Little** and **Great Rissington** wisely sit upon the hillsides of the valley some distance away from potential flooding. Others allow the river to skirt their boundary, such as Little **Barrington**, **Minster Lovell** and even the town of **Burford**, where the river crosses the bottom of the High Street.

From Witney the Windrush flows past Ducklington and Standlake before entering the River Thames at Newbridge, some way out of the Cotswolds National Landscape and 40 miles from its source.

1 THE RISSINGTONS & CLAPTON-ON-THE-HILL

A mile south of Bourton-on-the-Water, the Windrush is joined by the Dikler. The Dikler flows east of the Windrush first through the Slaughters and the Swells, before drifting through open meadows between Bourton and **Wyck Rissington**, a tiny scattered village that has escaped the ravages of modernisation and thoroughly deserves a detour. Approach it if you can from the east, down the hill from Wyck Beacon.

From the confluence of the two rivers, the Windrush wriggles for miles in a series of tight loops and squiggles. The valley floor is broad here, with your best sight of the river from New Bridge, on the road that links **Clapton-on-the-Hill** in the west with Great Rissington opposite. As you climb the hill towards the village from the Bourton to Great Rissington road, look back for some vintage sunsets melting over the village of Clapton.

Little Rissington and **Great Rissington** are sat partway up the valley hillside. A bridleway links the two, with views over the river valley. **Upper Rissington** originated as a featureless collection of married quarters for officers attached to RAF Little Rissington and once housed the famous Red Arrows flying display team. The connection with the Red Arrows is not forgotten in the tiny church of St Peter's, which stands alone in open fields. A window in the church with an unusual stained-glass Red Arrow aircraft remembers the lives of servicemen who served at the base.

¶¶ FOOD & DRINK

Lamb Inn Great Rissington ✆ 01451 820388 ⟨⟩ thelambinn.com. Rambling Cotswold stone country pub with large open-plan restaurant. Accommodation too. Great views from the pub garden over the valley. Try the lamb rump with artichoke, carrot and pearl barley or the goat's cheese tartlet with local asparagus, pea, broad bean, mint and new potatoes.

2 FARMINGTON & SHERBORNE

The villages of Farmington and Sherborne might not seem to have much to do with the Windrush Valley, set as they are at right angles to the river. Farmington, furthest west, sits on top of a hill with valleys and escarpments all around, unsure which way to turn.

Farmington frames a triangular village green and an octagonal-shaped pump house with stone columns to support its gabled roof. Built in 1874, the roof was 'presented' to the village in 1935 by the residents of Farmington in Connecticut, USA. A huge sycamore tree provides the shade for summer picnics. Close by, the village church has a clock that's very hard to tell the time by – it has no hands.

The village has been known for many years for the quality of the stone in the area, with Farmington stone a much sought-after product for making features such as fireplaces.

As the Sherborne Brook drops down the valley, it widens quite rapidly. As with so many villages around here, **Sherborne** is no exception to the

Cotswold prettiness, though this time it is in linear fashion, stretching for a mile alongside Sherborne Brook. Roughly in line with the middle of the village is a weir on the brook that was used as a sheepwash in bygone days, a sign once again of the significance of the wool industry in these parts.

"There will likely be chance encounters with plenty of wildlife, from wetland and farmland birds to a possible siting of an otter."

The focal point of the village is the very grand **Sherborne House** and the steeple of the village church next door. Sherborne House, once stayed in by Queen Elizabeth I, has been turned into a series of private apartments but the surrounding 4,000-acre **Sherborne Park Estate**, which is owned by the National Trust and has been used to film BBC *Springwatch*, is accessible to the public. Cars may park by Ewepen Barn, just off the A40, from where the National Trust has drawn out a series of walks. My favourite waymarked route here (follow the purple arrows) is through the Pleasure Grounds, a traditional parkland setting with fine views of the house and church, before darting off into Ragged Copse. The path exits this wood in the village centre, where you look out on to Sherborne Brook for a time, passing old stone cottages with long gardens brimming with vegetables, before returning to the parkland at the rear of Sherborne House and walking across fields to return to Ewepen Barn. At just over a couple of miles in length, it's a lovely walk to take with children and there will likely be chance encounters with plenty of wildlife, from wetland and farmland birds to a possible siting of an otter. The fabulously well-stocked village shop includes a delightful café serving coffees and homemade cake; this is a lovely place to stop.

3 WINDRUSH, TAYNTON & THE BARRINGTONS

Shortly after Sherborne Brook enters the Windrush, the river turns at right angles to flow east. On a hillside above, the village of **Windrush** clusters around a tiny green. The village was known for centuries for providing some of the best Cotswold stone, renowned for its longevity and used variously for St George's Chapel in Windsor in 1478 and for the Houses of Parliament in 1839. By 1911, however, the quarries were defunct, and are now marked by grassy knolls.

The **Barringtons** have a similar history, created as estate villages built upon the wealth of quarrying and stonemasonry in the area. Their location by the river aided their fortunes – barges full of the prized stone

A LITTLE CYCLE RIDE AROUND THE LANES

A more heavenly quartet of villages you'll be hard-pressed to find. Ignore the crowds of visitors around the Slaughters (page 170) and come to these Cotswold beauties for utter gorgeousness and a complete Cotswold scene. Collectively, Windrush, The Barringtons and **Taynton** will have you breathless in awe. The quality of the stonework, the variation in the style of houses from large Georgian frontages to tiny cottages, the architectural features (stone porches, archways, gabled windows), the wild and rumpled village green in Little Barrington with houses set back from the road, the hedgerows and little lanes and the countryside that surrounds them, including the River Windrush, of course: all these things combined make this tiny locale a joy to spend time mooching around. I've lived in this area all my life, and these villages still leave me dumbstruck.

Other than sat beside the Windrush at The Fox supping a pint, there's no access to the river in these parts. So, to appreciate the quartet at a leisurely pace, you can enjoy a cycle ride that joins the villages together.

Beginning on Burford's High Street (see opposite), travel north, crossing the Windrush and, at the roundabout, turn left onto the A424 signposted for Stow-on-the-Wold. Within 100yds, the A424 makes a sharp right-hand turn; continue straight on instead, signposted for Taynton. Note that these first few yards through Burford and the A424 are busy and extreme care needs to be taken. However, once off the A424 travelling towards Taynton, the roads become quiet country lanes.

Continue through Taynton to Great Barrington and descend towards the river, crossing at The Fox. Turn immediately right after the bridge to follow the road to Windrush. Once you've perused the village here, turn back along the road towards The Fox (or, for a longer ride, you could continue to Sherborne; page 208), then, at the T-junction (beside the bridge), turn right for Little Barrington. Once in the village, turn left along Middle Road, to take the lane on the south side of the Windrush back to Burford.

You can either stop at The Fox for a riverside pub lunch or, if you're taking a picnic, my recommendation is the village green in Little Barrington. Utter heaven!

were floated down the Windrush to the Thames and on to London. Barrington stone was used in prominent London landmarks such as St Paul's Cathedral and the Royal Hospital in Greenwich.

Little Barrington has a slightly warmer character than its more commanding northerly relation, the houses clustered together on the southern slopes of the river valley while **Great Barrington** stretches out north of the river and the extensive Barrington Park, hidden behind high stone walls.

¶¶ FOOD & DRINK

Fox Inn Great Barrington ✆ 01451 844385 ◈ thefoxatbarrington.com. A fine location on the banks of the River Windrush, with views across the river from the dining room and garden. Choose from braised beef short rib or belly of pork on the 'locally sourced' menu, or opt for classic pub dishes. Owned by Donnington Brewery. Tasteful and modern accommodation.

4 BURFORD

🏠 Greyhounds

Doorways, windows, roofs, chimneys – every aspect of every building is unique in Burford. I love wandering up and down the High Street gazing at all the little nuances that make up the architecture and always manage to find something that I've not seen before. It may be the arch over an alleyway, a tiny gabled window in a rooftop or something as simple as an ornamental doorknocker.

There's rarely a moment when the **High Street** is not lined with cars and thronged with visitors attracted to the mix of shops, from cookware to wood-burning stoves, garden ornaments to sporting antiques, as well as old-fashioned sweet shops and gourmet delicatessens (and a mention to The Madhatter Bookshop, with books attractively displayed, including a 'Man Cave'). As one of the oldest market towns in the Cotswolds, Burford's focus is this High Street, which climbs from an ancient stone bridge over the river, on which Queen Elizabeth I stood when she first saw the town. The view over the water meadows is alluring enough, though the bridge isn't especially pedestrian-friendly, being a traffic bottleneck. To appreciate the river a little better, head to **St John the Baptist Church**, with its churchyard by the water. It has historical importance as the place where three ringleaders from the political movement known as the Levellers were executed by Oliver Cromwell. Others faced their end in Oxford.

"I love wandering up and down the High Street gazing at all the little nuances that make up the architecture."

Like other Cotswold towns, Burford became known for its wool trade during the Middle Ages. While the northern slopes of the Windrush Valley across the river were perfect for sheep grazing, on Upton Down, southwest of the town, horses were the animal of choice, albeit a little later in history, when the Burford Races were second only to those at

Newmarket. Charles II came here with Nell Gwyn to watch the racing – the pair are thought to have had their trysts in the old Burford Priory, next to the river, and their son was named the Earl of Burford. The finest views are from the top of the High Street, south of the town, where you can look over the rooftops towards the northern slopes. Though do save time for a wander along Sheep Street, too, for an ogle and a further delectable display of fine Cotswold architecture. If you'd like some guidance, head to the Burford Tolsey Museum under the old market building, where you can scan a QR code for a one-mile self-guided circular walk.

SPECIAL STAYS

Greyhounds 19–23 Sheep St ✆ 01993 822780 ⌂ greyhoundsburford.com. On, arguably, the prettiest street in Burford. This 15th-century wool-merchant's house became the publishing house, until 2003, for The *Countryman*, a magazine about rural life. Three bedrooms in a house that's full of Cotswold character from the moment you arrive in the part-open, part-covered flagstoned courtyard. One-acre secluded gardens.

¶¶ FOOD & DRINK

Burford became an important coaching centre during the 18th century, with over 40 coaches a day trundling through the town. Its legacy is a vast number of places to eat and drink. This is my pick.

Angel at Burford Witney St ✆ 01993 822714 ⌂ theangelatburford.co.uk. A 16th-century Hook Norton Brewery pub and, with its secluded garden, the ideal escape from the bustle of the High Street. Slow braised pork belly with bubble & squeak cake, roast butternut squash and sage risotto with candied chestnuts or, from the bar menu, the 30-day-aged Angel burger with homemade tomato chutney. Three attractive bedrooms also available.

Bakery on the Hill 53 High St ✆ 01993 823898 ⌂ bakeryonthehill.uk. It's a tiny space but the bread, cakes and pastries sold here are made on-site, which you'll quite likely see happening. This artisan bakery serves breakfasts, brunch and light lunches using its own baked goods. Delicious quiche, too!

Hugo Lovage Patisserie 54 High St ✆ 01993 823578 ⌂ hugolovagepatisserie.com. Run by Michelin-trained pastry chef Cindy Kosmala, this is the place to come for sweet treats to take on a high-class picnic, as well as take-away lunch items. Cindy and her husband Hubert, who is head chef at nearby Swan at Swinbrook, are originally from South Africa and have made the Cotswolds their home.

Lamb Inn Sheep St ✆ 01993 823155 ⊗ cotswold-inns-hotels.co.uk. Comfy yet smart restaurant well known for the quality of its food. More informal dining in the bar, with all the character and distinguishing features expected of a Cotswold 'pub'. Dog-friendly accommodation too. The neighbouring **Bay Tree Hotel** is the more upmarket sister establishment run by the same group.

5 WIDFORD, ASTHALL, SWINBROOK & MINSTER LOVELL

🏠 **Three Horseshoes**

Following the Windrush east, it passes between four villages, Widford and Swinbrook on the north bank, Asthall on the south side and old Minster Lovell back on the north bank once again. Each has its own crossing point.

Widford, a medieval village, barely exists any more. You can just make out the lumps and bumps of the old buildings in the ground but the church of St Oswald's still stands forlorn. A footpath crosses the old site; you're literally passing through what was once someone's kitchen or hallway. But medieval is not old enough for Widford, for the tiny church is built on the site of a Roman villa; a mosaic was uncovered during restoration work in 1904. Take a look too at the large pond between the river and the church – it provides an atmospheric photo opportunity.

Further east is **Swinbrook**. It was dominated by the Fettiplaces for 500 years until the family line died out in 1805; nothing remains of their manor house but you can just make out the remains of the Italian terraced garden on the hillside close to St Mary's Church. Here you'll find grandiose statements of their self-importance – their gigantic tombs. More recently, Swinbrook was the home of the six aristocratic Mitford sisters, famed for much of the 20th century for their social lives, scandals and political persuasions, as well as their skills as novelists and prolific letter writers. Their father had Swinbrook House built for the family in 1926, 1½ miles north of the village. Four of the sisters – Nancy, Unity, Pamela and Diana – are buried in the churchyard. Deborah, the youngest sister, became the Duchess of Devonshire, restoring Chatsworth House in Derbyshire. However, while the Mitford sisters' story may end in Swinbrook, it certainly doesn't begin there. Having lived at their grandfather's house at Batsford (page 160) in Gloucestershire, they moved to Swinbrook's neighbouring village **Asthall** when their father inherited the Jacobean manor house there.

THE PICTURE TAKER/COTSWOLDS.COM

ARENAPHOTOUK/D

CAROLINE MILLS

THE PICTURE TAKER/COTSWOLDS.COM

Privately-owned **Asthall Manor** house and garden is not routinely open to the public but the manor's kitchen garden is a focus for courses, with practical tuition on nature-friendly gardening techniques alongside art workshops, mindfulness retreats and other events. It's a very fine classroom! There are volunteering opportunities in the garden, too, where all tools, gloves and training are provided, along with lunch if you're staying for a full day.

The countryside surrounding these hamlets is truly idyllic but it's the village furthest east that I enjoy most. **Minster Lovell**, or strictly **Old Minster** – modern Minster Lovell is on the south side of the river – does more than offer character. The old village is an inspirational place where the gentle river provides a backdrop to cricket on Wash Meadow, overlooked by a quintessentially English timber-framed pub adorned with cascading flowers, a narrow street lined with the most appealing thatched cottages and the spectacularly eerie ruins of a once grand manor house. **Minster Lovell Hall** tries to stand up next to St Kenelm's Church, on the banks of the Windrush, with ancient fishponds evident and an immaculately layered-stone dovecote close by. The hall was built by Lord William Lovell in the 1440s but was dismantled, in part, by 1750. Now the remaining blackened walls whisper tales of yesteryear, arched doorways hang in midair, empty windows whistle with the wind and moss grips the foundations trodden down with 300 years of footsteps.

The easiest way into the village is across the 15th-century bridge from the Burford to Witney road south of the river. But I love approaching from the northeast where fields are laid bare, where the Romans once trod along the course of **Akeman Street** and the views across the water meadows to the ruined hall and church make it all the more mysterious, especially when a mist hangs in the trees.

🧳 SPECIAL STAYS

Three Horseshoes Asthall OX18 4HW ✆ 01993 377500 ⌂ threehorseshoesasthall.com. Thoughtfully decorated with rustic charm and six bedrooms that are luxuriously comfy. Attention to detail everywhere. Views from the garden, lined with roses and smelly herbs,

◀ **1** View Sherborne Brook from a walk through the village of Sherborne. **2** Every building is unique in Burford. **3** Windrush is one of a cluster of beautiful villages in this area. **4** Step back in time at Cogges Manor Farm.

A Windrush Valley walk

✻ OS Explorer map 180; start: Old Minster Lovell, ⚲ SP322113; 5 miles; easy.

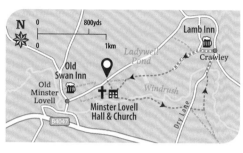

There's a fine walk across the water meadows around Old Minster Lovell, where you can brush past the weeping willows and wild mint that mount the banks of the River Windrush and where if you're lucky you'll catch sight of a swooping barn owl. From the small car park for Minster Lovell Hall, head southeast for the church and hall. Follow the public footpath southeast, past the ancient fishponds and across the river. The path continues along the foot of a small incline, close to the riverbank. Cross Dry Lane and take the bridleway (not the footpath) for 260yds before turning left to follow a small ditch. Turn right at Dry Lane for Crawley where you can stop at the Lamb Inn for a breather. With the pub on your right, continue to the end of the lane, which becomes a footpath across the river's northern meadows and Ladywell Pond, back to the start point.

are good for the soul; the River Windrush flows close to the pub. Large, bright and airy restaurant, also has a cosy bar area. Excellent breakfast and evening menu (try the heritage tomatoes, shallots and smoked-tomato dressing with basil pesto to start or lamb rump with summer veg, goat's curd and pea puree for a main). Part of Daylesford (page 245) Stays.

🍴 FOOD & DRINK

In addition to the Three Horseshoes:

Lamb Inn Crawley OX29 9TW ☏ 01993 708792 ⌂ lambpub.co.uk. Rustic-chic pub with superb food. The menu changes to allow for seasonal fare, with lots of slow-cooked food using ingredients produced within a matter of miles of the pub. Calves' liver and bacon with bubble & squeak, braised pig cheeks or rosti potato cake with grilled asparagus. Outdoors, food is cooked on a rôtisserie and in a pizza oven.

Old Swan Inn Minster Lovell OX29 0RN ☏ 01993 862512 ⌂ oldswan.co.uk. In Old Minster on the north side of the river, overlooking Wash Meadow and the medieval bridge. A beautiful boutique inn with all the Cotswold quirks of a historic pub. Serves gastro-pub food in atmospheric surroundings – cosy nooks and crannies with log fires and flagstone floors. Or dine outside in the stunningly beautiful gardens.

Swan Inn Swinbrook OX18 4DY ☏ 01993 823339 ⬧ theswanswinbrook.co.uk. A perfect location on the banks of the Windrush, one of the most idyllic locations of all Cotswold pubs, with a garden on the riverbank. Historic Mitford sister connections (the pub was once owned by Deborah, the Duchess of Devonshire); there are lots of photographs on the walls recollecting Mitford family life in a bygone age. Run by the same couple as the Kings Head Inn at Bledington (page 247).

6 WITNEY

While the Cotswolds were renowned for the wool trade, each town and village specialised in a specific aspect; in Barcheston it was tapestry, in the Stroud valleys, baize and broadcloth. In Witney, it was blankets. It doesn't sound like the most exciting of histories, but actually it was one that dominated Witney from the Iron Age until the Noughties. Blanket-making mills dot the Windrush all the way from Barrington and as far west as Worsham. The town had made a name for itself by the 17th century when there were a significant number of weavers and, latterly, blankets made elsewhere could not be named as a 'Witney blanket', as the title was synonymous with quality.

Most of the mills around town have disappeared now; the last blanket-making company, Early's of Witney, closed down in 2002. Although the mill chimneys have gone (except Early's), other buildings connected with the wool trade are apparent.

Of most significance is the **Witney Blanket Hall** at the north end of the long High Street, where the Witney Company (or Guild) of Blanket Weavers hung out. Keeping the town's traditions alive, the *"The museum, a 1,000-year-old anomaly tucked into a modern housing estate, is a great one for children."* hall reopened in 2015 and sells blankets once more, made by Cotswold Woollen Weavers (page 224). You can download a leaflet detailing the **Witney Wool and Blanket Trail**, a circular 2¾-mile walk, from ⬧ witneyblanketstory.org.uk/multimed/texts/WT00010.pdf.

Witney thrives, and the population has grown significantly despite the closure of the old mills. Seek out in particular **Church Green**, at the top of the High Street and the Market Place, beyond the curious **Buttercross**, a traditional market cross that was given a roof under which traders could sell perishable goods. Sheep were once herded into

HUFFKINS – A QUINTESSENTIAL COTSWOLD TEA ROOM

The Belgian buns have just come out of the oven. They release an appetising aroma, like warm bread, across the small bakery. Mary will ice them and place a sticky glacé cherry on top once they've cooled. But, for now, she's making Victoria sponge and chocolate brownie traybakes. That mixture smells heavenly, too.

At the far end of the bakery, Mark is making teacakes, placing soft, pliable hunks of currant-pricked dough in the bun moulder before spreading them out on a tray ready for baking. Thank goodness I'm wearing a face mask or Denise, the bakery manager, would see me licking my lips at the very thought of taste-testing everything. That will come later.

I'm in Huffkins craft bakery, a vital side to this quintessential Cotswold tea room business. Huffkins has been around for decades and is a part of the make-up of the north Cotswolds. The original bakery-tea room, in Burford (page 211), dates to the 1890s, though under a different name. It was renamed Huffkins sometime in the first half of the 20th century and, following only three changes of ownership in 100 years, was bought by the Taee family in 1998.

Over the next ten years, a further two tea rooms were opened, in Stow-on-the-Wold and Witney. Sons Joshua (as managing director) and Jacob latterly joined and expanded the business; now there are six tea rooms across the Cotswolds – additionally Cheltenham, Stratford-upon-Avon and Moreton-in-Marsh – plus three in John Lewis stores, and the new craft bakery in which I'm lip-licking.

Says Denise, 'We make all the tea-room treats here, from the teacakes and scones to traybakes, cakes, biscuits, bread, rolls and the biggest seller, our lardy cakes. All our core ingredients – flour, eggs, milk and cheese – are produced within seven miles of the bakery. The coffee and tea that we use in the tea rooms are roasted and blended in Witney, too. We bake with fresh yeast, meaning that there must be a slow proving process; no fast-acting agents are used, plus the shaping and moulding of all our products is a manual process.'

Later, I sit down to afternoon tea with MD Joshua to taste-test the supremely light and fluffy scones. Says Joshua, 'Our ethos is to focus on the highest quality, using local ingredients and to be an integral part of the community, where we feel Huffkins can add to the character of a place. We have members of staff who have worked for the business a long time, like Kate, who has been with us for ten years; her uncle Robert has also clocked up a dozen years. Our family ownership ethos is thread throughout the business.'

Huffkins is also supporting the Glorious Cotswold Grasslands initiative, sponsoring work to create and improve wildflower meadows within the area, particularly in Broadway. 'Every product sold with a bumblebee logo sows a square metre of wildflower meadow,' Joshua tells me. That includes the Huffkins Beesting, a sweet brioche bun with crème patissière, apricot jam and honey. Naturally, I have to taste-test one of those, too. Purely to help the wildflower meadows, you understand.

pens here ready for sale, and not all that long ago either – the middle of the last century rather than the Middle Ages. Sandwiched between two quiet roads lined with elegant stone merchants' houses, and punctuated with regularly spaced trees, Church Green is the perfect spot for a picnic, with the church of St Mary the Virgin standing at one end.

To the east of the church is the **Bishop's Palace**. Excavations have revealed the 12th-century manor house of the bishops of Winchester who ruled the town and farmed much of the surrounding area with sheep for the wool trade.

However, it's the river that really brought prosperity to Witney and you can get close to it at **Langel Common**, an island to the east of the town centre, about 200yds from the High Street. Cross right over the two stretches of river and you'll come to **Cogges Manor Farm Museum** (⌀ 01993 772602 ⌀ cogges.org.uk), where historic life is played out (including on screen; the farm turned into Yew Tree Farm in *Downton Abbey*). The first owner of Cogges Manor was clearly an important chap, as he's featured on the Bayeux Tapestry riding into battle at Hastings. The museum, a 1,000-year-old anomaly tucked into a modern housing estate, is a great one for children, with dozens of activities, but adults will appreciate the harmonious cluster of humble farm buildings with a fabulous kitchen garden and a riverside walk through ancient floodplain meadows.

¶¶ FOOD & DRINK

Fleece Inn 11 Church Green ⌀ 01993 892270 ⌀ fleecewitney.co.uk. Sit outside this Georgian building overlooking Church Green and relax in one of the best locations in town. Great gastro-pub food and good beers (though not necessarily a local brew).

Huffkins 35 High St ⌀ 01993 708155 ⌀ huffkins.com. Morning pastries, light lunches (rarebits, sandwiches, salads) and afternoon tea with award-winning scones, traybakes and cakes at this Cotswolds institution (page 218). My choice is the Beesting, a sweet bun made from a 15th-century recipe.

Part & Parcel 2–4 Market Sq ⌀ 01993 226016 ⌀ dodopubs.com. One of the excellent neighbourhood pubs from Dodo Pub Co, serving burgers (the rosemary chips are delicious) and pizzas. The upstairs is a dedicated co-working space.

Witney Blanket Hall 100 High St ⌀ 01993 706408 ⌀ blankethall.co.uk. Serves freshly made savoury pies and platters along with tea and cake in this historic 18th-century building. Opt for the 'Master Weaver's Lunch' – a hearty choice of pie, mash, pease pudding and gravy. Pine tables, old church chairs and seat cushions are made from 'patchwork' blankets.

THE LEACH VALLEY

The next valley west of the Windrush is that of the River Leach. Far shorter than the Windrush, its 18-mile stretch rises in the tiny hamlet of Hampnett (where the church has astonishingly rich Victorian stencilling, evoking the look medieval church interiors must have often had when freshly painted) and only passes through a handful of settlements, most of them taking their name from the river, before reaching the Thames just east of Lechlade close to Buscot Weir.

Leach Valley walk

✳ OS Explorer map OL45; start: Bouthrop Church, ♥ SP203053; 2.8 miles; easy

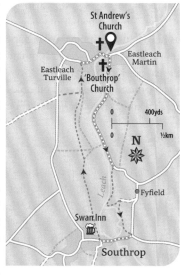

For an appealingly tranquil village-to-village walk along country lanes and riverside footpaths, take a circular amble from the Eastleaches via Fyfield to the equally idyllic village of **Southrop**, where you can stop for something to eat at the Swan Inn. The valley here is at its quietest, and arguably most scenic; by spending even a rewarding hour or two here, you can get to grips with the rural aspect of the Leach.

From Bouthrop Church, take the footpath through the churchyard and follow the lane (it's a very quiet country lane) south, signposted for Fyfield and Southrop. In just over half a mile, at a right-angled bend in the road, fork right onto a public footpath to follow the River Leach. In 275yds, turn left onto the footpath towards Fyfield. As you approach the village, take the footpath across open farmland to a road junction and turn right, across the Leach, into the village of Southrop.

Just west of the village, close to the footpath leading to the church on your left, turn right on a public footpath to head north, back towards Eastleach. You'll be rewarded with delightful views of the river. The footpath will take you between houses before arriving on the road; turn right to return to Bouthrop Church.

7 NORTHLEACH

Logically enough, the village of Northleach is in the north of the Leach Valley. Northleach is also the first settlement that the river flows through having sprung up from nearby Hampnett. You can follow the river between the two villages along a dog-leg of the Monarch's Way, which passes through Northleach.

The village grew up close to the Roman Fosse Way and when you're travelling along the Fosse, approaching the turning for Northleach, you soon get to appreciate the lie of the land and how steep and sudden the valley sides are for such a tiny river. At right angles to the Fosse, the village sprawls out along its High Street. A mix of tall 'town' houses with ruler-straight frontages mingle with dumpier cottages, squat to the ground, each one telling a tale of merchant or master versus minion.

Evoking its wool-rich days, in the Market Square stands a colourful sign marking the charter granted in 1227 allowing the village to hold an annual market. From then, its prosperity grew. Its wealth is obvious in the complexity and size of the **church of St Peter and St Paul**, a short stroll southwest of the Market Square. On approaching, the stained glass of the great east window, created only in 1963, reflects in such a way that it appears, like an optical illusion, to be falling out. From inside the building greens and blues change to reveal symbolism relevant to Northleach – woolsacks and shears, and the motif of a wool merchant. Memorials to dynastic wool merchant families fill the aisles and chapels. Many are remembered in memorial brasses buried into the floor and, in particular, a pair of tiny brasses pressed into the wall of a chapel.

The centre of Northleach is small and it doesn't take long to wander around. If you've arrived at the vast churchyard from the Market Place, exit via Church Walk and take a walk around School Hill, Town Row and College Row, which will deposit you back at the green, where you'll see one of Northleach's half-timbered buildings creeping into the fray of Cotswold stone.

¶¶ FOOD & DRINK

Ox House (The Curious Wine Cellar) The Ox House, Market Pl ⌀ 01451 860650 ⌂ curiousaboutwine.com. A real find. All the wines sold are from vineyards too small for the multi-nationals and each one is hand-picked by Mark Savage who visits the vineyards before choosing to sell the wine. Some great house reds and whites, and a wide price range. You can sip a glass of wine in the shop, or over a barrel or propped up at a bar made from wooden

IONUT DAVID/D

JOHN CORRY/S

wine crates. There are tables and chairs too if you wish to be totally civilised, or venture out to the vine-covered courtyard. Tapas-style nibbles, sausage rolls plus teas, coffees and pastries available too. If you don't fancy the wine on offer by the glass, select one of your own off the shelf, drink what you want there, and take the rest home with you.

Sherborne Arms Market Pl ✆ 01451 828186 ⌂ thesherbornenorthleach.com. Cosy town-centre pub in a charming stone property with beams, exposed stone walls and views to the eaves. Bar area with open fires. Separate restaurant serving simple but well-cooked British dishes, including offal and game.

8 THE EASTLEACH VILLAGES & FILKINS

After Northleach, the river flows steadily south, the valley sides remaining steep, through the village of Eastington then Lodge Park. Now owned by the National Trust, **Lodge Park** was a giant 17th-century playground. The lodge was never a residence but a grandstand built by John Dutton in 1634 to play out his passion for gambling and entertaining. The parkland is impressive, if windswept, and it's the only place that you can get close to the Leach before it reaches the Eastleach villages some miles further downstream. That is with one exception, at Sheep Bridge, where Akeman Street, the old Roman road from St Albans in Hertfordshire to Cirencester, crosses the river.

A few meanders further downstream and the little river passes between two heavenly idyllic villages in the Cotswolds (and, conjoined, one of my Cotswold favourites), **Eastleach Turville** on the west bank, and **Eastleach Martin** east of the river. Perhaps to distinguish the two, Eastleach Martin is also known locally as Bouthrop, although you'll be hard-pressed to find it named so on any map. The pair are noble oases of peace, and the river running through makes them all the more uplifting. As two separate parishes, the villages have two churches, no more than a stone's throw apart; it's just the river that separates them. Of the two, the tiny church of St Michael and St Martin, with its churchyard bordering the river, is the more quietly striking. The priest and poet John Keble – the famous Keble College in Oxford was built in his memory – was a curate here in the early 19th century. The church is only used once a year now, alternating annually between harvest and Christmas.

◄ **1** The former prosperity of Northleach is evident from the size of its church, St Peter and St Paul. **2** There are some peaceful riverside walks through the Leach Valley, including around Southrop. **3** The striking church of St Michael and St Martin in Eastleach Martin.

A footpath runs through the churchyard and along the riverbank, crossing over an old clapper bridge, known as Keble's Bridge, between the two villages. There's a wooden bench tucked by the riverside here and it is the most peaceful spot to sit among the wild flowers, listening to the dulcet tones of the river. Daffodils, ducklings and cow parsley line the riverbanks and there's an opportunity to dip your toe in the refreshingly cold water from the stone steps that descend into the river.

"There's a wooden bench tucked by the riverside here and it is the most peaceful spot to sit among the wild flowers, listening to the dulcet tones of the river."

On the tiny Broadwell Brook, **Filkins** is also well known for having one of the last links to the region's wool trade. Housed in an old mill and a series of striking stone barns around a sunny courtyard, **Cotswold Woollen Weavers** (GL7 3JJ ☎ 01367 860491 ⏿ cotswoldwoollenweavers. co.uk) is run by Richard and Jane Martin. Here wool is still woven into cloth – tweeds, flannels and saxonies (the finest merino wool); watch the processes and look at the design room upstairs where the team are working with some of the best-known fashion houses in the world. You can buy the pre-spun wool on spools if you like, but the temptation is in the shop downstairs – one room selling stylish clothes at pounds less

TAKING THYME AT SOUTHROP'S COOKERY SCHOOL

Southrop GL7 3NX ☎ 01367 850174 ⏿ thyme.co.uk

Rejuvenating the 150-acre Southrop Manor Estate from its once-crumbling existence has been a dedicated labour of love for Caryn Hibbert and her family. Alongside renovating neglected buildings using traditional craftsmanship has been the development of **Thyme Cookery School**. Considered a food school rather than a cookery school, it goes further than simply cooking, instead embracing the Cotswold countryside and looking at the story of food from source to sustainable production in addition to the enjoyment of serving, eating and drinking.

One part of the school's culinary philosophy is to encourage course leaders, chefs and class participants to work with fresh, seasonal and often locally distinct and traditional produce from small farms and artisans – classes usually begin in the kitchen garden. A love of the land and growing your own food is instilled. A seasonal programme of events is offered, though private food courses may be booked for individuals or groups.

than designer prices and the other with items for the home – fabulous rugs and blankets, cushion covers and throws, their tactile texture calling out from the shelves to be felt. A Cotswold tweed has been developed too, using colours that evoke memories of the landscape.

There is also a cosy café serving light lunches and homemade cakes with a sheltered orchard for sunny days and a small museum (free to enter) dedicated to textiles in the Cotswolds. I absolutely love this place, returning time and again to its quirky nature – the prehistoric ledgers of textile samples that line the walls, the snuggly throws piled high in the rug warehouse, the collection of pewterware alongside historic weaving apparatus and the sheer joy brought by keeping the very fabric of the Cotswolds alive.

¶¶ FOOD & DRINK

Thyme Southrop GL7 3NU ℰ 01367 850205 ⌚ thyme.co.uk. A choice of outlets under the Thyme umbrella. In the village centre, The Swan is a very attractive-looking pub with plenty of character and atmosphere and also the winner of plenty of awards for its outstanding food, which uses homegrown produce from the Thyme kitchen garden as well as lamb, pork and poultry from the farm estate. Sit outside on the village green to watch the world go by. Other places to eat on the estate include the Ox Barn and the Orchid House. Accommodation available on the Southrop Manor Estate, of which the Swan is a part.

THE COLN VALLEY

The River Coln rises at Brockhampton, east of Cheltenham. Like the Windrush, its character changes once it leaves the steep escarpments behind and begins to run through gentler territory. It too sweeps in a south to southeasterly direction, discharging its waters into the Thames west of Lechlade. The countryside through which it flows is the most rural of the five northern tributaries, and some of the least visited; the river never gets much wider than a few feet, the shallow banks and adjacent hay meadows teeming with wildlife.

9 WITHINGTON, CHEDWORTH & YANWORTH

Well, those Romans really knew a beautiful spot when they saw one, building one of their most important villas at Chedworth. They spent decades exploring this valley and the small part covered in this section deserves at least 24 hours of your time.

Once crossed by the main Oxford to Cheltenham road, the first village of any size that the Coln passes through is **Withington**. It's also the first of a string of transcendent villages, the beauty of which is difficult to comprehend without being here. The land once again twists and turns, each fold in the earth's surface never wishing to conform to uniformity.

"This vast expanse of ancient woodland, joined in the west by Withington Woods, grows on a steep slope of the Coln Valley."

Hence the village is squeezed between two steep ridges, the north wind funnelling down the valley; this is one of the highest parts of the Cotswolds and even on the valley floor, you're over 500ft above sea level. The village is dissected by an old disused railway line, the remnants of which are evident but a large lake through which the Coln flows has a few short yards of a footpath to wander along, just to the west of the dismantled line.

While the elongated village of **Chedworth** is wedged even tighter into a mile-long bottleneck of a valley, on a tributary of the Coln, Chedworth Roman Villa sits a mile north of the village. You can walk between the two using either the Macmillan Way or the Monarch's Way, and in doing so you'll pass through **Chedworth Woods**. This vast expanse of ancient woodland, joined in the west by Withington Woods, grows on a steep slope of the Coln Valley with masses of wildlife under the mostly beech canopy, including bluebells, primroses, wild strawberries, wild garlic, tawny owls, mammals, rare butterflies, adders and Roman snails. The Chedworth Nature Reserve falls within the woods, particularly in the area around the disused railway where you can see geological masterpieces and a tufa spring.

Chedworth Roman Villa (✆ 01242 890256; National Trust) is tucked on the edge of the woods, on a bank above the river. I love this place, not just for its location but also for the chance of understanding how the Romans – or at least some of them – lived. The layout of the villa is all here, with two bathhouses, hypocausts and some fabulous mosaics too, worthy of a visit simply to see the artwork and intricate patterns. Owned by the National Trust, it's a great place to take children, with lots of Roman-themed activities. Chedworth is by no means a conventional Roman villa. Uncovered in the 19th century, the whole place is an archaeological time-warp – it's not how they perform archaeological digs nowadays. Quaint little pitched roofs protect the shin-high remains of the villa walls, old barn-like structures shelter the mosaics and an over-conspicuous Victorian villa sits in the middle of it all housing a museum of once-buried 'treasure', very much in the spirit of a Victorian archaeologist's collection. Perhaps the most interesting aspects are the hypocausts with the mosaic floors peeled back in places to reveal this underfloor heating system, appearing like stone statues or a giant draughts board.

I would urge anyone not simply to drive straight to the villa, spend an hour there, then leave without exploring this beautiful section of the Coln. Take the time to picnic in the woods (or among the Roman ruins), and wander the quiet country lanes and the valley's footpaths through open, yet sheltered, meadows. If you are driving to the villa, the National Trust-signposted route takes you through the village of Yanworth. On your return from the villa, turn right just before the village and head down the valley's northern embankment, crossing the river at Yanworth Mill and exiting the valley at Fossebridge to see an alternative view of the valley that shouldn't be missed.

10 FOSSEBRIDGE TO BIBURY

Running beneath the Fosse Way at **Fossebridge**, the next section of the Coln Valley gives a good opportunity to get out on foot or to explore the lanes by bike, making the most of the two roads that run either side of the Coln to create a circular route between Fossebridge and Bibury. Off the Fosse Way, the first village you arrive at is **Coln St Dennis**, with its riverside church, where the strangely shaped tower has the look of a set of children's building blocks. The road then divides, running either side of the river, one

"The river is wide enough to need two double-arched bridges side by side, one carrying road traffic, the other for feet."

heading to **Calcot**, on a tiny ridge above, the other to **Coln Rogers** and its Saxon church. Two footpaths join these two villages, one crossing the river to meet up with the Coln St Dennis to Coln Rogers road, the other running along the eastern riverbank.

At the village of **Ablington**, the river is wide enough to need two double-arched bridges side by side, one carrying road traffic, the other for feet. There's access to the river here, its crystal waters reflecting a village that seems to have avoided the inescapable pace of modern life. This is your last chance to savour quiet solitude by the Coln before the onslaught of coaches and day trippers at Bibury.

The 19th-century craftsman William Morris once said that **Bibury** was the most beautiful village in England. I wonder if he would feel the same way now, as coachloads of tourists spill out across the village before 09.00. Generally speaking, they've come to snap a quick shot of the much-photographed **Arlington Row** before climbing back on board. The row originated as a 14th-century wool store and was later converted into a group of weavers' cottages. The American businessman Henry Ford (founder of the Ford Motor Company) tried to buy the entire row with the idea of shipping all the buildings to America where he would rebuild them in his history theme park; fortunately he was unable to, but he did get his hands on an old house in Chedworth which now stands, stone for stone, in Michigan.

You can reach Arlington Row, the epitome of Cotswold-esque architecture, by crossing the Rack Isle – a low-lying meadow in between Arlington Mill Stream and the River Coln. This tranquil, verdant meadow, now used to encourage rare water voles, frogs and kingfishers to habituate the area, was once a place for stretching out the drying cloth, hence its name.

There is more to Bibury than Arlington Row, however. If you've approached Bibury and Arlington from Ablington, following the River Coln, you'll have noticed a series of lakes as you enter the villages, with the famous, ivy-clad Swan Hotel opposite. These are the lakes of **Bibury Trout Farm** (⏾ 01285 740215 ⏾ biburytroutfarm.co.uk). The gift shop and children's play area make it rather commercial but you can still fish to catch your own supper or learn about the hatchery where up to six million brown and rainbow trout ova are spawned each year.

My favourite time of year to visit is during the winter months when hoar frost grips the skeletal webs of wild angelica and there's a greater chance of having the place entirely to yourself for a few moments. In any season though, the river is completely clear, and it doesn't take long to discover a couple of brown trout sunning themselves in the sparkling waters before whole shoals appear. Hunt too for the stone head of a Cotswold sheep hanging off the Saxon church; its give-away curly forelock is clear to see.

---

1 Rack Isle stretches up to Arlington Row in Bibury from the River Coln. **2** Marvel at the remains of the underfloor heating system at Chedworth Roman Villa. **3** St Mary's Church in Fairford has beautiful stained-glass windows. ▶

SS

NICK TURNER/COTSWOLDS.COM

¶¶ FOOD & DRINK

Inn at Fossebridge Fossebridge GL54 3JS ✆ 01285 720721 ⊘ fossebridgeinn.co.uk.
Highly recommended bar, restaurant and hotel adjacent to the Fosse Way with a riverside
garden on the banks of the Coln. The bar and restaurant have all the rustic features expected
of a Cotswolds pub and the food is superb. Breakfasts for non-residents are served as well as
cream teas. Accommodation too.

Mill Inn Withington GL54 4BE ✆ 01242 890204. Bizarrely, a Samuel Smith's-owned pub
(the brewery in North Yorkshire) but you're visiting the beautiful Mill Inn for its location,
tucked down a tiny country lane with a garden alongside the River Coln. The food is 1970s
'xyz and chips in a basket' but this is a welcoming and very popular pub nevertheless. One for
the summer.

11 BARNSLEY

The village of Barnsley sits midway between Arlington and Cirencester
on a wold four miles from both the River Coln and the next river along,
the River Churn. Here lived Rosemary Verey OBE, the internationally
acclaimed garden designer and writer who
drew up, among others, gardens for the
then HRH Prince of Wales and Sir Elton
John. Her own garden at the family home,
Barnsley House, was her most famous design,
attracting up to 30,000 visitors a year up until
her death in 2001. Today, the gardens remain
open to the public, but Barnsley House
itself is now a luxurious hotel. Rosemary Verey's head gardener, Richard
Gatenby, continues to work in the garden today, as does her grandson.

*"It was one of the most
important trade routes
for transporting wool
and a drover's road,
taking cattle from Wales
to market in London."*

Barnsley House is approached, like much of the village, from the
Cirencester to Bibury road that runs through it. But you may think the
back of the house looks more like the front of a house. Far from some
puzzling riddle, the main Cirencester to Oxford road in the 16th century
was actually the little track, known as Clacton's Lane, at the rear of the
hotel. It was one of the most important trade routes for transporting
wool and a drover's road, taking cattle from Wales to market in London.

12 RIVER'S END – COLN ST ALDWYNS & FAIRFORD

From Bibury both the River Coln and the ancient Salt Way head towards
a trio of villages: Coln St Aldwyns, Hatherop and Quenington. Of the
three, **Coln St Aldwyns** is my favourite, tucked as it is into a loop in the

river with the old lichen-covered cottages gathered together around a tiny village green.

There's a footpath from Quenington to walk south by the river and across water meadows for approximately one mile; thereafter the river flows through Fairford Park, a 4,200-acre estate. Though private, the estate is owned by the Ernest Cook Trust (Ernest Cook being the grandson of Thomas Cook, the very first tour operator), whose aims lie in the conservation and management of the countryside and providing educational opportunities for people to learn about the outdoors.

"I also like the fact that the bell ropes hang right in the centre of the church where the bellringing is clear for all to see."

A permissive footpath across the estate joins up with the aforementioned public footpath from Quenington, allowing you to walk along further stretches of the river and the little Pitcham Brook; a route map can be downloaded from the website ⊘ernestcooktrust.org.uk/discover-fairford.

The permissive footpath onto the Fairford Park Estate is also accessible from the little town of **Fairford**, at the top of the High Street, close to where the river ducks under two very pretty bridges. In some respects, it's a typical 'Cotswold town' though it receives less recognition – and considerably fewer tourists – than some of its popular counterparts.

For many Fairford means the RAF airbase, the location for one of the world's largest annual air displays, the Royal International Air Tattoo. And yet this quiet town is the antithesis of all this show of strength and force, the only strength shown in the town from the wool-trade wealth invested in the 15th-century church of St Mary the Virgin. It dominates the very attractive High Street, with its giant walnut tree at the entrance. Its near-complete set of medieval stained-glass windows are world famous, depicting scenes from the life of Christ, culminating in the Last Judgement. I also like the fact that the bell ropes hang right in the centre of the church where the bellringing is clear for all to see. Don't forget to pay your respects at the memorial for Tiddles, the church cat, in the churchyard. For the best view of the church, wander along the footpath to the west of the river.

Northwest of the High Street, close to the river, are the oxpens, ancient stalls where cattle once fed after a hard day's ploughing. They've been fully restored and the sunny courtyard is the perfect place for a picnic. You can also begin a riverside walk from here – via Back Lane.

Following the river until it reaches the Cotswold Water Park (page 264), it returns alongside a lake and back into the East End of town towards the Walnut Tree Field where the annual Fairford Festival takes place every June.

¶¶ FOOD & DRINK

Bull Hotel Market Pl 𝒥 01285 712535 ⊘ thebullhotelfairford.co.uk. Informal lunches and dinners served in the bar – slow cooked belly pork with hasselback potatoes, tandoori bavette steak, butternut squash risotto. Full selection of cask ales from Arkells Brewery in nearby Swindon. Trout-fishing breaks available – the hotel owns 1¼ miles of Coln riverbank.

THE CHURN VALLEY

The River Churn rises close to the tiny village of Seven Springs near Cheltenham and, despite it being a tributary of the Thames, is actually longer from its source to confluence than the Thames. It is therefore argued that this theoretically should be the head of the Thames.

Overall the Churn, which is the Thames's most westerly tributary, is only 16 miles long before its confluence near Cricklade where, bizarrely, it gets smaller as it approaches. It passes through a series of lakes at the impressive Cowley Manor hotel before being channelled between hills and wooded slopes taken up by, first **Colesbourne Park** and then Rendcomb Park.

North Cerney is its last village stop-off before reaching the historic town of **Cirencester**. From there, it's just a few more twists and turns until it passes through the Cotswold Water Park (page 264) before entering the Thames.

13 COLESBOURNE & NORTH CERNEY

The tiny village of **Colesbourne** appears on a bend in the river as the Churn turns south. The village is entirely consumed by **Colesbourne Park** (𝒥 01242 870567 ⊘ colesbournegardens.org.uk), a 2,500-acre estate with significant acreages of woodland. The park is renowned for its snowdrop collection, with more than 250 varieties of the Galanthus bulbs planted throughout. Visitors come from far and wide to wander through the gardens during the **Snowdrop Weekends** in February, when they can see the church, the waterfall where the Churn crosses the park, the woodland paths, and huge banks of snowdrops fluttering in the breeze. There are lakeside walks too, the bluest of blue waters reflecting further banks of little white stars. It is a glorious sight. Above all, this is a private home and you'll find the charming Elwes family (the snowdrop collection was begun in 1874 by the great-grandfather of the current owner) greeting visitors, selling jars of homemade jam, helping direct traffic and assisting with the charity afternoon teas. I thoroughly recommend a visit.

Elsewhere on the estate is the purpose-built **Foodworks Cookery School** (⌀ 01242 870538 ⌂ foodworkscookeryschool.co.uk), where some of the country's finest chefs take the classes and students can learn how to make the likes of fresh pasta or Lebanese cuisine.

From Colesbourne the Churn slides on through the valley and Rendcomb Park, before entering the village of **North Cerney**. Much of the village stretches up the eastern hillside while, unfortunately separated by the A435, the western riverbank includes the village's Norman church with its unusual saddleback tower and **Cerney House Gardens** (⌀ 01285 831300 ⌂ cerneygardens.com), a classic Victorian Cotswold garden: secret, romantic and full of old-fashioned everything. On a recent spring-time visit, bluebells and hellebores vied for attention with swathes of snowdrops in the woodland walk while the

"There are lakeside walks too, the bluest of blue waters reflecting further banks of little white stars."

parterre and borders of the walled garden were brimming with tulips and daffodils. My daughter loved the endearing little honesty-box kitchen with homemade cakes and a kettle to make your own tea or hot chocolate.

North Cerney is also known for its award-winning **Cerney Cheese**, in particular Cerney Ash, a soft goat's cheese that's coated with an oak ash and sea-salt mix. You'll find it for sale in many delis and outlets throughout the Cotswolds.

¶¶ FOOD & DRINK

Bathurst Arms North Cerney ⌀ 01285 831888 ⌂ bathurstarms.co.uk. Worthy of inclusion for its beautiful riverside garden, with tables beneath a cluster of weeping willows. Plenty of character inside. Pub and bistro classics with small plates (katsu bonbons with miso mayo; chicken & apricot terrine with toasted sourdough).

Colesbourne Inn Colesbourne ⌀ 01242 870376 ⌂ thecolesbourneinn.co.uk. Old coaching inn with two-acre gardens and rural views. Plenty of cosy corners, snugs and fireside seats. Try the char-grilled bacon chop with braised leeks and parsley sauce, or pan-roasted fillet of salmon, dill crushed potatoes and hollandaise. Accommodation available.

A cycle ride around secret valleys & hidden villages

I've put together a new cycle route that I thoroughly recommend to see some of the Cotswolds finest and most secretive valleys and hidden villages. These are not the villages that routinely make it onto the tourist trail and, save for the occasional tractor, you will have these lanes to yourself. There are pubs aplenty en route or with a short diversion (The Green Dragon Inn, for example, near Cowley) and some attractions along the way, too, like Cerney House Gardens and Chedworth Roman Villa. In total it's approximately 35 miles in length with plenty of hills for free-wheeling down or (as these are nearly all tiny valleys), pounding up. This is a contorted route, deliberately, to see these steep valleys, so, while it is only 35 miles, it's by no means easy-going riding. Allow a full day to appreciate the route – ideally, two days. Many of the lanes are little more than tracks – don't expect smooth tarmac for skinny wheels! However, you will come across some of the prettiest Cotswold villages and hamlets as you ride. The map (right) is broad, but gives a general guide of the route if you're plotting this on an app or marking up a more detailed OS map, so you can see the roads used in relation to others.

To begin, start in the tiny village of Coberley and take the narrow lane to Cowley (you could stay at striking Cowley Manor) then Brimpsfield. Continue on to Caudle Green, one of the Cotswolds' tiniest villages, crossing one of the initial streams that becomes the River Frome and the beginnings of the Golden Valley. Enjoy the view of the sharp valleys as you climb above and beyond the village.

Next it's on to Bisley (although I do recommend a detour to Miserden (page 292) for an extended ride), where you'll have views of the Toadsmoor Valley and a choice of pubs – though

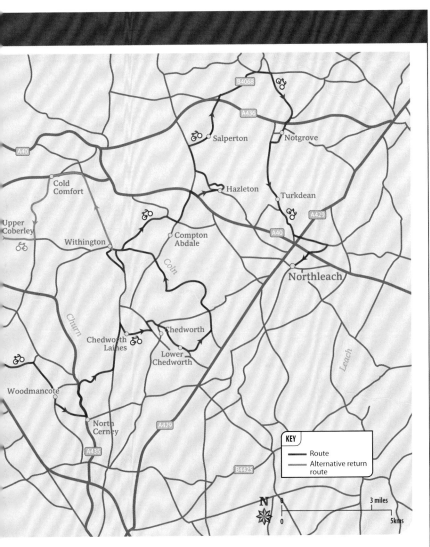

The Bear at Bisley is the nicer of the two. Don't forget to look at The Wells, a pagan place of spring water. From Bisley, take Limekiln Lane to Waterlane and continue to Frith Wood. It's a free wheel down to the hamlet (little more than a handful of houses) but you could make a short circuit to visit Far Oakridge, by taking the wooded lane to the right (signposted Far Oakridge and Chalford) just before the hamlet. From Frith Wood you'll descend then cycle ▶

A cycle ride around secret valleys & hidden villages (continued)

◀ through glorious beech woods as you make your way to Daneway Bridge. Along the way you'll pass by Daneway Banks Nature Reserve, a Wildlife Trust reserve that's worth stopping for to admire the rich calcareous grassland, and the views across Golden Valley.

At the Daneway Inn, where you can camp overnight in a glorious sun-soaked riverside meadow for a proper away-from-it-all off-grid experience (it's basic, not glamping), don't cross the River Frome (except to have a look at the river) but take Dane Lane to the north of the pub towards Miserden and Edgeworth. You'll begin with a steep climb through a wooded valley before levelling out onto open ground before turning right for Edgeworth and the next contorted valley; the junction is a mile or so beyond the Daneway Inn. Having turned right, the road to (and past) Edgeworth is one of the prettiest parts of the route, with views across to the church and the medieval Edgeworth Manor on the hillside as you descend into the Frome valley (again).

Head along Crabtree Lane and on to Duntisbourne Leer and then Duntisbourne Abbots, another glorious village, before heading northeast towards Woodmancote. You'll need to turn left just before the junction of the A417 to then pass beneath the main road and left again to run parallel with it. A quarter-mile after crossing beneath the A417, turn right for Woodmancote. You'll have views along the lane for some really knotted valleys and hillsides and one of the sharpest hill climbs en route; this is the chance to see the hidden Cotswolds and secret streams and rivers.

From Woodmancote, continue to North Cerney, where you can visit Cerney House Gardens (page 233) for a colourful breather. There's a woodland walk and walled parterres alongside borders brimming with perennials. The house is west of the main village, with a turning opposite the Bathurst Arms, which is another possible stop for a drink beside the River Churn.

Continue north along the Churn Valley (care required on the mile-long section of the A435) before turning off for Rendcomb – not forgetting to look back for stunning views from whence you came as you climb out of the village, in addition to the views you'll continue to see to the left and right.

Beyond the hill climb northeast out of Rendcomb, turn north along a straight road before the right turn for Chedworth Laines – a hamlet with a handful of houses – before dropping down and following the gentle valley, a tributary of the Coln, southeast through the villages of Chedworth, Bleakmoor and Lower Chedworth (the latter is by far the prettier of the three conjoined villages). Here you'll see a more open valley with hillside properties dotted across the countryside.

Heading northeast out of Lower Chedworth then north towards Withington, the road makes a sharp right-hand turn beside Yanworth Mill, where it crosses the River Coln. The Monarch's Way long-distance trail passes by here, and the valley is a marvellous spot for a picnic. The road then curves round above the valley floor, past Yanworth (do look across to this comely village if you don't make a short detour to it), with fine views over the Coln Valley and Chedworth Woods. There's also the opportunity to stop at Chedworth Roman Villa.

Continue to Withington (by now you'll be hard-pressed to decide which is the prettiest village you've seen en route), where you can enjoy a drink in the riverside garden at The Mill Inn. After, there's a steep ascent to the summit of Compton Hill (look north for wonderful views) then a steep descent to Compton Abdale, passing Stancombe Wood and Smallhope along the way.

Follow the road north out of Compton Abdale (signed Salperton and Hazleton) to cross the A40 (care needed) and take the road towards Hazleton, a village that's split by a small valley. The Cotswold stone walls are particularly fine here. Continue north and as you see a tall stone wall on your right, turn right between a pair of huge stone gate pillars into Salperton Park. Once in the park, the imposing house (and church) looms ever larger as you cycle towards it; the road darts left just before the main entrance (it's a private house, not open to the public). Leaving the park at the junction beside the war memorial, turn right to pass through the village of Salperton. It's a village I'd deem to be one of the top five in the Cotswolds.

Cross the A436 (care needed) and turn right onto the B4068 towards Naunton. At the crossroads southwest of Naunton, turn right (south) for Aylworth, passing through the village towards Notgrove. At Notgrove, a peaceful village that's part of a large farmland estate, you could stay overnight in one of the Notgrove Holidays' camping pods to make the most of the tranquillity before cycling through Turkdean, the last of the off-the-beaten-track Cotswold villages on this ride.

A mile south of Turkdean, be sure to take the left turn for Farmington. Follow the road to Farmington before making a sharp right turn towards Northleach. This route creates something of a dog leg but avoids the need to cycle along the A429, something I don't recommend doing. Finish your ride in the historic village of Northleach to look at the fine wool church and enjoy a drink at The Ox House, a very cosy wine merchants with a difference.

If you wish to make a circular route of a similar length, at Withington, head northwest to the A436. Turn left – taking care on the half-mile stretch of this main road – before turning left again, off the A436 just beyond the Kilkeney Inn, at Cold Comfort. Return to Coberley via Upper Coberley and Cowley. You will miss out on some fabulous scenery and villages by doing so, though!

MO WU/S

COTSWOLD DISTRICT COUNCIL/CORINIUM MUSEUM

CAROLINE MILLS

Green Dragon Inn Cockleford, Cowley ✆ 01242 870271 🖉 green-dragon-inn.co.uk. Very cosy Cotswold stone pub in a remote location on the banks of the Churn. Opt for the informal Mouse Bar (with furniture handcrafted by the famous Mouse Man of Kilburn) or the Lower Bar, each offering plenty of character and a menu that changes weekly (featuring dishes like fish pie in a creamy leek sauce with herb crust or Somerset brie and beetroot tart). Smart, modern accommodation. Village shop, too.

14 CIRENCESTER

🏠 **The Barrel Store**

Thousands of schoolchildren 'doing the Romans' are brought here every year to gain a better understanding of past lives. Understandably so, given that Corinium, to use its Roman name, was Roman Britain's second-largest city. Virtually nothing of the Roman town is now apparent, the central street plan dating from medieval times, although the **Roman Amphitheatre** still exists, a grassy arena adorned by wildflowers in summer just ten minutes' walk from the Market Place (just on the south side of the bypass): there's free access to the site. Externally, perhaps the best evidence is in the form of the roads on the outskirts that show why Cirencester was so important to the Romans, as a crossing point of several major roads – the White Way, bringing salt from Droitwich, the Fosse Way from Exeter to Lincoln, Akeman Street from St Albans and the Ermin Way from Gloucester to Silchester. Most of the remains of Roman Cirencester have been brought indoors, forming one of the best Roman museums in Britain. The **Corinium Museum** (✆ 01285 655611 🖉 coriniummuseum.org) houses thousands of artefacts and some vividly recreated Roman interiors, but for me, the highlight is the set of mosaics that were uncovered and carefully pieced back together. Cirencester boasts the largest concentration of Romano-British mosaics in the UK outside London; over 90 are known with many now housed in the museum. Numerous events and activities take place throughout the year for both adults and children, including guided Roman Cirencester town walks, booked through the museum or Cirencester Civic Society.

Today Cirencester centres around the vast parish church with its unique entrance through the medieval town hall, in the Market Place.

◀ **1** Many buildings in Cirencester's Market Place are painted in pastel hues. **2** The Corinium Museum in Cirencester houses some spectacular Roman mosaics. **3** Colesbourne Park is renowned for its snowdrops.

THE SPORT OF CIRENCESTER

Cirencester Park ℘ 01285 653225 ♂ cirencesterpolo.co.uk

It may be the sport of kings, but you may be surprised to learn that you don't need a king's ransom to watch a game. Matches at the **Cirencester Park Polo Club** take place virtually every day during the season from April to September, utilising any one of the six prestigious grounds in Cirencester Park. And while their website provides grid references for visitors arriving by helicopter, arrivals by road command an entrance fee of just £10 to £15 (depending on the month) per car at weekends regardless of the number of occupants; during the week you're likely to watch a match for free. It's recommended that you take a picnic and make an afternoon of it but for a few pounds extra per person you can collect day membership and have lunch in the members' restaurant and tea room. Or, if you really want to get involved, you can book a Polo Experience Day with full instruction for experienced riders and non-riders alike.

This town was also a major player in the medieval wool trade, as evidenced by the rich array of buildings framing the Market Place and the roads leading from it (including Blackjack Street with its veritable collection of eateries and independent shops and its own community feel); unusually, many of the buildings in the Market Place are pastel-painted – a rainbow of pale blues, pinks, greens and yellows sitting harmoniously together.

You could take a town map to be an efficient walker, but my advice is to ditch the map here and allow your head to follow wherever your feet take you for an amble. Most streets are so interesting architecturally, you'll find yourself wandering from one to the next as you take everything in.

From time to time you see little blue plaques pinned to the walls of certain buildings. These snippets of history give clues to what went on behind closed walls and are placed by the Cirencester Civic Society, whose waymarked town walk (follow the marks in the pavements) leads you to the smart town houses of Cecily Hill. It's on the west side of town, off Thomas Street, near the tallest yew hedge in the world (standing at 40ft high), and the bizarre neo-medieval Cecily Hill Castle, built in Victorian times. Cecily Hill is one of the most attractive streets, though my personal favourite is Coxwell Street, running east off Thomas Street. There's not a straight wall in the street, the buildings so wonky they'd make a structural engineer wince.

Beyond Cecily Hill are the fancy iron gates leading into **Cirencester Park**. This enormous expanse is five miles long and three miles wide. It is owned by the Bathurst Estate (over 13,500 acres) but permission is granted to walk or ride horses (no bicycles allowed) throughout the grounds between 08.00 and 17.00 each day. With its Broad Ride that extends into the horizon, woodland paths and wide avenues interspersed with huge specimen trees and vast grass 'meadows', it's the perfect retreat

"There's not a straight wall in the street, the buildings so wonky they'd make a structural engineer wince."

into the country while, initially at least, remaining in the town. Every July the park hosts the **Cotswold Show** (⊘ cotswoldshow.co.uk), one of the largest rural jamborees in the region's calendar, highlighting the very best of the countryside and the Cotswolds. Through entertainment and attractions, the ethos of the show is to foster links between town and country and to encourage a love, respect and understanding for the countryside and rural issues.

🛍 SHOPPING

My pick of the shops in Cirencester (most of which are on Black Jack Street).

The Coln Gallery 19 West Market Pl ⊘ 01285 659085 ⊘ colnart.com. Fabulous selection of artists' materials from paints and pastels to drawing accessories and sketchpads. High-quality craft supplies, too.

The Corn Hall Market Pl ⊘ cornhallcirencester.org.uk. Different days bring different things: in the former trading hall, there are antiques and collectables (Fri), local crafts (Sat), a vintage and artisan fair (one Sun a month) plus an indoor market (Sun–Thu).

Octavia's Bookshop 24 Blackjack St ⊘ 01285 650677 ⊘ octaviasbookshop.co.uk. Arguably one of the best children's bookshops in the UK; walk in here and you'll be inspired to become a child again. The bookshop does sell books for adults, but more than half the shop is dedicated to books for children of all ages, displayed with inspiration.

SPECIAL STAYS

The Barrel Store Brewery Court ⊘ 01285 657181 ⊘ newbreweryarts.org.uk. Fantastic upmarket hostel accommodation in Cirencester. The Barrel Store is a low-carbon eco-friendly hostel situated in a beautifully renovated brewery right in the centre of town. Up to 43 people can sleep across the 14 bedrooms, which are simple but very comfortable and use locally made products such as woollen throws from Cotswold Woollen Weavers (page 224).

There's a community room with self-catering kitchen and lounge. All bedrooms are en suite and provide great budget accommodation for families.

🍴 FOOD & DRINK

Cirencester has a lively farmers' market, held twice a month on the second and fourth Saturday morning, with producers from the surrounding countryside selling anything from cheese to chutney and charcuterie. Cirencester also has lots of very good places of all types to eat. Here's my pick.

King's Head Hotel Market Pl 𝒥 01285 700900. What choice. From breakfast and brunch or a steak sandwich in The Grill to dinner in the MBB Brasserie with its theatre kitchen. Plus afternoon tea to fill in the gaps. For excellent take-aways, use the **Corn Hall Deli**, also run by the King's Head. Accommodation available.

Malt and Anchor 4 Castle St 𝒥 01285 646343 ⊘ maltandanchor.co.uk. Multi-award-winning (National Fish & Chip Awards, including England Fish & Chip Restaurant of the Year 2023) fish and chip venue. MSC-certified sustainable seafood, and an exclusive pilsner lager with sales supporting The Fishermen's Mission.

Organic Farm Shop & Café Abbey Home Farm, Burford Rd GL7 5HF 𝒥 01285 640441 ⊘ theorganicfarmshop.co.uk. Very impressive farm shop selling produce from their own farm. Café serving organic food, inspired by the ten-acre vegetable garden surrounding it. Regular events including willow-weaving workshops, field-to-fork cooking days and wildflower meadow days. Accommodation (self-catering, camping, yurts) available.

Roots + Seeds The Old Kennels, Cirencester Park, GL7 1UR 𝒥 07873 621376 ⊘ rootsandseeds.co.uk. A very pleasant ten-minute walk from the town centre, through the grounds of Cirencester Park (or park at The Old Kennels Car Park for a 50yd walk). Restaurant opened in 2023 serving breakfast, lunch and dinner with all produce (except seafood) grown or reared within a 25-mile radius, including its own kitchen garden, on view. Roots + Seeds Deli opposite the restaurant.

THE EVENLODE VALLEY

The **River Evenlode** is the most easterly of the five Thames tributaries in this locale. Rising close to the town of Moreton-in-Marsh, it flows through a little corner of Gloucestershire before hopping over the county border into Oxfordshire. The river begins to gather pace at **Bledington**, cutting through wolds, dividing the Wychwood villages, skirting the vast – though not as large as it once was – **Wychwood Forest** before meeting up with its own tributary, the **River Glyme** close to **Woodstock**. It discharges into the Thames three miles northwest of Oxford near the village of **Cassington**.

The Evenlode is a relatively modern name for the river, its original title being the River Blade, hence the tiny village of **Bladon** through which the river flows. Powered boats are not allowed on any stretch of the river, so it is constantly peaceful as it drifts between villages save for the odd rumble of a train on the Cotswold Line, which uses the river valley. The beauty of the Evenlode was also immortalised by the Anglo-French poet Hilaire Belloc, who once wrote:

> The tender Evenlode that makes
> Her meadows hush to hear the sound
> Of waters mingling in the brakes,
> And binds my heart to English ground.
>
> A lovely river, all alone,
> She lingers in the hills and holds
> A hundred little towns of stone,
> Forgotten in the western wolds.

The villages are not forgotten now. This is commuter territory for Oxford and London, and houses here are some of the most expensive in the Cotswolds.

15 THE GLOUCESTERSHIRE EVENLODE

From its gentle beginnings in the 'marshes' around Moreton, the Evenlode flows past several villages but not through any one of them. The first, and one of the most peaceful (and beautiful), takes its name from the river. **Evenlode** is a square village with its heart centred around a small triangular village green overlooking the Norman church. Both Evenlode and the next, no less striking, village downstream, **Adlestrop**, lie on the east bank of the river valley, and like the 'tender' river, the land is gentle too, nothing dramatic, just perfect for being simple.

While Hilaire Belloc was writing about the river, Edward Thomas penned one of my favourite poems, his famous ode to the tiny village of Adlestrop. It describes an unremarkable train journey during which the train made an unscheduled stop at Adlestrop station. *Adlestrop* simply describes the sights and peaceful sounds of a summer's day in June 1914, witnessed from the railway carriage while waiting for the traveller's journey to resume. The station, about half a mile from the village, where the A436 crosses the railway line, fell with Beeching's axe in the 1960s, but the classic chocolate and cream railway sign hangs in the bus shelter at the entrance to the village approached from Evenlode. A bench originally on the platform is also there, with a plaque quoting the poem.

Adlestrop is one of those villages that you have to find. Off the beaten track, tucked against the bottom edge of a ridge of hills, it's sheltered from the elements and from stacks of tourists. It's a village definitely worth taking a wander around. Footpaths southwest of the village give views of the string of lakes in Adlestrop Park, though you can also head north on foot along the Macmillan Way, over Adlestrop Hill to Chastleton House (page 149). If, like Edward Thomas, you wish to linger for longer at the old Adlestrop station, **Larkswold Creative Workshops** ($\mathring{\partial}$ larkswold.com) are based at the former stationmaster's

WILD WETLAND AT DAYLESFORD

Daylesford Organic Farm Shop & Café Daylesford GL56 0YG ✐ 01608 731700
$\mathring{\partial}$ daylesford.com.

The air is so hushed, I'd be able to hear a pin drop – were it not for the tall grasses and sedges around me that create a soft pile.

In among the tussocks of meadow grasses are oxeye daisies, regal purple knapweeds and downy thistle heads. A dragonfly darts past over the reeded fen that reflects passing clouds, and a brimstone butterfly. Behind is a thicket of ash, sycamore, hazel, hawthorn, and beech. In front of me, the 'tender' River Evenlode, hiding beyond rosebay willowherb. Then, the soothing lull of cows tearing tufts of grass and the swish of tails.

I'm standing in a 17-acre water meadow on the Daylesford Estate. Daylesford is renowned for its organic credentials, with a huge following of loyal visitors that flock to its public-facing farm shop selling high-quality produce, most produced on the 2,500-acre farm. Few see the phenomenal work that takes place behind the scenes, including the creation of wetland that's proving valuable to the farm's biodiversity and routine conservation efforts – and to the taste of its cheese. I met with Daylesford's Head of Sustainability, Will Dennis, for a privileged tour to learn more about the wetland project and how it fits into the ethos of the wider farm.

The 17-acre field was taken out of rotation on the farm 15 years ago to restore it as a natural wetland area. Right beside the Evenlode, the meadow becomes a filtration system; it both filters and slows down the water flow, helping to prevent flooding in developed areas downstream. Explains Will, 'The meadow has three cycles. In autumn and winter, we allow the field to flood, creating habitat for migrating waders and ground-nesting peri-aquatic birds (ones that like to nest in wetland areas). The flooding house, where you can spend a few hours crafting while gazing out at the water meadows around the Evenlode. Workshops cover all types of art and crafts, from woodworking and ceramics to pen and ink or textiles.

Just south of Adlestrop, right on the county border, is **Daylesford**, the house and park once the home of Warren Hastings, the first Governor General of India and a large figure in the making of the British Empire. Daylesford today, though, is known for organic food, with the estate providing much of the produce for **Daylesford Organic Farm Shop**. It's far more than your average farm shop and the estate takes sustainability and the environment very seriously (see below). There's a cookery school on site, foodie and lifestyle events almost daily, farm visits, a café and restaurant and an organic spa. Food from the estate, however, remains the core focus, and it is sublime.

also channels nutrient-rich sediment into the grasses and reeds.

'In spring, the meadow is drained, leaving a diverse patchwork habitat of grasses and wildflowers that support a smorgasbord of insects for our summer visitors like martins and swallows. Then, in summer, our Gloucester cattle arrive on-site from neighbouring fields, giving them a richly nutritious pasture to graze.

'Wetlands like ours are an example of progressive farming in which the productivity of the land benefits grazing cattle and sheep, and they in turn enhance the meadow habitat for the species that rely upon it. We have counted more than 80 species of birds, including osprey, sparrowhawk, snipe, teal and mallard.'

As for the small herd of Gloucester cattle, a local native breed (and, with only 700 left in the UK, one of the rarest), their milk is used for Daylesford's Single Gloucester cheese, made in the creamery less than half a mile from the wetland meadow. Single Gloucester is a 'protected' (PDO; Protected Designation of Origin) full-fat hard cheese – it can only be made using the milk from the Gloucester breed and within the county. Says Will, 'I think the Single Gloucester cheese has a richer flavour after the cows have been grazing on the water meadow, thanks to the diversity of the nutrient-rich pasture.'

The cattle, alarmingly horned but reassuringly docile, look up, mouths rolling, as we pass. A quick, inquisitive glance, then they return to the rituals of grazing, and the soft sound of tugging at grass.

Note: To protect its biodiversity, the wetland area is not routinely open to the public. Look out for events at Daylesford that give behind-the-scenes insight, such as producers' lunches, tours of the market garden, cookery masterclasses, and floristry courses inspired by nature and the farm meadows.

West of the river lie the villages of first Broadwell and then the Oddingtons. **Broadwell** straddles a ford, the shallow waters making their way into the Evenlode, and many of the classic Cotswold cottages, farmhouses and stone barns are focused around a large green. As a reminder of the heady days when it was a 'wool village' owned by prosperous sheep farmers, its churchyard has a series of unusual 'wool-bale' tombs (there are others at Burford), where the tops look like strands of the very textile that created prosperity for the area. A pub completes the picture.

Broadwell needs time to be properly explored, especially if you're going to while away a few hours on the village green or dabble in the stream, but once satisfied that you've discovered every nook, take a stroll across the fields to the Oddingtons. **Upper Oddington** sits on two banks facing one another and while very attractive doesn't quite match its counterpart, **Lower Oddington**. From the village take a quick detour to the 'Church in the Woods'. The 11th-century St Nicholas Church is atmospheric enough simply for its lonesome location, buried in the surrounding woodland and along a no-through road. But inside the limestone walls are frescoed with a medieval Day of Judgement wall painting. It's so faint that the beige stencil-like artwork appears like an apparition seeping through the wall.

Two miles southeast is **Bledington**, the most easterly village in Gloucestershire. It's a village of two halves, with unremarkable recent 20th-century housing developments closest to the river – the county boundary – and the more attractive old part of the village housed around a green frequented by ducks that occasionally waddle to the little stream running through on its way to the Evenlode. The renowned Kings Head Inn provides the perfect backdrop and summer days will find locals and visitors strewn across the green enjoying the sunshine and the pastoral idyll.

ᵞ¶ FOOD & DRINK

Several pubs in the area are known either as the Fox Inn or the Fox and Hounds, showing variously the countryside's reverence for this creature or its past association with fox hunting.

Daylesford Organic Farm Shop & Café Daylesford GL56 0YG ☏ 01608 731700 ⌖ daylesford.com. The farm shop is renowned countrywide for its excellent produce, most of which comes from the estate, including fruit and veg from its market garden, cheese made in its creamery, breads, pastries and cakes from its bakery, and meat and poultry from the farm. There's a choice of café eating spaces (collectively awarded a Michelin Green Star), serving first-class breakfasts, lunches and occasional evening meals – all using produce from the estate.

Fox Inn Broadwell 🕿 01451 832134 🌐 thefoxbroadwell.com. Traditional village pub, owned by Donnington Brewery, in a great location overlooking the village green. Comfort food that's not pompously gastronomic and well-kept Donnington ales. Local produce a speciality.

Fox Inn Lower Oddington 🕿 01451 767000 🌐 thefoxatoddington.com. Under the Daylesford stable, all the requisites of a Cotswold country pub (flagstone floors, low ceilings and beams, log fire, comfy chairs, sunny courtyard garden) sensitively restored to minimise environmental impact (sheep's wool insulation and cattle hide from the Daylesford estate to make the leather seating; crockery made locally). Plenty of good food with a daily menu using produce from the Daylesford estate. Excellent accommodation too.

Kings Head Inn Bledington 🕿 01608 658365 🌐 kingsheadinn.net. An old cider house overlooking the village green and stream, a pub that is almost too perfect to be true. Superb atmosphere and a nice mix of regulars and locals, fine old furnishings and thoughtfully prepared food. Very attractive accommodation.

16 KINGHAM & CHURCHILL

When, 20 years ago, **Kingham** was judged by *Country Life* magazine as 'England's favourite village', it started attracting those looking for the right town and country balance – a quiet retreat in the countryside with a railway station nearby to make a quick exit to London. But, with its blend of thatched- and slate-roofed houses and village green, it has been something of a rural idyll long before celebrity musicians moved in or fever-pitch journalism made it known to the outside world.

Its near neighbour **Churchill** is further east, on an incline that makes its pinnacled church tower stand out for miles. However, this is 'modern' – since 1700 – Churchill, the old village was ravaged by fire on the lower slopes of the hill. Only the old church remains, where a **heritage centre** (🕿 01608 658603 🌐 churchillheritage.org.uk) is now explaining the history of the village and its two best-known sons William Smith, who created the first-ever geological maps of England and Wales, and the colonial administrator Warren Hastings (page 245). Close to the 'new' church in the village is an unusual-looking fountain with obelisks and flying buttresses, presented to the village in memory of the landowner who once owned the surrounding estates.

🍴 FOOD & DRINK

Kingham is fortunate to have two foodie pubs, both on the map for being at the forefront of gastronomic excellence.

Kingham Plough Kingham ☎ 01608 658327 ⌖ thekinghamplough.co.uk. Overlooking the village green, which is shaded by trees. Run by Matt and Katie Beamish (who also own The Crown Inn at Church Enstone and, nearby, The Hare at Milton-under-Wychwood), there's generous helpings of bar food and a changing restaurant menu with seasonal ingredients from farms and smallholdings within the Cotswolds and everything prepared in-house. Excellent accommodation, too.

Wild Rabbit Kingham ☎ 01608 658389 ⌖ thewildrabbit.co.uk. Part of the Daylesford (page 245) stable. Large Georgian farmhouse with comfortable, homely dining and drinking areas both inside and out. Theatre kitchen to watch the chefs at work using seasonal produce gathered daily from the Daylesford estate and other British farms.

17 THE WESTCOTES & FIFIELD

🏠 Bruern Farms

Just west of the villages of **Church Westcote** and **Nether Westcote** (whose hillside positions give commanding views over the Evenlode Valley) is Brookfield Ostrich Farm, home to the painter Irene Tyack and her **Yellow Hat Tribe Gallery** (OX7 6SJ ☎ 01993 832042). Her bold and vibrant paintings, depicting her little brigade of yellow-brimmed figures – you never see their faces – in all manner of environments bring vitality to any wall and have attracted a cult following. Irene is often in the gallery painting, so you can watch as she works while you browse the paintings and associated gift items. Says Irene, 'I love my little characters dearly. They have become a part of my life and I'm always thinking up new situations for them to be in. I bring out a new themed collection every year; the next setting will be the Caribbean, following a holiday I had there.' I like *Scarlett Fields*, a Cotswold scene of green hills, poppy fields and a little yellow-hat character sat among the poppies.

There are so many tiny villages in this area that rarely get a mention because of the few facilities (such as a pub) that they can offer tourists, and yet really shouldn't be missed – hamlets such as **Foscot**, **Idbury**, **Icomb** and **Sarsden**. These are the real Cotswold settlements, untouched by coach tours and gift shops. One such place is **Fifield**. It only takes 15 minutes to wander round the block – it is a rectangular-shaped village on a hillside with stone houses lining the four roads and, in the middle, St John the Baptist Church with a slender octagonal tower, unusual for the area, with spire. The D'Arcy Dalton Way runs through, which you can use to reach the **Foxholes Nature Reserve** close to the River Evenlode to the east. The 158 acres of woodland, known for its spring bluebells, grassland and wetlands, were once a part of the ancient Wychwood Forest. It takes a bit of finding but do persevere. Here you can listen to the numerous birds or look out for flora on the waymarked wildlife walks and permissive footpaths. Oaks, beech, silver birch and sallow tower above as does the sea of woodland ferns. The reserve can also be reached by car; there's a small layby on the Bruern Abbey road, and then a 500yd walk to reach it. To gain an overview of the reserve, the footpath connecting Idbury with Fifield offers hilltop views; it's extremely pretty with autumn colours.

For an alternative walk, one of the prettiest routes is to use the Oxfordshire Way through Gawcombe (just a handful of farm buildings), across the Westcote Brook to Bledington, where you can enjoy a drink at the Kings Head Inn. The easy-walking footpath takes you over the open meadows of the valley giving a sense of total seclusion.

🧳 SPECIAL STAYS

Bruern Farms Bruern ✆ 07966 437258 ◈ bruernfarms.co.uk. Quirky accommodation in an old grain silo that has been converted to offer space for six people with two en-suite double bedrooms and a sofa bed. Kitchen and living room plus outdoor garden. On a farm where biodiversity and community are at the heart. Excellent farm shop and café also on-site, serving breakfasts, lunch and cakes using produce from the farm (own venison, meat and flour) and other local producers. Lunch menu includes lamb tagine or the farm's venison sausages and mash. Lovely setting. And the blueberry flapjack is divine!

🍴 FOOD & DRINK

In addition to **Bruern Farm Shop & Café** (see above):

Feathered Nest Country Inn Nether Westcote ✆ 01993 833030 ◈ thefeatherednestinn. co.uk. This pub, completely rebuilt from an old malthouse, opened in 2010. It has won multiple awards since. Gastro-pub food with three AA Rosettes and everything, including the butter, made on the premises; open for lunch, high-quality afternoon teas and dinner. Cosy accommodation also available. Amazing views over the Evenlode Valley from the flower-filled gardens.

18 THE WYCHWOODS & CHARLBURY

In the 11th century the Wychwood Royal Hunting Forest covered much of west Oxfordshire. While it is a forest by legal definition rather than exclusively covered in trees, there is no doubt that much of the ancient woodland was steadily felled to make way for sheep pastures for the wool trade (names with 'assarts' indicate where). Several villages were already established, their names reflecting their woodland location: **Milton-under-**, **Shipton-under-** and **Ascott-under-Wychwood**. Between Milton and Shipton is the **Wychwood Wild Garden** (⌂ wychwoodwildgarden.org.uk), 12.5 acres of woodland owned by a local charity with a network of paths following a line of ponds and plenty of wildlife. It was originally a pleasure garden belonging to the Elizabethan Shipton Court, the impressive building that you cannot miss through the decorative gates alongside the A361.

Having flowed south since its source, the river turns east at Shipton and makes a wide, sweeping curve in which sits most of the remaining chunk of the Wychwood Forest. Some 1,700 acres of the forest come under **Cornbury Park**, where the former royal hunting lodge is, now a private house on folded, hilly ground. Deer roam free through the woodland and more open parkland, and provide many of the pubs and restaurants in the area with fresh venison. A public footpath and permissive cycle route runs through the estate, crossing a chain of six lakes which feed into the Evenlode. Park in the village of Finstock and take the footpath into the estate opposite the old chapel, on the Charlbury Road. Cornbury Park is also the venue for the annual **Wilderness Festival** (⌂ wildernessfestival.com). More than just a family summer music festival, there are talks and debates, theatre and arts, forest school and outdoor activities that make the most of the secluded surroundings like wild swimming, e-bike safaris and off-grid adventures in the woods. The festival is all about wellbeing and you'll find yoga classes and mindfulness sessions just as at home as hula-hooping for kids. There's scenic camping by the lakes and even an open-air lakeside spa.

As the river curves back round to continue its more easterly path, it skirts the very edge of pale-stone **Charlbury**, a very charming

---

1 The grand house and vast grounds of Blenheim Palace. **2** Building dry-stone walls with the Wychwood Forest Trust. **3** Thatched cottages in Kingham. **4** Daylesford Organic Farm Shop is known for its excellent produce. ▶

BLENHEIM PALACE/EXPERIENCE OXFORDSHIRE

CAROLINE MILLS

ANDREW ROLAND/D

DAYLESFORD ORGANIC

WYCHWOOD FOREST TRUST

The annual **Wychwood Forest Fair** celebrates the history, diversity and conservation of this area of countryside. It is organised by **Wychwood Forest Trust** (⌂ wychwoodforesttrust.co.uk), a charitable community organisation that helps to conserve, restore and plant new sections of the Wychwood Forest. The team are always looking for volunteers to help with conservation efforts on the Trust's six nature reserves, including Singe Wood (page 14), which has species of fungi found nowhere else in Oxfordshire, Wigwell Nature Reserve in Charlbury (page 250), Foxburrow Wood (site of the annual Wychwood Forest Fair) and the most recently acquired legacy, Gibbets Close Hill, a grassland site near Witney (page 217).

Maeve Bradbury, Development Manager for the Trust explained, 'We have joined up with Oxford University on a long-term project, monitoring our conservation efforts on Gibbets Close Hill, a piece of one-time degraded land, looking at natural succession versus deliberate planting. From the research project, we can determine which approach works best on this wonderful reserve with its amazing views.'

small market town on the valley hillside, filled with narrow lanes of rose-clambering cottages and grander Georgian houses along central Market Street. The town is home to the free **Riverside Festival** (⌂ riversidefestival.charlbury.com), held in summer on the Mill Field island, just to the west of town.

Charlbury is a lovely base from which to explore the Oxfordshire Cotswolds, either on foot, with the Oxfordshire Way passing through the town and the Wychwood Way close by (a useful way to get to neighbouring Stonesfield, page 253, and **Ramsden**, another of the Cotswolds forgotten-but-you-won't-be-disappointed villages). You can download details of three cycle rides from the Charlbury Community Website (⌂ charlbury.info), including the Wychwood Loop and two linear routes that utilise the Cotswold Line.

¶¶ FOOD & DRINK

Bull Inn Sheep St, Charlbury ✆ 01608 656957 ⌂ thebullcharlbury.com. A 16th-century freehouse with plenty of charm in the centre of town. Inventive menu, with dishes often cooked over a flame grill, using produce direct from farmers and growers. Cosy accommodation.

Café de la Post Chadlington ✆ 01608 676461 ⌂ cafedelapost.com. Village shop and welcoming café serving homemade food in the old post office. *Plat du jour* Friday nights and pizza nights on Saturdays. Wine nights and selling local Evenlode Gin. Also Café de la Gare at Charlbury railway station.

Lamb Inn Shipton-under-Wychwood ✂ 01993 832116 ✂ thelambshipton.com. Fine wines and well-kept beers. Extensive à la carte menu with small plates (buttermilk-fried chicken and aioli), starters and mains (calf's liver, onion gravy, mash, crispy bacon). Quite pricey but freshly prepared using seasonal produce direct from farmers, and game.

Royal Oak Ramsden ✂ 01993 868213 ✂ royaloakramsden.com. Former 17th-century coaching inn that was completely restored in 2020. Loads of character, including wood and flag floors, an oak-framed conservatory and courtyard garden. Relaxed dining (Malaysian pork bite with satay sauce; chargrilled Cajun aubergine steak; thyme-poached Kent apricots). Accommodation including the six-person Stable (love the handmade bunk beds).

Tite Inn Chadlington ✂ 01608 676910 ✂ thetiteinn.co.uk. Hillside pub with a very pretty terraced garden, which makes the most of Chadlington Ale, brewed less than a mile away. Starters include Charlbury Shed sourdough & smoked whipped lardo, and mains the homemade Tite Inn beefburger.

19 STONESFIELD & WOODSTOCK

Stonesfield was once one of the most important villages in the Cotswolds, providing some of the highest-quality roofing materials for buildings in the area, including many Oxford colleges. Stonesfield slate is not like a grey Welsh slate but slabs of Jurassic limestone known as pendle. As a sedimentary rock the limestone splits into slate-like pieces in frosty conditions, providing the stone is kept damp. Traditionally it was quarried or mined from Michaelmas until the end of January and, once dug out, would be covered with earth to keep it moist until a frost was imminent; the church bells would toll when a frost was expected. Many years ago, I had the chance to go into one of the Stonesfield slate mines where I had to crawl on hands and feet along the mine's cramped passages. Given that the workers toiled throughout the winter months, the work must have been tough in the extreme.

Evidence of Roman occupation in this area is apparent in many places but in particular, on the opposite side of the river from Stonesfield, there are the remains of **North Leigh Roman Villa** close to the riverbank. The ankle-high foundations of this aristocratic courtyard villa are pretty much all that remain (the location and the walk to it, with views over the Evenlode Valley and wooded cliffs behind, are phenomenal) except for its most special feature, a near-complete mosaic tiled floor. A grand statement, much of the house was once patterned with mosaic pavements and tessellated floors. This particular mosaic floor was in a formal reception room, and its geometric designs reveal intricate craftsmanship. The mosaic is protected from the elements by an unprepossessing but rather endearing corrugated-roofed building, which is opened occasionally. However, giant picture windows allow you to see the mosaic clearly at all times. Entrance is free, with access only from a knobbly footpath (not suitable for wheelchairs) 550yds from the road, just west of the village of East End. There's a lay-by for cars to park opposite the footpath.

Nearby **Combe** has a large central green upon which centuries-old seasonal festivities take place such as maypole dancing in spring and a summer fete. The charming village, filled with houses of slender mottled stone, is considered one of the most attractive in Oxfordshire. Take your pint from the Cock Inn (closed for refurbishment at time of publication, so do check prior to arrival) overlooking the village green and enjoy the tranquil atmosphere for a while. Look out for the majestic cedar of Lebanon, just to the east of the village green, close to the church.

My husband once worked on the Blenheim Estate (helping to build the timber bridges in the maze at the Pleasure Gardens) and he took me to see Notoaks Wood, a woodland on the estate that he planted over 30 years ago just to the west of Combe. Unsurprisingly, he commented that 'you'd hardly recognise it now', except for the excessive number of pheasants that appreciate the cover. 'They were there even when we planted.' He commented on planting up Combe Cliff with trees too, a mini Cotswold escarpment that lines the Evenlode Valley south of the village, and prominent from the river. 'It's so steep that we could barely stand up; we needed ropes to climb down and hold on as we planted.'

"The charming village, filled with houses of slender mottled stone, is considered one of the most attractive in Oxfordshire."

To the east of Combe is the small market town of **Woodstock**. It has been a popular place with tourists ever since the 18th century, with the building of adjacent Blenheim Palace and the subsequent arrival of wealthy guests attending engagements there. The town became a market for finery and a glovemaking industry took off. The history of Woodstock and the county is recollected at the admirable **Oxfordshire Museum** on the High Street, which charts everything that makes Oxfordshire what it is, from the geology of the area to Oxfordshire-based inventions. Free to enter, it has regular activities, many specifically aimed at children, and changing exhibitions. A pleasant rose garden at the rear provides a quiet place to sit for a cup of tea. The museum also provides a small visitor information centre where you can pick up a leaflet outlining the Woodstock Town Walk and historic stone wall plaques to locate. If you can't pick up a leaflet, I recommend a quick circular jaunt from Park Street along Chaucer's Lane, then Harrison's Lane, Brown Lane, through

A walk around Blenheim's Great Park

❋ OS Explorer map 180; start: Oxfordshire Museum, ♀ SP444167; approximately 4½ miles; easy

A visit to Blenheim Palace, a UNESCO World Heritage Site, easily takes up more than a day to do it justice if you're visiting the house and formal gardens alone, but the estate also includes 2,000 acres of parkland to explore. You can purchase a ticket for the park, allowing you to wander anywhere, or use a little-known entrance from the town and explore using the numerous public footpaths that criss-cross the estate.

The footpaths across the Great Park give outstanding views of the palace and vistas of the lake that Capability Brown was appointed to create. It gives the opportunity to get away from the crowds and the coaches that hang around the house and formal gardens – the majority of visitors don't step out into the park at all – and you'll find many delightfully peaceful spots to sit. Do bear in mind that the estate is private property and without an entrance ticket you must stick to the public footpaths. This circular walk through the Great Park begins outside the Oxfordshire Museum on the High Street in the centre of Woodstock.

With your back to the museum, walk right and turn right down Chancery Lane to Hoggrove Hill, a footpath. On reaching the main road, turn left along the Causeway where you see a green gate that looks like a private drive. Pass through this and the next green gate and you're in the grounds of Blenheim Palace.

Follow the track round to the right, which is a part of the Wychwood Way. There will be initial views across to the palace over Queen's Pool on your left. Continue along the track between the steep banks and make a 90-degree turn between the two rows of lime trees. This is one of the main symmetrical vistas with the palace behind you and the Ditchley Gate entrance far in the distance in front of you.

Pass over two cattle crossings and turn left at the second field boundary (marked with a fence). This is Akeman Street, the old Roman road that passes from St Albans to Cirencester and forms a part of the Wychwood and Oxfordshire ways. ▶

A walk around Blenheim's Great Park (continued)

◀ As you enter the first woodland, turn left and walk along the wooded track for approximately 500yds – look out for a small yellow footpath sign on the left (it's not that well signposted), which will take you out of the wood. Walk along the field perimeter towards another small woodland. With this next wood directly in front of you, turn left for approximately 100yds until you meet up with a metalled track. Turn right and pass through a strip of woodland before crossing the field through two kissing gates. Do not follow the metalled track around that leads to Park Farm on your right.

Through the second kissing gate, turn right and skirt round a small clump of trees. Continue until you come to the entrance of Park Farm. Follow the metalled track round to the left and where the track forks, turn back on yourself, following one track downhill. Continue until you have an open valley on your left and trees straight ahead. Turn left along the side of the valley. This is now one of the most secluded parts of the park.

At the end of the valley, with a steep bank on your left, turn left through a kissing gate and follow the path alongside the lake. From here as the ground rises slightly you will get views across the lake of the palace and the Grand Bridge.

Continue along the lakeside, past Fair Rosamund's Well and, with the Grand Bridge on your right, turn left when you reach the metalled track.

Continue for approximately half a mile along the track and at the cattle crossing turn right, over a stile. Follow along the fence until you reach the Column of Victory, erected shortly after the first duke's death. Pass by the column on your left and cross the rest of the field through the trees. Cross the stile and turn left for a short distance until you reach the small house on your right.

Follow the road around to your right (the first one that you came along when you entered the grounds) until you reach the green gate. You are now back where you entered the grounds to the Great Park. Retrace your steps back to the town centre.

the churchyard and then turn right to Rectory Lane, which will bring you back to your starting point.

Blenheim Palace

Woodstock OX20 1PP ℰ 0800 849 6500 ⊘ blenheimpalace.com

Brushing up against Woodstock is the huge **Blenheim Estate**, in the middle of which is Blenheim Palace, the seat of the Duke of Marlborough, aka the Spencer-Churchill family. We're currently on duke number 12, but it was the first duke who was granted the building of the house as

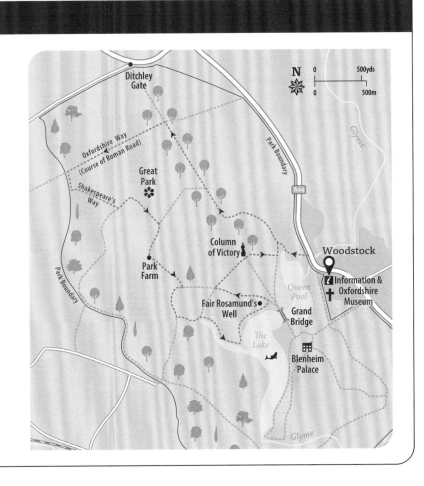

a gift from Queen Anne following his heroic victory over the French at the Battle of Blenheim in 1704. The hour of triumph is commemorated in one of the palace's finest treasures, the Blenheim Tapestry, just one of ten 'Victory' woven masterpieces.

The house is itself a masterpiece of Baroque, grand in scale and with all the pomp and stature inside and out that you'd expect from a symbol of victory. In 1874 Sir Winston Churchill was born here, an unexpectedly early arrival while his mother was visiting relations. It's also where he later proposed to his wife. There is a large, permanent exhibition on his life and work focused around the room in which he was born. Churchill, together with his wife and parents, is buried in the churchyard in the neighbouring village of **Bladon** (page 243), all their gravestones facing towards the Blenheim Estate.

While the house and grounds – including the Grand Bridge – were originally designed by the now celebrated, but at the time unqualified, John Vanbrugh, under the watchful eye of Nicholas Hawksmoor, the 2,000-acre grounds were later landscaped by Capability Brown. He created the two large lakes through which the River Glyme, a tributary of the Evenlode, flows; the two rivers meet on the estate.

ᵞᵞ FOOD & DRINK

Crown High St, Woodstock ☏ 01993 813339 ⊘ thecrownwoodstock.com. Modern interior combining touches of the traditional stone building. Watch pizzas being made with the wood-fired oven. Breakfast also served and accommodation available.

Orangery Restaurant Blenheim Palace. A beautiful, lofty and grand building within which to have elevenses, lunch or a decadent afternoon tea with freshly made sandwiches and a cake stand of homemade cakes, scones and petit fours. Only available with an entrance ticket to Blenheim but pre-booked tables are possible.

Woodstock Butchers/Grocers St, Woodstock ☏ 01993 812002/815955 ⊘ woodstockshops.co.uk. Fresh lamb and beef from the Blenheim Estate plus pork and chicken from farms in the Cotswolds. **Woodstock Grocers**, on the opposite side of the street, is a traditional greengrocers, a rare site in the Cotswolds, offering seasonal fruit and veg.

Woodstock Arms Market St, Woodstock ☏ 01993 811251 ⊘ thewoodstockarms.com. Very cosy central pub that's full of character and features. Breakfast, lunch and dinner (pea & mint soup; kiln-roasted salmon) available. Accommodation available.

Books for Mindful Travel

Bradt GUIDES

TRAVEL TAKEN SERIOUSLY

bradtguides.com/shop

BradtGuides @BradtGuides @bradtguides

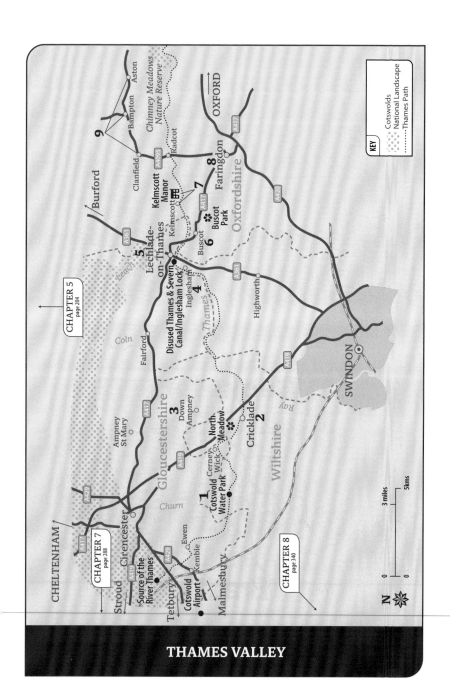

THAMES VALLEY

6
THAMES VALLEY

Where do you immediately think of as the Thames Valley? Reading, Goring, Marlow or Windsor, perhaps? The phrase has been usurped to represent a particular region between Oxford and London for politics, policy and organisation. How about Kemble, Cerney Wick or Inglesham? The true Thames Valley begins in rural Gloucestershire, 53 miles west of Oxford.

It's hard to imagine the source of the Thames being anywhere other than where it actually is, but the debate over its location divided opinion for many years and was even discussed in the House of Commons in 1937. Officially, the Thames Head is close to the Fosse Way between the villages of Coates and **Kemble**, a mile south of Cirencester. It remains dry for much of the year – though I've waded through in winter wellie boots occasionally, I've never seen it so much as trickle from the ground here most months of the year – while the source of the River Churn, at Seven Springs southeast of Cheltenham, could actually be the Thames's true source. It never dries up and, being longer to the confluence than the Thames, should theoretically be the main river.

It would be a brave soul to suggest change either to its route or its name now. The Thames is part of the British psyche. From the river's gentlest of beginnings, it seeps through the village of **Ewen** before winding through the old gravel pits that more recently have become the **Cotswold Water Park**. It soon gains water and is most definitely a reasonable stream when it reaches the edge of **Cricklade**, the first town on its journey. From there the river passes through flat open countryside with few villages to get in its way as if with a burning desire to become larger, fuller and more self-confident once the tributaries of the Coln and the Leach add to its stature. By the time it passes through **Lechlade-on-Thames**, the first town to bear its name, the river is navigable. Small marinas appear and the first of the locks, **St John's Lock**, is just east of the town where the reclining figure of **Old Father Thames** proudly watches over his adolescent child. Both Cricklade and Lechlade are Cotswold gems that often get overlooked by tourists concentrating on the big-name towns.

Within a few miles the river has all but left its Cotswold roots behind, passing through open vales rather than a valley lined with hills. Only when it comes close to Oxford does it show any signs of being a Cotswold river again, passing by suitably Cotswold-esque architecture, but by now the river has grown up, left its youthful home behind and continues its 215-mile journey to the North Sea as an adult responsible for grown-up boats and beautifying the grounds of dazzling, upmarket riverside properties. This chapter focuses solely on its youthful beginnings, until its meeting with the River Windrush (page 207) and the charmingly named National Nature Reserve, Chimney Meadows, once the river has passed by the **Buscot Estate** and **Kelmscott Manor**, the home of William Morris.

GETTING THERE & AROUND

The only **train** station hereabouts is at Kemble, though with this being right on the western edge of the locale, the station at Swindon is closer to some of the places mentioned in this chapter (Lechlade, Buscot and Kelmscott). **Great Western Railway** (⊘ gwr.com) operates trains from London, the southwest, Wales and the north via Birmingham New Street to Swindon. The station at Kemble is a spur between Gloucester and Swindon, so changes at either of these stations are likely. Kemble is the best station for walks close to the source of the river, along the Thames Path.

A frequent (at least hourly) **bus** service runs between Cirencester and Swindon stopping at South Cerney and Cricklade, while Lechlade is a stop on the Swindon to Fairford route. Cirencester and Lechlade also link up. However, as these bus services tend to stick to main roads, outlying villages are less well served. A bus service from Cirencester to Tetbury and Malmesbury stops at Kemble (including the railway station), useful for those wishing to reach the source of the Thames or walk along the Thames Path.

The obvious choice for **walkers** here is the long-distance Thames Path. Approximately 36 miles of the 184-mile footpath run through this area; this makes a good walking weekend, by breaking the journey into two and stopping at Cricklade and Lechlade or Kelmscott.

For those keen on **cycling** around the area, the Sustrans **National Cycle Network Route 45** runs from Cirencester to Cricklade. From South Cerney, 2½ miles south of Cirencester, the route is entirely traffic-free, using a disused railway line and passing through the Cotswold Water Park. It's all very flat and easy wheeling.

Elsewhere in the water park, cycling is useful for getting from A to B but the landscape is not particularly conducive to a really scenic bike ride, as most of the lakes are surrounded by tall hedges. In essence, this locale is great for level terrain but not the finest for amazing views.

 BIKE HIRE

Various companies offer bike hire throughout Cotswold Water Park including: **Discover Bikes** (⌀ discoverbikes.co.uk) at the Gateway Visitor Centre and Summer Lake; and **Bainton Bikes** (baintonbikes.com), at Lake 6 on Spine Road (East). The latter is self-service 24/7, using an app. Options of road and MTBs, e-bikes, child bikes/tag-along trailers, and tandems. Discover Bikes also offers repairs and service.

THE SOURCE – KEMBLE & EWEN TO CRICKLADE

I remember once, as quite a young girl, being driven past the vast RAF aerodrome at Kemble and, in one of those naive excitable childhood moments without concept of monetary value, wanting to buy it because I was told that it was threatened with closure and the Red Arrows display team, with which I was fascinated, would have to leave its base. The airfield was worth millions and I probably had little more than 50 pence pocket money saved.

The airfield has been renamed, rather grandly, as **Cotswold Airport** (⌀ cotswoldairport.com) and is now used by corporate jets looking to avoid the queues at major airports, as well as flying schools where you can take a pleasure flight and helicopters offering sightseeing tours. It's also a graveyard for decommissioned jumbos; from several miles away you can't help but notice the enormous tail fins of these monsters sticking up from the treeline. You pass right by the airfield on the Fosse Way.

But to view aircraft up close, visitors are welcome at the AV8 restaurant and sun terrace, where you can enjoy a meal while watching the flying manoeuvures; the restaurant has unrivalled views of the runway. There's also the opportunity to look inside the world's only complete **Bristol Britannia**, which also happened to be the world's first long-haul airliner, making record-breaking non-stop flights to Canada and the United States in 1957. Fully restored by a dedicated group of volunteers, open days to view the aircraft take place on selected weekends, with specific dates indicated at ⊘ xm496.com. The former British Airways Boeing 747 'Negus' (⊘ negus747.com), can also be visited for tours of the cabin and cockpit.

The source of the Thames is a few fields away from the airfield's perimeter fence. It's hard to tell simply by driving along the Fosse Way from Cirencester to Kemble that you are close to the source. There's rarely any water. Barely even a snake of sunken ground that suggests a river, and no sign or large arrow on the roadside that says, 'Source of the River Thames – this way'. Its official source is northwest of the Fosse Way, a mile from Cirencester in a far-flung meadow that you can reach only on foot. No car park, no fanfare, just a stone marking the spot.

The countryside is gentle and relatively flat here. The river, what there is of it now, bypasses the modernised village of Kemble, expanded owing to its proximity to the railway, and the linear village of Ewen. It's barely recognisable as a stream until it reaches the Cotswold Water Park.

1 COTSWOLD WATER PARK

Cotswold Water Park Information Centre Spine Rd East, South Cerney GL7 5TL
⊘ waterpark.org

Covering over 40 square miles of countryside, the Cotswold Water Park was once an area buzzing with heavy industry, extracting sand and gravel. Since the 1890s, when the first pits were dug to provide ballast for railway-line construction (in the 1960s aggregate from here was also used to build the M4 motorway), more than 150 lakes have been created. Owing to the high water table, any hole that was dug greater in depth than 12 inches would rapidly fill with water. Early forms of extraction would leave gravel behind beneath the water surface but the methods used have ultimately created havens for aquatic plants and a great habitat for insects, feeding bats and nesting birds. With relatively shallow, uneven-bottomed lakes that have irregular shorelines and several islands, much of the park looks like a natural part of the landscape rather than something entirely manmade.

However, don't expect to see much of the park simply by winding the car window down while driving along the roads that criss-cross between the lakes. Most lakes are surrounded by dense trees, and you'll see little of them without walking, cycling or, better still, getting onto the water. Each lake has a distinct 'use'. Some are used simply as a scenic backdrop to holiday lodges and houses, accessed only by residents. Others are specifically for various watersports such as sailing or for angling. But there are many lakes left to nature for migrating birds and wildlife projects that attract endangered species such as the water vole.

There are two sections to the water park – one between Fairford and Lechlade known as the eastern section, while the western section, the larger of the two, is concentrated around the villages of South Cerney, Somerford Keynes, Ashton Keynes and Cerney Wick.

For many visitors to the area, the first stop is the park's **Gateway Centre**, close to the A419. Centrally located between the two sections of park, it is like the nerve centre and is a useful stopping point to pick up free maps of the area from the Visitor Information Centre on-site, run jointly by the Cotswold Lakes Trust and Cotswold Canals Trust, use the facilities and sit in the rather pleasant eco-friendly green oak-framed building, which houses a café, overlooking one of the lakes. There's a convenient pizzeria on site – the views across 'Lake 6' (every lake has a number) are idyllic – and a very good, large branch of the Cotswold Outdoor chain, useful for picking up outdoor-activity clothing and gear. Also here is bike hire from Discover Bikes (page 263), where you can scan a QR code for directions to a selection of circular bike rides.

"In the summer it is the grass that is awash with electric blue damselflies, which have really taken to the area."

Numerous footpaths cut between the lakes, including the Thames Path National Trail, so there are plenty of opportunities to create a circular walk lasting a few hundred yards or several miles. One of the most pleasant is a simple walk around the **Neigh Bridge Country Park** in the west of the western section, close to the village of Somerford Keynes. It's an easy stroll along a path that surrounds one of the more secluded lakes and there are large lakeside areas suitable for picnics. It's also one of the best places in the water park to view wildlife. There's plenty of birdlife on the water, with winter migrants and spring breeders, but in the summer it is the grass that is awash with electric blue damselflies, which have really taken to the area. If driving, the car park for Neigh Bridge is accessed off the main arterial Spine Road.

Other places to spot wildlife within the western section of the park include Lower Moor Farm Nature Reserve, Shorncote Reed Bed, Coke's Pit Nature Reserve and Swillbrook Lakes Nature Reserve, the last a place to listen to nightingales. The park is renowned for birdwatching and is internationally important for migrating winter waterbirds.

The **Cotswold Lakes Trust** (⌀ waterpark.org) is responsible for the conservation of the area, working to improve biodiversity. The Trust organises events throughout the year including wildlife walks with field officers, fossil hunts and wildlife talks by distinguished speakers. They also hold regular volunteer days when anyone can muck in and help with conservation tasks.

ACTIVITIES WITHIN THE COTSWOLD WATER PARK

There are many different activities based around the water park, with numerous sailing clubs, watersports centres, 'boat' (in every shape and form) hire, birdwatching trips, etc. These provide merely a taste but you can discover more at the Gateway Visitor Centre.

Cotswold Country Park and Beach Spratsgate Lane ⌀ 01285 868096 ⌀ cotswoldcountryparkandbeach.com. Situated around two large lakes, the park includes the UK's largest inland beach with swimming lagoon. AquaVenture inflatable waterpark, hire of SUPs, kayaks, electric and rowing boats. Lakeside barbecue hire.

Cotswold Forest School ⌀ 01285 860867 ⌀ cotswoldforestschool.co.uk. Five acres of native woodland used for exciting outdoor activities, aimed particularly at children, such as woodland survival skills, camp craft, den building and woodland art. Workshops last for one day. Expect to get grubby.

Lakeside Ski & Wake Spring Lake ⌀ 01285 860606 ⌀ lakeside-ski.co.uk. Introductory wakeboarding and waterski sessions plus fun inflatable water rides.

South Cerney Outdoor Spine Rd ⌀ 01285 860388 ⌀ southcerneyoutdoor.co.uk. Sailing, windsurfing, kayaking, canoeing and stand-up paddleboarding, plus, on land, a high-ropes

1 & 2 Cotswold Water Park is an excellent habitat for birds – while also offering watersports, such as paddleboarding at South Cerney Outdoor Centre. **3** The stained-glass window in Down Ampney's All Saints' Church, commemorating 150 years since Ralph Vaughan Williams' birth. **4** Step inside the cockpit of a 1950s airliner at Cotswold Airport. ▶

COTSWOLDS.COM

ADRIAN BALCH

CAROLINE MILLS

course. Bring your own equipment for pay-and-play sessions, or get involved in taster experiences, holiday activities and courses for children/adults.

Tackle Den Lake 23 Wickwater Ln ℂ 01285 862716 ℂ tackleden.co.uk. Supply of day tickets to many of the angling sites within the Cotswold Water Park. Advice on local fishing knowledge and venues. Sale of tackle and bait.

⁙ FOOD & DRINK

Moos on Thames Manor Farm, Waterhay SN6 6QY ℂ moosonthames.co.uk. Farm vending machine selling organic milk and milkshakes. Glass bottles can be purchased from the vending shed, plus honey from the farm, grass-fed beef and organic cheese. It can be accessed a quarter of a mile off Thames Path National Trail, as well as by road.

2 CRICKLADE

Cricklade's Latin motto, derived from a 12th-century text on English history, is *in loco delicioso*, or 'in a delightful place', and I certainly wouldn't disagree.

For a town so small, its history is significant: it was created by the Anglo-Saxons as a fortified burgh for King Alfred to protect Wessex. Only 'North Wall' at the northern end of the High Street acts as a reminder of the town's defences. The town had its own royal mint, and coins from Cricklade, having been paid to the Vikings as ransom to prevent attacks, are in museums across Scandinavia.

"It has been managed in the same way for centuries, with a hay crop taken in summer to provide winter fodder."

Cricklade's High Street is a delight, a concoction of ageing stone and rendered buildings dating from the 15th century encompassing houses, shopfronts and old coaching inns. Wander up Church Street, west of the High Street, and you'll pass **Jenner's School**, with gabled windows in typical Cotswold style. It's best viewed from the churchyard at the rear where grass lawns show off the old school's stone façade to best advantage.

Allow time to look at **St Sampson's Church** too. There's a tiny stained-glass window on the wall of the south aisle that is so vibrantly scarlet red that I thought it had been lit from indoors. I found the lead panels, removed during repairs to the roof in 2009 and exhibited in the church, fun. On them are graffiti etched into the lead dating back to 1776, with drawings of shoes, hands that have been initialled by their artist, ships, rifles, a small bird and the elevation of a house.

One of the best places to view the church and its dominating bell tower in relation to the rest of Cricklade is from **North Meadow**, aptly, just north of the town and a short walk from High Bridge at the top of the High Street, designated as a National Nature Reserve and a Site of Special Scientific Interest. This traditional and ancient water meadow usually floods in winter, when nutritious minerals from the river are washed over the ground, creating perfect fertile ground for many wildflowers and grasses. It has been managed in the same way for centuries, with a hay crop taken in summer to provide winter fodder and then grazed by livestock that nibble down the tougher grasses allowing space for next year's wildflowers, in turn bringing out bees, butterflies, dragonflies and many hedgerow birds. But the meadow's most distinguishing feature is that it has the largest number of snakeshead fritillaries anywhere in the UK, representing 80% of the total fritillary 'population' and attracting crowds of people who come to walk among these delicate flowers.

The best time to see the fritillaries is during the second and third weeks in April, when the reserve manager takes guided walks through the flowers, explaining the meadow's history and pointing out other wildflowers along the way. You can find further information with exact dates and times, and book a walk, at ⊘ crickladecourtleet.org. uk. However, the 110-acre meadow is extremely attractive at any other time of year. To enjoy its beauty and differing characteristics, such as the riverside, pollarded willows or reed beds, three walks of varying length are marked out.

The main entrance to North Meadow is from the B4553, north of Cricklade. Cars should not park at the entrance but in the lay-by 100yds north. Better still is to walk from the town centre, using either the Thames Path heading west or via the short public footpath just north of High Bridge crossing the Thames.

ⓘⓘ FOOD & DRINK

Red Lion 74 High St ✆ 01793 750776 ⊘ theredlioncricklade.co.uk. Two menus for the bar (including chunky sandwiches and pizzas) and restaurant (braised beef brisket cottage pie; pan-seared calves liver with bacon mash). Championing beers from different microbreweries in the UK and abroad that rarely make it into large town pubs, including its own Hop Kettle Brewery. Close to the Thames, it's a good base from which to set off for North Meadow National Nature Reserve.

NORTH OF THE RIVER
– THE AMPNEYS

Unlike its Cotswold tributaries that frequently run through steep-sided valleys, the course of the Thames drifts through large, flat water meadows. Four miles to the north of the river is a small cluster of villages, the Ampneys – Ampney Crucis, Ampney St Mary and Ampney St Peter, the latter a no-through village with a delightful, squat church of Saxon origin. Put together the trio make an interesting detour from nearby Cirencester, with a collection of footpaths that allows a circumnavigation of all three. Ampney Crucis is the largest of the three villages but of note is **Ampney St Mary** and its separated church. The village, though centuries old, is modern by comparison with its 12th-century church. In 1349 the Black Death hit the original village hard and a new settlement was built a mile from the church. Nothing remains of the original village except the church standing alone by the side of Ampney Brook, a tiny tributary of the Thames. Known locally as the Ivy Church for the simple fact that it was covered with this creeper until restoration in 1913, the building has remained virtually unchanged. Its medieval wall paintings are remarkably well preserved.

"Nothing remains of the original village except the church standing alone by the side of Ampney Brook."

¶ FOOD & DRINK

The Crown at Ampney Brook/Wild Thyme & Honey Ampney Crucis GL7 5RS ✆ 01285 851806 ⌖ crownampneybrook.co.uk. Very popular 16th-century village inn turned boutique pub with menus and style to match. Menus use British produce (though not necessarily local to the Cotswolds). Good fixed-price menu Monday to Friday, noon to 18.00 (leek, potato and summer-herb soup with lovage pesto; Cornish crab and crème fraiche risotto). Private Dining Domes overlooking Ampney Brook. Accommodation available.

3 DOWN AMPNEY

While it retains the 'Ampney' name, the village of Down Ampney is three miles from its other namesakes, and is much closer to the Thames. It is also better known than its counterparts for being the birthplace in 1872 of the celebrated English composer Ralph Vaughan Williams. His father was vicar of All Saints' Church and Ralph was born at the Old Vicarage, a handsome house right in the centre of the village.

HUGH THE DROVER – A COTSWOLD OPERA

Ralph Vaughan Williams was most noted for his dedication to the collection and preservation of traditional English folk song. He searched for music that would otherwise have been lost because of its oral traditions.

His love of the countryside and the incorporation of traditional melodies within his own music led him to write his first opera, *Hugh the Drover*. A story about English life in 1812 and a love-at-first-sight relationship, it is the only opera ever to be set in the Cotswolds and includes typical Cotswold scene-setting at a fair.

Begun in 1910, it was not finished until after World War I, during which Vaughan Williams had witnessed the horrors of war on the front line in France, and subsequently amended the story. It was thought that his completion of a simple romantic tale using the English folksong traditions that he so loved was a therapeutic cleanser for all that he had seen.

The first public performance of *Hugh the Drover* was given in July 1924 by the British National Opera Company, conducted by Malcolm Sargeant.

The church, where his father preached and is buried, having died just three years after the composer was born, is tucked away from the village in a very pleasant spot surrounded by parkland and fields. In the bell tower is a superb exhibition about the life of Vaughan Williams created by the RVW Society while a stained-glass window was created to commemorate 150 years, in 2022, since the composer's birth. In dedication to his place of birth, Vaughan Williams named the hymn tune for 'Come down, O love divine' after Down Ampney. He died in 1958 and was buried at Westminster Abbey. His funeral included the hymn tune 'Down Ampney'.

Sitting opposite the churchyard is the disused RAF Down Ampney Airfield, which once hummed to the throaty sound of old Dakotas and played a significant part in both Operation Market Garden at Arnhem and D-Day. The Arnhem Memorial Window, an unusual stained-glass picture in the church illustrating a Dakota aircraft, commemorates the troops who were deployed from the airfield to Operation Market Garden.

"You can make a very pleasant short walk through fields and small pockets of woodland from the church entrance."

You can make a very pleasant short walk through fields and small pockets of woodland from the church entrance. Cross the noticeable parkland along the avenue of trees to meet with Old Road, then turn right to find a memorial that sits surrounded by Charlock Wood. It's a peaceful spot to sit a while before reversing the route to the church or along the length of Old Road into the village centre; turn left and left again to make a circular walk back to the church.

INGLESHAM TO KELMSCOTT

The Thames drifts east through open countryside past the villages of Castle Eaton and Kempsford and then takes a sharp turn north to meet with its tributary the River Coln at **Inglesham**. This is half a mile southwest of **Lechlade-on-Thames**, the first settlement downstream to take the name of the river, and where the Thames becomes truly navigable. Boats begin to appear, with the first of the river's locks, St John's Lock, just east of the town.

The river's route is no less winding than elsewhere though, curving through some of the flattest ground in the Cotswolds past the Buscot Estate and the tiny dead-end village of **Kelmscott**, where the Victorian designer William Morris once sought out a secluded hideaway house for a home.

4 INGLESHAM

There are two parts to Inglesham – Upper Inglesham that's split by the very busy A361 and simply Inglesham, north of its neighbour, and the part that I'd like to focus on. There's very little here, just a few surviving buildings from a medieval village 'protected' by a bend in the River Thames, but it's an important place nonetheless. Drive too fast along the A361 south from Lechlade and you'll miss the inconspicuous turning to the one access road; a tiny wooden sign points in the direction of a remote 13th-century church.

St John the Baptist Church, with Saxon origins, is significant though. A series of remarkable medieval wall paintings – and the church itself – is likely to have crumbled to dust but for one man, William Morris. In 1887 he discovered the church in a state of disrepair, fell in love with the building and vowed to restore it. The restoration project was one of his first having founded the Society for the Protection of Ancient Buildings, an organisation still extant that is based upon Morris's principles to restore 'old and interesting' buildings in a sympathetic way, using appropriate, traditional materials.

Rather than arrive by car – there is no official parking, and the road is extremely narrow – the most appealing route is from Lechlade, crossing ancient water meadows using the Thames Path, which passes the entrance to the church.

Another intriguing building, close to the tiny village, is at **Inglesham Lock** (which you would pass if using the Thames Path to the church). Close to where the River Coln meets the Thames, there is the entrance to an old, disused canal. This was the Thames and Severn Canal, a waterway that helped to join the two mighty rivers together until 1927. Inglesham Lock, one tiny section of the canal that has recently been restored, is the point at which river and canal met and by it is the **Round House**. The unusual dwelling, built in 1790, was lived in by the canal lengthsman who would manage the lock and the first stretch of canal. Horses were stabled on the ground floor while the ingenious inverted roof (providing it didn't leak) collected rainwater for domestic use. It is one of five lengthsman's round houses along the disused canal with others at Coates, Chalford, Cerney Wick and Marston Meysey.

5 LECHLADE-ON-THAMES

Lechlade gets overlooked by mass tourism even though the A361 from Burford to Swindon passes through, meeting with the road from Cirencester to Faringdon. But that in itself, together with the Thames, shows the town's importance as a trading post with a fascinating history. And today, there are some quirky shops to nose around.

There is, albeit buried, evidence of Bronze Age, Iron Age, Roman and Saxon living within the vicinity but much of what you see today, especially around the High Street and the Market Square, is elegant town houses built using the wealth created by the town's trade. The Salt Way from Droitwich ended in Lechlade with the salt then loaded onto boats to be shipped down the Thames to London. The ancient drovers' road, the Welshway, also arrived at Lechlade, where livestock were either sold off at one of the markets or, like salt, shipped down the river to London.

"Indeed, as a highway the Thames was as important to the town as any of the converging roads."

Indeed, as a highway the Thames was as important to the town as any of the converging roads. The river was dredged, deepened and widened downstream from Lechlade as early as 1235 to allow London barges to pass. The riverside wharves were busy loading stone, cheese (made around Cricklade) and corn bound for the capital and other major cities such as Bristol and Liverpool via the Cotswold canals. Anglers, pleasure boats and swans now use the river.

The charming 12-seater Inglesham launch provides private charter trips between May and October from St John's Lock. These are run by the Cotswold Canals Trust, and money raised from the river trips goes towards continued restoration of the canal. If you prefer to spend longer enjoying the river, Canadian canoes and kayaks can be hired from Cotswold Canoe Hire (⌀ cotswoldcanoehire.co.uk) next door to the Riverside Inn. Hire is available for a few days or even a week in addition to by the hour, so you can really take your time to get to know the area; a particularly lovely stretch to canoe along is from Cricklade or Castle Eaton, navigating the section of the river that boats can't access, down to Lechlade. Furthermore, you can camp overnight at Second Chance Touring Park (⌀ secondchanceholidaypark.co.uk), six miles west of Lechlade with direct access to launch your canoe on the river.

Spanning the Thames, **Ha'penny Bridge** was built in 1792 when a halfpenny was the toll levied from the small square tollhouse on the Lechlade side. Cattle and people were charged in addition to carts. From the Riverside Park next to the bridge you can get a very attractive view of the town, with the wharf, the bridge and the spire of St Lawrence's Church; this is a prime picnicking spot and the place to pick up the Thames Path to Inglesham. Views to the west incorporate the sight of Inglesham Church in the distance, across the meadows.

"A particularly lovely stretch to canoe along is from Cricklade or Castle Eaton, navigating the section of the river that boats can't access."

Lechlade celebrated 800 years of market status in 2010. The weekly market that once thrived on the through-trade has long gone but an antique and vintage market takes place once a month and the brick façade of the New Inn – one of the few brick buildings in the centre of town – still sports the archway through which stage- and mail coaches would start their journey to London.

In the corner of the Market Square stands the majestic **church of St Lawrence**, its spire a landmark for many miles. The church was originally known as St Mary but Catherine of Aragon, whose estate included Lechlade Manor, insisted that it be renamed after a saint from the Spanish region of Aragon. A pomegranate, Catherine's symbol, is carved into the huge church door.

It was the poet Percy Bysshe Shelley who wrote most notably about Lechlade. He was so taken with the church that in 1815 he wrote *A Summer Evening Churchyard: Lechlade, Gloucestershire* while staying at the New Inn. The path through the churchyard is known as **Shelley's Walk**, from where you can take a fine circular walk out of town. My preference is actually to start from Ha'penny Bridge and walk east along the Thames Path until you reach the Trout Inn close to St John's Lock, then return using the ancient, raised causeway across the water meadow just north of the Thames, where you'll gain superb views of the church spire, finally reaching Shelley's Walk. In the centre, a wander along Sherborne Street, bridging the west and northern arms of the High Street, is also worth a wander to give you an idea of the mix of architectural styles in the town.

St John's Lock and Old Father Thames

Half a mile east of Lechlade is **St John's Lock**, the first lock on the navigable stretch of the Thames. The lock takes its name from the medieval priory dedicated to St John the Baptist that once stood where the Trout Inn is now. Close by, St John's Bridge, built in 1229, was one of the first bridges across the Thames to be built outside of London.

Overseeing the lock is the stone statue of **Old Father Thames**. The reclining figure, shovel swung over his shoulder, was commissioned for London's new Crystal Palace Exhibition in 1854. Bought by the Thames Commissioners following the exhibition, the old man was placed at the source of the river until being relocated to St John's Lock.

Following the flow of the Thames, half a mile from St John's Bridge is **Cheese Wharf**, a 180-degree loop in the river close to which warehouses, in the early 19th century, stood brimming with cheese from north Wiltshire and Gloucestershire. Between 2,000 and 3,000 tons of cheese were sent down the Thames to London annually. The warehouses are gone and there's enough space to pull off the road to stop: it's a very pleasant place to watch ducks dabbling by the shallow banks of the river.

¶¶ FOOD & DRINK

The centre of Lechlade is not blessed with pubs offering menus warranting mention here. However, the Riverside Inn and New Inn both offer riverside gardens, as does the Trout Inn, a mile out of town on the Faringdon Road. My pick (of the gardens) is the New Inn; sadly the Riverside has been laid with imitation turf. Otherwise, pick up some excellent picnic goodies from **Cutler & Cashin**, a butcher, greengrocer and deli on Oak St.

Crown Inn High St ☏ 01367 252198. A drinker's pub with settles and log fires. No food served, though visitors (buying a drink) are welcome to eat their picnic in the secluded pub garden.

New Wave Brasserie & Bar High St ☏ 01367 252677 ☍ newwavebrasserie.com. A fish and seafood restaurant serving produce from mostly British waters: Maldon and West Mersea oysters, Cornish crab and lobster, New Wave fishcakes with aioli. Also operates a fish market on the covered outdoor patio on Fridays.

Sourdough Revolution High St ☏ 01367 253122. Bakery and restaurant serving and making – you guessed it – sourdough alongside many other tempting treats. Morning pastries and choux buns plus delicious fresh-made lunches (cumin-roasted carrot and cannellini bean salad with parsley, red onion, chilli and coriander hummus) and sourdough pizzas.

6 BUSCOT & BUSCOT PARK

🏠 **Lock Cottage**

Faringdon SN7 8BU ☏ 01367 240786 ☍ buscotpark.com; National Trust

Three miles east of Lechlade, Buscot Park, owned by the National Trust, remains the family home of Lord Faringdon, who lives in and administers the house and grounds. The house therefore feels alive and, despite the opulence and grandeur of the architecture and interior design, there are personal touches. Not least in the Faringdon Collection, a significant portfolio of art, furniture, ceramics and *objets d'art*, which is displayed in the house and to which Lord Faringdon continues to add with contemporary works. The collection includes artwork by Rembrandt, Reynolds, Rubens and Van Dyck. But perhaps of greatest importance given the proximity of the estate to Kelmscott is the representation of 19th- and 20th-century British art, in particular some Pre-Raphaelite masterpieces: Edward Burne-Jones's famous series *The Legend of the Briar Rose,* depicting *Sleeping Beauty*, panels the walls of the saloon while hanging in the Pre-Raphaelite Rooms is Rossetti's portrait of *Pandora*, modelled by Jane Morris, the wife of William Morris (page 279). There's also a very fine watercolour of Buscot by Eric Ravilious.

Outside, paths through the parkland and pleasure grounds fan out towards two large lakes with fishing allowed (day tickets purchased on site). Each path creates an intriguing vista, pulling you further into the pleasure grounds, where themed gardens and sculptures break up the asymmetrical lines. I particularly enjoy the Swinging Garden, an intimate roundel like an oasis among the trees, lined with swing seats for gentle contemplation. So, too, the formal Water Garden, created by the celebrated garden designer Harold Peto. And the walled kitchen garden is always filled with strikingly colourful borders.

"There's something equally refreshing about moving away to the quietness of the nearby weir pool and riverside picnic area."

The National Trust also owns **Buscot**, a tiny one-street village with a mix of tantalisingly attractive brick and Cotswold stone houses. The river and its southern water meadow form a natural development barrier; you must park in the small car park provided in the village and walk the hundred yards or so to the river.

The tempestuous noise of **Buscot Weir** is therapeutically energetic. You can stand on a small bridge directly above the weir and watch the frothing foam just beneath your feet, a fearsome reminder of the power of water. It's hard to talk above the natural noise so it's best simply to watch in awe. However, there's something equally refreshing about moving away to the quietness of the nearby weir pool and riverside picnic area. While the currents of the river should not be underestimated, the weir pool is a renowned spot for a refreshing outdoor dip.

This whole stretch of the Thames is strikingly scenic and deserves savouring slowly. Turn left from the weir pool along a riverside footpath and you will come to Buscot Church, separated from the remainder of the village. Virtually on the banks of the river, the church is renowned for its very attractive stained-glass windows designed by Edward Burne-Jones. The figures in both *The Good Shepherd* and *Faith, Hope and Charity* are noticeably in the Pre-Raphaelite style.

Turn right by Buscot Weir and you can follow the Thames Path for two miles to find another church with Pre-Raphaelite connections, at the site of the deserted village of **Eaton Hastings**. The windows here were designed by William Morris, Ford Madox Brown and, again, Edward Burne-Jones. They were all installed by William Morris's interior-design business, Morris, Marshall, Faulkner & Co, latterly Morris & Co.

I love this stretch of the Thames between Buscot and Eaton Hastings, where the only noise comes from an occasional swan gliding into land

STOCKER1970/S

JACEK WOJNAROWSKI/S

SAL

FARINGDON COLLECTION TRUST, BUSCOT PARK

on the swirling water and the odd plop of some mythical creature in among the river weed. Teasels are splashed with the pink of rosebay willowherb and vetch, and willows droop over the riverbanks.

It's believed that one of the most famous of William Morris's designs, 'Willow Bough', was inspired by walks in the area from his home at nearby **Kelmscott**. A four-mile waymarked circular walk from Buscot Weir, the **Willow Walk** (follow the signs with a willow leaf), makes the most of the Thames Path and other local footpaths through water meadows north of the river. It passes through the village of Kelmscott.

▌▌ SPECIAL STAYS

Lock Cottage Buscot ⊘ nationaltrustholidays.co.uk. Owned by the National Trust, this is a very sweet one-bedroomed (sleeps two) lock-keeper's cottage right beside the Thames at Buscot Weir and Lock in the tiny National Trust-owned village of Buscot. Wonky walls, low ceilings and latch doors all add to the character of the stone property, but it's the pretty garden overlooking the river and the walks along the Thames Path that are the lure here.

▌▌ FOOD & DRINK

There is a tea room at Buscot Park (with a fine mural depicting life on the estate worth looking at) but my pick is one in the village of Buscot itself.

Buscot Tea Rooms 6 Buscot ⊘ 01367 250329. Tiny tea shop in the centre of the village serving good freshly prepared snacks (quiche, ploughman's, sandwiches) and superb cakes and cream teas. Pretty tea garden too.

7 KELMSCOTT MANOR & KELMSCOTT

Kelmscott GL7 3HU ⊘ 01367 252486 ⊘ kelmscottmanor.org.uk

Just yards from the north bank of the Thames, 1½ miles east of Buscot, is Kelmscott, another 'secluded' village in remote farmland. William Morris, the craftsman central to the Arts and Crafts Movement, believed the village to be 'heaven on earth' when he first discovered it. He chose **Kelmscott Manor** as a summer house to get away from the stresses of

◀ **1** The Thames, spanned by Ha'penny Bridge, has always been important to the town of Lechlade. **2** St John the Baptist Church in Inglesham has some remarkable medieval wall paintings. **3** Kelmscott Manor was the home of the Arts and Crafts Movement's William Morris. **4** The art collection at Buscot Park features some masterpieces, such as Edward Burne-Jones's Briar Rose series.

his successful but busy interior-design business and London life. At first he merely rented the notably homely manor (actually a farmhouse), with his artist friend, the Pre-Raphaelite painter Dante Gabriel Rossetti. Rossetti felt that the property and the surrounding countryside were ideal for painting in; his studio can be seen on the upper floor. But his attentions towards Morris's wife, Jane, created friction and Rossetti moved out. Ultimately, William Morris bought the property outright and he created a family home.

Morris loved the house for its pureness – it had been virtually untouched since its building in 1600. He found not only peace and sanctuary from the village and the countryside but inspiration, and much of his work, both in the house and throughout his world-famous designs, shows evidence of this. His designs seem more meaningful having seen his house and the environment within which he chose to live his life.

"He found not only peace and sanctuary from the village and the countryside but inspiration."

I find the house soothing because it is so evidently a creative family home with almost every aspect worked upon or created by a family member or friend. The furniture, rugs, bedspreads, embroideries, paintings, wall hangings, are all personal. There are Pre-Raphaelite paintings on the walls by his friends Rossetti and Burne-Jones, and tapestries by his daughter May, one of the finest embroiderers of her generation and a celebrated craftswoman in her own right. Cushion covers are the work of his wife and daughter, the wallpaper the work of Morris himself. Every room of the house shows artistic expression and a love for the building.

The gardens are no less inspiring. There is nothing grand or formal about them; they make a very restful place to stop for a while where sunny glades and courtyards, alluring pathways through the undergrowth, hidden corners beneath shady fruit trees and delicate roses that scent the stonework can be found.

The main car park for visitors is approximately 10 minutes' walk from the manor, though the most evocative first glimpse of the house is arriving on foot from the Thames. A 180yd footpath links the two.

William Morris, his wife and two daughters are all buried in the churchyard in Kelmscott, his grave like a giant Cotswold stone ridge tile. Morris helped to restore the church and his fabric is used on the altar, while the kneelers are derived from his *Strawberry Thief* design.

⃛ FOOD & DRINK

Kelmscott Manor Tearoom Within the farm buildings at William Morris's home, this is a comfortable restaurant and glorious courtyard for wholesome lunches (homemade soup and light bites) and teas, using produce from the gardens and nearby farms.

Plough Inn Kelmscott ✆ 01367 253543 ⌂ theploughinnkelmscott.com. Useful stopping point for those visiting Kelmscott Manor or walkers on either the Thames Path or the Willow Walk. Very attractive pub with lovely garden. Classic British comfort food with bar (try the pub-made Guinness and treacle bread) and à la carte (pork belly, creamed carrot and potato mash, kale) menus. Attractive accommodation.

RADCOT TO THE WINDRUSH

Once the River Thames has drifted beyond Kelmscott, one can argue that the landscape doesn't look much like the Cotswolds at all. Gone are the contorted valleys and hilltops. In place, a wide open and ultra-flat plain that has sufficient space to be filled with a river ten times the size that the Thames is at this stage. It's still a diminutive river, unrecognisable for those only familiar with its Berkshire or London stature.

South of the Thames, with the exception of Faringdon, one can't claim to be in the Cotswolds. The Vale of the White Horse and north-facing ridge of Lambourn Downs sees to that. But step into the villages to the north, like Clanfield, Bampton and Aston and, though far removed from the western escarpment in mileage, you'll still find Cotswold-esque character.

8 FARINGDON

I'm not going to pretend that the little market town of Faringdon is extraordinary in its beauty. Recent town planning has much to answer for; a brush with its outskirts, even much of its interior and you'll wonder why I've included it here. It's not a town that warrants travelling any great global distance for exclusively. But there is an attractive, if very small, core around the Market Place that, should you be nearby, warrants some time.

"A fine market house on pillars, the Old Town Hall, is the focal point of Market Place and dates from the 17th century."

Faringdon was granted a market charter by King Henry III in 1218. A fine market house on pillars, the **Old Town Hall**, is the focal point of Market Place and dates from the 17th century. Its painted walls match the style of many of the buildings within the historic area of the town, a delightful mismatch of brightly coloured and pastel-painted buildings along London Street and Church Walk.

To the north of Market Place is **All Saints' Church**, notably wide and low with a squat tower. The Cotswold stone church lost its steeple during the English Civil War, courtesy of a cannon ball.

On the east edge of Market Place is **Faringdon Museum**, which, highlighting the history of the town, explains the connection with one-time resident Lord Berners. The eccentric aristocrat, composer and artist lived at Faringdon House (not open to the public) from 1930 to 1950 and socialised with friends the Mitford Sisters (page 161), composer Igor Stravinsky and artist Salvador Dalí, who all visited Faringdon.

Outside the museum is a three-sided stone bench with an unusual diving-bell sculpture and riddle-like words from Lord Berners. The bench observes Berners' friendship with Dalí, who reputedly wore a diving suit during a visit to the town, which was given to him by Berners at the opening of the first surrealist art exhibition in London.

In spring, particularly, **Badbury Hill** to the west of Faringdon is a place for a fine walk. The National Trust-owned woodland, an Iron-Age hillfort, offers one of the finest places in this locale for bluebells. For a walk at any time of year, follow the public footpath off Stanford Road to **Faringdon Hill**. There are wonderful views from the hilltop, which was a Royalist camp during the English Civil War, and the thicket of Scot's Pine, oak and beech is a shaded place for a picnic. In the centre of the thicket is **Faringdon Folly** (⌀ faringdonfolly.co.uk). The brick mock-Gothic structure, run by volunteers of the Faringdon Folly Tower Trust, was built by Lord Berners. A small exhibition highlights its history, but climb the 153 (I counted!) wooden steps to the viewing point at the top to look out over the Thames floodplain and Cotswold Hills to the north and northwest, with incredible views south of the nearby White Horse of Uffington. You really are at the extremities of the Cotswolds here.

ⵟ FOOD & DRINK

Old Crown Coaching Inn 25 Market Pl ✆ 01367 242744 ⌀ theoldcrowncoachinginn.com. Double AA Rosette award for culinary excellence for its fine-dining experience. In addition to a dinner menu (gazpacho mousse, black olive, basil and garlic focaccia to start; venison loin, king oyster, celeriac, shallot with summer truffle to follow; pineapple tarte tatin to finish), there's also an epicurean seven-course tasting menu.

9 CLANFIELD, BAMPTON & ASTON

While Faringdon lies to the south of the River Thames, to the north, on land beyond the floodplain, is a delightful cluster of villages, first **Clanfield** then, travelling east, **Bampton** and **Aston**. They're reached from Faringdon by crossing Radcot Bridge, the oldest standing on any stretch of the river, dating from circa 1200.

Clanfield, recorded in the Domesday Book of 1086, was occupied a century or so later by the Knights Templar who established the first hospitaller in Oxfordshire here. Today, the village continues to provide copious amounts of hospitality amid the pretty Cotswold stone houses that line the main road. There's a choice of village greens upon which to park a bottom for a picnic beneath weeping willows and, in spring, amid daffodils.

To the south of the village lies Friars Court (⌀ friarscourt.com), a 16th-century moated property on the site of the former hospitaller. Though not routinely open, its exceptional three-acre gardens and small museum are accessible on certain public open days throughout the summer.

Within the village is Windmill Farm (⌀ adventureplus.org.uk), which offers retreats, adventure holidays and outdoor conservation education, often with a Christian background, for children, adults and families. It's also the base for the West Oxon Canoe Club. For experienced paddlers and newcomers, there are opportunities to paddle on the Thames with qualified instructors every Wednesday evening from May to October.

"There's a choice of village greens upon which to park a bottom for a picnic beneath weeping willows."

Neighbouring Bampton, the largest and, in my humble opinion the prettiest of this trio of villages, receives the greatest share of visitors to this area. That's thanks to location scouts who regarded the village's attractiveness worthy of turning Bampton into Downton for the global television series and film, *Downton Abbey*.

The place to visit upon arrival is Bampton Community Hub (⌀ bamptoncommunityhub.org), in the Old Grammar School on Church View. The restored building houses Bampton's extensive archives, a permanent display on the filming of *Downton Abbey* in the village, a gift shop and around three temporary exhibitions a year on a multitude of themes. The hub is run for residents and visitors by a passionate team of volunteers, and I caught up with a couple of lovely ladies on duty during a recent visit there. We chatted for the best part of an hour about this and that, chewed the rag about living in the Cotswolds, and, more specifically, Bampton; they were wonderfully generous with their time. 'If you'd like to head upstairs, you'll get a wonderful view into Mary's Garden,' it was recommended – the garden of character Mary Crawley in *Downton Abbey* (the Old Grammar School became the village hospital in the series). As it happened, I was keen to learn more about the long tradition of morris dancing in Bampton with no fewer than three morris-dancing sides. Explained the volunteer, 'Various quarrels over the decades has led to the formation of three separate teams of dancers. On the Spring Bank Holiday Monday, they all compete for a day of dancing around the village from early morning until long into the evening. Each team resides at one of the three pubs in the village, and on that Monday, any former pubs (there were once thirteen) may also offer a barrel of beer to the dancers.

"On the Spring Bank Holiday Monday, they all compete for a day of dancing around the village from early morning until long into the evening."

'We also have SPAJERS, the Society for the Preservation of Ancient Junketing, a charity that organises the annual Shirt Race on the Saturday of the Spring Bank Holiday weekend. Teams of two in fancy dress (originally a nightshirt) must take it in turns to push each other in un-powered transport like an old pram or bed from pub to pub to down a half pint of ale. Funds raised go towards an annual outing for the village pensioners. The nationally renowned Bampton Opera performs every summer in the village, showcasing little-known 18th-century works. And, on Christmas Eve, the Bampton Mummers perform a historic mummer play.'

Alongside a map of *Downton Abbey* film scenes, visitors can pick up leaflets from the Hub on self-guided walks around Bampton, highlighting historic buildings and locations. That includes the triangular Market Square, within which the town hall is home to WestOxArts (⌂ westoxarts.com). There's always an exhibition of work

1 Faringdon Folly offers beautiful views over the Cotswold Hills. **2** Bampton town hall is home to WestOxArts, which offers exhibitions, workshops and art sales. **3** Radcot Bridge, built in 1200, is the oldest bridge over the Thames. ▶

DRONESKI IMAGING/S

SILVI SCHAUMLOEFFEL/WEST OX ARTS GALLERY

CHRIS LAWRENCE TRAVEL/S

by local artists, the opportunity to purchase local artwork and take part in workshops and events like jewellery making, embroidery and life drawing.

For more art, neighbouring Aston warrants a visit. Here, established close to half a century ago by Jane and Stephen Baughan, **Aston Pottery and Gardens** (astonpottery.co.uk) designs, manufactures and decorates its vast collection of hand-stencilled pottery. The creamy kitchenware, which celebrates the British countryside with rustic prints of garden birds, wildlife, farmyard animals, flowers and insects, is sold in an excellent gift shop adjacent to the pottery studio.

To entice customers into the timber-framed gift shop (also made using handmade bricks) from the road, Jane and Stephen created a vibrant flower garden hemmed in only by the Cotswold stone wall at the entrance. That garden has since been extended, offering a riot of spring and summer colour across six areas, including a Hot Bank of perennials in shades of red, orange and yellow and a 236ft-long Pleached Hornbeam Walk with double flower borders and a Dahlia Border showcasing more than 130 varieties. All 8,500 plants are grown on-site each year. Visitors may wander the gardens at will, though guided garden tours take place throughout the summer.

"On a walk at dusk you might just catch a glimpse of a magical barn owl hunting."

To end a visit to this area, I recommend a good walk at **Chimney Meadows** (bbowt.org.uk/nature-reserves/chimney-meadows), two miles south of Aston. This ancient landscape is, at 760 acres, the Wildlife Trust's largest nature reserve in Oxfordshire. The species-rich floodplain meadows that make up the reserve, extending to the banks of the River Thames, are filled with wildflowers while its wetland areas are an important feeding and breeding ground for wading birds. Part of the site is designated as a National Nature Reserve (NNR), too.

There are recommended public and permissive footpaths throughout the reserve from a small car park at the northwest entrance. These link with the Thames Path National Trail, where you'll find a picnic area close to Shifford Lock. Bird hides and a Thames Observation Platform have been constructed, allowing uninterrupted views of ground-nesting birdlife at the NNR as well as views along the river. On a walk at dusk you might just catch a glimpse of a magical barn owl hunting.

Seasonal guided walks are offered and there are regular volunteering opportunities to help with work on the reserve.

🍴 FOOD & DRINK

There's no shortage of places to eat and drink in the area, particularly in Bampton where there are three pubs (**Morris Clown** is legendary for being a 'locals' pub serving good beer but no food and where you might get to watch the traditional Oxfordshire game of Aunt Sally), two coffee shops including Lynwood & Co and a French bistro. Too many to detail here, but this is my selection:

Aston Pottery & Gardens Aston ✆ 01993 852896 ⬒ astonpottery.co.uk. Excellent daytime café in a purpose-built building from which guests can see the gardens (see opposite). Lunches include a selection of warm quiches (leek and Oxford Blue cheese; bacon and mushroom; beetroot, goat's cheese and walnut etc), salad bowls and soup. Large selection of cakes (I can vouch for the chocolate and Guinness , which I have devoured several times!). All homemade on the premises, including the soda bread and rolls.

Blake's Kitchen Clanfield ✆ 01367 810660 ⬒ blakeskitchen.com. Third-generation bakery and post office making sourdough loaves, cinnamon buns, cakes and sausage rolls (and much more). Brunch and lunch with sandwiches and 'goodness bowls' of salad. Lovely outdoor seating area overlooking the village green beneath a giant festoon-lighted tent.

Double Red Duke Clanfield ✆ 01367 810222 ⬒ countrycreatures.com/double-red-duke. Very popular boutique pub with rooms in a former 17th-century wool-merchant's house. Seasonal menus with daily specials, specialising in open-grill meat and fish dishes (lamb rump, grilled peas and mint; pork tomahawk with burnt-apple puree). Not the cheapest option in the area, but a dining experience.

Fleur de Lys Bampton ✆ 01993 223160 ⬒ fleurdelys-bampton.com. In the centre of pretty Bampton, this large Georgian townhouse became a French bistro in 2023, with an interior to match (toile wallpaper, wooden bistro chairs, feather-plume ceiling lights). Breakfast, lunch and dinner plus a good prix-fixe Menu du Jour (Mon–Fri lunch). Moules frites, pork rillette, croques, French onion soup and bouillabaisse make this a welcome change to the British menus seen at most pubs in the area, though you can still get 'Le Full English' for breakfast. Classy, French-styled accommodation.

Trout at Tadpole Bridge Buckland Marsh ✆ 01367 870382 ⬒ butcombe.com/the-trout-at-tadpole-bridge-oxfordshire. On the banks of the River Thames beside, unsurprisingly, Tadpole Bridge. Cosy bar with wood panelling, flag floors, exposed Cotswold stone walls and armchairs beside log burners. Menu of British classics including Sunday lunch. Fabulous riverside garden with boat moorings. Boutique accommodation.

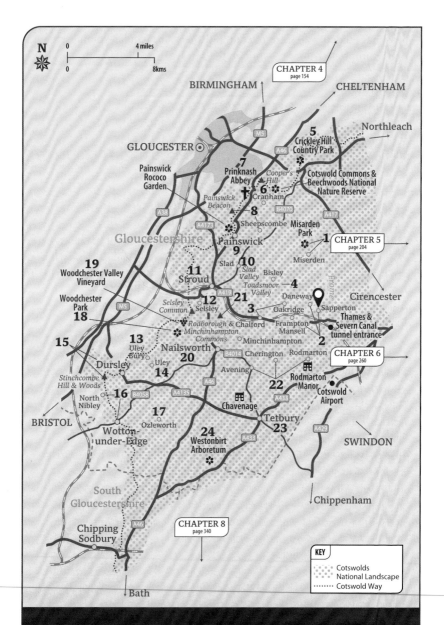

7
THE SOUTHERN COTSWOLD SCARP & FIVE VALLEYS

While the northern and eastern areas of the Cotswolds are cosy, gentle and lay claim to soft undulations, the southern Cotswolds are rugged, raw and wild. Sharp escarpments and gauged river valleys twist and bend with absurd frequency, funnelling cold winds and trapping fog. In between the contorted valleys and giant beech woods, high ground amasses creating rough commons, superb for bracing walks and views.

There's an edgier feel to the area too. Where the softer wolds of the northern Cotswolds belie their rural heritage of rearing sheep and selling wool with the odd farmstead and squire's manor house dotted across the countryside, here is the corresponding industrial landscape. Cloth mills, originally powered by the area's fast-running waters, lined the valley floors and the steep escarpments meant that builders had nowhere to go but up. Consequently, the houses of the workforce cling limpet-like to the valley sides.

Having skirted around Cheltenham, the western escarpment continues to run south from **Crickley Hill** towards **Stroud** and then on towards **Dursley** until it reaches the graceful city of Bath. This section of the escarpment has some of the most dramatic views in the Cotswolds, over the Severn Valley and into Wales.

In the hinterland, the area around Stroud is known as the Five Valleys. Synonymous with the cloth industry, each of the five valleys follows small streams; to the east there are further valleys, unconnected to the cloth industry, that are completely dry. There are no giant rivers here. North of Stroud is the **Painswick Valley**, its western ridge making up a part of the main Cotswold escarpment. Northeast is the **Slad Valley**, made famous by the author Laurie Lee, who lived there for much of his life.

To the east is the **Frome Valley**, otherwise known as Golden Valley when it edges ever closer towards Stroud and, like a northerly spur from it, the **Toadsmoor Valley**. Running due south of Stroud is the **Nailsworth Valley**. At first it is as steep as its neighbours but gradually the land begins to flatten and the odd barbed spur escapes, such as at **Woodchester** to the west and towards Avening and **Tetbury** to the east.

The area of the Five Valleys is unique in Britain. The whole landscape is bizarre and intriguing. I love visiting – and yet I'm glad to escape to the high ground of **Rodborough** and **Minchinhampton commons** or to stand on top of the escarpment and breathe in great gulps of air.

GETTING THERE & AROUND

The only main **train** station in the locale is at Stroud. **Great Western Railway** (⏣ gwr.com) operates services from London Paddington via Swindon. From the southwest and Wales, services are via Gloucester. Trains from Birmingham and the north are operated by **Cross Country Trains** (⏣ crosscountrytrains.co.uk); a change at Gloucester is required. A local train service, also operated by First Great Western, runs to the Cam and Dursley station from Bristol and Gloucester. The station is actually three miles from the centre of Dursley.

As one of the main meeting points, most **bus** journeys in the area begin and end in Stroud. Regular services operate from Stroud to Cheltenham along the Painswick Valley, to Nailsworth, Tetbury and Dursley. There are only limited services along the Frome Valley, with most daily buses stopping at Chalford. An hourly service operates from Gloucester to Dursley and from Dursley to Bristol via Wotton-under-Edge. Most buses keep to the main roads, so alternative modes of transport are essential for finding those out-of-the-way places.

The continuation of the Cotswold Way is naturally the focal point for **walkers** here as it utilises the full length of the western escarpment for stunning, far-reaching views. But there are plenty of opportunities to pick a short stretch of the long-distance route for a there-and-back walk – look at the scenery to the west walking one-way, and to the east on the way back, because you won't want to miss any of it. My recommendation would be sections around Crickley Hill, Painswick Beacon and Hawkesbury. Alternatively, there are now several circular walks that use some of the most scenic parts of the Cotswold Way. As designated waymarked walks, full instructions for them can be downloaded

TOURIST INFORMATION

Painswick St Mary's Churchyard
Tetbury 33 Church St ✆ 01666 503552
Wotton-under-Edge The Heritage Centre ✆ 01453 521541

from the National Trail website (⌖ nationaltrail.co.uk/otswold-way). Fourteen of these walks are within this locale, with each one graded for ability and, most, no more than four or five miles in length.

Off the Cotswold Way, some of the best walking is on Selsley, Rodborough and Minchinhampton commons, southeast of Stroud. They provide space and give bird's-eye views of the landscape and how the valleys interconnect. Most of this of course is hill walking; my pick of the valleys is the Frome Valley around Sapperton and Daneway. You can easily add this on to the flatter sections of ground east of Sapperton, where Sapperton Park and the extensive Bathurst Estate provide some very peaceful woodland walks. The **Laurie Lee Wildlife Way**, developed to celebrate the centenary of the author's birth, covers five miles around the Slad Valley where he spent his childhood and much of his latter years. It takes in places important to Lee and is punctuated with ten posts inscribed with his poetry. This really is a wonderful signposted walk; one not to be missed.

There's no getting away from it – **cycling** is hard work in this area unless you stick to the valley floor, but you would be denying yourself some of the most dramatic of Cotswold scenery to do so. The Sustrans **National Cycle Network Route 45** provides traffic-free cycling through Golden Valley and the Nailsworth Valley. The six-mile Stroud Valleys Trail uses a traffic-free section of the route from Stonehouse, west of Stroud, to Nailsworth.

The Stroud District Cycling Map, available from ⌖ stroudtown.gov. uk/visitors, grades all the roads in the area according to their suitability for cycling. However, if you're not as fit as you once were and think a helping hand to get you up the hills would be good, Five Valley Cycles e-bike hire is based in Nailsworth.

BIKE HIRE & REPAIRS

Cyclists are well served in this part of the Cotswolds, with bike shops and repairs in Stroud, Brimscombe, Dursley and Nailsworth in addition to the following bike hire/services.

The Bikeworks Frogmarsh Mill, South Woodchester ✆ 01453 872824 ⬦ thebikeworks. co.uk. Bike hire, sales and repairs.

Five Valley Cycles 5 Cossack Sq, Nailsworth GL6 0DB ✆ 07518 677589 ⬦ fivevalleycycles. co.uk. E-bike hire plus bike sales, repairs and servicing.

Veloton Cycles 22 Market Pl, Tetbury ✆ 01666 504343 ⬦ veloton.co.uk. Bike sales, servicing, repairs. Cyclists' coffee shop.

THE FROME VALLEY (GOLDEN VALLEY)

The River Frome bubbles from the ground a good way northeast of Stroud, close to the village of Brimpsfield and the old Roman road, Ermin Way. It flows due south for six miles past the small villages of Miserden and Edgeworth, collecting riverlets from other dart-like valleys on its way.

At Sapperton the river changes course, turning west towards Chalford, where the Frome Valley becomes better known as the Golden Valley, so called because of the money generated by the processing of wool. At the peak of production, in the 19th century, the Frome powered 150 mills. Some are still evident today in the steep-sided valley, though used as shops, warehouses and dwellings, in what was once a teeming hub of industry. Two of the prettier villages at the end of the valley closest to Stroud are **Thrupp** and **Far Thrupp**, partway up the northern hillside, with views across to Rodborough Common.

1 MISARDEN PARK & MISERDEN

Why Misarden Park comes to be in the village of Miserden and how or why the change of vowel came to be seems a mystery. But regardless of spelling or pronunciation, the estate-owned village is perhaps the most attractive in the whole of this locale, perched on top of the extremely steep valley and looking across to Warren Hill, Fishcombe Bank and right along both the Frome Valley and its thickly wooded neighbouring spur.

Miserden is an estate village that you have to get to rather than pass through. But once there, numerous footpaths take you to the point where the two valleys unite, and from which you can make several very enjoyable streamside and woodland walks, or head to the more southerly village of **Edgeworth**, where you can walk through one of the most delightful sections of the Frome Valley. There's also a series of downloadable walks, including to Misarden Park Lake through which the Frome flows, available on the estate website (see below).

One of the main reasons for going to the village is to visit **The Garden at Miserden** (✆ 01285 821303 ⊘ miserden.org). While the striking 17th-century Cotswold stone manor house, with external additions by Sir Edward Lutyens, is closed to the public, the Arts and Crafts-style gardens provide sublime vistas of the house and the valley over which it looks.

I find this one of the most beautiful of all Cotswold gardens, in the most tranquil of settings. The last time I was there it was pouring with rain but the spectacle really lifted the spirits and I noticed that, despite being late in the summer season, the garden was still filled with colour at a time when other gardens were not. The long, wide traditional borders (some of the longest in any private garden), filled with roses, dahlias and many more perennials, are eye-opening in scale, the formal parterre extraordinarily restful. I love the tiny row of gnarled old apple trees, their trunks and branches cloaked in moss, creating an avenue not dissimilar to the famous Dark Hedges in Northern Ireland. This continues right into early autumn when the leaves of the specimen trees within the arboretum begin to change their hues on the lower slopes.

> *"The Arts and Crafts-style gardens provide sublime vistas of the house and the valley over which it looks."*

🍴 FOOD & DRINK

Glasshouse Café Miserden GL6 7JA ⊘ miserden.org. Wonderful café located in historic greenhouses, filled with light throughout the year. Comfy sofas and wood-burning stoves in winter; outdoor setting in summer. Within the grounds of The Garden at Miserden but accessible without the need to visit the (paying) garden. Large selection of homemade cakes and light bites with hot drinks and a wine bar.

2 SAPPERTON, DANEWAY & FRAMPTON MANSELL

Of the three villages, **Sapperton** and **Frampton Mansell** stand on the hillside above the Frome Valley while the tiny hamlet of **Daneway**, no more than a pub and a couple of houses, sits on the valley floor between the two. This trio make an excellent combination to visit together, with plenty of opportunities to walk between them. Sapperton in particular is a walker's dream. On the southern side of the valley, now that the river

A short walk in Sapperton

✳ OS Explorer map 168; start: Bell Inn 📍 SO949033; 2 miles; easy, but sturdy footwear required

Much of Sapperton and the surrounding land is a part of the vast Bathurst Estate. My pick of possible short walks around the village uses the Broad Ride and is two miles long. As its name suggests, it's a wide avenue, as straight as a ruler, which, if you followed for its full five-mile length, would deposit you in the centre of Cirencester. The grass is often long so boots or stout shoes are advisable.

Turn left out of the Bell Inn at Sapperton and walk through the village to the T-junction opposite Sapperton Lodge. Turn right and in 50yds turn right down Broad Ride, which is signposted as a bridleway. Continue along the Broad Ride, through open parkland and crossing a quiet road, for three-quarters of a mile. You'll begin to get views over the Frome Valley. As the Broad Ride finishes, with dense woods in front of you, turn right along the narrow lane. At the crossroads, go straight across into the village, past the school on your left. With the church on your left, turn right to return to the Bell Inn.

has turned a corner, there are superb views from the village over the valley below, which is crammed with beech trees.

A picturesque, short trek runs between the welcoming **Bell Inn** in Sapperton and the riverside **Daneway Inn**, next to the Daneway Bridge. You need to decide whether you wish to begin at the bottom and do the appreciable climb to Sapperton first, before supping a pint overlooking the valley, or whether to take the downhill leg first and then summon up the energy for the return climb in the Daneway Inn by the banks of the Frome.

An alternative, longer two-pub walk without a hefty climb is from the Bell Inn at Sapperton, following the course of the Thames and Severn Canal using the **Macmillan Way** through Hailey Wood. For Sapperton is where the disused Thames and Severn Canal (page 310), having followed the Frome Valley from Stroud, turns a corner to meet up with the section of canal that uses the Thames Valley to Lechlade. But to link the two sections it was necessary to build a tunnel between Sapperton (or actually Daneway being on the valley floor) and Coates. Completed in 1789, the **Sapperton Tunnel** was at that time the longest canal tunnel and, at 3,817yds, remains the third longest in Britain today. In places the tunnel is 200ft below ground level; the section of the Macmillan Way runs above much of the course of the tunnel.

The Tunnel House Inn (closed for refurbishment at the time of publication), originally built to accommodate the workers building the canal, sits in the middle of nowhere just yards from the classical-designed portal at the tunnel entrance. Another, less ornamental portal is at the Daneway entrance to the tunnel. Further walks along the canal towpath, using a section of the Wysis Way, can be accessed from the Tunnel House Inn, but be careful when walking with young children as the empty canal is deep and the sides sheer.

¶¶ FOOD & DRINK

Bell Inn Sapperton GL7 6LE ℘ 01285 760298 ◌ bellsapperton.co.uk. A friendly pub in the heart of the village with a very pretty front garden providing good views over the valley. A convenient base from which to walk. Very good food (veg and meat from the Cotswolds) with British classics. Accommodation available.

Crown Inn Frampton Mansell GL6 8JG ℘ 01285 760601 ◌ thecrowninn-cotswolds.co.uk. Good-looking Cotswold-stone pub and front garden with incredible views over the Frome Valley. Cosy inside too, with log fires and very good gastro-pub food (venison leg steak with potato rosti, confit carrot, crispy shallots, autumn vegetables and bearnaise butter). Ales from local Stroud and Uley breweries. Accommodation available.

Daneway Inn Daneway GL7 6LN ℘ 01285 760297 ◌ thedaneway.pub. Very traditional riverside pub with simple but nourishing lunchtime and evening food. Come for the location to sup a pint more than anything. Secluded, 'wild-camping' campsite (tents only) 200yds down the valley among the trees.

Jolly Nice Farm Shop & Kitchen Frampton Mansell GL6 8HZ ◌ jollynicefarmshop.com. A destination food venue that's worth travelling for. This extensive farm shop, created from a series of yurts, run by the Wilson family, sells meat, ice cream and other produce from its own farm in Westonbirt plus fruit and veg and much else of high quality that's supplied from local farms and food/drink producers. Also on-site, The Hive is a café during the day and bar at night (piano and log-burning stove in a separate yurt). Also a funky drive-through when you're on the go.

NICK TURNER/COTSWOLDS.COM

CAROLINE MILLS

CAROLINE MILLS

3 OAKRIDGE & CHALFORD

🏠 The Old Vicarage at Oakridge

There are just three crossing points over the Frome between Sapperton and Chalford. All the roads running along the valley and across the river are incredibly narrow, often single track, but they provide a constantly changing view.

Chalford and its conjoined neighbour, France Lynch, have oft been described together as an alpine village. A touch over the top, for although steeply sloped, timber chalets on rocky mountains it's not; Chalford has a unique character. While the old block-shaped mills of yesteryear, with their symmetry of windows and tall chimneys that poke just above the road line, spread along the valley floor – now the Golden Valley – confined weavers' cottages are crammed against the cliff-like hillsides. Cars need to breathe in to ride down the warren of tiny lanes, no wider than a sheet of cloth – even the High Street struggles with two cars side by side. Chalford is made for walking, not cars, if your calf muscles will withstand the gruelling hill climbs. Life, one imagines, must have been tough for the weavers and their donkeys that plied the hillsides carrying materials. Rack Hill, in the centre of the village, is where the cloths were spread out on racks to dry.

There are walks along the towpath by the disused canal and at Chalford Wharf, just below the church, one of the five roundhouses along the Thames and Severn Canal that were used as lengthsman's cottages. As a private residence, this one is particularly well preserved.

💼 SPECIAL STAYS

The Old Vicarage at Oakridge Oakridge Lynch, Stroud GL6 7NS ✆ 07789 224595 🖥 oldvicarageoakridge.com. You've a choice of self-catering accommodation here in addition to comfortable B&B: there's a very sweet cottage for two that sits in the grounds of and adjacent to an attractive listed Georgian house (the old vicarage). The single-floor cottage was once the staff quarters for the house and retains original flag floors, oak beams and heritage glazing in the windows. High quality modern fixtures and fittings including a kitchen, living/dining area with wood-burning stove, kingsize bedroom with Hypnos mattress and en-suite. Original artworks on the walls from the owner. It's that wonderful, I'd like to move in! In the

◀ **1** Barrow Wake offers fine views across the grasslands and wildflowers to Crickley Hill. **2** The well-preserved roundhouse at Chalford. **3** The Garden at Miserden, with its colourful flowers, is a peaceful setting.

garden, with private outdoor seating area overlooking the Frome Valley, is a beautifully hand-crafted shepherd's hut (new in 2023) with wood panelling, handmade oak doors, oak dining table and kitchen area and a cosy alcove double bed (Hypnos mattress). Log-burning stove. Combi oven/grill, fridge. Washroom with shower, basin and toilet and toiletries.

4 THE TOADSMOOR VALLEY

Residues of old mills lie along the Toadsmoor Valley, a pencil-thin gorge with little more than the width of the road that winds down it for space. The valley runs north to south, like a spoke off Golden Valley. Tight-knit and secluded, it has plenty of good walks through the beech woods on its western slopes, which waft with the smell of wild garlic in early summer.

At the head of the valley is **Bisley**, a charming village that, before the wool trade, was more important than Stroud or any of its neighbours. The town has a bizarre story to tell: the legend of the Bisley Boy. In 1542, Henry VIII came to visit Over Court, reputedly a royal hunting lodge where his daughter Elizabeth was staying. While Henry was out hunting, the young princess fell ill and died. Rather than explain the tragic event to the king, courtiers buried her swiftly and substituted a like-for-like 'replacement' with red hair, except that the 'new' princess was a boy. It's believed that's why the Queen never married, went bald and requested that no post-mortem should be carried out on her body upon death! In a later twist, a Reverend Thomas Keble confessed that during restoration work to Over Court in 1870, he found a stone coffin with the remains of a little girl in Tudor dress and, respecting the original story, ordered the remains to be buried secretly once more.

Queen Elizabeth indeed once owned the house, which still stands in the village, as so many properties did once belong to the crown, but that is about the closest link. The Gothic writer Bram Stoker wrote about the legend/hoax in his book, *Famous Impostors*.

THE PAINSWICK VALLEY & THE SLAD VALLEY

The lie of the land north of Stroud looks like a part of the left hand: if the Painswick Valley is the index finger, a tiny spur around Sheepscombe is the knuckle and the Slad Valley is the thumb.

Having bypassed Cheltenham in a ring, the main Cotswold escarpment turns south and you begin to get spectacular westerly views from **Crickley Hill**, **Barrow Wake** and **Cooper's Hill**. The Painswick Valley proper begins in **Buckholt Wood**, a beechwood nature reserve of national importance and the source of the tiny Painswick Stream. Further views are obtained from the next high point, **Painswick Beacon**, followed by the exquisite town of **Painswick**. Opposite is the knuckle, where Sheepscombe is enveloped by further significant beech woods.

Below Sheepscombe is the thumbnail, the head of the Slad Valley and, roughly on the thumb joint, the village of Slad, the location of Laurie Lee's autobiographical *Cider with Rosie*. The two digits are webbed as well, for there is little between the valleys, each one pushing against the other.

5 FROM CRICKLEY HILL TO COOPER'S HILL

Crickley Hill is one of the best places in the Cotswolds to see the strata of oolitic limestone; the hill cliffs have the thickest section in Britain of pea grit, a particular kind of poor-quality limestone that is made up of pea-like nodules brimming with fossils. The area around the hill is a country park with beech and oak woods, grassland, old quarries and an archaeological site where 5,000 years of occupation are exposed, featuring a Neolithic causewayed enclosure and an Iron Age hillfort. Five circular trails from the car park are waymarked, variously including the hillfort, the parkland, a short trail for families, the scrubs and the steepest section of the park on the edge of the escarpment.

"The area is named after an Iron Age burial chamber discovered by quarry workers at the end of the 19th century."

Just south is **Barrow Wake**, a viewpoint and picnic spot with some of the finest views across to the Malverns and to Crickley Hill, where you can see the limestone strata of the cliffs even more clearly. Right on the edge of the escarpment, it's a windy spot and the slopes are inevitably steep, but there's plenty of flora and fauna enjoying the limestone grassland including, in late summer, vast swathes of rare electric purple devil's-bit scabious. The area is named after an Iron Age burial chamber discovered by quarry workers at the end of the 19th century.

As the escarpment continues south, grassland turns to dense woodland, in particular filled with beech trees, for which this part of the Cotswolds is most renowned. Witcombe Wood covers much of the escarpment as it folds around to create a crescent shape towards Cooper's Hill. To see how the scarp curves round, follow the road from Little Witcombe to **Great Witcombe Roman Villa** (free access, unstaffed). Here, partway up the ridge and below the Cotswold Way, are the remains of a once-grand house and bathhouse built around AD250 within a large country estate. Little is left – just the low-lying outline of some of the walls, but it is a contemplative place to take in the surroundings: villa sites were often chosen for their views, and this has steep pastures and woodlands as a backdrop, with Gloucester, a villa town of Roman origins, in the near distance. There is a small car park for the villa but the remaining 150yds must be made on foot.

The line of high ground continues to **Cooper's Hill**, facing north right on the end of the crescent before the escarpment takes a dramatic turn south. It's one of the most jaw-dropping points of the Cotswold ridge. If the gradient of the escarpment were not steep enough, Cooper's Hill then appears to sit on top, with a 1 in 2 incline beneath. As this is common land, you are entitled to walk on the hill – and the Cotswold Way passes along its foot – but what is all the more remarkable is that hundreds of people, who one can only assume must be bordering on insane, throw themselves down this slope every year in pursuit of a giant wheel of Double Gloucester cheese. The annual **cheese-rolling** event, which takes place every spring bank holiday at the end of May, is a highlight of the quirky Cotswold calendar.

"The annual cheese-rolling event, which takes place every spring bank holiday at the end of May, is a highlight of the quirky Cotswold calendar."

Getting to Cooper's Hill at any time of year is tricky. There is a tiny car park along the narrowest of single-track roads off the A46 from Brockworth, and up a steep incline up the side of the escarpment. The best access route is on foot along the Cotswold Way, and there's a particularly fine signposted circular walk from Cranham that takes in Cooper's Hill.

6 CRANHAM

South of Cooper's Hill and running east to west, sandwiched between the A46 Cheltenham to Painswick road and the Birdlip to Bisley road, is Buckholt Wood. The lie of the land appears not to know which way to turn, darting this way and that. The wood is of international importance, demonstrating some of the finest ancient beech in Europe and making up a part of the **Cotswold Commons and Beechwoods National**

Nature Reserve. The wood is a joy to wander through – even if some of the paths are steep – a chiaroscuro of wide tracks and light-filled open woodland against dense shades of bottle green. On its floor are bluebells in spring and rare orchids in summer, spiders and snails found only in ancient woodlands and rare butterflies such as the white admiral. I'm particularly fond of family walks in this wood – and in the neighbouring Brockworth and Cooper's Hill woods. In spring, the luscious canopy of lime-green leopard's spots above your head creates a cathedral-like roof, while in autumn and winter it's a fabulous crunchy-leaved walk.

Adjoining the woods is **Cranham Common**, also part of the national nature reserve. The 48-acre piece of hillside is classic unimproved limestone grassland, grazed using traditional methods and issuing cowslips in spring, orchids in early summer and later in the year, knapweed, harebells and wild thyme. You may come across the rare rufous grasshopper, a very localised species with distinctive white-tipped, club-shaped antennae, or hear the skylarks singing above your head. It's an ideal place for a picnic – I've particularly noted a bench on the single-track road that crosses the common and connects the two parts of **Cranham** village. It's one of the best spots to view the autumnal changing colours of Buckholt Wood.

7 PRINKNASH ABBEY

Prinknash Shop & Café GL4 8EX ✆ 01452 812066 ⌖ prinknashabbey.org

West of Buckholt Wood, tucked into the escarpment, is Prinknash Abbey, accessed off the A46 Cheltenham to Painswick road. The Benedictine monks live at St Peter's Grange, a tranquil medieval manor house in the grounds of the estate.

Naturally, it's not open to the public other than for religious services and retreats. However, the Monastery Shop and Café is open to the public, selling monastic gifts and items made by the monks (Prinknash

"In between, work involves the blending of incense – the oldest incense-blenders in Europe still operating."

is apparently famous worldwide for its incense, and, Prinknash Pottery, though no longer produced by the monks, is highly collectible), together with books. It's housed in a not very spiritual-looking building, an old 1970s prefab office block that was once used by the Prinknash Pottery. But don't let that deter you from visiting: the café, serving delicious cakes, biscuits, breakfasts and lunches all made on the premises, has a restful quality, playing recordings of gentle monastic chants and with easy chairs where you can sit quietly. Make time, also, to visit the walled Monastery Garden. It's a work in progress as it is gradually being restored by volunteers from the Stroud Valleys Project (page 309). It too is a restful, sheltered spot, with views across the uninhabited valley, a colourful butterfly garden created by the Gloucestershire branch of Butterfly Conservation, soft fruits and raised beds plus very attractive apple arbours.

GRAZING THE COTSWOLDS

A lack of traditional grazing by animals over the years allows coarse grasses and scrub to take over an area of land, which prevents low-lying grasses, herbs and many of the limestone-loving flowers from peeking through and regenerating. These flowers, herbs and mosses, often unique to the Cotswolds, also flourish on poor, brashy soils; they do not thrive on 'improved' grassland that has been enriched by fertilisers or treated with herbicides.

Over the last 20 years, the National Trust has been utilising cattle and the age-old techniques of grazing to keep scrub under control and to gradually restore, conserve and enhance chunks of unimproved limestone grassland that makes the Cotswolds so distinctive. That practice has evolved into The Stroud Landscape Project, with long-term objectives and a vision of a climate-resilient landscape.

David Armstrong, the project's Delivery Manager, explained, 'What began as a project on Trust-owned sites has expanded to become a landscape-scale conservation project. It involves the National Trust delivering conservation and habitat creation not only on its own sites across the Stroud Valleys, but working with other partners [such as Natural England, Butterfly Conservation and Gloucestershire Wildlife Trust] and private landowners to ensure we create a more connected landscape.

'Creating greater connectivity means bigger, better, more joined-up quality habitats. This means that species can move across that landscape in response to changes in the environment such as global warming and climate change, but also in response to small issues on sites that could lead to local extinctions. It means that populations are more robust. While the project began with the calcareous grasslands – and these remain the focal point – our work has extended to the hedgerows, wood pasture and woodlands, too, as important wildlife corridors.

'Hence, we are harvesting wildflower seed from donor and recipient sites on and off NT land, then offering local landowners that seed – and some of our cattle for grazing – together with appropriate advice as a comprehensive grassland restoration service.'

Matt Watts, the Farm Manager in charge of the conservation grazing herd, added, 'We use

A small display details the lives of the monks at Prinknash – a day that begins at 04.40 and with seven calls to prayer. In between, work involves the blending of incense – the oldest incense-blenders in Europe still operating.

8 SHEEPSCOMBE & PAINSWICK BEACON

If you want to survey Painswick from afar before heading into the town there are two particularly fine places from which to do it. The first is the

the cows to prepare the ground for wildflower seeding. Then, for meadows that are further on in the restoration stage that don't need wildflower seed, the cows are used to take out the scrub and encroaching grass.'

For this, the Trust selected and has grown a small herd of Belted Galloway, a native British breed of cattle that requires conserving in its own right. 'They are incredibly hardy cattle so can remain outdoors all year round, they're thrifty, are good for slopes and rank grass. They're also docile, which is good for our visitors', continued Matt. 'We have roughly 105 pedigree cattle grazing over 930 acres of Cotswold grassland at 23 sites.'

'One example of grazing management', explained Project Manager Lisa Edinborough, 'is the reintroduction in 2020 of the Large Blue butterfly (the rarest of the UK's native blue butterflies, which disappeared from Minchinhampton and Rodborough commons 150 years ago). The Large Blue likes limestone grassland, but we had to make sure that we had created the right conditions on the Commons before reintroducing the butterfly. Cattle were used to graze the scrub first, to allow the relevant plant and insect species to thrive to give the butterfly the best chance of survival upon its reintroduction. This has been a huge partnership project with multiple agencies. The population and spread of the butterfly from the initial site on Rodborough Common are being closely monitored, and early indications suggest that it has been successful so far.

'For a venture as big as the Stroud Landscape Project, patience is required. There is no immediate visual change. We're working with nature and so many factors can affect what we're doing. But we have objectives planned through until 2030, and a vision to have created a biodiverse, climate resilient landscape within the Stroud area by 2050.'

The Project is always looking for volunteers; you can pick and mix different tasks including scrub clearance, as cattle checkers, or habitat surveying (with training from the Trust); see ⊘ nationaltrust.org.uk/stroud-landscape-project.

Places where you are likely to see these cattle grazing while on a walk are at Rodborough and Minchinhampton commons, Haresfield Hill, Cranham Common, Sheepscombe, Woodchester Park and Crickley Hill.

road to **Sheepscombe**, to the northeast, and on a valley nodule. A tiny stream splits the pretty village, with houses on both hillsides. From there you can take walks into the vast surrounding beech woods that are part of the Cotswold Commons and Beechwoods National Nature Reserve. In *Cider with Rosie* Laurie Lee describes how his Uncle Charlie helped to plant some of these woods.

The hillsides here are some of the steepest in the Cotswolds; they appear almost vertical from the **Ebworth Centre**, the area hub for the National Trust. There's a moderate two-mile walk that can be taken around this traditional Cotswold farm estate with viewpoints towards Cranham Common and Sheepscombe Common. An information panel at the centre details the walking route; otherwise follow the orange waymarkers from the car park.

The second location is **Painswick Beacon** to the north of the town. An area of common land, this high point is ideal for walking, filled with scrub and woodland, native juniper bushes (which are in national decline), wild flowers and butterflies. And in contrast to the beech woods, the beacon is covered with a good mix of pines, chestnut, ash and field maple. Having been quarried years ago, the ground is lumpy and intriguing – you never know quite where the next view is coming from. The official beacon is on top of an Iron Age hillfort, the ramparts of which are remarkably clear. Views from here are quite something, over Painswick, **Haresfield Hill** (another of the Cotswolds' high points and over which the Cotswold Way passes) and westwards over the Severn Vale. From the beacon you begin to realise how vast an area (by English standards) Buckholt Wood and the beech woods around Sheepscombe occupy. There's a golf course at Painswick Beacon too and one of the greens fits snugly into the hillfort's ring as if to protect the golfers from marauding armies of hill walkers. Actually, the defences have already been breached, as a footpath runs right through the middle.

¶¶ FOOD & DRINK

Butcher's Arms Sheepscombe ✆ 01452 812113 ⟡ butchers-arms.co.uk. On the north side of the valley, this is very much a traditional village pub smothered with roses and hanging baskets in summer. Traditional pub-grub menu (steak and chips; sausage and mash). Good views and a pretty pub garden. Dog-friendly. A great stop-off on walks in the area (you'll need to replenish energy with all the steep hills!).

9 PAINSWICK

Approaching Painswick on the road from Cheltenham, it's as if the church spire of St Mary's is piercing the tarmac in front of you. A surreal entrance down New Street ('new' in 1428), a composé of fine Georgian façades and chimneys galore, you begin to appreciate how special this bite-size town is, perfect for exploring in an afternoon.

The absolute must-visit is the churchyard, celebrated for the significant number of sadly crumbling chest tombstones (plus the 18th-century town stonemason's pyramid tombstone; you can't miss it) and the 200-year-old lollipop yew trees, which legend says will always remain at 99 in number. Inside the elegant church, along the north aisle, are the graffiti of a disgruntled Puritan soldier who, in 1643, was imprisoned here during a disastrous English Civil War siege of the town. Charles I had his headquarters in the adjacent court house for some time.

"This is a town to look out from, with views of the more open valley hills to the east from many of the attractive streets."

This is a town to look out from, with views of the more open valley hills to the east from many of the attractive streets such as Hale Lane and the memorably named Tibbiwell. It's also an arty town, attracting artists whose studios appear here and there, notably Rupert Aker's, named The Loovre (it's the old public conveniences), creating oil paintings of local Cotswold scenes. There's also a collection of studios within **The Painswick Centre**, where you can see artists, including painters, textile artists and jewellers, at work.

I chatted with Isabella Hughes, a lino-printing artist who had just graduated from university and was setting up her studio. The keen surfer and skateboarder was already busy creating her first design, ready to colour-up the blank studio walls. 'I plan on creating murals with narratives and symbols associated with Painswick in a funky medieval style,' she says. 'They'll be fun; I can't take them too seriously, and I love primary colours, so they'll be bold, too.'

Painswick Rococo Garden

Painswick ✆ 01452 813204 🖉 rococogarden.org.uk

A half-mile walk from the town centre, Painswick Rococo Garden is acknowledged as one of the finest examples of Rococo theatricality left in Britain. Its restoration since the 1980s, when it was overgrown and abandoned, has been little short of miraculous, returning it to the way it looked in its flamboyant heyday. The various follies and architectural delights from which to enjoy numerous vistas create an atmosphere that you're unlikely to find anywhere else in the Cotswolds. A circular walk is best to appreciate all the nuances of the garden. Snowdrops smother the woodland banks in January and February, replaced by thousands of tulips and fritillaries in April, heritage roses in June and carpets of naturalised cyclamen later in the year.

¶¶ FOOD & DRINK

Painswick has a morning market (⊙ 08.15–09.45) every Thursday in the Painswick Centre car park on Bisley Street, supporting local producers within five miles of the town; on sale are bread, pastries, coffee, eggs, meat and cheese.

Arts Café Bisley St ⊘ painswickcentre.com/cafe-shop. A light and bright café that serves a particularly good cup of tea plus homemade cakes, from individual sponges to traybakes and scones. Quiche and paninis. Lots of artwork by local artists for sale on the walls.
Falcon New St ✆ 01452 222820 ⊘ thefalconpainswick.com. Very good British and European fare served all day, including morning coffee and afternoon tea. Pea and mint tortellini, with basil, peas and pine nuts; beef carpaccio, with parmesan, honey and figs. Owned by the Balfour Winery in Kent, which makes excellent English fizz that's on the wine list. Comforting surroundings with wood-panelled bars and sofas. Accommodation with views over St Mary's Churchyard.

10 THE SLAD VALLEY

♠ Furners Farm

Like its neighbours that make up the Five Valleys, the Slad Valley once bustled with cloth mills until 1820. The evidence has largely gone and the hillsides around the playful Slad Brook have returned to a rural idyll.

While the outskirts of Stroud are pushing their way up this short valley, the only other settlement is the ribbon village of **Slad**. This is where the poet Laurie Lee spent his Edwardian childhood and where his autobiographical book *Cider with Rosie* is based. He is also buried

1 Enjoy views across the valley from Painswick Beacon. 2 The Stroudwater Textile Trust is keeping the area's textile traditions alive. 3 The impressive Painswick Rococo Garden.
4 A cheese-rolling event is held every May on Cooper's Hill. 5 Buckholt Wood near Cranham has some of the finest ancient beech trees in Europe. ▶

NICK TURNER/COTSWOLDS.COM

STROUDWATER TEXTILE TRUST

PJ PHOTOGRAPHY/S

PJ PHOTOGRAPHY/S

PJ PHOTOGRAPHY/S

in the village churchyard and, prior to his death, was a familiar figure in the area. Despite the prolific attention that's given to his life and work, there is no physical museum or exhibition to look at in the village (instead you need to visit Stroud, where a tiny corner of the Museum in the Park (see opposite) is given over to the author). Better is to walk the fields and slopes that Lee did as both a child and adult to gain a sense of his work; the **Laurie Lee Wildlife Way** (page 291) was created by the Gloucestershire Wildlife Trust (⌀ gloucestershirewildlifetrust.co.uk) to celebrate the centenary of Lee's birth, and there are ten poetry posts to find along the way. The route includes walking through Laurie Lee Nature Reserve, an ancient woodland, and on to the summit of Swift's Hill, for extraordinary views along the valley.

"Like its neighbours that make up the Five Valleys, the Slad Valley once bustled with cloth mills until 1820."

As it was one of those books that seemed to be forever on the exam syllabus in schools, I refused to read *Cider with Rosie* for many years. Finally picking up a copy latterly, I could read it without the need to dissect every sentence structure and appreciate Laurie Lee's sublime descriptions of the countryside around the Slad Valley. He describes it as living in a 'bean-pod'. Visit this valley and you'll understand exactly what he means.

Despite Lee's understandable protestations about development, the Slad Valley is still very much a get-away-from-it-all destination. And you can do just that at **Furners Farm** (⌀ furnersfarm.co.uk) an organic smallholding with bed and breakfast in the depths of the Slad Valley. It is, no less, the old cider farm in *Cider With Rosie*.

🧳 SPECIAL STAYS

Furners Farm Elcombe, Slad GL6 7LA ☎ 01452 813216 ⌀ furnersfarm.co.uk. Approached along a twisting single-track lane on the steep eastern slope of the Slad Valley, overlooking Slad. Guest accommodation (one room, king-size double or twin beds) is on the ground floor of a renovated farm cottage, detached from the main house though breakfast is served here. On the route of the Laurie Lee Wildlife Way.

🍴 FOOD & DRINK

Woolpack Inn Slad ☎ 01452 813429 ⌀ thewoolpackslad.com. The pub immortalised in *Cider with Rosie* and a haunt of Laurie Lee in adult years. A traditional Cotswolds pub for both drinkers and diners. Good food with classics and more on a menu that changes weekly: mussels in cider, cream and leeks; mutton chops with lentils; panna cotta with apricots. Veg provided by Lypiatt Park in Stroud. Stunning views from the rear garden.

11 STROUD

You only need to see how the Five Valleys all come together to realise that Stroud has, for centuries, been an important meeting point. It developed late, by comparison with other Cotswold towns – not surprisingly given the inhospitable landscape before any forms of transport became available.

Today it thrives on being different (it's a town of brick and stone for starters and has a rugged feel in comparison to, for example, the towns of the north Cotswolds) and has carved a niche for itself as a bohemian place, shunning large chain stores and embracing the independent ones (Loose zero-waste shop; Stroud Valleys Project eco-shop; Stroud Bookshop (new books) and Fireside Bookshop (secondhand); Weven not-for-profit folk crafts and weaving). The weekly **farmers' market** – held every Saturday – is first rate, and one of the first ever to be introduced in the UK at the beginning of the renaissance for good, local food. Organic and fresh, local produce abounds throughout the town.

Stroud's rise came as the centre for the cloth-making industry and while this may have waned, there are at least some mills remaining. But the contemporary Arts and Crafts movement, in particular textiles, is important here and pride in locally made goods is huge. **Made in Stroud** at 16 Kendrick Street (✆ 01453 840265 ⊘ madeinstroud.co.uk) is one of the most popular shops in town, selling locally made crafts and gifts.

My favourite place to visit in Stroud is the excellent **Museum in the Park** (✆ 01453 763394 ⊘ museuminthepark.org.uk). Set up in a 17th-century mansion house that was built by a wealthy clothier, it's a fascinating

"It developed late, by comparison with other Cotswold towns – not surprisingly given the inhospitable landscape."

museum that provides a potted history of the Stroud valleys in addition to an art gallery and regular exhibitions. Free to enter, it's well attuned to families, with children's discovery trails and child-friendly displays.

There are some extraordinary oil paintings, highlighting the town of yesteryear, including *View of Wallbridge*, c1790, which always catches my eye for its depiction of the Stroudwater Navigation Canal

THE COTSWOLD CANALS – A RESTORATION PROJECT

In the 18th century two canals, the **Thames and Severn Canal** and the **Stroudwater Navigation**, were built to create a 36-mile stretch of waterway that linked up the rivers Severn and Thames. It made a formidable and important journey for goods to be transported from towns on the Severn to London. Merging in Stroud, the pair became known as the Cotswold Canals.

The Stroudwater was the first to be built, between 1775 and 1779, with the Thames and Severn Canal completed a decade later. But the River Severn is considerably lower than the Thames and a flight of locks was required to reach the summit at Daneway, near Sapperton (page 293), where one of the longest canal tunnels in Britain was built.

The Cotswold Canals were an incredibly important and busy thoroughfare for goods but competition from the railways during the latter half of the 19th century caused decline and by 1927 the Thames and Severn Canal was closed, followed shortly after by the Stroudwater. With the canals neglected they soon became derelict.

Today restoration is uppermost in the mind of the **Cotswold Canals Trust** (⊘ cotswoldcanals.org), which owns parts of the canal including Inglesham Lock, considered the gateway to the Cotswolds from the Thames. Several sections of the

and rows of Stroud Scarlet dyed broadcloth hanging out to dry on the hillside behind. Displays allow you to really get to grips with the history of the cloth industry; how Stroud and nearby Dursley became famous for making broadcloth, a heavy felted fabric that was used for regimental soldiers' uniforms, the covering of billiard tables and more recently tennis balls. Much of the cloth was dyed with strong colours that became known as 'Stroud scarlet', the classic colour for a soldier's uniform, 'Uley blue' and 'billiard table green'. But by 1900 only 20 mills had survived and by the end of the 20th century only one major manufacturer remained. Stroud was also the birthplace of the lawnmower, inspired by the rotary shearing machines used to cut the surface of cloth in the local mills.

The **Stroudwater Textile Trust** (⊘ stroudtextiletrust.org.uk) is committed to keeping the textile traditions of the area alive, organising textile events, preserving historic machinery and providing courses on weaving, felt-making and dyeing. They also organise a series of mill visits between April and September each year, where you can watch – and have a go at – some of the processes required to make cloth.

canals, most notably around Stroud, are fully restored but the ultimate aim is to restore the full length of both canals, using volunteers to clear undergrowth, rebuild locks and repair walls.

Said David Le Bourgeois, volunteer at the Wallbridge Visitor Centre in Stroud, 'The vision of our founding members in 1972 was the canal's restoration for boats. That still holds true; however, it's latterly become apparent the importance of the restoration for walkers, who now have 11 miles of towpath for walks, while the canal has also become a wildlife corridor.'

Working parties meet four times a week, including volunteer drop-in sessions for anyone that happens to be in the vicinity. The Trust really needs enthusiastic people, whether regular or over the course of a volunteering holiday, to restore and maintain locks and sections of the canal, and clear towpaths.

For those that prefer a leisurely boat trip or a guided walk along the canal, these help to generate income to keep the restoration project going. Volunteers can approach through the website or by dropping into one of the visitor centres at Wallbridge in Stroud (open six days a week) and at Saul (open every weekend). Both have excellent displays highlighting the current stage of the long-term restoration.

However, my favourite part of the museum is the tiny Laurie Lee corner where you can become immersed in his luxurious language. A chair sits beside a small, old-fashioned range; there are knick-knacks and books – all by Laurie Lee of course – and sound extracts from his most famous work, read by the author.

¶¶ FOOD & DRINK

Stroud **Farmers' Market** takes place every Saturday but there's also an **organic market** held every Friday and Saturday in the Shambles Market, off the High Street, and a market held on the first Sunday of every month.

Little Ginger Deli & Café Kendrick St ✆ 01453 790664. Offering a delicious range of fresh salads, homemade quiches, sausage rolls (plus vegan option) and cakes. Excellent cup of tea, too.

Star Anise Café Gloucester St ✆ 01453 840021 ⊘ staraniseartscafe.com. Very popular café specialising in nutritional food with a philosophy to use wholesome, organic, local and seasonal produce. Includes organic beers and wines too. Predominantly vegetarian with daily vegan and gluten-free options.

Woodruffs Organic Café 24 High St ✆ 01453 759195 🖱 woodruffsorganiccafe.co.uk. Established in 1998, this was Britain's first totally organic café. Mainly vegetarian menu (barbecue 'Boston' beans, eggs and mushrooms) with options for allergy sufferers. Good, wholesome and appetising food with plenty of choice. Organic tea and coffee.

THE COTSWOLD SCARP – THE DRY VALLEY?

Southwest of Stroud the landscape has a very special quality. This is a continuation of the Cotswold ridge but there is no way of finding uniformity at any point. The ridge meanders like an ageing river, except that there is no river, at least not of any note or length. And within these meanders are knuckles of miniature valleys clustering together.

Every so often prominent hills such as **Downham Hill** and **Cam Long Down** are dotted about, the effects of land slippage when the crust of the Cotswold ridge was tilted up onto its side millions of years ago.

12 SELSLEY TO ULEY BURY

Leaving Stroud on the B4066 to Dursley requires an instant and dramatic climb, passing through the village of **Selsley**, on the cusp where the Nailsworth Valley and the Cotswold escarpment meet. Particularly noticeable in the village is the French-looking (though a copy of the church in Marling, South Tyrol) saddleback tower of **All Saints' Church**, which catches the sunlight at a time when the surrounding hills are in shadow. The stained glass here was one of the first major commissions granted to William Morris. Windows include the work of Morris together with his Pre-Raphaelite friends, Dante Gabriel Rossetti and Edward Burne-Jones. Each artist designed one of the three triptychs on the south side of the nave while the rose window, above the west door, is the work of Morris himself.

From Selsley the main road actually runs part of the way up the westerly hillside of the Nailsworth Valley, and to its west is **Selsley Common**. At the centre of the common is the top of the ridge that divides this valley from the western edge of the Cotswold escarpment. It is rich in the wildflowers – and therefore birds and butterflies – most associated with the limestone grassland of the Cotswolds. Formerly quarried, the land dips and rises and, owing to the natural curve of the land, you get one view disappearing as another arrives. Yes, there are views over the Severn Vale and the Forest of Dean but what's best about the common are the views over Stroud and other valleys, the walks and picnicking opportunities, despite the often windy conditions.

Beyond the common are Pen Hill and Pen Wood, filling a loop in the distorted ridgeline and, on the other side of the road, the home of the **Bristol and Gloucester Gliding Club** (∂ bggc.co.uk). On a fine day, you'll see the gentle, giant gliders whistle overhead, and you can have a go, too. Close to the edge of the scarp, it's the perfect place for gliding, the pilots (members of the club include world and European champions) using the warm currents that rise off the ridge for soaring. Trial flights provide a 15- to 30-minute soar with a fully qualified instructor above the Cotswold scarp, arguably the best way to see it – and you'll get to take hold of the controls.

There's a picnic area at the 778ft-high **Coaley Peak Viewpoint**, with the scarp dropping like a thunderbolt below. While munching on a sandwich, you can easily make out Sugar Loaf Mountain in Wales and the Malverns. On this site is **Nympsfield Long Barrow**, an exceptionally fine example of a Neolithic chambered tomb, which is in the shape of a cross despite being pre-Christian by 5,000 years. When excavated, the communal grave was found to contain the skeletons of 17 men, women and children and was possibly used for the ritualistic sacrifice of animals too. **Hetty Peglar's Tump**, one mile south, is another fine example, and it still has its roof. At 120ft long and 84ft wide it's big enough to crawl into. There is no parking at the tump so to reach it, park at Coaley Peak Viewpoint and walk along the Cotswold Way.

¶¶ FOOD & DRINK

Caper Bristol & Gloucester Gliding Club, GL10 3TX ∂ caper.org.uk. On the airfield of BGGC, this restaurant makes everything, including its homemade spice blends, preserves, marinades and pickles. Middle Eastern, Mediterranean and Asian cuisine, with vegan, vegetarian and local, free-range meat options. Opposite the Cotswold Way, making this an excellent stop-off between Uley and Selsley.

13 ULEY BURY

Making the most of a promontory between the edge of the scarp and knobbled valley is the scheduled Ancient Monument of Uley Bury. The large, 32-acre Iron Age hillfort once was home to an industrious farming community that made woollen cloth and early coinage. As a prime example of unimproved grassland, the terraced structure is grazed using traditional methods to stop the encroachment of trees and walkers are not allowed in the centre. But you can walk the full distance around the mile-long ramparts using the circular bridleway for jaw-dropping views.

I've taken several walks here over the years and, in addition to the profusion of common blue and gatekeeper butterflies and coppery gold damselflies, I'm always struck by the views over the Severn Vale on the northwest side and those over the Ewelme Valley to the southeast.

"You can walk the full distance around the mile-long ramparts using the circular bridleway for jawdropping views."

But by far the most captivating aspect is the short stretch of rampart facing the southwest. On occasion my children and I struggle to stay upright on the edge of the rampart as the wind hits this projecting side of the escarpment hard. But the views over the landmark hills of Downham Hill (or Smallpox Hill locally), Cam Long Down and Peaked Down towards **Stinchcombe Hill** are out of this world. I don't know what it is about these protruding luscious green hummocks in an otherwise relatively flat landscape below the escarpment, but I fell in love with them instantly the first time I saw them. We met an elderly man on the tip of the bury who has lived in the area for years. He described how in springtime these mounds become highlands as the mist envelops the valley: 'The tops peek out and the mist swells up and down like the ocean.' This southwest corner of Uley Bury he described as having 'one of the finest views in England'. I agree.

To visit Uley Bury you can park at the northeast entrance, where you can also pick up paths to visit the very steep **Coaley Wood**, owned by the Woodland Trust. This is an alternative route to visit Hetty Pegler's Tump.

14 ULEY & OWLPEN MANOR

The village of Uley sits in the Ewelme Valley, a stubby valley upon the eastern side of the Cotswold escarpment. The knobbly contours of the land ambling in and out create a series of plump, green cushions, fringed with woodland. The village is strung along the Stroud–Dursley road and is made up of many fine clothiers' houses in typical Cotswold style. Like its counterparts, this valley was caught up with the boom of the cloth-making industry, and Uley blue cloth, used for military uniforms, was unrivalled from the 17th to the early 19th century. Today the village is better known for its **brewery** (⏀ uleybrewery.com), producing ales such as Uley Bitter and Hogshead, using water from the Cotswold springs that feed the Ewelme. The beers are sold in pubs within the local area, but you can visit the brewery on pre-booked dates for an Evening with a Brewer to try a range of beers while learning its history.

A mile to the east of Uley, tucked into a secret spur of its own, is **Owlpen Manor** (✆ 01453 860261 ⏀ owlpen.com). Known as one of King Charles's favourite places in England, the beauty of the Owlpen Estate defies words. Its location is so hidden that you cannot see it from Uley Bury, despite the 'whole' of the Ewelme Valley being laid out before you. The Tudor manor house is an architectural gem that was left untouched for centuries until sympathetic restoration began early in the 20th century during the Arts and Crafts Movement.

The gardens, like the house, have received acclaim from many of Britain's greatest garden designers, including Vita Sackville-West and Gertrude Jekyll. Of historical importance, it's the most complete garden of the Stuart period open to the public, containing seven formal hanging terraces together with further additions made by the present owners along 'old English' traditions. Box parterres, immaculately clipped hedges and moss-lined stone walls frame borders rich with colour. Visitors can wander through the idyllic estate-owned village and peaceful valley too, with miles of walks through the surrounding beech woods.

¶¶ FOOD & DRINK

Old Crown Inn 17 The Green, Uley ✆ 01453 860502 ⏀ oldcrownuley.co.uk. Traditional country pub on the village green at the top end of the village. Serves ales from Stroud Brewery and simple fare – hot pork roll, loaded potato skins, plus 'pie and a pint' night on Tuesdays.

15 DURSLEY & STINCHCOMBE WOODS

Dursley is an extraordinary Cotswold town in that it doesn't have that typical look or quaint charm so connected with the towns of the Cotswolds. A refreshing change, it's made up of buildings in a mixture of styles, ages and materials. Sitting in the Cam Valley, to the east of and beneath Stinchcombe Hill, it is really the conjoined triplet of both the larger town of Cam to the north and Woodmancote to the south,

NICK TURNER/COTSWOLDS.COM

MARTIN FOWLER/S

JOHN CORRY/S

NICK TURNER/COTSWOLDS.COM

sandwiched between the two. With **Walkers are Welcome** status, and an annual walking festival, Dursley is a popular start point for various walks including the 14-mile circular Lantern Way, which links the town with the villages of Coaley and Uley.

Parsonage Street, Dursley's main, pedestrianised shopping street down which the Cotswold Way runs, has been taken over by a plethora of charity shops and low-cost supermarkets but remains endearing nonetheless. Dursley's most iconic building is the pillared Market House, built in 1738, now used as the town hall and the location for the monthly farmers' market. An interesting little **Heritage Centre** opposite the Market House gives a thousand years of history and showcases many locally made objects from the town's industrial past.

Southwest of Dursley is **Stinchcombe Hill**, a protruding limb of the Cotswold escarpment. Its rim is lined with woodland but the top is a windy wilderness, used partly by the Stinchcombe Hill Golf Club and by walkers on the Cotswold Way, which skirts around the edge. In my view it's a must-visit place if you're in this part of the Cotswolds; a long, narrow road takes you from Woodmancote to the centre of the hill – don't park in the first car park that you come across, near the clubhouse, as it's for members of the golf club, but continue until the road stops where there's a second, public car park. A circular walk known as the **Korea Friendship Trail** (in partnership with a long-distance trail in South Korea) around the rim of the unevenly shaped down will provide astonishing if wind-blown views, particularly at Drakestone Point, one of the most westerly points of the Cotswold escarpment. But close to the golf clubhouse, the Cotswold Way passes right by a very pretty triangular green, perfectly sheltered for a picnic.

A mile from Stinchcombe Hill, approached along the same narrow road, is the predominantly beech **Twinberrow Wood**. During the winter there are glimpses of Dursley below but in spring the woodland floor comes alive with bluebells and wild garlic. Within the wood, a **Sculpture and Play Trail** is aimed at encouraging more people to visit and particularly to develop imaginative play among children. The

---

◀ **1** The Iron-Age hillfort of Uley Bury. **2** The Tudor Owlpen Manor is hidden away in a beautiful setting. **3** The Tolsey Clock in Wotton-under-Edge was erected in honour of Queen Victoria. **4** Woodland-lined Stinchcombe Hill offers some spectacular walking on the Cotswold Way.

various sculptures and artworks that crop up along the trail have been created by many different community groups and organisations such as the Girl Guides, a nearby residential care home (where the residents have provided some fascinating stories from their own childhood memories of visiting the woods, displayed on the trail), an art group and local schools. There are activities too, such as the 'Friendship Circle': simple enough, you sit on logs and talk to one another, sharing a woodland story. A proportion of the trail is accessible to wheelchairs and pushchairs.

¶¶ FOOD & DRINK

Leaf and Ground Dursley Rd, Woodfield GL11 6PP ✎ 01453 393007 ⬧ leafandground. com. A destination venue with café and deli in a new oak-framed building, offering 20 acres of hillside walks with views and pop-up shops with local artists. Pick up a picnic from the deli counter or choose from the varied kitchen menu (from ham, egg and chips to Palestinian musaqa'a, lamb kofte and mussels steamed in Dunkertons cider).

Old Spot Inn Hill Rd, Dursley ✎ 01453 542870 ⬧ oldspotinn.co.uk. Wide selection of real ales and hearty home cooking of traditional fare. A popular pub with locals. Useful for the Cotswold Way, which passes by the entrance.

16 WOTTON-UNDER-EDGE & NORTH NIBLEY

As its name implies, **Wotton-under-Edge** sits at the edge of the Cotswold escarpment. Yet its position is not quite that simple, for it also spreads up the hillsides of the small Tyley Valley that runs at right angles to the escarpment, the pair crashing into one another right beneath the feet of the town. You'll realise during any exploration that you are constantly walking up or down a hill.

Like Dursley, Wotton is not picture-postcard stuff, but a working town with a welcoming spirit and a mix of architectural styles. In the centre is the little stream that flows down the valley, once used by dyers to change the colour of broadcloth. Wotton too was completely taken over by the woollen industry from the 13th to the 19th century and was originally one of the most important woollen towns in the area. Women would spin the wool while the men wove the yarn into cloth – there's a string of weavers' cottages on the Culverhay, close to the parish church.

Long Street and the High Street, to the west of the stream, are the main shopping areas, with plenty of interesting independent shops, the impressive Tolsey Clock erected in honour of Queen Victoria, and eateries to occupy a wander. But head down Market Street, off the High Street, and you'll come across three buildings of note. The first is the town hall, where the farmers' market takes place on the first Saturday of every month and Wotton's 'Town Hall Teas' are held. Next door is the **Electric Picture House**, an intimate 100-seat cinema run by the community with volunteer helpers, showing both popular and unusual films in state-of-the-art digital format. It's a cinema like no other and is certainly worlds apart from the multiplexes. Next door is the **Heritage Centre**, a tiny building crammed with interesting bits and pieces.

Again run by volunteers, it's free to enter. You'll really get to grips with the history of the area there. Have a look at the exquisite 3D fabric map of the town, made by the Women's Institute in 1979. Also in the centre are leaflets on numerous local walks, including three 'mill walks' of two, five and seven miles long, pinpointing the remains from the woollen industry along the way.

Elsewhere look out for the **Perry and Dawes Almshouses**, built in 1630 along Church Street. Accessed through an archway, there's a very pleasant little grass courtyard where you can sit and the sweetest tiny chapel to visit. Inside, two stained-glass windows draw the eye – a tiny commemorative window made in 2005 that's filled with daffodils and roses, and the other showing the town's dependence upon sheep, wool and the clothing trade.

Approaching Wotton-under-Edge from Stinchcombe, you pass through the village of **North Nibley**. It's no more or less remarkable than any other village, but on the hillside above is the **Tyndale Monument**. At 111ft tall, the tower can be seen for miles around – including from Stinchcombe Hill – and was built in memory of William Tyndale, the first translator into English of the New Testament in 1525. Though born in North Nibley, Tyndale was strangled and burned at the stake in Belgium for heresy upon the orders of Henry VIII. However, in 1540, just four years after Tyndale's death, his work was used as the basis for four translations of the Bible, including the king's official 'Great Bible' and in 1611 the King James version, still in use today. The monument is accessed up a steep path just to the south of the village.

¶¶ FOOD & DRINK

Town Hall Teas Town Hall. Every Sunday Wotton's town hall is taken over by local community organisations that put on a spread of homemade cakes and refreshments to raise funds for various causes. Having run for many years, the teas are proving ever more popular, attracting people from afar.

Wotton Farm Shop Bradley Rd ⌀ 01453 521546 ⌂ wottonfarmshop.co.uk. Superb shop with on-site butcher selling homegrown (from the farm) fruit and veg in addition to other produce from the county. The on-site kitchen makes cakes, pastries, soups and ready meals while the Potting Shed café has a lovely ambience and is my pick of places within Wotton for a quick lunch bite.

17 OZLEWORTH & THE LAST OF THE COTSWOLD SCARP

Parallel with the Tyley Valley, at the bottom of which is Wotton-under-Edge, a neighbouring valley spreads similarly from the northeast and pushes against the western escarpment. Likewise, there's a tiny stream that cuts through this quiet and secret valley, barely touched by human habitation, with the undulating hills either side appearing like soft, green pillows just as at Uley and Owlpen. And one tiny lane carves its way along the Ozleworth Bottom valley floor and up the steep bank to Ozleworth. This minuscule hamlet consists of little more than three or four modest houses and **Ozleworth Park**, surrounded by parkland and 12 acres of handsome gardens with neat box-enclosed parterres. These are privately owned (and not open to the public) but within the park grounds, and accessible all year round, is **St Nicholas of Myra Church**, managed by the Churches Conservation Trust. You cannot get near with a car but must walk (or ride) along footpaths and bridleways to reach it. Wonderfully atmospheric, tucked against the side of one of the most unspoilt valleys in the Cotswolds, in a walled garden and surrounded by parkland, this tiny, squat building exudes a sense of peace. It has an unusual hexagonal tower of irregular proportions; no two walls are the same width. It's most noticeable from inside when you gaze up to the tower ceiling.

At the top of the valley ridge, and best accessed from Wotton-under-Edge, is **Newark Park** (⌀ 01453 842644; National Trust), owned by the National Trust. As a Tudor hunting lodge and later expanded into a Georgian country house, Newark Park has plenty of history, but its glory is its location overlooking this wild but lusciously green and partly wooded valley. A series of permitted walks through the estate, including former deer parks, allows you to explore this otherwise inaccessible part of the valley, devoid as it is of public footpaths.

Ozleworth Bottom is almost the last of the extended valleys running at right angles to the western ridge. From here, the Cotswold escarpment compresses itself into a thin band that runs due south, passing the tiny villages of Hawkesbury, Horton, Little Sodbury and Old Sodbury. The little lanes that follow the ridge between the villages provide some spectacular westerly views, although it's a little surreal to be seeing the large expanses of Bristol and Yate close by.

One of the best outlooks is from the **Somerset Monument**, close to the village of Hawkesbury Upton. Not dissimilar to the nearby Tyndale Monument, it was erected in 1846 in memory of General Lord Robert Somerset, a soldier whose ancestral home was at nearby Badminton (page 346) and who had a distinguished military career fighting at the Battle of Waterloo.

Chipping Sodbury is the last of the Cotswold towns along the ridge – or actually sitting just below the ridge – before Bath. As 'chipping' was a word that meant 'market', unsurprisingly Chipping Sodbury was an important market town during medieval times and a meeting point on the Bristol to London road. While the town has expanded over the years, joining up with the town of Yate, the very wide main street through Chipping Sodbury, aptly named Broad Street, remains extremely attractive, with a mixture of Cotswold stone and neatly painted buildings. Walks on **Sodbury Common**, north of the town, provide marvellous views of the Cotswold ridge.

THE NAILSWORTH VALLEY

Stroud spreads down the first mile of the Nailsworth Valley, sandwiched between Selsley and Rodborough commons. The Nailsworth Stream lines the valley floor, once marshland, so early inhabitants stuck to the steep valley sides. Villages such as **Woodchester** and the town of **Nailsworth** have only really developed since the 17th century, when the woollen industry took off here.

On the eastern slopes tiny villages, all connected to the cloth industry, hug the steep hillside. It's as if everything is in miniature here – tiny, terraced former weavers' cottages line the narrowest of lanes. You can make a very picturesque day out by linking together hamlets such as Littleworth, Amberley, Theescombe and Watledge, where the poet W H Davies, whose poem began the introduction to this book, spent his final years. Walking constantly on the slope can be tough, but the roads, many of which are designated as Quiet Lanes where horseriders, cyclists and walkers take priority over cars, are sufficiently narrow and twisty that you have to go slow either when driving (small cars required) or cycling. Make the most of the requirement to be unhurried and soak up the views as you progress from village to village.

To the west, two further tight-knit valleys run at right angles to the Nailsworth Valley. The wooded **Woodchester Park** fills up the more northerly of the two, while the **Newmarket Valley** just below remains totally untouched with no roads along its floor and only the village of Nympsfield at its western end for habitation.

18 WOODCHESTER PARK

To the northwest of Nailsworth is Woodchester Park, a lost 18th- and 19th-century landscape park that takes up most of a steeply sided valley. For 200 years, until the mid 19th century, the park was the seat of the Ducie family who designed and constructed the landscape park around their home, since demolished. It included formal gardens and large fishponds as well as carriage drives providing panoramic views over the estate. During the late 19th century the estate, under new owners, was planted with trees, which have now matured, creating a new wooded park.

The National Trust now owns Woodchester Park and visitors can wander through the 400-acre estate all year round, free of charge. The Trust is performing a gradual restoration of the park, thinning out some of the plantations to create the vistas that there once were.

"Their enchanting boathouse, built in the early 19th century and used by the family for picnics and boating parties, was restored in 1998."

It is an idyllic place, regardless of tree count, to go for a walk, either through the shaded beech woods, annually filled with bluebells and wild garlic, or through the more open glades and pastures alongside the string of five lakes created by the Ducie family. Their enchanting boathouse, built in the early 19th century and used by the family for picnics and boating parties, was restored in 1998.

The Trust has created a series of walks throughout the estate from the pick of two entrances – either the Buckholt car park (not to be confused with Buckholt Wood some 13 miles north), accessed off the B4066

Stroud to Dursley road, or the Tinkley Gate entrance, off Tinkley Lane from Nympsfield. Of the two, walks are directly into the woods from the Buckholt entrance while the Tinkley Gate entrance affords a birds-eye view across the top of the valley from open grassland meadows (and a café) before making the steep descent on foot to the valley floor. My favourite is the 3½-mile circular Boathouse Walk (waymarked from the Buckholt entrance) that makes the most of the vistas from both the lakes and woods. Although manmade, the lakes are most attractively unspoilt in appearance.

Woodchester Mansion

Nympsfied, Glos GL10 3TS ℰ 01453 861541 ⬦ woodchestermansion.org.uk

Hidden among the trees in this secluded valley, a mile from any road, is one of the most secret houses, the 19th-century Victorian Gothic Woodchester Mansion. To me, it's also one of the most memorable houses in the Cotswolds, indeed Britain, made all the more special because it will never be completed.

Woodchester Mansion has no glass in the windows, limited staircases and barely any floors. It is not a derelict ruin, though the masterpiece was mysteriously abandoned mid construction in 1873. The listed building, completed externally but not internally, is an extraordinary architectural exhibit, the craftsmanship second to none, and your imagination is required to finish the house. Intricately carved corbels, butted against the walls, stand ready to receive vaulted ceilings that never materialised, Gothic arches are part-finished and the marks of the builder's pencil are poised for a non-existent completion. Time really does stand still here.

Only one room was ever finished and to a lower standard of work not seen anywhere else in the house, having been hurriedly completed to receive a dignitary who unexpectedly accepted an invitation to visit. It makes the remaining abandonment all the more poignant. But the roof of the house is occupied now – by two nationally important colonies of bats recorded in the hundreds. Live footage of both greater and lesser horseshoe bats can be seen from the webcam in the Bat Room.

Various events and children's activities are hosted regularly throughout the summer, both in connection to bats and Victorian history. Like the park, access to the house is from the Buckholt entrance off the B4066 Stroud to Dursley road, close to the village of Nympsfield. Visitors may walk the mile from the car park to the house or use the free minibus.

¶¶ FOOD & DRINK

There's a café at the Tinkley Gate area of Woodchester Park. Woodchester Mansion has a small tea room in one of the uncompleted rooms but it can get very busy. The Rose and Crown at Nympsfield is the nearest place to eat otherwise.

Old Fleece Woodchester ✆ 01453 872582 ⊘ food-club.com. Wood panelling and timber floors make this old inn warm and inviting. A mix of British and continental food on the menu with plenty of choice for light meals or something more substantial, with much of the produce coming from the neighbouring historic orchard owned by the pub.

19 WOODCHESTER VALLEY VINEYARD

⌂ Woodchester Valley Vineyard

Convent Ln, Woodchester ✆ 07523 967219 ⊘ woodchestervalleyvineyard.co.uk

It's long been known that the Romans introduced vineyards to England and, with a Roman villa discovered at Woodchester, there's every likelihood this included planting vines on the slopes of the Nailsworth Valley. It's one of the reasons why Gloucestershire-child Fiona Shiner chose to plant an acre of vines in the valley, at Amberley (page 330).

The vines grew well and the first few bottles to come from the vineyard tasted pretty good, so she planted a few more, encouraged by learning that the 12th-century historian William of Malmesbury recorded that the Cotswolds were planted with more vines than anywhere else in England, including two acres at 'Stanhouse' (now Stonehouse), also recorded in the Domesday Book of 1086.

Woodchester Valley Vineyard now has 58 acres of vines across three sites within the Stroud Valleys, including at Stonehouse; walkers along the Cotswold Way will walk among the vines here.

Climbing the western slopes of the Nailsworth Valley south of Woodchester is the largest block of vines. Here, Fiona built a winery where she and winemaker Jeremy Mount create internationally recognised, award-winning sparkling and still wines. I joined one of the regular vineyard tours and tastings in the purpose-built tasting room.

1 Stroll among the vines at Woodchester Valley Vineyard. **2** A boathouse by one of the lakes at Woodchester Park. **3** Woodchester Mansion is one of the most memorable houses in the Cotswolds. **4** You can't help being drawn in to William's Fish Market and Food Hall in Nailsworth. ▶

WOODCHESTER VALLEY VINEYARD

MIKE GRASSMYER/D

WOODCHESTER MANSION TRUST

NICK TURNER/COTSWOLDS.COM

The views are very special – across the Nailsworth Valley to Rodborough and Minchinhampton commons and the village of Amberley, where it's possible to see the first vines that Fiona planted on the razor-sharp escarpment. Above are the glorious, wildlife-rich limestone grasslands of the commons.

Guests were welcomed with a glass of the vineyard's 'Cotswold Classic' sparkling wine as tour guide Aby explained the story of English wine, the history of the vineyard and how the wine is made before a tour outside to see the wines and the winery. The harvest was about to kick-off, and the grapes hung plump and juicy in neat rows. Staff were preparing the winery equipment – stainless-steel tanks and oak barrels – ready for the first pressing. But I could not keep my eyes off the immense views. The vineyard occupies an exceptional spot and, with *terroir* the all-important word with winemaking, Aby described the Cotswold limestone brash as being very similar to that of Burgundy.

There are numerous options for tutored tastings, local cheese and wine evenings, a Sunday afternoon tea option and 'Fizz and Chips' nights (Aby's favourite). Vineyard tours and events must be pre-booked but if you simply wish to sample a bottle (I particularly recommend the still Pinot Rosé and the sparkling Reserve Cuvée), these can be purchased from the Cellar Door Shop on Bath Road (the main A46 from Stroud to Nailsworth) in Woodchester.

🧳 SPECIAL STAYS

Woodchester Valley Vineyard Woodchester GL5 5HR ✆ 07808 650883 ⌂ woodchestervalleyvineyard.co.uk. A rare opportunity to stay within a vineyard setting in the Cotswolds. Three options: the Vineyard Barns have three double-level suites for two with terraces to enjoy views of the Nailsworth Valley; Woodchester Valley House sleeps up to 12 with a terrace and garden facing the vines; and The Retreat, in a secluded spot within the vineyard, sleeps four.

20 NAILSWORTH

Of all the towns in the Five Valleys, I find Nailsworth the most rewarding. It has an industrial heritage, in both wool production and quarrying stone, and yet retains the Cotswold charm and good looks seen in the towns of the north Cotswolds. The stone is much paler here than in the north and east, and was often quarried underground rather than in open pits. Its quality was renowned, coming out of the ground in large blocks that were good for carving, used in stately homes and even the Houses of Parliament, while the rubble was used to build the quaint weavers' cottages on the hillsides.

But Nailsworth is better known for its mills – 12 in total dotted along the valley, each one used for a different process of woollen cloth manufacture. Like the mills of Stroud, it was most closely associated with producing the West of England cloth for military uniforms, lengths of scarlet-dyed material regularly seen stretched out to dry on the valley slopes. All the mills have either been demolished or changed to other uses today but **Dunkirk Mill** on the northern edge of town is a good surviving example. It's now used for residential flats but next door is a museum, run by the Stroudwater Textile Trust, in which you can see Gloucestershire's largest working waterwheel, still driving traditional textile machinery. At **Gigg Mill**, you can visit the Weaving Shed, also run by the Trust, to try your hand at weaving. **Egypt Mill**, close to the town centre, is used as a hotel and restaurant where you can see the two waterwheels, while Days Mill still stands right in the centre of Nailsworth, along the old market street.

For its size, Nailsworth has an impressive mix of independent shops and places to eat. The open nature of Old Market and the Town Square running parallel with Fountain Street, the main thoroughfare, doesn't make the town feel closed in. And yet the hills are never far away, with Minchinhampton Common just to the east and the road climbing up the hillside from Nailsworth known locally as 'the W', indicating the number of sharp hairpin bends required to reach the top. Alongside is the **Nailsworth Ladder**, an even steeper footpath that links the town and the common, with a gradient of 1 in 2¼ in places.

¶¶ FOOD & DRINK

Foodies are spoilt for choice in Nailsworth, with great delis for picnic goodies, gastro-pubs, cosy restaurants and more upmarket dining.

Egypt Mill Bridge St ✆ 01453 833449 ⌂ egyptmill.com. Superb location on the banks of the Nailsworth Stream, Egypt Mill was once used for cloth manufacture; there's a small, rear terrace overlooking the stream. Watch the two 'working' waterwheels as you eat in the comfy restaurant with flagstone floors, beams and sofas. Accommodation available.

Tipputs Inn Tiltups End, near Nailsworth GL6 0QE ✆ 01453 839949 ⌂ tipputsinn.co.uk. An old coaching inn and barn, full of character. Most produce used comes from within a ten-mile radius, including longhorn beef. This is 1½ miles from Nailsworth town centre on the Bath road; Tiltups End is so named because overladen carts travelling from Nailsworth to Bath would tilt up while trying to climb the escarpment.

Wilder Market St ℘ 01453 835483 ⌂ dinewilder.co.uk. Everything is handmade on the premises, from fresh pasta to chocolates and ice cream to bread. Quality of produce and flavour is of the utmost importance to the owners of the three AA Rosette restaurant, who try to source all their ingredients from the Cotswolds and southwest of England. Accommodation at Wild Garlic Rooms on Cossack Square.

William's Fish Market & Food Hall Fountain St ℘ 01453 832240 ⌂ williamsfoodhall. co.uk. You can't help but be drawn into this shop and restaurant, such is the sight of fresh food through the plate-glass windows of this timber-framed building right in the centre of Nailsworth. Choose from the deli, sumptuously fresh fish and meat counters for take-away treats or eat in the restaurant, naturally specialising in fish and seafood but with plenty of other options.

THE COMMONS & SKINNY VALLEYS

At Nailsworth, the Nailsworth Valley actually splits into two further valleys running southwest to Kingscote and southeast towards **Avening**, where it begins to curve north towards Cherington and Aston Down. These are the feeder streams for the Nailsworth Stream, ultimately flowing into the River Frome at Stroud. Having curved around to all but meet up with the Golden Valley in the north, an area of high ground is encapsulated, creating **Rodborough and Minchinhampton commons**.

Southeast of the Nailsworth Valley the land remains gently undulating in the main, nothing like the gouged-out landscape of the Five Valleys. Except that here and there are sudden reminders – or pre-empters – of these dramatic escarpments and valleys, where pencil-thin, elongated relations suddenly flare up among the hills. One such dry valley begins close to Kemble, near Cirencester, and runs southwest to **Tetbury**. The main Cirencester to Bath road follows its course. A similarly dry valley runs through the **Westonbirt Estate** towards Tetbury, finally picking up water just before entering the town.

21 RODBOROUGH & MINCHINHAMPTON COMMONS

Between the Nailsworth Valley and Golden Valley, the land rises sharply with Rodborough Common, closer to Stroud, and Minchinhampton Common, keeping the pair apart. They are very popular valleys with walkers and picnickers for the views over the Five Valleys but, owing to the lie of the land and the distance between viewpoints, you'll never see everywhere all at once. Head to the west side of **Rodborough Common** to look over Stroud, the Painswick Valley and Selsley Common, and the east side for a view of Golden Valley overlooking Thrupp and Brimscombe. The west side of **Minchinhampton Common** gives the best views of Nailsworth, while from the east side you can see up the Toadsmoor Valley and further along the Frome Valley. From up here you get the sense of how tightly compact all of these valleys are.

The commons are superb for walking and, as common land, you can walk pretty much anywhere you like; my walk almost always includes

GIFFORDS CIRCUS

✆ 01451 820378 ⌀ giffordscircus.com

If you think of 'the circus' as huge big tops, impersonal arenas and depressed elephants, think again: Giffords Circus is different. A truly traditional show that turns up on village greens and commons in and around the Cotswolds, this is an intimate and unashamedly old-fashioned extravaganza, a tiny ring in a tiny tent with rickety wooden benches where you'll have the night of your life. Each show is both visually attractive and electrifying. For children and adults alike it is utter, spine-tingling magic.

The traditional atmosphere is intensified with the burgundy-and-gold show wagons that surround the tent too – you buy your programme and bag of sweets from a costumed seller in a painted caravan. And during the interval the tea tent sells homemade cakes, locally made Cotswold ice cream and proper tea, all from appropriately patterned Emma Bridgewater crocks. Circus Sauce, the show's 60-seat travelling restaurant, pops up in a tent near the main top, where the audience can enjoy a spectacular starlit circus dinner with the artistes after the show, an attraction in its own right with fresh and local ingredients used for the three-course meal.

Each summer brings a new and unique show full of musicians, jugglers, clowns, acrobats and wirewalkers performing breath-holding stunts. I was privileged to meet Nell Gifford, who set up the circus with her then husband Toti in 2000, while writing the first edition of *Slow Travel The Cotswolds*. At the time, Nell said, 'We always aim to create outstanding quality shows for a rural audience. We're from the area, we live in the area and Gifford's Circus is very much a part of the Cotswolds'. Sadly Nell passed away from breast cancer in 2019 but her spirit, love of horses and passion to put on an amazing spectacle continues in the shows, with the circus still very much a part of the Cotswolds. You can read about Nell's career as a circus artist and owner on the Giffords Circus website.

a beeline for **Winstones Cotswolds Ice Cream** (Bowham, Stroud, GL5 5BX ✆ 01453 873270 ⊘ winstonesicecream.co.uk), the dreamiest cornet with an inland view you can imagine – blackberries and cream is always top of my list, closely followed by honey and ginger. But these are some of the best examples of Cotswolds' unimproved limestone grassland where cows roam free, and consequently some of the best places to view the accompanying wild flowers, including 13 species of orchid, and butterflies (I spotted six different species in a short space of time on my last visit) rarely seen in gardens these days. For alternative but equally pleasing views of the Golden Valley, take a ride along the lane between Swellshill and Butterow, via Bagpath. The road has been designated as a Quiet Lane. There's no room for speed; this is a road to enjoy slowly.

From the common you can quite easily walk to **Minchinhampton**, a quiet old market town on the eastern edge of the hilltop. Its streets and buildings, including the arched Market House, are very enticing and the High Street is a heady mix of Cotswold gables and Georgian façades with barely a modern intrusion in sight. Perhaps the most striking of Minchinhampton's buildings is **Holy Trinity Church** in Bell Lane. The church tower is like a truncated cone topped with a coronet, although its design is not the original idea. The tower has a square base and should have remained square to the top but cracks began to appear as it was being built and so changes to its shape and appearance were necessary. Inside the church are several eye-catching brasses that you can take rubbings of for a few pence (you need to ask the verger in the house next door first); bring your own supplies of paper and crayons.

"The High Street is a heady mix of Cotswold gables and Georgian façades with barely a modern intrusion in sight."

Don't miss visiting the two pretty villages of **Amberley** and **Box**, both clinging to the edge of Minchinhampton Common. Both have that therapeutic Sunday morning feeling every day of the week. You can make up a circular walk by starting on the common and combining these two with a stop-off in Minchinhampton for a bite to eat.

⅋ FOOD & DRINK

For such a small town, Minchinhampton is very well endowed with good places to eat or buy food. L Taylor & Sons butchers on The Cross is revered by locals for miles around, and a country market sets up every Wednesday morning at the Market House. And don't forget to stop and buy an ice cream from Winstones, in between Rodborough and Minchinhampton commons, when out for a walk: the family have been making delicious ices since 1925.

Black Horse Inn Amberley GL5 5AL ✆ 01453 872556 ⌂ theblackhorseamberley. co.uk. A tiny pub with a tiny bar but which nonetheless has a garden with excellent views across the Nailsworth Valley and the commons. The menu is basic (chilli, burgers, curry, scampi and chips) but come here to drink in the views during a stomp around Minchinhampton Common.

Bear of Rodborough Rodborough Common GL5 5DE ✆ 01453 878522 ⌂ cotswold-inns-hotels.co.uk. Attractive and imposing building on top of the common. Dine in the Library Restaurant, take afternoon tea in the cosy lounge or have a drink and a 'bar meal' (gastro-pub food) in the Bear Bar. Accommodation available.

Henry's Coffee House & Dairy Market Sq, Minchinhampton ✆ 01453 703269 ⌂ orderhenrys.com. Run by the family behind Stroud's Woefuldane Dairy, the shop stocks its own handmade organic cheeses, milk and other dairy produce all sourced from the Ravenhills' small organic farm half a mile from the shop, plus freshly baked bread, morning pastries and coffee. Tiny coffee shop with convivial atmosphere.

The Kitchen High St, Minchinhampton ✆ 01453 882655 ⌂ thekitchenminch.co.uk. Family-run café and tea room where all the food, from cakes and biscuits to pâtés and chutneys, is made on the premises. Ingredients are sourced from local producers. Very popular with locals.

Old Lodge Minchinhampton Common ✆ 01453 832047 ⌂ food-club.com. One of two Cotswold Food Club pubs and restaurants, offering food in convivial surroundings and delightful gardens overlooking (in the middle of) the common. Sharing platters (Indian veg; antipasti and baked camembert) and a seasonal menu. Six en-suite bedrooms.

Ragged Cot Cirencester Rd, Minchinhampton ✆ 01453 884643 ⌂ theraggedcot-minchinhampton.com. Half a mile east of Minchinhampton, a country pub with food that makes the most of the farms and local food producers. Try the pan-fried Cotswold rack of lamb with shepherd's pie bonbon or tempura sprouting broccoli with almond granola.

22 AVENING, CHERINGTON & RODMARTON

Across the **Avening Valley** south of Minchinhampton is **Avening**, a hilly mill town at the extremities of the cloth-making area. A thousand years ago it was owned by a Saxon nobleman who rejected the advances of a young girl in Flanders. She, Matilda, went on to marry William the Conqueror, and in so doing was able to inflict revenge on her former suitor by confiscating his estate. Feeling remorse upon the nobleman's

JOHN CORRY/D

THE CHAVENAGE HOUSE PARTNERSHIP

NICK TURNER/COTSWOLDS.COM

JOHNNY HATHAWAY

death, she requested that the church at Avening be built. It's one of the fine buildings that you can still see today, along with some of the old mills and the handsome houses of the mill owners.

At the far end of the valley is the tiny village of **Cherington** where the feeder springs for the Avening Stream run through Cherington Pond on their way to the cloth mills. The pond was built in the 18th century to provide fishing for the manor house but today, in among woodland, it is a quiet nature reserve. A public footpath runs around the pond, from which you can create a short circular walk along a part of the valley and back to the village.

Rodmarton Manor

Rodmarton GL7 6PF ✆ 01285 841442 ⊗ rodmarton-manor.co.uk

Approaching Rodmarton Manor through the entrance gates, and finding the many-gabled house curving around a courtyard, you would be forgiven for believing that it had stood there for centuries. In fact, the house dates back only to 1909, when it was built at the request of the Biddulph family, who still reside there today. Ernest Barnsley, a well-known figure in the Arts and Crafts Movement and who was responsible for much of the Arts and Crafts buildings in nearby Sapperton (page 293), led a group of craftsmen, taking 20 years to complete the house using traditional skills in woodwork, metalwork, needlework, painting and gardening. It was one of the last country houses to be built in the traditional style using local materials and local craftsmen, and when all the work was done by hand.

But the work didn't stop there, for once the house was built, it was furnished in the Arts and Crafts style too, with all the furniture and furnishings made by eminent craftsmen, much of it in the workshops at Rodmarton. All this craftwork remains in the house. But despite the extraordinary amount of notable artwork, it is still, refreshingly, very much a lived-in house.

I find it a joy to wander through. On my most recent visit the house was used as an exhibition space by the **Gloucestershire Guild Of**

◀ **1** Minchinhampton is an enticing market town, with an unusual truncated church tower. **2** Avening Church was commissioned by Matilda, wife of William the Conqueror. **3** Chavenage, near Tetbury, has some striking interiors, with stories to tell. **4** Westonbirt Arboretum is a Grade I Historic Landscape of International Importance.

Craftsmen (⊘ guildcrafts.org.uk) for its annual Crafts Alive event. Members display exquisite work from ceramics and mixed media artwork to calligraphy and textiles, highlighting a continuation of the Arts and Crafts movement.

Outside the eight-acre gardens are uplifting too. Originally designed as a series of rooms, each has a unique feel, while retaining the overall character of the garden. Traditional cottage plants mix with chiselled topiary and mossy stone walls, wide borders and pathways draw the visitor to some other 'room', and then another. Losing your bearings is quite likely with all the pathways and hedges, so find a focal point on the house and stick with it.

23 TETBURY

The very yellow **Market Hall**, antiques and His Royal Highness King Charles III are always my immediate thoughts when I think of Tetbury, a town that in 1633 was 'given' to its inhabitants by the then lord of the manor and a delegation of seven feoffees, or trustees, accountable to the townsfolk, were appointed to look after property.

Though less authoritative than they once were, feoffees still perform some duties around the town including looking after the magnificent Market Hall, built in 1655. Like other Cotswold towns, Tetbury made its wealth through the wool trade, with a prospering market taking place from the 12th century onwards, at first in The Chipping, but later in and under the pillared Market Hall. It remains the most prominent building in town, with its distinctive illuminated clock and colourful floral displays.

Other prominent buildings in town include **St Saviour's Church** on the Avening road, a medieval-style Victorian building with an unusual roofline for the area and the thickest of Cotswold stone roof tiles. It was built for the poor of the parish who could not afford to pay for seats in Tetbury's other church. In 1975 the building was struck by lightning, damaging the roof and bringing the weathercock crashing to the ground. Inside was found a poem, dated 26 June 1848, by the maker William Sealy:

Will'm Sealy Made this Cock,
The wind that blew will make it work,
The place where it is to stand,
The Lord preserve it with His Hand.

Records show that Sealy was a working smith in business in the Market Place as an ironmonger, brazier and nail manufacturer.

St Mary's Church has a spire that can be seen for miles around. Built in 1781, the church has an elegant Georgian interior with panelled galleries, box pews and grand slender columns. It also has a modern, yet fitting, entrance that catches you unawares with contemporary paintings and 'Magnificat' in giant gold lettering above the door. Look, too, for the small exhibition in the church of old photographs. There are some wonderful pictures of the church spire being taken down and rebuilt in 1890, with some very dodgy-looking wooden scaffolding that doesn't look as if it would pass 'health and safety' today.

St Mary's has also made efforts to create a wildflower haven right in the centre of town, having planted the churchyard with 300 English bluebells, hundreds of

"It provides a tiny retreat from the bustling shopping streets, where antique and interior-design shops play a prominent role."

snowdrops, carpets of cyclamen and many perennial wildflowers. It provides a tiny retreat from the bustling shopping streets, where antique and interior-design shops play a prominent role, particularly down Long Street.

Long Street is also the address for HRH King Charles III's flagship **Highgrove Shop** (✆ 0333 222 4555 ⌖ highgrovegardens.com), a very popular destination among visitors to the town. Inside is the Highgrove Collection of gifts, with products inspired by aspects of the house or gardens on his private estate.

For another address worth visiting, **Chavenage** (✆ 01666 502329 ⌖ chavenage.com), just to the west of Tetbury, is not to be rushed.

WOOLSACK RACES

Every spring bank holiday Monday, Tetbury revives an old tradition of gruelling hard work when men and women compete in the Woolsack Races. The location is **Gumstool Hill**, where fraudulent traders received a watery punishment at the ducking-stool. Competitors race from the Crown Inn at the top of the hill to the Royal Oak at the bottom carrying a bag of wool on their shoulders, weighing a staggering 65lbs. But that's not the half of it, for they then pass the bag to a team member who must climb back up the hill – with a gradient of 1 in 4 in places – still carrying the sack. A plaque in the wall close to the Crown Inn marks the start and finish line.

HIGHGROVE GARDENS

highgrovegardens.com

A mile south of Tetbury is **Highgrove**, the private residence of HRH King Charles III and Queen Camilla. For many years the king has opened up his beloved gardens, developed and maintained enthusiastically while embracing organic principles, to the visiting public. Guided tours of the gardens must be booked in advance and all proceeds go towards the Prince's Foundation. I thoroughly recommend a visit; every aspect is mesmerically inspiring but the Cottage Garden, Wildflower Meadow and Kitchen Garden are particularly beautiful. The gardens are the king's passion, and he has a direct hand both in the design and the work. Guests may visit the Orchard Room during their visit, surrounded by the paintings created by His Majesty, for lunch or afternoon tea – all using organic ingredients, sometimes from the gardens themselves.

With the king's passion about keeping heritage crafts and rural skills alive, The Prince's Foundation also runs Highgrove Traditional Crafts, a series of training programmes, on the estate, with workshops for beginners, advanced learners and community-focused activities. Courses include textiles, for example weaving and lacemaking, furniture making and wood carving, and garden-inspiration workshops such as floristry, natural-yarn dyeing or drawing.

The Elizabethan house is very good looking from the outside, with its mottled Cotswold stone simplicity, but inside is full of stories to tell. The house has been used in recent years for notable TV dramas, including the BBC's *Poldark*.

¶¶ FOOD & DRINK

With so many top-quality farms and food producers in the area, it's not difficult to find outlets selling fresh local food here. For a picnic area and pleasant out-of-town walk along a minuscule valley, head to Preston Park, next to the old railway station, accessed from The Chipping.

Hobbs House Bakery 18-20 Church St ⌀ 01666 504533 ⌀ hobbshousebakery.co.uk. Traditional bakers, passionate about making real, artisan breads. Sandwiches made to order, handmade pastries and some of the best coffee in the Cotswolds. Useful for picnic provisions. Shops also at Chipping Sodbury and Nailsworth.

Martin & Malthouse The Chipping ⌀ 07388 572982. Family-run café, deli and bottle shop with communal tables. Sells fruit and veg from Close Farm, on the Duchy Estate on the outskirts of Tetbury, organic wine, and olive oil from the family's farm in Greece.

Snooty Fox Market Pl ✆ 01666 502436 ⊘ snooty-fox.co.uk. Overlooking the Market Hall, with pavement tables outside and a warm, comfy lounge-like bar inside. Informal restaurant serving classic British food: slow-cooked pork belly, apple and parsley mash, and cider sauce; pan-roast chicken supreme with fondant potato and thyme jus.

24 WESTONBIRT ARBORETUM

Westonbirt GL8 8QS ✆ 0300 0674890

⊘ forestryengland.uk/westonbirt-the-national-arboretum

Westonbirt Arboretum is registered as a Grade I Historic Landscape of International Importance. Robert Stayner Holford, one-time owner of the Westonbirt Estate, began to plant trees in the 1850s and laid out the grounds using a blueprint known as the Picturesque Landscaping Style, the argument being that the best way to improve a landscape was to apply the principles of painting. The collection, of course, has been added to and extended, but you can still make out those principles in the Old Arboretum, with disappearing perspectives in the long, stately avenues that look towards Holford's mock-Elizabethan mansion, colour against the skyline and vistas.

Yet the area around Westonbirt has something unique in the Cotswolds. Split by a small, dry valley, the arboretum has two contrasting areas, as it sits on two differing soil types – the alkaline limestone to the east of the valley, where the Old Arboretum is, and, to the west, an acidic, sandy soil where the Silk Wood was planted. The differing soils have enabled a large variety of trees and shrubs to become established. While the Old Arboretum contains many rare and exotic specimen trees from around the world, Silk Wood provides themed groups such as the native tree, the oak, ash, cherry and national Japanese maple collections.

"Numerous trails lead around the arboretum but every so often you'll come across natural play features where fallen trees and log pathways make toys."

Every month provides something specific to look at, with many seasonal events taking place throughout the year, including guided walks, art-and-craft workshops relating to trees and the natural environment, and wellbeing days. The Forestry Commission is keen that the arboretum is not just a place to look at trees but to encourage people, in particular children, to use woods as places of activity. Numerous trails lead around the arboretum but every so often you'll come across natural play features where fallen trees and log pathways make toys and where children are encouraged to build dens, using their imagination to make the most of the natural resources around them.

An area of wildflower meadows, The Downs, separates the two woodlands, unexpected for an arboretum of some 2,500 tree species. You'll gain a good view of these from the **Treetop Walkway**. The 330yd-long step-free walkway makes it accessible for all, rising to a height of 43ft. There are information panels to fire the imagination whatever the age, without dumbing down the science of trees. I find the walkway a work of art. The wood and metal structure gracefully soars above the ground, curling through the upper branches of the trees, allowing you to reach out to the canopy, see high-up pine cones close up, cross the wobbly rope bridge to a lookout and climb up to the 'Tree Hotel', a crow's nest for even greater views across the arboretum.

'Over the road' is **Westonbirt House and Gardens** (✆ 01666 881373 ⌂ holfordtrust.com). Maintained entirely independently from the arboretum, this is the original home of the Holford family, an imposing house with both formal Italianate gardens and surrounding pleasure grounds. The house and gardens are open to the public from June to October on a limited number of specific days, providing an opportunity to see the opulent furnishings and interior décor.

¶¶ FOOD & DRINK

On site at Westonbirt is the **Westonbirt Kitchen Restaurant and Smokehouse**, serving good, home-cooked and wholesome food, including a traditional pizza oven fired by Westonbirt wood. There's also a small café and a picnic area. Just yards from the entrance is the **Hare and Hounds Hotel** (✆ 01666 881000 ⌂ cotswold-inns-hotels.co.uk), where Jack Hare's Bar serves fresh, seasonal fare from nibbles and sandwiches to more substantial meals. The Beaufort Restaurant is a more elegant dining experience. Children are welcome. Accommodation available.

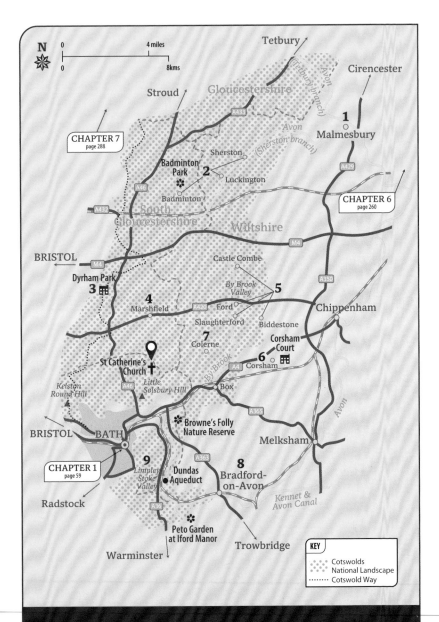

WILTSHIRE COTSWOLDS

8
WILTSHIRE COTSWOLDS

For some, Wiltshire is more associated with Salisbury Plain and the Vale of the White Horse than the Cotswolds, but a reasonable chunk of the Cotswolds does fall into the county. Because the area is less known, its quiet, untouristy nature gives quite a sense of discovery.

Towns such as **Malmesbury, Corsham** and **Bradford-on-Avon** all have their own character and just a day spent in each should leave you feeling that you'd like to spend longer. But it's the countryside that is the jewel here, much of it appealingly remote. In the north of this locale, above the M4, the land lends itself to open wolds – Malmesbury sits on top of one of them. But below the M4 corridor the land begins to twist and turn again, providing sharp ridges and secret valleys around the edge of Bath.

One of the best valleys for exploring is **By Brook**. In the north, close to its source, it is relatively well known and tourist orientated, including **Castle Combe**, one of the great showpieces of the Cotswolds. But further south it uncovers equally worthwhile villages such as **Ford** and **Slaughterford**, with plenty of opportunities for walks off the beaten track.

I've sneaked north Somerset and a tiny snippet of Gloucestershire into this locale too, for the ridges of hills know no authoritative boundaries, and secrets such as **St Catherine's**, which lies within 10yds of the Wiltshire boundary, are too good to miss by being overly picky about where the dotted line falls.

When exploring this area, I met a man who had been stationed at one of the barracks near Corsham while performing his National Service in the 1950s. He reminded me of the important role that the military has played here over many years – there are still several military bases and operational units in the area. He told how, on a Friday evening, the roads for miles around, in particular the London road (now the A4 between Bath and Chippenham) out of Bath, were lined with personnel trying to thumb a lift to go home for the weekend.

GETTING THERE & AROUND

To catch a **train**, **Great Western Railway** (⌀ gwr.com) run services to Bath Spa from London, the south, the southwest and the north (the last two via Bristol Temple Meads). There are also direct services to Bradford-on-Avon from London and Cardiff on the **Wessex Main Line** along with local services to Bradford-on-Avon from Bath and Trowbridge on the **Heart of Wessex line**, also run by Great Western Railway.

National **coach** firms stop at Bath. There are local bus services between Bath, Corsham, Bradford-on-Avon and Malmesbury but such journeys around the area can be tortuous, lengthy affairs with many changes or so infrequent as to be virtually useless for tourists.

While the Cotswold Way just skirts around the west side of Wiltshire, there are plenty of opportunities for **walks** in the Wiltshire Cotswolds. Many can be gentle strolls utilising grand estates such as those at Dyrham Park and Corsham Court. But the most notable are the **Macmillan Way**, which passes right along the By Brook Valley from Castle Combe to Box, and the **Limestone Link**. Joining the Cotswold Way at Cold Ashton, it passes through one of the quietest, most unspoilt valleys in the Cotswolds before crossing the River Avon and continuing on its way along the Limpley Stoke Valley. It's a great alternative for walking to Bath (turning onto the towpath of the Kennet and Avon Canal at Bathampton) in place of the final stretch of the Cotswold Way.

For **cyclists**, a useful, dead-straight section of former Roman road is the 12-mile rural byway section of the **Fosse Way**; this begins close to Crudwell, three miles north of Malmesbury, and ends just north of the By Brook Valley, close to Castle Combe. Where the byway ends, the Fosse Way continues as a quiet country road until it reaches the outskirts of Bath close to Batheaston.

---

i TOURIST INFORMATION

Bradford-on-Avon 50 St Margaret's St ⌀ 01225 865797 ⌀ bradfordonavon.co.uk
Corsham Arnold House, 31 High St ⌀ 01249 714660
Malmesbury Town Hall, Cross Hayes ⌀ 01666 822143 ⌀ discovermalmesbury.life

A particularly attractive traffic-free cycle ride runs between Bath and Bradford-on-Avon. It's a part of the **National Cycle Network Route 4** and uses the towpath of the **Kennet and Avon Canal**, which runs alongside the River Avon. It's a popular route that involves running on the flat through the Limpley Stoke Valley, with its wooded slopes either side and a stop-off point midway for a drink at the Dundas Aqueduct.

BIKE HIRE

Towpath Trail and TT Cycles Elm Cross Business Park, Bradford-on-Avon BA15 2AY
℘ 01225 867187 ⌀ ttcycles.co.uk. Cycle hire including adults' and children's bikes, trailer bikes, child seats and helmets. Bike sales and repairs at TT Cycles bike shop.

THE YOUNG AVON VALLEY TO MALMESBURY

The town of **Malmesbury** clusters around the River Avon, which ultimately flows south to Bradford-on-Avon and west to Bath and Bristol. But before it reaches Malmesbury, its young life begins in two halves, the Tetbury branch, obvious enough, and the Sherston branch, which flows from the southwest, rising just over the county border in Didmarton and on to Sherston before meeting up with its twin. A prominent tributary also flows into this river at Sherston, whose source rises within the grounds of the great **Badminton Estate**. It is this Sherston branch of the Avon, together with its tributary, that I'm focusing on here.

1 MALMESBURY

As a defensive location, Malmesbury has an ideal position upon a hill sandwiched between the two branches of the River Avon. Iron Age settlers were the first to make the most of its natural assets. While today the Dyson headquarters is left vulnerable outside the town's defences, at the heart of Malmesbury is its magnificent abbey, visible for miles around and dwarfing all other buildings in the town.

What can be seen today of **Malmesbury Abbey** is only a third of its original size, having, in the 12th century, been built in a cruciform shape. Over the centuries, bits have dropped off and never been replaced. A tower, taller than that on Salisbury Cathedral, was added but fell down, and what remains is essentially the nave, with the transepts – and the

A walk around Malmesbury

Allow 1½ hours minimum.

Begin at the distinctive, octagonal **Market Cross** at the top of the High Street and walk through the Tolsey Gate into the **Abbey precinct**, where you'll come across the grave of Hannah Twynnoy who, according to her gravestone, was mauled to death by an escaped circus tiger in 1703. Coming out of the graveyard by the Old Bell Hotel, walk down Abbey Row, where you'll catch glimpses of the town and the Sherston branch of the River Avon below.

At The Triangle, turn right into the Gloucester road and almost immediately left along St Mary's Street, to the charming **Horsefair**, where an illegal market used to run to dodge the town market's toll.

Leave Horsefair via West Street and, at the end, turn right into Bristol Street. Take the first left into Foxley Road and cross over Turtle Bridge, taking in the views of the town from the Avon. Just past the bridge, turn left onto a footpath that crosses **King's Heath**, the water meadows that were given to the town by King Athelstan. Follow the footpath and the river – these are some of the prettiest views of the town – until you come to a bend in the river with a tiny footbridge. The bulge in the river is called **Daniel's Well** and is great for a summer paddle.

Cross over the footbridge, passing the backs of residential gardens and climb the steep steps back to the Market Cross. Continue past the cross into Oxford Street where, at its end, you'll see **Tower House**. Among the former houseguests were Henry VIII and Charles I but the tower atop was not built until the 19th century, as an observatory. Turn right into Cross Hayes, one of the old marketplaces, and then left into Silver Street. The land falls away sharply at the bottom as you walk down Back Hill Steps towards the Tetbury branch of the **Avon**. Within yards, the two branches of the river join together.

Turn right into St John's Street, past the **almshouses** and then left where there's a pretty 12th-century stone archway, once the entrance to a medieval hospital. Cross the river using St John's Bridge, where you'll see the old mills that were originally used for wool, but turned to silk production 200 years ago as the wool trade declined. Just over the bridge turn into Cuckingstool Mead and walk through to **St Aldhelm's Mead**. This is a great place for a picnic, as the rustle of giant poplar trees overshadows the noise of the nearby road. The park is overlooked by meadows at the western end, while towards town are the backs of the terraced houses above. Their endearing gardens slope down to a spur of the river, where plum trees dangle in the water.

At the playground, turn right and climb up to King's Wall, a delightful narrow street of old stone houses that heads back to the High Street. At the junction with the High Street, look down its lower section where you'll see the terrace of old millworkers' cottages before turning left to return to the Market Cross.

monastery – long gone. Since the 16th century, the abbey has been the parish church and inside has an inspiring sense of grandeur, with soaring ceilings. Yet outside, signs of its piecemeal neglect are clearly evident. The south porch once had remarkable stone carving, sadly now decaying. From the peaceful Cloister Garden, on the north side, the stone ruins are more obvious, where pigeons roost silently in prayer along the precipice of arched window frames, and pink-tinged valerian clings to life from rocky edges, the stunted posts of once-grand archways and giant flying buttresses left suspended.

On Tuesday evenings bell-ringing practice takes place; you'll be able to hear them, wherever you are in the town.

"From the peaceful Cloister Garden, on the north side, the stone ruins are more obvious, where pigeons roost silently in prayer."

Of the remaining stained-glass windows, one features the abbey's benefactor, the 'Flying Monk'. In 1010, inspired by the jackdaws who roosted at the abbey, Brother Eilmer strapped wings to his arms and legs and 'flew' from one of the abbey towers. The experiment was not greatly successful and after gliding about 200yds he fell, breaking both his legs. Banned by his abbot from making another attempt, Eilmer lived on another 50 years or so to become a distinguished scholar. The townsfolk have since taken the budding pilot to their hearts.

You can find out more about the abbey and the history of the town at the **Athelstan Museum** (✐ 01666 829258 ◇ athelstanmuseum.org.uk), named after Athelstan, the first 'King of all England' who requested that he be buried in the grounds of the abbey. The museum, which is free to enter and run by volunteers, is bite-sized and gives the first-time visitor a good introduction to Malmesbury, including, of national significance, the history of Malmesbury lace. Within the museum collection, I particularly like the pictorial map of Malmesbury which was created in 1646 during the English Civil War. The map (which is a reproduction; the original, owned by the Warden and Freemen of Malmesbury, is tucked away) provides remarkable detail of the town and its then defences; it even has the positions of the cannons and look-out posts.

¶¶ FOOD & DRINK

Malmesbury has numerous independent shops along its High Street, together with an exciting mix of very good cafés, pubs and restaurants. There's an artisan and farmers' market held every Friday at the Market Cross.

The Abbey Kitchen Malmesbury Abbey ☎ 01666 826666 🖱 malmesburyabbey.com. A therapeutic and inspiring place to relax on sofas within the north aisle of the abbey. Homemade cakes and Fairtrade coffee.
Birdcage 2 High St ☎ 01666 825505. Restaurant with quirky interior. Specialising in artisan thin-crust pizzas, each named after a street in, or with some other link to, Malmesbury. Imaginative toppings, with more than 25 to select from.
Old Bell Hotel Abbey Row ☎ 01666 822344 🖱 oldbellhotel.co.uk. Reputedly the oldest purpose-built hotel in England (built in 1220), today offering traditional Cotswold comfort. Two restaurants have informal and formal dining for lunches and evening meals, while afternoon tea can be taken in one of the lounges or outside on the secluded garden terrace. Beetroot gazpacho with goat's cheese mousse; ruby-red beef with malt-glazed carrot and green sauce. Accommodation available in individually styled rooms.

2 SHERSTON, LUCKINGTON & BADMINTON

Winding southwest, back towards its source, the Sherston branch of the Avon skirts around **Sherston**. The focal point of this village is its broad High Street lined with Cotswold stone houses. Every July, Sherston holds an annual carnival, the highlight of which is a French-style boules tournament.

The Romans occupied this area, with the Fosse Way running just to the east, and the remains of a villa were found close to the village, but Sherston's history really comes alive with the Saxons. The Danish king Canute and his men advanced on the village in 1016 but were met by John Rattlebone, so named afterwards because his knockout blows caused the enemy's bones to rattle. The Danes retreated. John Rattlebone has been the village hero ever since and is celebrated at the village pub, the Rattlebone Inn.

"Its uncharacteristic colour co-ordinated yellow lime-washed houses seem more in keeping in west Somerset than the Cotswolds"

You can use a two-mile stretch of the Macmillan Way to walk from Sherston to its southerly neighbour, **Luckington**. In doing so, you'll pass by the church and through the grounds of the attractive Queen Anne-period Luckington Court. The Wiltshire/Gloucestershire border lies just to the west of Luckington, dividing the Badminton Estate and **Badminton Park**. The village of **Badminton** is impressive enough and makes a refreshing change from all the stone villages in the area. Its uncharacteristic colour co-ordinated yellow lime-washed houses seem more in keeping in west Somerset than the Cotswolds. Badminton Park remains essentially private, but a **public footpath** – a metalled track that is perfect for pushchairs and wheelchairs – runs straight through the park linking Badminton with Little Badminton. The there-and-back stroll provides ample opportunity to watch the deer that roam the park, and to take in the views of the lake and the grand house, home of the Duke of Beaufort, but a five-mile circular walk has also been created with instructions on the Cotswolds National Landscape website (⊘ cotswoldsaonb.org.uk; look under Self-Guided Walks). The private gardens connected to the house are opened for three days in April, June and September (open days are posted at ⊘ badmintonestate.co.uk).

Badminton is, of course, best known for its annual horse trials (⊘ badminton-horse.co.uk), one of the most prestigious events in the cross-country eventing calendar, attracting top riders from across the world, including royalty. It was also the birthplace of badminton when, in 1873, the game was introduced to guests at Badminton House as 'the Badminton game', even though versions had existed for centuries under several guises throughout the world. The nearby Bath Badminton Club cemented the new game by drawing up the first set of written rules in 1877.

¶¶ FOOD & DRINK

The King's Arms Didmarton GL9 1DT ⊘ 01454 238245 ⊘ butcombe.com/the-kings-arms-gloucestershire. Just across the border, in Gloucestershire, in the very pretty village of Didmarton, The King's Arms is a cosy place to sit by the fire in winter or enjoy the rose- and lavender-bordered garden in summer beneath vintage-striped parasols. Food is excellent, served either in the attractive restaurant (leather-buttoned banquettes and mood lighting) or the more rustic bar area. The outdoor wood-fired pizza oven serves up pizzas in summer. Butcombe beers (from nearby Bristol) on tap. Accommodation too.

Old House at Home Burton SN14 7LT ⊘ 01454 218227 ⊘ ohhpubs.co.uk. Ivy-clad pub with abundant internal character. Select from a choice of bar snacks or main menu, with masses of choice, including game. Very popular for Sunday lunch. Usefully placed for nearby Badminton.

Rattlebone Inn Sherston SN16 0LR ⊘ 01666 840871 ⊘ therattlebone.co.uk. Named after the village hero, a 17th-century village pub enjoyed by locals. There's plenty of character, with exposed stone walls and beams, inglenook fireplaces and various nooks and crannies. The main restaurant is housed in an atmospheric old barn and serves up modern interpretations of pub classics and locally sourced produce.

DYRHAM & MARSHFIELD

Having run pencil-thin for several miles between Hawkesbury and Old Sodbury, the Cotswold escarpment begins to broaden again at Dyrham, creating a great knotted lump as it nears Bath. Fighting armies have used the prime vantage points, overlooking the Avon and Severn valleys. In AD577, for instance, the Battle of Dyrham took place when a West Saxon army, under the authority of Cuthwine and Caewuln, sprang an attack on the Britons of the West Country, making use of an Iron Age fort on Hinton Hill, just north of Dyrham. Three kings of the Britons were killed and, in so doing, Cuthwine and Caewuln took the cities of Bath, Cirencester and Gloucester.

3 DYRHAM PARK

⌀ 0117 937 2501; National Trust

Television and film producers clearly love the Cotswolds and none of it more so than Dyrham Park. My first encounter of this house, with its imposing deep golden façade, was through the film *The Remains of the Day*, when political dignitaries drew up to the entrance to be waited upon by Anthony Hopkins. More recently, the house has played host to *Sanditon*.

"In contrast to the wildness of the landscape park, the West Garden is a suntrap, perfect in the warmer months."

The Baroque mansion sits at the foot of the Cotswold escarpment, sheltered by a bend in the ridge. Its landscaped deer park takes up almost 270 acres of the escarpment, including Hinton Hill, where the Battle of Dyrham was fought. Visitors may wander here throughout the year to enjoy the views over Bristol and the Severn bridges, though if you've visited previously and enjoyed seeing the roaming deer, which had been in the park since it was enclosed in 1620, don't expect to see them this time; sadly the entire herd had to be culled after contracting TB in 2021.

The National Trust lays on a small electric bus to take you down the long, sweeping drive to the house but, if you're able, winding your way down the escarpment on foot, stopping at Neptune's Statue to soak up the view of the house below or following the Prospect Walk, is by far

1 Malmesbury's magnificent abbey dates from the 12th century. **2** Badminton is famous for its horse trials. **3** Beautiful Dyrham Park has been used as a setting in TV and film. ▶

EMANUELE LEONI/D

BADMINTON HORSE TRIALS

CAROLINE MILLS

the best approach. Then you'll encounter the changing landscape as you descend: the Frying Pan Pond, a relatively recent addition in 1833, and the Old Lodge buildings where there's a picnic area.

Inside, the huge rooms have changed little in decoration since William Blathwayt transformed the house and estate in 1691. An introduction to the property informs visitors that he acquired his wealth – and the opportunity to renovate the house – through sugar and coffee plantations and the slave trade. His taste was for Dutch everything (the landscape park once included a Dutch garden, now disappeared) and the house is filled with Dutch decorative arts, with a large collection of Delftware. Consequently, one of the best times to visit is in April or May, when the gardens are brimming with tulips.

In contrast to the wildness of the landscape park, the West Garden is a suntrap, perfect in the warmer months for lazing around on the lawns, in the orchard – filled with perry pears, daffodils and wild flowers – or around the pools. Events are often put on here to tempt you to linger a while longer and enjoy the rear views – actually the original entrance – to the house. Or simply return as frequently as you can to watch the long-term redevelopment of the garden take shape, including garden elements taken from a 17th-century engraving of the property by Dutch draftsman Johannes Kip. You can see a copy of the incredible engraving in the Stable Courtyard; it really is a treat.

4 MARSHFIELD

Southeast of Dyrham is Marshfield, a large village positioned at the top of a south-facing ridge and overlooking a green moonscape of undulations and wooded valleys. Its layout is of one long, long High Street, off which are numerous thin burgage plots, a medieval land-rental system consisting of a house and a thin plot of land behind. When I first visited Marshfield I was astounded by its beauty and had visions of its High Street, like so many other locations in the Cotswolds, being used as a film set. The extensive street, which runs virtually the full length of the village, is made up predominantly of graceful Georgian façades, with numerous architectural features such as balustrades on roofs and scalloped porches. The fascinating street names such as Sheep Fair Lane and Touching End Lane give an indication of

"Positioned at the top of a south-facing ridge and overlooking a green moonscape of undulations."

THE MARSHFIELD MUMMERS

Every Boxing Day, the village tradition is for 'The Paper Boys', a seven-strong troupe of 'boys', to perform a mummers' play. The troupe, costumed in strips of paper, begin in the Market Place and process along the High Street, performing their five-minute play several times along the route. The story is based loosely – oral traditions without anything written down mean that the play has evolved over time – on the legend of St George and the Dragon, but remains a fertility rite. According to tradition, therefore, women may not perform.

The troupe is made up of villagers, ideally those whose families have lived in the village for generations.

village history – it was granted market status in 1234 – encouraging you to explore further, away from the High Street. And close to the church is a magnificent tithe barn, now converted to a private house.

¶¶ FOOD & DRINK

Catherine Wheel High St, Marshfield ✆ 01225 892220 ◌ thecatherinewheel.co.uk. Handsome Georgian building with an inviting restaurant and bar. Classic British dishes and a more creative menu (fennel, peach and feta salad with pumpkin pesto; lamb tagine; chicken chasseur with mustard mash). Exposed walls and roaring log fires make winter visits cosy or there's a sunny patio for summer. Accommodation too.

THE BY BROOK VALLEY

A 12-mile-long tributary of the River Avon, By Brook provides a backdrop to some of the choicest villages. Its spaghetti-like tangle of meandering loops is unusual for a river so small, and its gracefulness and therapeutically quiet sound make it an ideal companion for walking. Its steep valley sides are reminiscent of other areas of the Cotswolds and indeed its water was important in powering the 20 mills that once worked hereabouts during the years of the wool trade. When wool declined, many of the mills were used to make paper instead; now they have all disappeared.

Beginning close to the village of **Burton**, By Brook sidles through **Castle Combe** and then on to **Ford**, **Slaughterford** and **Box** before joining up with the Avon at Batheaston.

The roads between all of these villages and their neighbours are small and narrow, ideal for fairly hilly cycling or pottering about slowly by car.

5 CASTLE COMBE, FORD, SLAUGHTERFORD & BIDDESTONE

Creating a tour out of these four villages provides the ideal opportunity to explore them all, for while Ford and Slaughterford are free of tourist attractions, they should not be missed, and neither should the countryside that surrounds them. Views unveil themselves abruptly, for example as you drop down from Thickwood towards Slaughterford, turning a corner and suddenly coming across the sweetest little stone bridge across By Brook, the roadsides brimming with wildflowers.

The furthest north is **Castle Combe**; vehicles need to approach the village from the north and park in the dedicated visitor car park. However, if you're on foot or cycling, I find the most impressive way to arrive is from the south, either along the little lane that runs startlingly close at times to the gorge-like valley below or along the Macmillan Way footpath, which runs close to the stream. The attractiveness of the village is renowned, tucked as it is into the valley, and its unblemished array of Cotswold cottages really pull the crowds.

"The view from the bridge across By Brook, at the lower end of the main street, is one of the most photographed in the Cotswolds."

The view from the bridge across By Brook, at the lower end of the main street, is one of the most photographed in the Cotswolds, but sadly that's all many visitors tend to see before moving on. At the top of the main street is the 14th-century market cross, where wool was once sold – Castle Combe also had its own mill and made its wealth from the wool trade – with the Castle Inn behind.

But take a short walk just out of the village and you'll see more of Castle Combe. With the Castle Inn on your right, walk under the arch at the far end of the hotel and turn left, walking parallel with the drive to the Manor House Hotel. At the end of the lane, turn right past Gardener's House and up the hill (it becomes only a footpath). Duck under a small, stone footbridge and up some steps. Turn left at the stile. You'll begin to see the village the way most visitors don't – looking across to St Andrew's Church (with one large and three small turrets) with woodland in the background and the old apple orchards of the Manor House Hotel in the foreground. Continue along the (often muddy) path, skirting the woods and with the perimeter wall of the hotel grounds on your left. Within 200yds you'll come to a gate, arriving at a golf course. Stick to the footpath as the land suddenly opens out into a grand estate with grassland areas that are full of wildflowers in summer. Reaching a tiny footbridge across By Brook, you'll have the stream and the surroundings to yourself with the possible exception of the occasional golfer. You can either continue along the Macmillan Way and create a circular walk re-entering Castle Combe from the south or take the 10-minute walk back to the village to enjoy a drink in one of the pubs or tea rooms.

Ford is the next village on the route of By Brook, closely followed by **Slaughterford**, a disjointed village on the valley side with a very handsome church set among meadows. The houses drift down to the stream, which – rather than crossing at the end of the village – you can follow through the imposing Backpath Woods. This is, I think, the ideal route to reach **Biddestone**. Approximately two miles to the east of both Ford and Slaughterford, Biddestone is one of the most sought-after villages in Wiltshire for property buyers and prices are some of the highest in the area. Reaching it you'll understand why, with its wide main street, lined with some very good-looking stone houses, plus a village green and duck pond in the centre. It's a pleasant spot to sit, open a flask of coffee and enjoy the ducks' company for a moment or two.

¶¶ FOOD & DRINK

The pavement tables of the **Castle Inn** have one of the best views in Castle Combe, overlooking the market place. The **Manor House Hotel**, set well back in its own grounds, provides a sumptuous afternoon tea and formal Michelin-star dining. A walk, as suggested opposite, will introduce you to the hotel's orchard and kitchen garden, which supply the hotel kitchens.

White Horse Biddestone ☎ 01249 713305 ♿ whitehorsebiddestone.com. Village pub with a great location by the village green and duck pond. Standard bistro-style pub fare (burgers, fish and chips, salads) but come to drink outdoors and take in the atmosphere of this most charming of Cotswold villages.

6 CORSHAM

Often overlooked in favour of other Cotswold towns simply because they happen to be better known, Corsham is every bit worth visiting, not least because it is filled less with tourists and more with locals – although it was filled with 18th-century-costumed actors during the BBC's filming of *Poldark*, despite the town being far from the Cornish setting of the TV drama.

PETER JARVIS/D

LC CAPTURES/S

MARTIN FOWLER/S

THE BURLINGTON BUNKER

It's hard to imagine idyllic little towns like Corsham being a seat of power, but things are not always what they seem. For beneath the surface, in the abandoned stone quarries under Box Hill, is the Burlington Bunker, also known as Site 3.

In the 1950s parts of the old Spring Quarry were developed as a central Government War Headquarters, where the politicians would adjourn in the event of a nuclear strike. The underground bunker was radiation-proof and consisted of a street with Whitehall ministries on each side and included a pub (the Rose and Crown), a bakery, laundry, kitchens and enough facilities for 4,000 government ministers and civil servants.

The bunker was decommissioned in the early 1990s but remained a decoy site until 2004. Indeed, many of the underground quarries continue to be used for various purposes, from defence stations to storage of the world's finest wines.

Right on the eastern edge of the Cotswolds, Corsham too made its wealth through the wool trade, but being slightly away from the river and without the means to drive mills, the market town stuck to the less industrial tasks of spinning and weaving. The 17th-century row of **Flemish cottages** on the High Street was built for weavers who came from the continent.

The town also made a name for itself through the quarrying of high-quality Bath stone, a pale, creamy-coloured limestone that is significantly different in both colour and texture from the stone of the northern Cotswolds. The industry still continues today in quarries close to the town, with Bath stone remaining an ever-popular choice for building.

The partly pedestrianised, flagstoned **High Street** is full of attractive façades, with the neo-Georgian town hall, originally built as a market hall, perhaps the most elegant, although the gabled Flemish cottages do perhaps rule with their charm. The street has a good range of independent shops and eating places; I particularly like the **Made in Corsham** shop, housed in the town hall, where delicious preserves made by a local primary school teacher sit side by side with attractive craftwork from the town's former practice nurse.

Fifty yards from the southern end of the High Street are the 17th-century **Hungerford Almshouses and Schoolrooms**, Grade I-listed

◀ **1** Castle Combe is notoriously picturesque. **2** Corsham's High Street has some beautiful façades. **3** Colerne's church has a distinctively tall tower.

and some of the best-preserved structures of their kind. The buildings were built to an extremely high quality, and of a scale or lavishness previously unknown for buildings of this nature. The almshouses are still lived in but you can visit the schoolrooms, which contain many of their original 17th-century fittings. One-hour guided history tours of Corsham are available from the tourist-information centre in the High Street.

Corsham Court

✆ 01249 701610 ⌘ corsham-court.co.uk ⏱ see website

Topping both the High Street and the almshouses is Corsham Court, where the countryside meets the town. Accessed just 100yds from the High Street via Church Street, the Corsham Estate was a royal manor during Saxon times and was later owned by royalty in Tudor times too. But the existing house is Elizabethan, built in 1582, with extensions and alterations in the late 18th century. It has belonged to the Methuen family for eight generations; you can see the family crest carved into the exterior walls.

"To walk the park without visiting the gardens means missing out on the formal herbaceous borders and the folly in the form of a ruined castle"

The Methuens have been avid collectors of paintings; inside is a distinguished collection of Old Masters from the 16th to 19th century with works by Van Dyck, Filippo Lippi, Granacci, Reni, Reynolds and Romney. It really is extraordinary in scale, with more than 160 paintings to view. The artworks hang in, among others, the Picture Gallery, a room of striking red silk damask-lined walls commissioned for the purpose and which was designed, along with the other state rooms, by Capability Brown. Brown, along with Sir Humphry Repton also landscaped the parkland and gardens, building a Gothic-style bathhouse in the grounds, planting avenues and numerous specimen trees, some of which still survive. Two public footpaths cross the park, where you can catch sight of the 13-acre lake that Brown had planned but was not finished until 40 years after his death.

To walk the park without visiting the gardens means missing out on the formal herbaceous borders and the folly in the form of a ruined castle – built to screen a part of the High Street. You'd also miss the glorious peacocks that roam the gardens and who have become a symbol of Corsham. Quite unfazed by people, they hang around the entrance steps to the court, and also promenade along Corsham's streets, perfect speed-reducing measures. Look out for the huge, knobbly yew hedge beside the Court, too.

For an alternative walk on the west side of town, close to **Pickwick** – from which Charles Dickens gained the ideas and names for *The Pickwick Papers* – a friend of mine who lives in the town tells me that strolling up Middlewick Lane and along the footpath to Pickwick Lodge and the woods behind is 'absolutely gorgeous, especially in winter'.

¶¶ FOOD & DRINK

Corsham has numerous places to eat and drink, some considerably better than others.

The Greenhouse Restaurant Wadswick Green SN13 9RD ℘ 01225 220148 ⟁ rangefordvillages.co.uk/the-greenhouse. Well off the beaten track and behind closed gates with an intercom system, this is a modern restaurant with copper tables lit by copper pendants and swish furnishings coupled with commissioned artworks of the Cotswolds. Relaxed, all-day dining means you can kick back for morning coffee or linger over lunch.

The Methuen Arms 2 High St ℘ 01249 717060 ⟁ butcombe.com/the-methuen-arms-wiltshire. A former nunnery that's now a multi-award-winning pub that prides itself on fresh, seasonal food. Lunch and supper menus (pea and mint dumplings with ricotta and spring-vegetable broth; pressed ham hock and pistachio terrine with coal mayo). Accommodation too.

Mother & Wild High St, Corsham SN13 0HB ℘ 01249 712515 ⟁ motherandwild.com. Charming, cosy restaurant in an old town house (exposed stone walls, historic leaded-light windows, rustic tables) serving bistro food including pizzas and small plates using produce from the county and neighbouring Somerset. Sweet little garden for cocktails.

7 COLERNE & ST CATHERINE'S

On the opposite side of the valley to Corsham, standing on the ridge, is **Colerne**, a delightful village that tends to get bypassed by tourists. Yet the views from here out across the By Brook Valley and across to Box are spectacular; you can even make out the lights of Bath at night.

Its prominent hilltop position, with its water tower and distinctive church tower, also makes it a landmark from which to gather your bearings in the area. And standing beneath the church tower, you'll notice that the clock has only the hour hand, one of only a few churches in Britain to do so, including Westminster Abbey. **Frank's Wood**, along Eastrip Lane to the east of the church, is a relatively new community

A remote valley walk via St Catherine's Church

❅ OS Explorer map 155; start: the Fosse Way 1½ miles north of Batheaston ♥ ST797706; 5½ miles; moderate

From the Fosse Way 1½ miles north of Batheaston and virtually opposite the turning for Colerne, turn onto the road signposted for Rocks East Woodland, a 100-acre wood with signposted trails that you can walk for a fee. Take the first left on a tight turn. The road descends sharply through very attractive hillside beech woods that remind me more of Scandinavia than the Cotswolds, somehow different from those around the Stroud valleys. Water oozes from springs with the forest floor smothered in ferns, bamboo, common comfrey

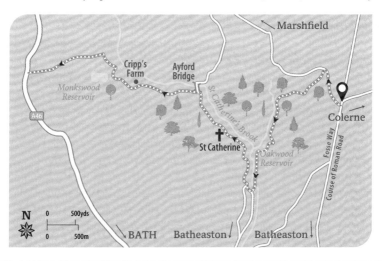

woodland. Planted in 2000 in memory of a villager, it's very pleasant to wander through, with young oaks and field maples just above head height, but its rim is also one of the best spots to view the valley.

East of the village is **Colerne Park and Monk's Wood**, a 132-acre woodland and SSSI owned by the Woodland Trust; you are welcome to wander through it. On the western slopes of the valley, its trees provide cover for many rare woodland plants such as meadow saffron, toothwort, green hellebores, lily of the valley and star of Bethlehem. Down by the river is Weavern Farm (weavern meaning 'wavering', a description of the meandering river), a derelict property now but once the site of Weavern and horsetails making the most of the damp conditions, the smell sublime, patchy sunlight stroking the leaves. A series of small lakes, occupied by numerous waterfowl, come into view and there are a couple of public footpaths here to delve further into the woods.

Once out of the woods, continue along the narrow, twisting lane for half a mile progressing deeper into the valley, past Oakford Reservoir, where the lie of the land begins to change and further hillsides begin to encroach on the complex landscape. Take the next right, which appears to bend back on itself, and within yards right again. The lane necessarily bends with each curve in this secluded valley. In a mile, on your left is **St Catherine's Court**, a Tudor manor house that looks out across the valley. The house is privately owned and you can do little but admire its beauty as you pass, but next door **St Catherine's Church** stands out among the area's buildings. Its entrance is through ornamental gates of some grandeur hung upon carved stone pillars, and whenever I visit the tiny courtyard is filled with flowers. The view across the valley is magnificent from the churchyard, but inside is the jewel. The church remains a shrine to Captain William Blanchard, a former owner of St Catherine's Court, who died in 1631.

Carvings of him and his wife kneel on top of a marble tomb but the decoration that surrounds them is inspirational, with a peacock blue, medieval red-and-gold painted pulpit and mosaic tiles patterned with gold, greens and soft reds on the walls and the altar screen.

Having visited the church, continue on until the road takes a left bend and begins to climb. Look back at the sweeping views along the next remote valley of green pastures and swathes of woodland. Climbing past the end of Monkswood Reservoir don't forget to catch a bird's-eye view of the lake below once the little lane runs along the hillside above. Within yards the land comes to a junction with the busy A46 and your moment of seclusion is over.

Mill, where fulling for the wool industry took place, followed in 1793 by paper manufacture.

This area is perfect for a walk where you're unlikely to see another soul. Access from Colerne is via Thickwood. A quarter-mile past Thickwood, turn right towards Euridge Manor Farm and park at the end of the lane.

West of Colerne and the Fosse Way, a knotted cluster of valleys covers the landscape. You're only 10 minutes from Bath here (a climb up **Little Solsbury Hill**, immortalised in words by songwriter Peter Gabriel, will provide sweeping views of the city) and yet to be in among the valleys feels deliciously remote. I took a gentle drive and walk in the relatively confined area and it's best described by what I saw on my visit (page 358), but this is no place for rushing. I can happily spend the day walking here.

BRADFORD-ON-AVON & THE LIMPLEY STOKE VALLEY

In the far southern tip of this locale and right on the border with Somerset is Wiltshire's other Cotswold gem, **Bradford-on-Avon**. This is the Bristol Avon, not the same river as the Avon that flows through Stratford in the north of the Cotswolds. From Bradford the Avon flows west and then curves north, running through the **Limpley Stoke Valley** and taking the **Kennet and Avon Canal** with it to Bath. So very different from other parts of the Cotswolds, there are lots of alternative activities here, like taking a canoe on the canal or watching boats cross the remarkable **Dundas Aqueduct.**

8 BRADFORD-ON-AVON

Although on the very fringes of the Cotswolds, few towns could be more Cotswold-like, with weavers' cottages huddled up the hillside and steep paths that once took the workers to the mills lining the river. Bradford, or 'Broad Ford' as it was in Saxon times, has its fair share of agreeable architecture and enticing corners.

The river and its medieval stone bridge in the centre of town combine to make a notable focal point from which emanates so much of interest. As a starting point, climb up **Silver Street** and look back, where you'll see great views of the town, the spires and turrets, cupolas and pinnacles. Silver Street is one of the main shopping streets, along with Market Street, though this is the main thoroughfare through town and can get ridiculously busy with traffic. From Silver Street, climb Coppice Hill. It's a very quiet no-through road lined with appealing stone cottages and at the top are the most unusual remains of a very grand Wesleyan chapel built in 1818 with only the façade remaining, containing giant window arches and a substantial portico entrance.

Between Coppice Hill and Silver Street is **The Shambles**, one of the shortest streets in town, yet with a number of tiny shops crammed together – including a minute Tardis-like bookshop, a deli and a café, each shop decorated with baskets of hanging flowers.

From Market Street cross over to **Church Street** and follow the road to the end, passing by the weavers' cottages and more stately clothiers' homes. Next to the river is **Abbey Mill**, the last cloth mill to be built in Bradford, in 1875. However, its opening almost signalled the closure of a 700-year industry of wool and cloth manufacture and just 27 years later, the mill closed. The Royal Cycling Corps and Australian Forces occupied its vast bulk, a classic chunk of stone and glass, during World War I. The building has more recently been renovated and converted to retirement apartments but remains very stately reflected in the river.

At the end of the street are two churches almost side by side. On the right is the tiny but tall Saxon church of St Laurence, the oldest surviving building in town. It is still used as a place of worship, though with a dozen people standing inside it's crowded. Bizarrely the church was once 'lost', having been redeveloped into a school and overshadowed by other buildings. It was not until 1856 that a local clergyman came across some old records and discovered the building to be a 10th-century church.

"It's a very quiet no-through road lined with appealing stone cottages and at the top are the most unusual remains of a very grand Wesleyan chapel."

If you want to extend a walk to see more of the town's appealing terraces and obtain magnificent views, continue from the Saxon church along Church Lane, past The Chantry and past Barton Orchard. Climb the steps and turn left before climbing beside the sky-high wall and a small sign to **St Mary Tory**. Turn left along Tory to the diminutive and restful pilgrim chapel. The car-free Georgian terrace of Tory – and the tiny terrace of St Mary Tory, where you can sit awhile – is one of the most beautiful I have seen in England: portico entrances and flowers erupt from cracks in the wall and pavement; each property has a tiny hillside garden and the most incredible views over the town, extending to the Westbury White Horse and Salisbury Plain.

Otherwise, the main parish church sits pleasantly by the river, which can be crossed at McKeever Bridge (renamed after the London 2012 Olympic Games to celebrate the achievements of gold medallist sprint kayaker Ed McKeever) to take a waterside walk to **Barton Farm Country Park**. This is the place to spend a lazy afternoon paddling in the backwaters of the Avon or relaxing on a picnic rug. Across the very handsome ancient packhorse bridge is a wildflower meadow left for walkers to enjoy the rural surroundings within minutes from the town centre. But take a look in the immaculate **tithe barn**, for which superlatives are of little use. Built in 1341, this is cathedral-like in stature, 168ft long and 33ft wide. Its roof of thick Cotswold stone tiles weighs over 100 tons alone, supported by an astounding lattice of timberwork.

¶¶ FOOD & DRINK

Bridge Tea Rooms Bridge St ♪ 01225 865537 ♂ thebridgetearooms.co.uk. Not just a place to eat but also one of Bradford-on-Avon's major tourist attractions; visiting these tea rooms is a must if you like old-school service. A former blacksmith's cottage dating from 1502, you step back to a bygone age as you walk through the door. Under the low ceilings, costumed waitresses serve light meals and afternoon teas during the day followed by candlelit dinners in the evenings. Twice winner of the prestigious Tea Guild's 'UK Top Tea Place', they really do know how to serve tea correctly – with a selection of 34 different teas and tisanes.

Lock Inn Frome Rd ♪ 01225 868068 ♂ thelockinn.co.uk. Vibrant and quirky canalside café that's something of an institution. Sizeable breakfasts that sort out over-indulgence from the night before, snacks, lunches and dinners served in the multi-coloured café, the tugboat (on the canal) or in the canalside garden, sheltered under the trees. Plastic tablecloths rule. Beer on draught and local Bath ales. Canoe hire by the hour or day too.

The Weaving Shed 3 Bridge Yard ♪ 01225 866519 ♂ weaving-shed.co.uk. A striking building of wood and glass beside the River Avon with an open-plan seating area and open-plan kitchen, so you can see what's being prepared for you. Everything is made in-house with a modern twist on classic British dishes.

9 LIMPLEY STOKE VALLEY & THE KENNET & AVON CANAL
🏠 Rowley Cottage at Iford Manor

Three miles southwest of Bradford-on-Avon is **Iford Manor Garden** (♪ 01225 863146 ♂ ifordmanor.co.uk ☉ Apr–Sept, variable days), an architecturally styled garden created by the celebrated garden designer Harold Ainsworth Peto, who bought the manor in 1899. His style of mixing fragments of old buildings and sculptures is shown off to dramatic effect on the steep hillside overlooking the River Frome. Rock gardens mingle with Roman columns, statues gaze over formal terraces and windows in walls peer at silent pools. Specimen trees are

1 Iford Manor Garden was created by celebrated garden designer Harold Ainsworth Peto. **2** The medieval stone bridge is a focal point of Bradford-on-Avon. **3** The entire length of the Kennet and Avon Canal is accessible to boaters, cyclists and walkers. ▶

MARIANNE CARTWRIGHT-HIGNETT/IFORD MANOR

DOUBLELEE/S

GEORGESIXTH/D

used architecturally too. Italian influence is everywhere and one of my favourite areas is the Cloisters, an atmospheric courtyard building at the far end of the garden where fluttering pink clematis flowers and sweetly scented roses are entwined with the graceful marble columns. The garden is used annually for an intimate summer jazz festival.

A more idyllic setting for a house and garden is hard to find, with the mellow stone house sited beside the gentle River Frome and the garden climbing the hillside behind, offering views over the valley hillside pastures. The narrow lanes are ripe for peaceful walks and cycle rides, and there are three miles of woodland footpaths through the Iford Manor Estate, which was used as a location in the BBC's *Wild Isles* (2023) with Sir David Attenborough. A bite to eat at the new café and restaurant is worthy reward following a walk in the area; the garden can also be approached via a 25-minute walk from Freshford train station.

> *"One of my favourite areas is the Cloisters, an atmospheric courtyard building at the far end of the garden."*

The **Kennet and Avon Canal** lies just a half-mile north of the garden and has a stirring backdrop passing through the green pasture and forested Limpley Stoke Valley. Explorers of the area are spoilt for choice, with the entire length of the canal and its towpath between Bradford-on-Avon and Bath accessible to boaters, cyclists and walkers. Within a matter of three miles, the canal boasts two aqueducts – the Avoncliff and Dundas – carrying water sky high over the railway and the Avon. Both notable feats of engineering, their existence stopped the requirement for numerous locks and makes a boat journey much less arduous.

The **Dundas Aqueduct**, with its smooth balustrading above the river, represents beauty in industrial design. It was built from Bath stone in the 18th century, although the chief architect and engineer for the project wanted to use brick, feeling that the stone would not be a sturdy enough material. But stone won the day; as some of the main users of the canal were going to be local quarry owners, it would have been a slight on their industry to transport their stone over a brick-built structure.

Those not walking from Bath or Bradford-on-Avon can park in the small car park at the **Brassknocker Basin** to reach the Dundas Aqueduct. This is where the former **Somerset Coal Canal** joins the Kennet and Avon, a link to carry 'black gold' from the Somerset coalfields to Bath and Bristol. The canal lasted for less than a hundred years in the 19th century and only the few yards, used as the Brassknocker Basin, remain. There's a small, free exhibition about both canals at the basin and a place to hire canoes, electric boats and narrowboats for the day. But if you'd prefer someone else to skipper a boat while you sit back and enjoy the scenery, the **Kennet and Avon Canal Trust** (⌀ katrust.org.uk) also plies the water with MV *Barbara Maclellan*, a handsome narrowboat used for public boat trips between Bradford-on-Avon and Avoncliff, giving visitors the chance to explore this weavers' village, where two of the old cloth mills remain. It's a relaxing 2-hour round trip, and the volunteer crew will tell you all about the countryside and the natural world that you pass through, including their dedication to keeping the Kennet and Avon maintained. Their passion and enthusiasm for the canal shines through.

At the northeast end of the Limpley Stoke Valley, close to the village of Bathford is **Browne's Folly**, a nature reserve with SSSI status and of great importance within the area. It's also a fabulous place to go before visiting Bath, as the views of the city from the cliff-like slopes are some of the best you'll find; it's the place to see how the city is laid out. Run by the Avon Wildlife Trust, the nature reserve covers an area where former quarrying of Bath stone has created many giant sunken holes and caves. Much of the area is now covered with mature woodland of mixed, native species, a children's natural playground with lots of space to build dens.

"The views of the city from the cliff-like slopes are some of the best you'll find; it's the place to see how the city is laid out."

Following the main path, walk to the far end of the wood until you reach a fence. You can turn left for the actual Browne's Folly, a tall tower sadly misused and looking rather forlorn, or pass through a black kissing-gate and down the steps to walk out onto open scrubland. Be careful of steep drops at the cliff face, where you will find the wonderful views of Bath and the hills beyond, Bathampton Down on the other side of the valley, as well as views south down the Limpley Stoke Valley. A footpath – there are actually numerous tracks – runs for a mile along the top of the ridge, providing a regularly changing view among the low-lying shrubs and bushes.

Browne's Folly is accessed off the Bathford to Monkton Farleigh road but there's a very, very steep hill (1 in 4) out of Bathford to negotiate. An off-road car park for the reserve is just near the brow of the hill.

SPECIAL STAYS

Rowley Cottage at Iford Manor nr Bradford on Avon BA15 2BA ✆ 01225 863146
⌂ ifordmanor.co.uk/stay. Within the grounds of Iford Manor, this beautiful Cotswold stone
cottage (once the stables to the manor but completely refurbished in 2022) sleeps six in
three en-suite bedrooms. Guests have access to the Grade I-listed Iford Manor Gardens all
year round while enjoying the cottage's own small garden for al-fresco dining. A truly blissful
place to stay.

¶¶ FOOD & DRINK

The Cross Guns Avoncliff BA15 2HB ✆ 01225 862335 ⌂ crossgunsavoncliff.com. Attractive
pub in a fabulous setting on the banks of the River Avon in secluded Avoncliff. The terraced
garden sits right beside the river. The food is standard pub fare but then it's the location for a
quiet drink that you're coming for.

Iford Manor nr Bradford on Avon BA15 2BA ✆ 01225 863146 ⌂ ifordmanor.co.uk. A
fabulous addition to the area, developed during the Covid lockdown. The café and restaurant
are housed in a Cotswold stone and oak-framed building within a walled garden, with a
lovely sunny courtyard. Seasonal ingredients are sourced from the garden and wider estate
where possible and all food is prepared on the premises. Delicious light bites (Scotch eggs;
heritage tomato and goat's cheese tartlets; salads) and cakes served in the café with more
substantial meals in the restaurant. Sunday jazz lunches and supper clubs, too.

INDEX

Entries in **bold** refer to major entries; those in *italics* refer to maps.

THE BRADT STORY

In the beginning

It all began in 1974 on an Amazon river barge. During an 18-month trip through South America, two adventurous young backpackers – Hilary Bradt and her then husband, George – decided to write about the hiking trails they had discovered through the Andes. *Backpacking Along Ancient Ways in Peru and Bolivia* included the very first descriptions of the Inca Trail. It was the start of a colourful journey to becoming one of the best-loved travel publishers in the world; you can read the full story on our website (**bradtguides. com/ourstory**).

Getting there first

Hilary quickly gained a reputation for being a true travel pioneer, and in the 1980s she started to focus on guides to places overlooked by other publishers. The Bradt Guides list became a roll call of guidebook 'firsts'. We published the first guide to Madagascar, followed by Mauritius, Czechoslovakia and Vietnam. The 1990s saw the beginning of our extensive coverage of Africa: Tanzania, Uganda, South Africa, and Eritrea. Later, post-conflict guides became a feature: Rwanda, Mozambique, Angola, and Sierra Leone, as well as the first standalone guides to the Baltic States following the fall of the Iron Curtain, and the first post-war guides to Bosnia, Kosovo and Albania.

Comprehensive – and with a conscience

Today, we are the world's largest independently owned travel publisher, with more than 200 titles. However, our ethos remains unchanged. Hilary is still keenly involved, and **we still get there first**: two-thirds of Bradt guides have no direct competition.

But we don't just get there first. Our guides are also known for being **more comprehensive** than any other series. We avoid templates and tick-lists. Each guide is a one-of-a-kind expression of an expert author's interests, knowledge and enthusiasm for telling it how it really is.

And a commitment to wildlife, conservation and respect for local communities has always been at the heart of our books. Bradt Guides was **championing sustainable travel** before any other guidebook publisher. We even have a series dedicated to Slow Travel in the UK, award-winning books that explore the country with a passion and depth you'll find nowhere else.

Thank you!

We can only do what we do because of the support of readers like you – people who value less-obvious experiences, less-visited places and a more thoughtful approach to travel. Those who, like us, take travel seriously.

Bradt GUIDES

TRAVEL TAKEN SERIOUSLY